The Cardinal's
the General's Cross, the Martyr's Testimony
and Other Affirmations

The Cardinal's Sins,
the General's Cross, the Martyr's Testimony
and Other Affirmations

For Eric,
Adelina
and Aurora Loqui —
All good wishes, and warm regards —
The peace and joy of the Lord be
always with you —

GREGORIO C. BRILLANTES

Greg Bultes —
January 18, 2009

ATENEO DE MANILA UNIVERSITY PRESS

ATENEO DE MANILA UNIVERSITY PRESS
Bellarmine Hall, Katipunan Avenue
Loyola Heights, Quezon City
P.O. Box 154, 1099 Manila, Philippines
Tel.: (632) 426-59-84 / Fax: (632) 426-59-09
E-mail: unipress@admu.edu.ph
Website: www.ateneopress.com

Book design by JB de la Peña
Cover design by BJ Patiño

The National Library of the Philippines CIP Data

Recommended entry:

Brillantes, Gregorio C.
    The cardinal's sins, the general's cross,
the martyr's testimony and other affirmations
/ Gregorio C. Brillantes. - Quezon City : ADMU
Press, c2005
1 v

        1. Philippine essays (English). 2. Journalism.
I. Title.

PL5546 899.21'04 2005 P044000764
ISBN 971-550-474-4

To Maríalu Brillantes

and for Luis Cabalquinto, Monica Feria, Ani Habulan,
Norma Japitana, Henry Leung, Gabriel Mañalac, Jr.,
Joan Orendain, Evangeline Pascual, Elena Roco,
Carmen Sarmiento *and* Domingo Soriano

Contents

Contents

Ancient and Ever New

Critical Conditions

Last Laughs

Titles

An Introduction of Sorts

"WITH ALL DUE RESPECT," says my faithful reader, critic and nephew, Erwin, "it's no good, lousy. The Martyr's Cross, the General's Sins, the Cardinal's Testimonies or Testimonials and Other Afflictions. . . You owe this book and all literate Filipinos a better title—not too long, something short and smart, and easy to remember."

"Too long? But that's the point, exactly," I say. "What the book's all about, what makes it different. People will stop in their tracks and notice it and remember to buy and read it—the book with the title that's not too hard to forget."

"Still and all, Tito G., I think a shorter title is in order," says Erwin (whose second name ought to be Rommel and not Albert, after either his dad or Saint Albertus Magnus, Albert the Great of Cologne—the 13th-century Dominican theologian and scholastic philosopher whose works enriched Aristotelianism and the natural sciences, and whose feast day is November 15—since he was named, and this I know for a fact, from the day he was baptized, after the German general, Feldmarschall Erwin Rommel, the "Desert Fox" of World War II fame, the bold, brilliant commander of the Afrika Korps that in 1941–43 battled the British and then the Anglo-American armies from El Alamein and Tobruk and through the deserts of Libya in retreat to northern Tunisia after being driven back from Egypt and Suez, which Hitler coveted as the gateway to the oil fields of the Middle East and the Caucasus; the Wermacht general who during the Allied invasion of Normandy commanded Army Group B, under Gerd von Rundstedt, who revoked his strategy of massing Panzer divisions behind the beaches, thus ensuring the German debacle of D-Day, June 6, 1944, a few weeks after which Rommel himself was wounded in a strafing attack by Spitfires—the legendary fighter planes that won the Battle of Britain in the summer of blood, sweat and tears, in 1940—and following his recovery was implicated in the plot to assassinate Hitler, and rather than be court-martialed and executed as a traitor chose to commit suicide by cyanide on October 14, 1944, and be memorialized as a hero not of the Nazis or the Third Reich but of the German nation, the master of desert warfare, the dashing, decorated general wearing aviator-like goggles that weren't German-issue but taken from a British command vehicle in El Alamein, as portrayed in movies made after the war: by James Mason in *The Desert Fox,* 1951; by Mason again in *The Desert Rats,* 1953; Werner Heinz in *The Longest Day,* 1962; Christopher Plummer in *Night of the Generals,* 1967; Karl Voglen in *Patton,* 1970; Wolfgang Preiss in *Raid on Rommel,* 1971), an infotech executive—*sapientia et eloquentia*—and investment consultant on the side—it's "not money, but the love of money when you don't have it, that needs a root canal," Erwin likes to quote Kierkegaard, P. J. O'Rourke or Pope Paul VI—and an A.B. Interdisciplinary Studies dropout from the Ateneo de Manila University (which is not to be confused with as it is distinct and distinguished from the Ateneo de Manila, according to some Jesuits and most of the alumni over age 50: the Ateneo Municipal de Manila as it was first titled, established as a secondary school by Father Jose Fernandez Cuevas on the grounds of the city primary school, the Escuela Municipal on Calle Real, that Governor-General Fernando de Norzagaray had requested the Jesuits—expelled from the Spanish empire in 1768—to administer upon their return to the Philippines, in 1859; the Ateneo Municipal that offered a five-year program leading to the Bachillerato dedicated to the Jesuit Ratio Studiorum which affirmed the primacy of language and literature—Spanish, Latin, Greek, English and French—over studies in philosophy and the sciences, the course which Rizal pursued, graduating with a bachelor's degree in 1877; the Ateneo which removed "Municipal" from its official name in 1908, when its partial state subsidy was dissolved and it became a private college; the Ateneo de Manila which the Jesuits of the New York Province administered beginning in 1912; the Ateneo of the Sodality of Mary and the Catechetical Instruction League, the Social Order Club and the Chesterton Evidence Guild, the annual Shakespeare play and the elocution and oratorical contests, the class retreats and the philosophy orals and the NCAA, not UAAP, champions—the Ateneo that transferred to Padre Faura in 1932 after a fire razed its Intramuros buildings, and eventually in 1952 from the war-ruined, post-liberation Ermita campus to Loyola Heights in Quezon City, where it was inaugurated, transformed, expanded as a university in its centennial year, 1959, with what remained of the old Ateneo, the College of Arts and Sciences, becoming coeducational, the girls and/or women taking over, administratively, academically, extracurricularly but not athletically or sportingly, in 1973 or soon after the constitutional authoritarian F. E. Marcos declared martial law and turned the nation upside down, even the old, the original Ateneo in spirits and in troth, in gender and faculties, etc.; the Ateneo of Fathers Francisco de Paula Sanchez, Pablo Pastells, Jose Vilacalara, Joaquin Vilallonga, Federico Faura, Vicente Balaguer, Estanislao March, Francis Byrne, John Hurley, Joseph Mulry, Forbes Monaghan, John Delaney, Henry Irwin, William Masterson, Leo McGovern, James Meany, Harry Furay, Thomas Cannon, Kyran Egan, Martin Casey, James Reuter, Bartholomew Lahiff, Raymond Gough, John Carroll, Horacio de la Costa, Pacifico Ortiz, Jose Eliazo, Miguel Bernad, Jaime Bulatao, Jose Cruz, Augustine Bello, Maximo David, Benigno Mayo, Luis Candelaria, Lino Banayad, Vitaliano Gorospe—Spanish, American and Filipino Jesuits who all together represent the history of the Ateneo, the history of the Filipino nation; the Ateneo de Manila of Jose Rizal, Gregorio del Pilar, Antonio Luna, Baldomero Roxas, Claro M. Recto, Cesar Bengzon, Narciso Pimentel, Vidal Tan, Jr., Vicente Araneta, Gabriel Daza, Manuel Colayco, Cesar Basa, Ramon Cabrera, Arsenio Lacson, Teodoro Locsin, Leon Ma. Guerrero, Ambrosio Padilla, Francisco Rodrigo, Raul Manglapus, Jeremias Montemayor, Rafael Roco, Moro Lorenzo, Chole Gaston, Bobby Littaua, Frank Rabat, Luis Javellana, Manuel Lim, Jr., Vic Silayan, Totoy Avellana, Max Soliven, Tony Manuud, Leo Benesa, Gaby Mañalac, Domingo Soriano, Matt Roa, Henry Leung, Jimmy Dy-Liacco, Greg Imperial, Vic Diaz, Ben Bautista, Jesse Paredes, Emil Jurado, Reli German, Gary Lising, and the honorary high school alumnus, Joseph Estrada).

(All the above stuff in parentheses would suggest the wide range and abundant variety of the subjects, topics and themes contained in this book; and all the things you could pick up from reading this compilation—by the way, a selection that's only a third of the load submitted to the publishers, cut down for reasons of space, inflation and printing costs—all sorts of things, varied kinds of knowledge, ideas, information, argument, commentary, illumination, gratification, aggravation, nostalgia, humor and déjà vu, in the essays, articles, columns, reviews and such that first appeared in various publications: the *Philippines Free Press, Asia-Philippines Leader, Veritas, Focus, National Midweek, Philippine Graphic* and other journals since defunct or still in circulation, to the publishers and editors of which the author hereby gives many heartfelt thanks—for their interest, generosity and encouragement.)

"Let's think of a better title," Erwin says. "Like, Beyond All Forgetfulness."

"Sounds familiar—seems like I read that somewhere before."

"How about Fly High? Or, maybe, Down from Loyola Heights . . ."

"But this is not the *Guidon*. And it's also for the rest of the country—people from La Salle, San Beda, Letran, St. Theresa, St. Paul, Assumption, Maryknoll, I mean, Miriam, St. Esco, UP, UST, FEU, UE, Adamson."

Erwin calls a couple of days later: "I've got it! Prose to Press. Kin and friends from Pangasinan will pronounce it Prose to Praise. The folks, too, in Cebu, Leyte and Bohol. It's sure to maximize readership addiction and profitability."

"Is that your hangover talking?"

"One more try," says Erwin. "Your book has landed from outer or inner space, cyberspace, wherever. An identified printed object. And it announces to all mankind, on the world-wide Web, no need to click—Take Me to Your Reader. Smart and global, gotcha."

"I kind of like that," I say. "Make it Readers. Plural. It'll do for a subtitle."

"Suit yourself, sir," says Erwin.

G. C. Brillantes

Lives and Legends

Rizal and the Jesuits:
A Convergence at Bagumbayan

IN A MAN'S LIFE, A CERTAIN YEAR may be the most crucial and significant: the turning point when human destiny is set in a definite and final if often imperceptible direction. This was true of Jose Rizal, who was, contrary to what some of us might think, neither divine nor mythical, but recognizably human: a life thus rendered all the more real, admirable and enduring in the memory of our people.

In the life of Rizal, what year was the most important and fateful, impelling him more than any other toward December 30, 1896?

With the hindsight of history, his biographers might point to 1882, when Rizal traveled for the first time to Europe. The Continent then was a glacier melting and cracking under the heat of secular ideas which the real-life prototypes of Padre Damaso and Padre Salvi could only denounce as subversive, abominable, diabolical—a dangerous realm whose influence, in the judgment of the friars, would turn Rizal into a political and religious heretic deserving of condemnation by court-martial and death by firing squad.

If Rizal had not sailed for Europe in 1882—if, it might be argued, he had then decided at the age of 21 to stay home half a world away from the battleground of ideas that was Spain, France, and Germany in the late 19th century, his life and our country's history would have taken a radically different course.

He in all probability would have remained, simply, Dr. Rizal the eye specialist, one more placid and prosperous alumnus of the Royal and Pontifical University of Santo Tomas. He might have lived to end his days as a harmless, philosophical septuagenarian with a clinic in Binondo or Ermita, and perhaps a hospital or two later named in his memory, and professional chairs in ophthalmology instituted in his honor. He might have survived into the 20th century and become the grand old man of the American regime or the Commonwealth, sipping brandy on nostalgic afternoons with Francis Burton Harrison or Manuel Quezon, perhaps writing his memoirs in comfortable retirement from the presidency of the University of the Philippines.

2

But there was 1882, and the steamer *Salvadora*, and the journey to Europe, to Barcelona and Madrid and Berlin, to the Propaganda Movement and *La Solidaridad* and the intellectual ferment generated by the Renaissance, the French Revolution and the Enlightenment. And it all made a tremendous difference in Rizal's life, and in the lives of his countrymen and the history of the Filipino nation.

And then there was the year 1884, when Rizal embarked on another journey that was perhaps even more decisive and fateful than his voyage to Barcelona. It was also the most perilous journey Rizal was to undertake: he could not have chosen an enterprise more fraught with danger than the writing of a novel exposing the evil hypocrisies of the friar-dominated regime. Others had died on the gallows, or by the garrote, or by musketry, for less insolent crimes.

While his friends and fellow expatriates presumed that he was as usual preoccupied with his studies, Rizal kept to his room, in a boardinghouse in Madrid, one night in 1884. And by some mysterious alchemy known only to the artist he began writing the story of Ibarra and Elias, Maria Clara and Sisa. "Only a novel," thus might his more pragmatic compatriots have exclaimed in impatient disgust. "Only a novel"—but the *Noli me tangere* and its sequel would prove to be far more explosive and deadly than all the dynamite that Simoun could have planted in the walls and foundations of Malacañang.

If, in 1884, it might again be argued, Rizal the lyric poet and writer of political and literary essays had not turned novelist; if, in that year in Madrid, he had confined himself to writing those cultural essays expected of him by the Circulo Hispano-Filipino—what a difference that would have made in his life and the history of the nation!

But there was 1884, and the night he began to write, not another lyric poem or polemical essay, but a novel: "On the last of October Don Santiago de los Santos, popularly known as Capitan Tiago, gave a dinner"—and the course of his life and our history would never be the same again.

And there was, finally, 1896. In terms of tension and conflict, the speed, intensity and number of events, 1896 was the high point, the climax, the most decisive year, for Rizal as well as the colonial society in which he lived and the regime that condemned him to death. All the years from Calamba to the cell in Fort Santiago were but a prologue leading up to the last and greatest moment of his life, on that December morning 86 years ago.

IT IS SHORTLY AFTER 6:30 in the morning. The sky is cool and growing brighter over the Noble and Ever Loyal City as Jose Rizal is escorted out of Fort Santiago by a detachment of Spanish soldiers. A bugler and a drummer precede him as he walks with a calm, unfaltering step through the gate called Postigo and out into the Paseo de Maria Cristina along the western ramparts of Intramuros. He is in a black suit with his elbows bound loosely behind him.

In the folk consciousness as well as in the more sophisticated remembrance of his countrymen, the image of Rizal on his way to meet the firing squad is that of a solitary, Christ-like figure surrounded by his enemies. Rizal alone against the fury of an empire that is itself about to expire—the tableau is romantic, melodramatic, intensely theatrical.

But a second unblinking and dispassionate look at the scene— the kind of scrutiny the analytical, relentlessly observant Rizal would himself prescribe—shows us that he is not alone among his enemies. He is not bereft of human companionship, even now, moments before the bullets from the Remington rifles will smash into his back and his now astonishingly calm and untroubled heart.

There are three men walking in step with him, three Spaniards, but they are neither his judges nor his executioners. He talks to them as a man would to old friends come to say goodbye. He remarks on the beauty of the December morning; and as he gazes at a building along Calle Orzobispo behind the ancient walls, he recalls the years— the "happiest" in his life—spent at the Ateneo Municipal de Manila.

Behind him and to one side is Luis Taviel de Andrade, his legal counsel in the court-martial. On either side of him walk two priests in black cassocks. As Rizal positions himself with his back to the firing squad, one of the priests says some comforting words and reaches out a crucifix for him to kiss. The words of the priest are the last human words Rizal will hear in this life, on this earth.

The anticlerical onlookers at the execution grounds on this December morning may find it strange, absurd, scandalous, a terrible farce and mockery, that Rizal should be accompanied and comforted in this moment by Catholic priests. Why, has Rizal not been persecuted and condemned to death by a regime dominated by priests? Who are these priests with Rizal, why are they here at all?

True enough, Fathers Estanislao March and Jose Vilaclara are Spanish priests, but they are not Spanish friars. They are Jesuits from Rizal's alma mater, the Ateneo; and Jesuits are not friars—a distinction not lost on Rizal and the nationalists and revolutionaries of his generation. This fact makes all the difference, in this hour in this field called Bagumbayan, to Rizal no less than to our country.

The presence of these Jesuits by the side of Rizal as he goes forth to his death is what bids us to return to 1872, that inclines us to the proposition that, with the exception of 1896, the year 1872 was the most decisive and meaningful period of his life. It was a year that may be said to have contained all of his future. For 1872 was when two events, two developments, made their imprint on Rizal's character and spirit in a way that no one and nothing could erase, in a manner more profound and irrevocable than a voyage to a distant continent, the writing of a novel, the loneliness and pain of exile.

In February of 1872, Fathers Gomez, Burgos and Zamora were executed for their alleged complicity in the Cavite Mutiny. The fate of the three priests so affected the young Rizal that years later, in 1889, he would write to Mariano Ponce that "without 1872, Rizal would now be a Jesuit . . ." As Jose Rizal, S.J., with his formidable talents, his versatile genius, he would have doubtless become one of the most eminent figures of the Church in the Philippines and in the Society of Jesus. He did not become a Jesuit; but in 1872 he began what proved to be a profound, dramatic, fascinating and, it would now seem to us, indestructible relationship with the Jesuits.

Many pages have been written, and rightly so, on the influence of Jose Burgos in the political evolution of Rizal. Little comparatively has been said of the role of the Jesuits in the intellectual and spiritual formation of Rizal—a role which cannot be ignored in the study of the whole man, not just this or that fragment of the man according to the style of a season, the theme of a celebration.

IN JUNE OF 1872, or scarcely three months after the executions of the martyr-priests, Jose Rizal was enrolled in the Ateneo by his brother, Paciano, who, incidentally, deserves more than the virtually forgotten niche to which our history has relegated him. In 1872, Rizal and the Jesuits began to see and acknowledge the merit of the other—a process, an association, a spirited dialogue and debate that reflected nothing less than the religious and political forces at work in Rizal's life and in the Philippines of his time.

The ties that bound Rizal to the Jesuits and the Jesuits to Rizal were to be subjected to the tug and stress of doubt, disappointment, distrust, even animosity. But history suggests that the same bonds held fast, they were never completely broken. Rizal himself regarded the Jesuits, as a religious order if not always as individual priests, with affection and respect long after he had left their college and his youthful faith.

Only once, it would seem, did Rizal write critically of his friends and teachers at the Ateneo, when he referred to them in the *Noli* as trailing behind the "cart of progress" in spite of their accomplishments in the natural sciences. Significantly, he did not say that they would block or overturn the cart, as he might have said of those ordained preachers who lorded it over the estate of Calamba and the campus of Santo Tomas.

Precisely because of this relationship, and regardless of whether this was desirable or not, salutary or not, the Jesuits could place their signature, as it were, on Rizal's life, his works and his death. In this light, surely, we who wish to know Rizal more truly would do well to make the acquaintance of this Catholic company of priests who append after their names the letters "S.J."

The *Societas Jesu*, the Society of Jesus, the largest and most militant, the most gifted and capable, and also the most maligned and controversial order in the Church, can be said to have begun in 1521, a year, as it happened, of tremendous import for both Spain and the Philippines.

When Magellan discovered a Southeast Asian archipelago for the Spanish crown, a Basque on the other side of the world discovered that there was a king far greater and more worthy of his service than the Spanish sovereign. While Magellan the invader lay dying on Mactan Island, a soldier named Iñigo de Oñez y Loyola lay wounded in a castle in northern Spain, one of his knees having been shattered by a cannon ball in a battle against the invading French.

As a student at the Ateneo, Rizal must have read about Ignatius Loyola—how the convalescing warrior read the life of Christ and the lives of the saints, how he was converted and gave up the life of a knight and courtier to become a hermit in Manresa, and then a student much older than his classmates at the universities of Alcala and Salamanca. There was one episode in his life that must have impressed the young Rizal—the Inquisition suspected Ignatius of heresy and put him in prison, his feet in chains. After his imprisonment, Ignatius proceeded to take his Master of Arts at the University of Paris, for like

Rizal, Ignatius believed that education, the disciplined formation of intellect and will, must precede any reforming of man and society.

To this end Ignatius fashioned the *ratio studiorum*, a program of studies built around Latin, Greek, the humanities, science and mathematics. This was the course leading up to the Bacchiller en Artes that Rizal began in 1872 and in which he would reap many a *sobresaliente* until his graduation from the Ateneo, in 1887.

The *ratio* was designed to imbue the student with an intense devotion to the Christian faith even as it stressed a progressive mastery of every subject, an aspect which would inspire the liberal arts course of the modern university. Rizal's faith in a personal God, his rejection of agnosticism as an alternative to Christianity, his preference for political evolution rather than revolution, his fondness for logic and disputation, his development as poet, essayist and novelist: all this one might ascribe to the Jesuit *ratio*.

It is cause for some wonder, at least: would the schoolboy from Calamba have fared better, would his talents have found more skillful guidance and inspiration under the instruction, say, of the Spanish Dominicans?

As the shock troops, the "light cavalry" of Catholicism, the men of Loyola were in an exposed and vulnerable position, and incurred the ire of governments, royal houses and dynasties. In 1773, Pope Clement XIV heeded mounting protests in France, Portugal and Spain, and disbanded the Society. Their enemies in Spain, fanatically conservative, had earlier succeeded in having them expelled from the Philippines, in 1768. This banishment was not by any means an unusual experience. Since their founding, there is hardly any country where they have not been banned or suppressed.

Had the Society not been restored by Pius VII in 1814, there would have been no Ateneo for Rizal. The Jesuits were back in Manila by 1859, when they established the Ateneo Municipal, the college the Spanish authorities would threaten to close down for producing "patriots and revolutionaries." Jesuit alumni, indeed, enough of them anyway since Voltaire, tend to be as original, nonconformist and controversial as their mentors.

RIZAL'S OWN REBELLION, his turning away from the Catholicism of his childhood and early youth, has been recorded in the exchange of letters between him and the Jesuit Pablo Pastells.

7

Father Pastells, one surmises, must have felt a sense of admiration, perhaps even humility, when he realized that he was dealing, not with the mind of simple piety, but with the intelligence and reason of the Jesuits' most brilliant graduate. In his letters from Dapitan, Rizal has left us a stunning self-portrait—of a Renaissance man who was at home both in scholastic philosophy and Darwinian science; a 20th-century Christian in the prison of the 19th, already drawn toward that wider, deeper, more humane and ecumenical Christianity which the Church itself would eventually proclaim at the Second Vatican Council, in our time.

He believed in a God who reveals Himself, Rizal wrote to Father Pastells, in "that nature which surrounds us on every side . . . that revelation which speaks to us and penetrates us from the moment we are born until we die . . ." In his intimations of a faith which recognized the presence of God in the world and in the evolution of this world, Rizal foreshadowed the coming of one of the greatest Jesuits who has ever lived—Pierre Teilhard de Chardin, scientist, mystic and philosopher.

A French Jesuit who died in 1955, Teilhard de Chardin was a paleontologist, cosmologist and evolutionist who saw the universe as evolving irresistibly toward a higher consciousness. His lifework was the reinterpretation of Christianity in the light of evolution, which to him derived its thrust and direction from God and which would culminate in Christ as the "Omega Point," the goal and perfection of mankind.

Like Rizal, Teilhard was persecuted for his ideas, his vision of man and the universe. His books were banned by church authorities in Rome, and he was subjected to the torments of censorship, surveillance and exile. And like Teilhard, Rizal too has been vindicated by time, history and the pronouncements of the Church, specifically on the question of science and religion.

This vindication of Rizal should be of special interest to those who would know more about one of the most important developments of our century—the reconciliation between science and faith. Today, notes the Jesuit theologian Ladislaus Boros, science and religion are no longer hostile. As Rizal himself might have put it, faith no longer slays the scientist; and science, in turn, has ceased to be the mortal enemy of religion, as it was once believed to be, in the days of Galileo and, later, of Darwin.

The first principle of the modern Christian attitude to science, according to Father Boros, is that every truth regarding man and the universe is of divine origin; thus it is impossible in principle for religion and science to contradict each other. As physicists and astronomers reveal to us a universe of breathtaking dimensions, from subatomic particles to galaxies, quasars and pulsars on the farthest boundaries of space-time, "the more powerful the human mind becomes, the greater we can conceive God to be."

All this has been made possible by the new humility adopted, almost simultaneously, by science and religion. Astronomers have discovered that the universe is expanding, that the galaxies are speeding away from one another and that this expansion is the result of a cosmic explosion 15 to 20 billion years ago. The Big Bang, as it is called, shows that though they differ in language and details, the astronomical and biblical accounts of the origin of the universe are essentially the same.

The universe is not eternal, it had a beginning. The chain of events leading to the formation of galaxies, stars, planets, life on earth and, eventually, the creature called man, began at a definite moment in time. From nonexistence the universe came into existence in a flash of light and energy. What force, what power produced that cosmic explosion? Science can only admit that it cannot pierce the ultimate mystery, which belongs properly to the realm of faith.

Furthermore, recent developments in science and technology have resulted in a radical change in man's view of the material world, a view once dictated by the mechanistic physics of Newton. The new physics founded by Paul Dirac, Neils Bohr and Werner Heisenburg, which demonstrates that matter is not inert and solid but consists of waves and particles of energy, has rendered obsolete the centuries-old scientific dogmatism concerning space and time, cause and effect. There is infinitely more to the world, to reality, than what our senses or even our most sophisticated instruments can perceive.

There is room in the cosmos for the invisible, the mystical, the supernatural, as has long been claimed by the religious traditions of the East and West. And in addition to the revelations of atomic and subatomic physics is the humbling knowledge that the same physics, in spawning the specter of a nuclear holocaust, has demolished forever the 19th-century materialist dogma, already badly battered by two world wars, that science can lead only to the progress and well-being of mankind.

As for religion, the insights of science, particularly in the matter of evolution, have helped dismantle those medieval structures and attitudes in the Church which failed to distinguish between the message of salvation and the form of the message, between meaning and manner of expression. In spite of St. Augustine's quite modern view of evolution, most theologians until the time of Pius XII adhered to a literal interpretation of creation and the garden of Adam and Eve, in Genesis.

The world and man, it was contended, came into existence whole and entire from the hand of God—in 4004 B.C., according to Anglican Archbishop James Ussher in the 17th century. Life and consciousness could not have undergone stages of development toward more complex forms and more superior modes of being. The result, among other things, was a rigid, triumphal authoritarianism which a Christian humanist and evolutionist like Rizal found totally unacceptable.

But to paraphrase Galileo, the world does move, the universe evolves, and so does the Holy Roman Catholic Apostolic Church. The God of the Bible, the theologians now tell us, is also the God of Evolution. Partly in response to the challenge of Marxism, Rome has become more human, more humane, and committed to that evolution toward fuller truth and knowledge which reflects the evolution of species. Post-Vatican Council Catholicism has shed much of what Rizal called, in a letter to Father Pastells, "that pride (which) has always shown itself in the ideas of imposition."

In 1896, Father Vicente Balaguer, S.J. could intone with dogmatic severity: *"Extra Ecclesiam Catholicam nulla datur salvus.* Outside the Catholic Church there is no salvation." In 1971, Father Pedro Arrupe, the Superior General of the Society of Jesus, would declare: "The fact is that the world has changed; hence we too must change if we wish to be of service to others as we should." In 1981, Father Joaquin Bernas, then Provincial of the Jesuits in the Philippines, could affirm: "What we are trying to avoid is a kind of imperialist papacy. In the light of present economic and political conditions, and from the point of view of a deeper understanding of the nature of man, we cannot be of service to the faith without promoting the cause of justice. That is the acid test. There can be no love of God without love of man."

In the forefront of the new Christian humanism are the Jesuits. Not surprisingly, from their ranks arose the great scientist and philosopher who, probably more than anyone else in our time, hastened the coming of what Rizal foresaw in Dapitan and expressed in his letters and his poems: the evolution separately and then convergence of science and faith.

But Pierre Teilhard de Chardin was to live and write in a more enlightened age; and it was left to the Spanish Jesuits of the Province of Aragon to try to bring Rizal back to what Austin Coates calls the "little Catholicism of obedience," though surely there was nothing "little" in a matter that concerned death and eternal life. Which brings us back once more to the morning of December 30, 1896.

IT IS A DAY FULL OF QUESTIONS, conjectures and possibilities for us who would truly honor Jose Rizal. But for Rizal himself, all such surmises and questions appear to be over and done with as he walks with the drummer and the troops to the place of execution called Bagumbayan. His expression, his words, his gestures are those of a man of absolute honesty and sincerity, a man at peace with himself, with his conscience. He does not have the fearful, defeated look of a man crushed by the night-long vigil of those "terrible Jesuits."

But the questions, the conjectures haunt us still as we reflect on that December morning almost a hundred years ago. And they all revolve around that controversy which concerns not so much Rizal perhaps as the Jesuits who came to his death cell—the Jesuits Sederra, Viza, Rosell, Vilaclara, March, Faura and Balaguer. Sometime during the night, did Rizal, as Father Balaguer was later to claim, sign a document declaring himself a Catholic and retracting whatever he had written that was contrary to his "condition as a son of the Church"?

Many an argument for and against the retraction has been propounded—arguments that might bring a smile to Rizal's lips could he but hear them in whatever realm he now dwells. For these claims and counterclaims must contend with a mystery impervious to Rizal Day perorations and doctoral dissertations: to dissect it, to uncover it for all the world to see, is to try to make visible the invisible, to utter the unutterable. But perhaps we can try to examine the edges of the mystery without ever hoping to penetrate into its heart, into the silence, the secret which Rizal carried with him to that region "where he who reigns is God—*donde el que reina es Dios.*"

The evidence, which Rizal biographer Leon Ma. Guerrero pronounced as valid and acceptable in any court of law, would indicate that Rizal did sign the document of retraction. Was it "impossible" for Rizal before his death to have returned to the Catholic faith? "New" documents, torrents of footnotes, do not necessarily lead to the truth; wisdom does not require a long bibliography. Let us not be so dogmatic then as to deny, despite the reasonableness of the original evidence, at least the possibility of the retraction.

Because of prayer, grace and good will, great and honorable men may choose to be reconciled with the Church—the Church finally recognized, despite the distorting haze of human frailty, as the pledge and proof of God's compassion. And such reconciliation or reconversion can take the better part of a lifetime, a few days or hours, or a few seconds. It is less a matter of duration than of intensity. A century after the bitter anticlerical passions of the 1890s, it is neither prudent nor fashionable to reject even the probability that Rizal chose to die in the faith.

To this proposition one might add a speculative footnote or two that may well bring another smile to Rizal's lips—Rizal, in signing the document formally restoring his relationship with the Catholic Church, was being "Jesuitical," not in the pejorative sense of unscrupulous cunning, but in that other rational, Ignatian sense of defining and clarifying the truth, of distinguishing one category of truth from another. And an indication of the precise distinction is to be found in the phrase, "contrary to my condition as a son of the Church," contained in the document.

Anything that was not contrary to that condition Rizal had no need to retract, and therefore in truth and in effect did not retract. The phrase itself Rizal could have suggested or chosen with a half-amused Jesuitical smile as he and Father Balaguer discussed the formula of retraction.

His political convictions, his passionate belief in the freedom and independence of his people, did not contradict, on the contrary they affirmed that condition, that membership in a Church whose true nature, vision and essence, after all, are not Spanish or colonial but Catholic, apostolic and universal. Rizal in the end thus showed himself to be still a son of the Jesuits, methodical and exact, lucid and logical, keenly aware of distinctions, of the difference between form and substance, essence and accident; between the political and the religious; between "frailocracy" and authentic Catholicism; between the Church of Archbishop Nozaleda and Governor-General Polavieja, and the Church of the Apostles, Martyrs and Saints: the Church in evolution toward greater love and service of humankind.

It is not so strange and startling, after all, that the Jesuits should walk with Rizal to his martyrdom, that Rizal should speak and listen to them in the last hours and moments of his life. There is a certain inevitable aptness, grandeur and nobility in that scene at Bagumbayan which suggests the convergence of material and spiritual forces as perceived by Pierre Teilhard de Chardin. From Lapu-lapu the arrow of Filipino consciousness had ascended to its highest point in Rizal the Christian humanist, evolutionist and visionary; and from Manresa and Paris the Jesuit spirit had arced and descended to a convergence with Rizal, on December 30, 1896.

That scene, that moment of convergence between Jose Rizal and the Jesuits, would remind us that reason and faith, science and religion, are allies in the same human enterprise, and that nationalism, patriotism, need not be anti-Catholic or agnostic or atheist. Love of country can be, as it has been for many Filipinos, for many generations, unmistakably Christian. In a time of new heresies and controversies, new dogmas and dispensations, it can also be—*nunc et semper*—Jesuit.

(*Weekend,* 1982)

Don Emilio's Cross

"DESPITE THE LOVE AND FRIENDSHIP Jesus showed toward his twelve disciples, one of them turned out to be a traitor," Gregorio Cadhit said.

He sat with several other men under a tree, there on the beach in the bright and windy March afternoon. The longboats were taking such a long time coming in over a rough sea from the warship anchored two miles out. Telling a story in a joking tone—it was just Cadhit's way of passing the time, entertaining the men, now that the very dangerous and nearly disastrous mission was over.

"The traitor was Judas," Cadhit went on, his expression roguish, provocative. "He sold the Lord for thirty pieces of silver."

Cecilio Segismundo, suddenly agitated, stood up. "What? Why are you telling us this?" he demanded. "What is the point of your story?"

"Well," Cadhit said with a sly grin, "what I am relating has its parallel in the capture of the president of the Republic."

"What parallel?" Segismundo asked, his voice rising, belligerent.

"Well," Cadhit said, "the twelve apostles of Jesus were like us. Don Emilio is like Jesus Christ and you are Judas."

His face twisted as if from a blow, Segismundo drew his revolver. Just as quickly, Cadhit pulled out his gun.

They stood muttering curses, glaring at each other, ready to shoot it out. The men around them drew back, some crying out in alarm.

Col. Frederick Funston, chatting with the other American officers, noticed the commotion and strode up to the two men. He spoke a few words, motioning them to holster their revolvers. They obeyed him. No shots were fired, no blood spilled on the warm sand.

Finally, the longboats from the U.S. Navy gunboat *Vicksburg* heaved through the surf and slid onto the beach. The men who had come in the morning from Palanan some six miles inland and had waited half of the afternoon to be ferried out to the ship now started boarding the boats—Emilio Aguinaldo and his aides, Col. Simeon Villa and Dr. Santiago Barcelona, the three having been taken prisoner in Palanan two days earlier; their captors, led by Colonel (soon Brigadier General) Funston and the other American officers, Capt. Henry Newton, Capt. Russell Hazzard and his brother, Lt. Oliver Hazzard, and Lt. Burton Mitchell; the Spaniard Lorenzo Segovia, Funston's intelligence operative; the former "insurgents" recruited for the mission, Hilario Tal Placido, Dionisio Bato, Gregorio Cadhit, and the courier who had surrendered to the Americans, Cecilio Segismundo; and the contingent of mercenaries, 78 so-called Macabebe Scouts.

Twilight came swiftly on the Pacific shore of Isabela, below the wild, desolate eastern slopes of the Sierra Madre. It was past six in the evening of March 25, 1901, before the last of the Macabebe squads had clambered up the gunboat's gangplank.

For the return trip, the *Vicksburg* did not follow the southern passage of the voyage out, which would have taken the ship back along the eastern coast of Luzon and through San Bernardino Strait to the Sibuyan Sea between Bicol and Mindoro. This time the gunboat with its load of weary, bedraggled but triumphant soldiers and their distinguished prisoner steamed around northern Luzon and then south off the Ilocos, La Union, Zambales, Bataan, and on to Manila—a voyage that took all of two days and three nights, the *Vicksburg* docking at the mouth of the Pasig River at sunrise on March 28, 1901.

During all that time at sea, there was ample chance, as both Aguinaldo and Funston would suggest in their memoirs, for the fallen president of the first Republic and the U.S. Army colonel from Kansas to be better acquainted.

Right from the start, according to both in their recollections years later, it seems the Filipino leader and the American officer had developed a measure of respect if not friendship for each other, on that portentous journey from Palanan to Manila at the beginning of the new century.

"The prisoners were treated with the greatest courtesy, being entertained in the officers' mess, and sitting about on deck whenever they desired," Funston recalled, and as Aguinaldo and his captor talked about whatever then might have weighed on their minds, perhaps over goblets of amiable wine or brandy, a kind of affinity grew between them that might have salved the possible conspirator's unease of one, and the defeat and dejection of the other: an augury of the more amicable strands of what would come to be called Philippine-American relations.

NO AMICABLE REMEMBRANCE, whether Filipino or American, is that brief but highly symbolic incident on that remote shore almost a century ago—Gregorio Cadhit's "little joke" about Judas and Cecilio Segismundo's outrage.

The near-fatal exchange and confrontation, all in Tagalog, was first recounted by an aide of Funston, Maj. William Brown, in a dispatch to Vice President Theodore Roosevelt, arch-foe of Aguinaldo and the "insurrectos." Brown must have heard of the aborted duel from Funston or another officer with the expedition, as he had remained on the *Vicksburg* while the troops and the prisoners waited to be taken aboard.

The same scene as sketched above is recreated by journalist and historian David Haward Bain in *Sitting in Darkness: Americans in the Philippines* (Houghton Mifflin, 1976). The title of this eminently readable history of the Aguinaldo-Funston encounter against the backdrop of the Philippine-American War is from Mark Twain, as Bain himself tells us.

In an essay seething with righteous anger and bitter sarcasm, "To the Person Sitting in Darkness," Twain assailed the "imperialistic aggressions" of the British in Africa, the Germans in China, the Russians in Manchuria and Port Arthur, and beginning in 1898 the Americans in the Philippines.

The world powers, the United States in particular, wrote Twain, professed to have the "Blessings of Civilization" such as liberty, justice, honesty and mercy ready for "export" to China, the Philippines, South Africa and other presumably benighted and uncivilized countries. But these "Blessings" were just "a pretty and attractive display of our civilization, which we reserve for Home Consumption, while inside the bale is the Actual Thing that the Customer Sitting in Darkness buys with his blood and tears and land and liberty. That Actual Thing is, indeed, Civilization, but it is only for Export."

Twain asked: "Shall we go on conferring our Civilization upon peoples that sit in darkness, or shall we give these poor things a rest?"

About the Filipinos then fighting the United States in a war to save their newborn Republic—a war that would rage for more than four years, kill 4,300 American troops, 16,000 Filipino soldiers, and through pestilence, famine and other battle-related causes claim the lives of 200,000 civilians—Twain wrote, alluding to Commodore Dewey's deception and the U.S. Army commander Gen. Thomas Anderson's double-dealing at the expense of the trusting and impressionable Aguinaldo:

"We had lent them guns and ammunition; advised with them; exchanged pleasant courtesies with them; entrusted our Spanish prisoners to their humane and honest hands; fought shoulder to shoulder with them against the common enemy; praised their courage, praised their gallantry . . . borrowed their trenches, borrowed strong positions which they had previously captured from the Spaniard; petted them, lied to them—officially proclaiming that our land and naval forces came to give them their freedom and displace the bad Spanish Government—fooled them, used them until we needed them no longer, then derided the sucked orange and threw it away."

On reading Twain's fierce denunciation of those cunning and violent "Exporters of Civilization," Bain had to wonder at such disgust and bitterness—as if the once peaceable creator of Tom Sawyer and Huckleberry Finn had been "personally betrayed, along with some sacred American ideals." And he continued to wonder, he has confessed, until the American war in Vietnam compelled "a full understanding of that war that had been relegated to footnotes in history books but had once stirred Twain so."

THE SENSE OF A NATION embarked on an immense, murderous deception against an already much abused and grievously wounded people would have likely stirred Twain more and roused him to greater fury. The celebrated novelist turned polemicist must have read the dispatches from the war correspondents or Gen. Arthur MacArthur's headquarters in Manila, on Aguinaldo's capture and its aftermath—including that bit about Segismundo's betrayal—only after the publication of his "Sitting in Darkness" piece in a popular weekly.

Whether as believer or scoffer—he had announced, with cheerful mockery, that he had no use for the Scriptures—how vehemently Twain might have seized on the devilish trickery that entrapped Aguinaldo, infernal grist for his satiric mill. He might then have written a more ferocious indictment inspired by Cadhit's "parallel"—Segismundo as the Traitor prodded by Gringo Pharisees to deliver the victim to his executioners, except that el Presidente, Don Emilio, wore no martyr's crown, and lived to carry his own cross, through the stations of more than a half-century.

In any event, Twain would later make up for his failure to deal with the manner of Aguinaldo's capture and that nasty little epilogue on the beach—which summed it all up for the Filipino cause—the betrayal by Aguinaldo's courier, the treason and treachery of Segovia, Tal Placido, Bato and Cadhit, who had all soldiered for the Revolution and fought under the banner of the Republic; the stratagem employing forged "insurrecto" letters, fake prisoners of war and a company of Macabebe mercenaries that President William McKinley and Gen. Arthur MacArthur could only hail and justify. Twain would take on all this, in his "In Defense of General Funston," published in the *North American Review* in May 1902.

Twain drew an admiring portrait of the Filipino leader, paid tribute to "Aguinaldo's government and the law-abiding character of his subjects," praised the patriotism and courage of his generals and his troops. They continued to ambush and shoot and bolo American boys who only wished to educate them with a Krag, but "they were fighting for their country's independence, the brightest and noblest of all causes, and that is an inspiration which is able to lift up even little people and make them fine and great."

A momentary lapse there, it would seem: a touch of Yankee patronizing of the Little Brown Brother waiting in ambush or just sitting, wasting away in darkness. But Filipinos still at war, still fighting for freedom and homeland, even perhaps Aguinaldo himself, who had by then sworn allegiance to the United States, should have been reassured. His American advocate was in fine form as he ripped with a vengeance into Funston's ruse, "the whole abominable exercise."

As the column of Filipino "reinforcements" approached Palanan with Funston and the four other American officers posing as prisoners of war, a scout was sent forward to ask for food. Aguinaldo promptly obliged, dispatching rice, carabao meat and other provisions to the raiders about to swoop down on his camp. "Every detail of Funston's scheme"—except for this begging for food from his humane and unsuspecting quarry, Twain pointed out—"has been employed in war in the past and stands acquitted of blame by history. By the custom of war it is permissible . . . for a brigadier general (if he so chose) to persuade or bribe a courier to betray his trust; to remove the badges of his rank and disguise himself; none of them is new, all of them have been done before, although not by a brigadier general. But there is one detail that is new . . . It has never been resorted to before in any age of the world, in any country, among any people, savage or civilized . . . When a man is exhausted by hunger to the point where he is too weak to move, he has the right to make supplication to his enemy to save his failing life; but if he takes so much as one taste of that food—which is holy, by the precept of all ages and all nations—he is barred from lifting his hand against that enemy for that time.

"It was left for a brigadier general of volunteers in the American Army to put shame upon a custom which even the degraded friars respected. We promoted him for it.

"This is the first time in the annals of the human race that that gracious custom has been smitten in the face.

"Aguinaldo's capture was legitimate in all details but one. But the one detail annuls the whole matter, and it seems to me that he is cleanly and clearly entitled to his liberty as is any man in the Philippines as elsewhere."

Maybe it was mostly tongue-in-cheek, this "tribute" to Frederick Funston by one of the most trenchant pros in the ironic industry; but if it was, Samuel Clemens' bushy, salt-and-peppery moustache helped him keep a straight farce.

There is nothing of record concerning what Fred Funston, once known as a hard-drinking barroom brawler around San Francisco, considered doing about Twain's sardonic accolade. As for Aguinaldo, who was observed to have begun studying English a day after his capture, in his detention room in Palanan, and who might have managed later to read *Harper's Weekly*—what if the proper and predictable revolucionario had been instead as cunning as a serpent, as wise as a dove, so that when his enemy came to ask for rice, he sent forth Remington bullets and Mauser rifle bayonets?

But it was not that kind of finale. Fate and history, character and destiny and Frederick Funston, with the collaboration of a company of turncoats, renegades and mercenaries, scripted what another era, which had already slouched to these islands and borne to Manila the promise of Hollywood illusions, might have called a different kind of movie.

TO FREDERICK FUNSTON as chief planner, plotter and strategist of the Palanan operation, it must have been nothing less than high adventure calling for uncommon boldness, audacity and derring-do. All these components the crafty, gutsy colonel got, along with enough falsehood, betrayal and deception to persuade President Aguinaldo to lower his guard and his security troops to welcome the enemy, their rifles not loaded as they presented arms in unwary formation in the Palanan plaza, on that March day of infamy.

The story of Aguinaldo's capture has been recounted by Funston, Segovia and Don Emilio himself. Aside from the memoirs of these principal protagonists, there were the dispatches of the New York, Boston and other correspondents, articles in the journals of the period, papers by contemporaries, the works of American and Filipino historians. But from Edwin Wildman's *Aguinaldo: A Narrative of Filipino Ambitions* in 1901 and Raymond Bridgeman's *Loyal Traitors* in 1903 to Antonio K. Abad's *Ang Pagkanulo Kay Heneral Emilio Aguinaldo* in 1919 and James Freeman's *The Capture of Aguinaldo* in 1927; from Teodoro Agoncillo's *History of the Filipino People* in 1977 to Leon Wolff's *Little Brown Brother* in 1981, David Haward Bain's *Sitting in Darkness* in 1984 and Stanley Karnow's *In Our Image: America's Empire in the Philippines* in 1989, each and every chronicle of the Palanan operation has had to hark back to the Funston narrative more than any other source. For the best of historical reasons: Funston could write interestingly of both the overview and the immediate scene, having worked as a reporter and feature writer between college and the army. He was a keen observer of landscape and atmosphere, and a scrupulous note-taker as well, having spent some seven years on assignment as government botanist and explorer in desert, jungle and arctic terrain.

In a tone and style that contrasted with Aguinaldo's dispirited inadequacy ("It is difficult to give you a detailed account of what happened outside the house during the confusion . . .") and Segovia's pompous subservience and self-serving, translated awkwardly from the Spanish ("Really, our march from Casiguran to Palanan was foolhardiness . . . but we, either owing to our strength of will power, or desire to capture Aguinaldo . . . undertook the overbold and hazardous task . . ."), Funston's venture into history covered the whole momentous enterprise—from the chance discovery of Aguinaldo's hidden sanctuary to the expedition's return to Manila, where a dumbfounded Arthur MacArthur, roused out of his bed in Malacañan Palace by Funston's early arrival, received the captive President of the Republic routed and ruined, the fallen leader of what the Americans derided and dreaded as the "Philippine Insurrection."

For Funston, it all began, as usually happens in the course of human events of tremendous consequence, with a note, a message—in this instance, a telegram.

"It was the 8th day of February, 1901," writes the commanding officer of the Fourth District of the U.S. Army's Department of North Luzon, "and in the room that served as an office in the headquarters building at San Isidro [Nueva Ecija], I was going over the morning's work with the adjutant-general of the district, Capt. Edward Smith, when there arrived a telegram that for the moment disturbed our equanimity . . ."

The wire came from Lt. James Taylor who commanded a company of the U.S. 24th Infantry Regiment based in Pantabangan, some 65 miles to the northwest, in the western foothills of the Sierra Madre.

Taylor's message was that "a small band of insurgent soldiers had voluntarily presented themselves to him," Funston continues, "and that the man in command had stated that he was the bearer of dispatches from Emilio Aguinaldo to certain subordinates in Central and Southern Luzon. The letters addressed to Baldomero Aguinaldo, Jose Alejandrino, Urbano Lacuna, Pablo Tecson, Simon Tecson, Teodoro Sandico and other insurgent leaders were in cipher . . . and evidently signed fictitiously, though in a handwriting that resembled Aguinaldo's."

The bearer of dispatches from Aguinaldo was Cecilio Segismundo, from Dupax, Nueva Vizcaya, formerly a constable under the Spanish in Manila before the Revolution, later a corporal and courier attached to Aguinaldo's security company under Maj. Nazario Alhambra. He had not been wounded or captured in battle. He had not been tortured, let alone "water-cured," by the Americans.

But he was "foot-sore and very hungry," and 26 days after setting out from Palanan with his companions he seemed ready to collapse, sick and tired of it all, the war, the constant fear and danger, the hard life in the hostile highlands.

Segismundo knew the town *presidente* or mayor of Pantabangan and sent the official a distressed note. The official was "in the service of the Americans," writes Funston, "and strongly counseled him to present himself to the commander of the local garrison, and give up the correspondence in his charge, and in fact attach himself to the chariot of progress and become an Americanista. I don't suppose the loyal presidente put it just that way, but that is what he meant."

After a few more days hiding in a forest, and further "diplomacy" from the unnamed Americanista collaborator and Lieutenant Taylor, Segismundo surrendered—yielding not only his foot-sore, demoralized self, but the pouch of secret directives from Aguinaldo. What decided him in the end to hand over the crucial dispatches, which would disclose Aguinaldo's whereabouts to the Americans? Could he not have summoned one last desperate surge of patriotism, loyalty and duty, and destroyed the dispatches before surrendering? (And that unidentified mayor of Pantabangan—was he ever exposed and pilloried for encouraging the courier to turn traitor?)

Funston then directed that "the leader of the insurgent band, with the letters that he had given up, be sent to San Isidro at all possible speed." In less than two days, he arrived with his American cavalry escorts at Funston's headquarters.

Segismundo struck Funston as "a very intelligent Ilocano" who looked at him straight in the eye when answering questions "frankly and apparently without reserve, and seemed to be telling the truth and keeping back nothing." The candid, cooperative courier talked about his "recent adventures" in Spanish, which Funston, too, spoke quite well. Without being asked, the corporal come down from the mountains seemed ready to do the colonel's bidding.

Thus did Cecilio Segismundo—Cadhit's "Iscariot," who didn't slink away in terrible anguish and despair to hang himself, but went on to claim his reward of $300 and a commission in the Philippine Scouts—in this way did the courier from Palanan signal the beginning of the end of Aguinaldo's fugitive life and liberty.

DURING HIS FIRST INTERROGATION at the U.S. brigade headquarters in San Isidro, Cecilio Segismundo had talked willingly enough— "frankly and apparently without reserve," Colonel Funston noted: the ingenuous candor of the betrayer.

As the courier from Palanan told it to the American commander—"after being well-fed"—his story was that he had been "attached to Aguinaldo's headquarters and had been with him for many months . . . On the 14th of January, accompanied by a detachment of twelve armed men of Aguinaldo's escort, he had left with a package of letters to be delivered to Urbano Lacuna, the insurgent chief of Nueva Ecija province, who was to forward to their final destination those that were not meant for him."

After a "terrible journey" across mountains and jungles, they had run into an American patrol near Baler, and lost two men. Desperate, without food and civilian support, the small band had been reduced to six by desertions and disease when they came down from a high mountain pass in the Sierra Madre to the lowlands, reaching the outskirts of Pantabangan 26 days after setting out from Aguinaldo's camp. The bone-weary, starved survivors hid out in a barrio forest,

22

and Segismundo, who knew the town presidente, had gotten in touch with the helpful Americanista collaborator . . .

Then—this probably inventive touch of a Pilate added to Cadhit's Judas is mentioned in Bain's *Sitting in Darkness*—"I am glad to wash my hands of this business," Segismundo said as he handed over his pouch of dispatches to the Americans in Pantabangan.

Frederick Funston continues his own narrative: "Segismundo then went on to tell of conditions at Palanan. Aguinaldo with several officers of his staff and an escort of about fifty uniformed and well-armed men had been there for several months . . . The residents of the town and most of the soldiers of his escort were not aware of his identity. He passed himself off as 'Captain Emilio,' and those who did not know him supposed that he was merely a subordinate officer of the insurrection."

The official correspondence that Segismundo said was from the Filipino President and Commander in Chief should be more revealing, Funston realized—if it could be decoded. Still skeptical—the dispatches could be an "insurrecto" ploy to make Aguinaldo's forces appear far stronger and more extensively deployed than they actually were—Funston ordered "a squad of burly soldiers" to hustle the courier away and help him "round out his story."

According to one of the colonel's aides, Segismundo spent "an agreeable afternoon in an empty house" telling everything that he knew about Aguinaldo and the camp in Palanan. Aguinaldo would claim in his memoirs that his messenger had been subjected to the "water cure" at least twice before the Americans finally believed his story. It was as though the old revolucionario reminiscing in Kawit could not accept the notion that his own trusted man had sold out the Revolution, the Republic and his President while having merienda with a squad of sociable gringos.

In any event, Funston and his aides were thoroughly convinced that the Aguinaldo communications were genuine. Composed in what seemed to be, at best, impenetrable Tagalog combined with algebraic equations, they had to be deciphered and translated, fast—but "the cipher letters completely balked us for many hours," recalls Funston.

FOR A WHOLE DAY and late into the night, Funston, his adjutant, Capt. Edward Smith and the Spaniard Segovia sat around a table racking their brains, drinking strong coffee to keep awake.

It was Funston's intelligence operative who broke the code and sealed Aguinaldo's fate as dawn was breaking—aptly enough, and as though foreordained, for Lazaro Segovia y Gutierrez, born and bred in Madrid, had brought to the task all the knowledge and skills, the wiles, cunning and insights he had gained as a renegade, a turncoat, a defector twice over.

Originally an officer with a Spanish regiment in Manila at the time of the Castilian surrender to the Americans in August 1898, Segovia crossed over to Aguinaldo's army two months later, after a failed bid to emigrate with his Filipino wife to some Latin American country. He ended up offering his services in May 1900 to the U.S. Army in the person of Frederick Funston, then in command of a regiment of Kansas Volunteer Infantry fighting in Central Luzon. The Colonel, recognizing "a kindred spirit," had since made Segovia his "trusted aide, translator, guerrilla strategist and spy."

Segovia found the key word in the cipher—the Tagalog for "ammunition" (*munisyon*), with each letter represented by a number—in Aguinaldo's dispatch to Gen. Teodoro Sandico. The breakthrough enabled Segovia to unravel the whole system—the Tagalog alphabet in reverse corresponding to numbers, with some letters assigned random or arbitrary figures as a fool-proof device.

The three correspondence analysts toasted the "peerless and versatile" Segovia's decoding feat with a round of whiskey. On the brink of collapse from going without food and sleep for 20 hours but "wildly enthusiastic," they went on to finish deciphering and translating practically all of the dispatches shortly before noon.

What he now beheld, Funston recognized jubilantly, were "the plans of one man who, for what seemed to be a long time, had been the head and front of the insurrection against the authority of the United States."

The deciphered letters made no mention of their place of origin but contained references to a valley in Cagayan and a route through Isabela to a wilderness on the Pacific coast—and the only inhabited place in that far corner of Northern Luzon, the former Franciscan mission outpost dedicated to Santa Maria Magdalena: Palanan. They were signed "Colon de Magdalo," Aguinaldo's Masonic nom de guerre, confirming for Funston conclusively that "these communications could come only from one who was recognized as the leader of the insurrection, as they gave positive orders to officers of the highest military rank."

THE MOST INTERESTING OF THE LOT—"the one that was the final undoing of its writer," Funston remarks—was the letter addressed to the Filipino leader's cousin, Gen. Baldomero Aguinaldo, who commanded the resistance forces in Cavite.

Baldomero was directed to proceed to the "Center of Luzon," displace Gen. Jose Alejandrino as regional commander, and order Generals Urbano Lacuna, Tomas Mascardo and other military chiefs operating in the area to send reinforcements to Palanan.

"I do not have enough people," Aguinaldo had written his cousin. "Send me about 400 men . . ." The courier Segismundo, it was indicated, would guide the detachment to the President's sanctuary beyond the hidden valley and the wilderness . . .

The orders to Baldomero Aguinaldo were for Funston the summons to plan an operation for the capture of Don Emilio, el Presidente, who for over a year following his rear guard's last stand at Pasong Tirad had eluded the pursuing Americans in the northern highlands of Luzon. Funston spent another sleepless night—"By morning I had thought out the general features of the plan . . . and on asking Segismundo whether it was in his opinion practicable, he replied in the affirmative. There were now all sorts of details to work out"—and the most crucial of these involved the expedition's approach to Palanan.

Filipino outposts along the trail leading eastward over the mountains from the valley in Cagayan would warn the Aguinaldo camp of any advance from that quarter. A landing by ship in the vicinity of Palanan would be as perilous and futile for Funston's crew. Any vessel off the coast even at night was likely to be detected and drive Aguinaldo into a mountain fastness deeper inland.

"It was settled beyond the possibility of a doubt," writes Funston of the projected hunt for his all-important quarry. "So the only recourse was to work out a stratagem, that is, to get him under false colors."

The stratagem in broad outline was approved by Funston's immediate superior and mentor, Gen. Lloyd Wheaton. In Manila, the supreme commander, Gen. Arthur MacArthur (father of Douglas of "I Shall Return" fame), gave the scheme his somewhat doubtful permission.

The driven, daredevil cavalry colonel took three weeks to assemble the plans, personnel and equipment for the mission, and procure those necessary deceptive colors.

For the benefit of Aguinaldo before he could be brought to bay and taken alive, letters and signatures were to be forged— by Segovia and Roman Roque, another "insurrecto" turncoat and a clerk-interpreter at Funston's headquarters in San Isidro. The most impressive of the fabricated correspondence would bear General Lacuna's purported signature, on official stationery with the letterhead "Brigada Lacuna" that the Americans had acquired weeks earlier from an abandoned Filipino command post in Nueva Ecija.

More than any other document or evidence, the fake Lacuna letter, so crafted as to look perfectly authentic and to be delivered in advance of Funston's column, would assure Aguinaldo that "reinforcements" were indeed on the way. The bogus Lacuna contingent would thus gain entry into Palanan, and be welcomed even by Don Emilio, whose aides and security troops would then be quickly overpowered or mowed down, if the mission should be so favored by the fortunes of war . . . So went the general thrust of the plan that Funston and his team would reveal to their Filipino cohort only when the expedition itself was under way.

The infantry company supposedly being sent by General Lacuna would consist of 78 Macabebes (traditional mercenaries employed by the Spanish, now in the service of the Yanquis) posing as Filipino loyalist soldiers; their make-believe officers, the former "insurrectos" enlisted by Funston for the mission—"Colonel" Hilario Tan Placido, "Major" Dionisio Bato, "Lieutenant" Gregorio Cadhit and "Sergeant" Cecilio Segismundo; Lazaro Segovia likewise in the guise of an "insurgent" officer; and the five Americans—Funston as mission commander, Capt. Harry Newton as vice-commander, the brothers Capt. Russell Hazzard and Lt. Oliver Hazzard, and Lt. Burton Mitchell—cast as prisoners of war captured after an encounter with an American patrol on the fictitious march from General Lacuna's camp to Palanan.

At seven o'clock on the evening of March 6, 1901, or a month to the day after Colonel Funston and the surrendered courier Cecilio Segismundo had their first agreeable meeting in San Isidro, Nueva Ecija, the thousand-ton U.S. Navy gunboat *Vicksburg*, with the special force of 88 officers and men on board, pushed off from its berth at the mouth of the Pasig, and steamed across Manila Bay and out past Corregidor . . .

26

AN HOUR LATER, as the *Vicksburg* changes course southward off Batangas, Lazaro Segovia, stretched out in a hammock on the lower deck, begins to feel seasick.

The heat and the movement of the ship are to blame, the 23-year-old Spanish soldier and adventurer will recall later, in his own account of the expedition. Unfortunately, he reflects, he was not born for the sea. For other things, perhaps, like changing armies and loyalties, but this he does not say.

In search of fresh air, Segovia struggles to the upper deck. He steps carefully among the Macabebe troops sitting or lying about on the dark deck, and looks around for "a soft, comfortable place." He wants to know if the forward thrust of the ship is "harder" at the stern than at the bow. A sympathetic sailor decides the matter for the "extremely unwell" Segovia, guiding him to a spot amidships that seems more level and steady than the rest of the gunboat.

He and the sailor chat for a long while, which does him good. About to doze off in his cozy nook, he hears his name being called. Lieutenant Mitchell comes up to tell him that he is wanted by Colonel Funston. He goes down to the Colonel's cabin.

The bearded, wiry, five-foot-four Funston looks up at the tall Spaniard. "Hi, Segovia, how are things going?"

"Everything's all right, Colonel—except for my head and stomach."

"What's the matter? You already seasick?"

"No, not really," Segovia chuckles, unwilling to show any weakness. "But I may soon be if the ship keeps on rocking like this."

"Very well," says Colonel Funston, "tomorrow the people here must be told the objective of our expedition. You will inform your fellow officers. Captain Newton and Captain Russell will tell the Macs. You must keep alert, eyes and ears open, Segovia. Play close attention to anything both parties might say, scouts and native officers, about this mission. We must be absolutely sure about their sentiments . . ."

"Rest assured, Colonel. I'll take care of that, sir. Anything suspicious I'll report to you at once. I'll be watching them."

"Very good, Segovia. Hey, you don't look well. You'd better get some rest. Tomorrow the real work begins. Good night."

"Good night, Colonel."

Segovia returns to his comfortable nook on the upper deck. He cannot stop thinking of the mission, their objective, and past midnight he is still awake, on the blacked-out ship slicing through the dark sea, under an overcast sky with a smudge of a waning moon . . .

In Palanan, far away to the north, in the schoolhouse by the river that serves as his headquarters, on a carved four-poster bed that Col. Simeon Villa somehow hauled from somewhere across the mountains, Emilio Aguinaldo sleeps soundly—he does snore, sometimes with a loud strangled rasp or choking groan that wakens and worries Dr. Santiago Barcelona lying on his mat across the room. If in his deep sleep on this night Don Emilio dreams at all, it is perhaps of his coming 32nd birthday: a fiesta like last year's celebration in Bontoc, with band music, horse races, amateur dramas, serenades, the rigodon and other dances, a banquet and over a hundred invited guests, including General Tinio and General Mascardo and Colonel Joaquin and Major Quijano and other senior officers based in other provinces, soldiers from the outposts on the trail from the mountains, various village leaders and prominent citizens of Casiguran town some 90 miles to the south and not far from a desolate stretch of coast where, on March 14, 1901, on a night filled with rain and the sounds of a rising sea, Colonel Funston and his men will land from the *Vicksburg* to begin their trek to Palanan, to the Fil-American double-cross and capture and captivity of Emilio Aguinaldo.

(Graphic, 1999)

The Phenomenon of Teilhard de Chardin

TWELVE YEARS AGO, ON EASTER SUNDAY in New York City, a tall, gentle, white-haired French priest with wise, pensive eyes on the finely sculpted face of a nobleman was struck down by a heart attack. A month earlier, he had told friends of his hope that when God saw fit to take him, it would be on the Day of the Resurrection.

Father Marie-Joseph Pierre Teilhard de Chardin (Tay-ar d' shar-Dann) died at 73 as he had lived for most of his life—an exile. His exile, in more senses than one, was not just from kin and country. Forbidden to teach and publish his works as a scientist during his lifetime, he spent years separated, as it were, from the contemporary current of history, probing into the secrets of rocks and bones millions of years old in the remotest corners of the earth. He was, for all his assurances of fealty, estranged from the official thinking of his religious superiors and the institutions of Rome. The Vatican at one time issued a formal warning, a *monitum*, against the dangers to the Faith posed by his reinterpretation of Christianity in the light of evolution, which to him was no mere theory but the existing and indispensable key to the meaning of the universe. Not a few of his companions in the Society of Jesus viewed the man, if not with alarm, at least with puzzled skepticism; and even fellow paleontologists—scientists whose particular discipline is the study of past geological periods as known from fossil remains—considered him an enemy of accepted methods and ideas. To learned men within and outside the Catholic Church, he seemed to be working against the greater glory of science and religion.

Thus, when Pierre Teilhard de Chardin died, the absence of pomp and ceremony at his funeral, aside from being a tradition among the Jesuits, might have been regarded by the more worldly as a fittingly obscure end for a man deserving of oblivion: the world would hear no more of him. The service at St. Ignatius Church in New York, we are told, was "simple to the point of poverty." There were no more than ten mourners, and only one, Father Pierre Leroy, accompanied the body on the 75-mile trip to the Jesuit cemetery at St. Andrew-on-the-Hudson. The priest-scientist who had traveled far and wide over the earth, farther perhaps than any other man if we take into account journeys of the mind unreckoned by miles or even light-years, rests there today, under a stark headstone among others similarly fashioned, at the edge of a forest.

A photograph of the austere cemetery illustrated an article on Teilhard de Chardin by John Kobler in *The Saturday Evening Post,* in 1963. Three dates are inscribed in Latin on the headstone, beneath the name Pierre Teilhard, S.J. ("de Chardin" was added to the original family name after a 19th-century marriage): born May 1, 1881; entered the Society of Jesus, May 19, 1899; died April 10, 1955. In the fall the winds tear the last leaves from the forest and scatter them between the rows of tombs.

Today the winds of change and renewal are blowing through Christendom, the late Pope John XXIII, in his own words, having opened wide the windows of the Church: a metaphor Father Teilhard would have appreciated, for he had a passion, a poetic feeling for wide open spaces, gulls on the wing, skies and far-ranging horizons. And one of the moving spirits behind these winds, no less than Pope John himself conceded, is the Jesuit Teilhard. Indeed, the tone of the Second Vatican Council, with its stress on the need to "bring the Church into step with modern times," its optimism and its hopes for Christian unity, and more recently, Pope Paul VI's concern with the "development of peoples," appear to reflect Teilhard's influence, grown wider and more pervasive since his death.

In an essay on Christ and the universe written in the last year of his life, Father Teilhard had observed that "if the truth appears once, in one single mind, that is enough to ensure that nothing can ever prevent it from spreading to everything and setting it ablaze." The truth as the priest and scientist perceived it is no longer confined to unpublished manuscripts guarded by the Holy Office. More than a million copies of his ten published books have been sold; difficult, labyrinthine, controversial, his style nothing less than the involved reflections of a scientific Joyce or mystical Faulkner, he is being read by Christians and the faithful of other creeds, atheists, unbelievers, agnostics, and the merely curious. Bibliophiles of any number of faiths who give up on Teilhard in Chapter 1—"The Stuff of the Universe"— of his most famous work, *The Phenomenon of Man*, reserve for him a place of honor among their Kierkegaards, Sartres, and Bertrand Russells. Far from complete, posthumous publication of his writings is being supervised by an international committee composed of, among others, historian Arnold Toynbee, the nuclear physicist Robert Oppenheimer, biologist Julian Huxley and man of letters Andre Malraux. No less than men of science and philosophy, the writers of our time have paid tribute to his singular influence. He was the model for the philosophical Father Tassin in Romain Gary's novel, *The Roots of Heaven,* which, appropriately enough, deals with the splendor and nobility of a form of animal life in the African veldt; and for the brilliant and humble Father Telemond in Morris West's *The Shoes of the Fisherman*. Flannery O'Connor used as the title of her last collection of short stories Teilhard's mystical axiom: "Everything that Rises Must Converge."

In Europe and South America, associations dedicated to propagating his ideas have sprung up, and his vision of mankind has inspired numerous studies, interpretations, conferences, symposiums in various countries, not to mention the adulation of Marxists who see in his philosophy a confirmation of their own doctrines on the socialistic and collective future of mankind. One of his most outspoken admirers is the Communist Roger Garaudy, head of the Center of Marxist Studies in Paris and one of the leaders of the current dialogue between Christian and Communist intellectuals in Europe. For his part, the French-educated Catholic President of the African nation of Senegal, Leopold Sedar Senghor, would advance Teilhard's ideas as an antidote to communism. Marxism, according to Senghor, might "cure our underdevelopment," but "it could not satisfy our spiritual hunger. Father Teilhard enabled us to transcend the paradox of materialism and spirituality." The Jesuit thinker who proclaimed that "the most humanized groups appear always, in the end, as the product not of a segregation, but of a synthesis," has found ardent champions, thanks to Senghor, among the political leaders and intellectuals of the African continent where, one recalls with a certain awe at the profound aptness of it all, the phenomenon of man that so obsessed Teilhard is said to have had its mysterious beginnings more than a million years ago.

IN AN AGE OF STRIFE, CLASS CONFLICT, disintegration, dark forebodings and the ever present danger of nuclear war, the appeal of Teilhard de Chardin derives mainly, it would seem, from the boundless optimism of the man and all his works. To begin with, evolution to him was not a process of blind chance leading, inevitably, to that solar doomsday billions of years from now when all energy will have been expended, the hydrogen atoms of the sun will have been consumed and the sun itself will have expired into a cold cinder. This, as Teilhard himself was well aware, is what science says is the fate of our world.

"I believe in science," he wrote, "but up to now has science ever troubled to look at the world except from without?" Since evolution was a process planned by God, He must have provided, according to Teilhard, a kind of energy that transcended the laws of thermodynamics and would prevent "universal decay." This "radial" or spiritual energy, which acted on the "Inside of Things," or consciousness, he went on, is capable of producing higher forms of life ad infinitum, thus reversing the spiraling descent, as of a spent rocket, of the world into a cold, immobile darkness.

With this energy, the universe is constantly ascending, so to speak, striving to perfect itself. The stages of evolution, from the pre-life of atoms and molecules, to life in plants and animals, to consciousness and thought in man, attest to this irresistible thrust toward perfection. And evolution does not end with man as he is today, the complex creature that moved Hamlet to both rhapsodic praise and ironic dismay: beyond present life and consciousness lies hyper-life, the threshold of which, Teilhard believed, 20th century man has just entered: "Something is happening to human conscious-ness. It is another species of life that is just beginning."

The chief attribute of this new species is thought, and thought has generated around the earth a new layer which Teilhard called the "noosphere" (from the Greek term for mind: *noos*), a layer as real and recognizable to him as the hydrosphere, of water, and the atmosphere, of air. As if anticipating that other prophet of modern communica-tions, Marshall MacLuhan, he wrote of "the earth not only covered by myriads of grains of thought but becoming enclosed in a single thinking envelope so as to form, functionally, no more than a single vast grain of thought. . ." Enclosed in this "thinking envelope," the noosphere, men are destined to be united: "on a round planet they keep meeting, they intermarry, they interbreed—communication is inevitable." As social progress brings about an intensification of the noosphere, men will in time arrive at the culminating synthesis of evolution, borne there by a unique quality of "radial" energy, the love of the "cosmic Christ." United in and by this love to form a kind of universal mind, the human race will then be united with the Omega Point: God: the final end of evolution and of the world.

Teilhard coined another word, "noogenesis," for the movement that would take the human race to the point of final convergence. "Noogenesis rises upwards in us and through us unceasingly," he wrote in the concluding chapter of *The Phenomenon of Man*. "We have pointed to the principal characteristics of that movement: the close association of the grains of thought; the synthesis of individuals and of nations or races; the need of an autonomous and supreme personal focus to bind elementary personalities together, without deforming them, in an atmosphere of active sympathy. And, once again: all this results from the combined action of two curvatures—the roundness of the earth and the cosmic convergence of mind—in conformity with the law of complexity and consciousness.

"Now when sufficient elements have sufficiently gathered together, this essentially convergent movement will attain such intensity and such quality that mankind, taken as a whole, will be obliged—as happened to the individual forces of instinct—to reflect upon itself at a single point; that is to say, in this case, to abandon its organo-planetary foothold so as to shift its center on to the transcendent center of its increasing concentration. This will be the end of the fulfillment of the spirit of the earth.

"The end of the world: the wholesale internal introversion upon itself of the noosphere . . . detaching the mind, fulfilled at last, from its material matrix, so that it will henceforth rest with all its weight on God-Omega."

As "our planet approaches the final stage of maturity," Teilhard prophesied, "evil . . . will be reduced to a minimum. Disease and hunger will be conquered by science and we will no longer need to fear them in any acute form. And, conquered by the science of the earth and human sense, hatred and internecine struggles will have disappeared in the ever-warmer radiance of Omega. Some sort of unanimity will reign over the entire mass of the noosphere. The final convergence will take place in peace. . ."

In the book's epilogue, he wrote with lyrical confidence: "Christianity is the unique current of thought, on the entire surface of the noosphere, which is sufficiently audacious and sufficiently progressive to lay hold of the world . . . in an embrace, at once already complete, yet capable of indefinite perfection, where faith and hope reach their fulfillment in love. Alone, unconditionally alone in the world today, Christianity shows itself able to reconcile, in a single living act, the All and the Person. Alone it can bend our hearts not only to the service of that tremendous movement of the world which bears us along, but beyond, to embrace that movement in love. . . .

"The palpable influence on our world of another and supreme Someone. . . . Is not the Christian phenomenon, which rises upwards at the heart of the social phenomenon, precisely that?

"In the presence of such perfection in coincidence, even if I were not a Christian but only a man of science, I think I would ask myself this question."

Because his triumphant vision little stressed such doctrines as original sin and divine grace, orthodox theologians have been quick to detect the odor of heresy in his works. Father Jean Danielou, a renowned Jesuit in his own right, and one of the theological experts who served at the Vatican Council, observes that a man should base his life on the hope of individual salvation rather than on the certainty of an evolutionary movement carrying humanity to absolute perfection in the remote future. The agnostic Julian Huxley, who wrote the introduction to the English translation of *The Phenomenon of Man,* voices the viewpoint of fellow scientists when he asserts that he finds it "impossible to follow (Teilhard) all the way in his gallant attempt to reconcile the supernatural elements of Christianity with the facts and implications of evolution." Huxley points to certain possible shortcomings: "The biologist may perhaps consider that in *The Phenomenon of Man* he paid insufficient attention to genetics and the possibilities and limitations of natural selection . . . the social scientist, that he failed to take sufficient account of the facts of political and social history." Other critics have attacked him for his "sheer mysticism" and his faith in human progress and the certainty of universal survival in the shadow of the Bomb.

Perhaps it was to detractors who would question his optimism that Teilhard addressed these words, in a letter to a friend:

"I do not see man as a static center of the world, but as the axis and leading shaft of evolution, which is something far finer, because in you and me, through matter, the whole history of the world is in part reflected. The trouble, as I keep emphasizing, is that we don't look far enough. It's the old problem of seeing. We are continually inclined to isolate ourselves from the things and events that surround us, as though we were spectators, looking at them from the outside, not elements in what is going on.

"If I say the word history, your mind probably races back six thousand years. That's the most—and that's because you are thinking of history in terms of dates and recorded events. But when you see history in its proper perspective, it's far longer. In the history of the world's evolution 30,000 years are like a flash. I have concentrated so much on the past, on the earliest phases of the universe before even man existed, because I believe it helps to give us surprising visions of the future. Man is no more static than the world, for he too, like the world, is evolving all the time.

"In the books which I read as a boy, man was presented to me as an erratic object in a disjointed world, a conscious being standing

34

like an actor before an unconscious backcloth. This is where as a scientist I feel bound to make a protest.

"I am optimistic about man—and I am not forgetting the bombs that were dropped on Nagasaki and Hiroshima. Let me say why. Nothing on earth will ever saturate our desire for knowledge, so that as we advance toward a human era of science, so we shall find it will be eminently an era of human science. You will have the paradox where man, the knowing subject, will perceive at last that man, the object of knowledge, is the key to the whole science of nature. In short, man is the solution of everything that we can know. To decipher man is to try and find out how our world was made and how it ought to go on making itself. . . ."

And on another occasion, he wrote on his favorite theme:

"As soon as the universe admits thought within itself, it can no longer be merely temporary nor can there be limits to its evolution. It must, from its very structure, progress into the absolute. Hence, whatever appearance of instability we may find in life, and however impressed we may be by its strict attachment to the spatial dimensions that delimit it and the forces that disintegrate it, one thing above all is certain (because it is as certain as the world itself): namely, that Spirit always will, as it always has, make sport of every sort of determinism and chance. It represents the indestructible portion of the universe."

THE WORSHIP OF THE DURABLE, the indestructible, seemed to have always been a dominant quality of his temperament. As a boy in the tiny mountain village of Sarcenat, in the French province of Auvergne, "he looked always for durability in his possessions and was not greatly attracted by the frail coloring of butterflies or the evanescent beauty of flowers," writes Father Pierre Leroy, who worked with Teilhard in China, in an introductory essay to *The Divine Milieu*. He collected commonplace objects which he called his "idols": a little metal rod, a plow-spanner, nails, shell casings. "I withdrew into the contemplation of my 'God of Iron,'" he was to reveal later. "Why iron? Because in my childish experience nothing was harder, tougher, more durable than this wonderful substance. There was about it a feeling of full personality, sharply individualized."

But iron, the boy soon realized with despair, could be consumed by rust: "I had to look elsewhere for substitutes that would console me. Sometimes in the blue flame (at once so material, and yet so pure and intangible) flickering over the logs in the hearth, but more often in a more transluscent and more delightfully colored stone: quartz or amethyst crystals, and most of all glittering fragments of chalcedony such as I could pick up in the neighborhood." He and his father, who demanded of his eleven children "active cooperation in a disciplined family life," went on long walks in the countryside gathering specimens of rocks and minerals. This early concern with the durable, and the sense of spirit pervading matter, were to shape his vocation as a priest and scientist.

At 18 Pierre Teilhard entered the Jesuit novitiate at Aix-en-Provence. Three years later, in 1902, he embarked on the first of the many journeys of his life: the religious orders were expelled from France by the anticlerical government, and he and his fellow-scholastics found refuge on the English island of Jersey. When not immersed in his philosophical studies, he went on scientific excursions around the rocky island, armed with a geologist's hammer and a naturalist's magnifying glass. In 1905 he was sent to teach physics and chemistry at the Jesuits' Holy Family College in Cairo, where he endeavored "to deepen and extend his still imperfect knowledge of geology and paleontology."

Egypt's strangeness, "nature in its richness and diversity," exerted on him a strong fascination, and perhaps part of it was already the call of Asia: "The East flowed over me in a wave of exoticism; I gazed at it and drank it in eagerly—the country itself, not its peoples or its history (which as yet held no interest for me) but its light, its vegetation, its fauna and its deserts." At the same time, as if to suggest that henceforth his preoccupations would be not merely with what he called "the cosmic in the solid state," he was filled with "a sense of fulfillment, ease and of being at home" by the "world of electrons, nuclei and waves," which he studied and taught. "There was the dawning attraction of the nature of plants and animals; and, underlying everything, one day there came my initiation into the less tangible (but how exciting!) grandeur brought to light by the researches of physics. On both sides I saw matter, life and energy: the three pillars on which my inner vision and happiness rested."

The physics of atomic structure prompted in him the thought that "to escape the inexorable fragility of the manifold," one might "take refuge beneath it. . . . Thus we may gain the world by renouncing it, by passively losing self in the heart of what has neither form nor dimension." But he was too much of a Christian dedicated to action, notes Father Leroy, to succumb to the "eastern" solution: not for him the attraction of losing one's identity in a vague impersonal universe. Shortly after, in England where he was sent for the last stages of his Jesuit training, he realized more than ever the "oneness, solidity and intensity" of the universe: "at sunset in particular . . . the Sussex woods seemed to be charged with all the 'fossil' life that I was then looking for, from cliffs to quarries, and in the clays of the Weald. Sometimes it seemed to me as though suddenly some sort of universal being was about to take on shape in nature before my very eyes."

The Jesuits had returned to France, and he was by then an ordained priest and attached to the paleontological laboratory of the Paris Museum of Natural History, when World War I broke out. He served as a stretcher-bearer in a Moroccan regiment. The horrors of war could not diminish his Christian faith and mystical ardor. After days of carnage at the front, he wrote to a cousin, Claude Aragonnes: "I'm glad to have been at Ypres. I hope I shall have emerged more of a man and more of a priest. And more than ever I believe that life is beautiful, in the grimmest circumstances—when you can see God, ever-present, in them." The front line was not simply "the exposed area corroded by the conflict of nations, but the 'front of the wave' carrying the world of man toward its new destiny. When you look at it during the night, lit up by flares, after a day of more than usual activity, you seem to feel that you're at the final boundary between what has already been achieved and what is struggling to emerge."

A Christian who saw God even in the midst of forces that denied Him, he also proved himself a man of superlative courage. For valor he was awarded the Military Medal and made a Chevalier of the Legion of Honor. He volunteered often to serve in the forward trenches, and retrieved the bodies of fallen comrades "on ground torn by shellfire and swept by machine guns." A fellow soldier asked him how he managed to keep so calm in battle; he replied with a smile: "If I'm killed, I shall change my state, that's all." He would remark later that the reality he found as a stretcher-bearer would be with him forever "in the great task of understanding creation and how it must become more and more sanctified."

At war's end Father Teilhard returned to his scientific studies, earned his doctorate at the Sorbonne, was appointed professor of geology at the Catholic Institute in Paris. The novelty and daring of his lectures began to arouse an enthusiastic following, to the dismay of his superiors, who were only too glad to grant him permission to leave Paris and join a paleontological expedition to China sponsored by the Museum of Natural History and directed by another Jesuit, Father Emile Licent. At the start of what he called his "Asian Adventure," the major goals of his life, says Julian Huxley, were clearly indicated: "Professionally, he had decided to embark on a geological career, with special emphasis on paleontology. As a thinker, he had reached a point where the entire phenomenal universe, including man, was revealed as a process of evolution, and he found himself impelled to build up a generalized theory or philosophy of evolutionary process which would take account of human history and human personality as well as of biology, and from which one could draw conclusions as to the future evolution of man on earth. And as a dedicated priest he felt it imperative to try to reconcile Christian theology with this evolutionary philosophy, to relate the facts of religious experience to those of natural science."

A sea voyage from Marseilles took him to Tientsin, the northern Chinese port not far from Peking, in 1923, and in a China "more unsettled than ever," he spent a whole year absorbed in the discovery and study of fossil deposits, in the process "consolidating his dangerous thoughts." That such thoughts served only to confirm his convictions as a priest rather than weaken them is a measure of the depth of his unique vision: it was during this period, in the remoteness of the abandoned hills and canyons of the Ordos Desert of Mongolia, that he composed his poetic masterpiece, *The Mass upon the Altar of the World*:

"Since once again, Lord—though this time not in the forests of the Aisne but in the steppes of Asia—I have neither bread, nor wine, nor altar, I will raise myself beyond these symbols, up to the pure majesty of the real itself; I, your priest, will make the whole earth my altar and on it will offer you all the labors and sufferings of the world.

"One by one, Lord, I see and love all these whom you have given me to sustain and charm my life . . . those who surround me and support me though I do not know them; those who come and those who go; above all, those who in office, laboratory and factory, through their vision of truth or despite their error, believe in the progress of earthly reality and who today will take up again their impassioned pursuit of the light. . . .

"Christ of glory, hidden power stirring in the heart of matter, glowing center in which the unnumbered strands of the manifold are knit together; strength inexorable as the world and warm as life; you whose brow is of snow, whose eyes are of fire, whose feet are more dazzling than gold poured from the furnace; you whose hands hold captive the stars; you, the first and the last, the living, the dead, the re-born; you who gather up in your superabundant oneness every delight, every taste, every energy, every phase of existence, to you my being cries out with a longing as vast as the universe: for you indeed are my Lord and my God."

He returned to France, only to find himself barred from teaching: his Jesuit superiors had come upon the two closely written pages on which he had set down for a young colleague his views on original sin, which he tended to regard not as a historical fact but as a mere theory to account for the existence of evil. He was ordered to limit his endeavors to scientific research abroad, and ever the obedient Jesuit, "deeply wounded but submissive," in the words of his friend Father Licent, often depressed but bearing with patience "trials that might well have proved too much for the strongest of us," hiding his suffering and abandoning himself to "Christ as the only purpose of his being," he returned to China, where he was to live and work, with brief visits to France and the United States, and expeditions to Africa, India, Burma and Java, for more than twenty years. As scientific adviser to the Geological Survey of China, he collaborated with outstanding paleontologists of various nations and beliefs, made important contributions to the knowledge of paleolithic cultures in China and neighboring areas, and played a major role in the discovery of the 300,000-year-old skull of Peking Man, *Sinanthropus*, one of the greatest anthropological finds of the century.

Glimpses into the life of the Jesuit explorer during this period Claude Aragonnes gives us in her preface to Teilhard's *Letters from a Traveller*: "Field work always had an enormous attraction for him. Although he had to spend so much time in the laboratory, he was essentially a scientist of the open air, and to touch Mother Earth—as in the Greek myth—made him feel younger. . . He was always ready to go anywhere. . . .

"He was often a pioneer in uncharted regions. Teilhard the naturalist, geologist and paleontologist had to become an expert in topography, zoology, botany and ethnography. As he journeyed he studied the different races he encountered, their mentality, habits and culture. And this over vast territories. The China which he traversed in every direction from 1923 to 1940 was still the old immemorial China in which long caravans made their way along mere tracks, the China in which road and rail were still almost unknown— the Mongolian and Gobi deserts, the banks of the Hwang-Ho and the Yangtze, the lost corners of Honan and Shansi . . . it was no small thing to lead expeditions into those lost regions. . . .

"When he emerged from the interior and arrived at Peking, Pierre Teilhard found a totally different China, a China brimming with intellectual and political ferment and an intelligentsia avid for knowledge and emancipation. This China welcomed scientific research and hence foreign scientists—Americans, Swedes, Danes, Germans. The value of Pierre Teilhard's specialist collaboration was immediately recognized . . . Convinced that the internationalism of science was to be one of the mind's greatest achievements, he served as a link between the cosmopolitan elements which made up Peking society between the two wars. He had many friends in the legations and the embassies. . . .

"Ceaseless travel meant continual meetings. One day Pierre Teilhard came across a friend in some remote corner of the globe. He greeted him so warmly that the other expressed mild surprise. 'Why am I so happy?' said the traveller. 'Why, because the earth is round!'"

It was at friendly gatherings in the Peking of the 1930s, according to Father Licent, that one saw the "real" Teilhard: "his mere presence brought an assurance of optimism and confidence. He had, too, that sort of mind that needs to retain and even multiply its contacts with the world outside . . . he had to discuss his way of seeing things with other people.

"Not that his conversation was always serious or pitched on a high level. He was often, on the contrary, lively, cheerful; he appreciated good cooking and a good story. . . He had a fine sense of humor: his face would light up like a child's at a good joke; and if sometimes he could not resist an inviting target for his sly wit—after all, on his mother's side the blood of Voltaire flowed in his veins—it was done with such unaffected good humor that no one could take it in bad

40

part. It was one of his outstanding characteristics that he never gave way to bitterness, not even when decisions were taken that prevented the dissemination of his ideas. . . ."

DURING ALL THIS TIME he was writing his books and his essays: the prohibition to publish he could accept, but nothing could stop him from writing. "If I ceased to write," he said, "I would be a traitor." *The Phenomenon of Man* was completed in Peking, in 1940. Rome would not relax its ban on the publication of his controversial manuscripts, and on his return to France after the last world war, in 1946, although elected a member of the Academy of Sciences, he was forbidden from accepting any academic post. But convinced by a sympathetic Jesuit, Father Raymond Jouve, that the vow of poverty did not cover manuscripts, he appointed a literary executor who would take charge of publication outside his order, after his death.

From South Africa in 1951, where he was on an expedition for the Wenner-Gren Foundation for Anthropological Research based in New York, he wrote to the General of the Jesuits in Rome, the Very Rev. John Janssens, explaining, "with the frankness that is one of the Society's most precious assets," why he believed there was no contradiction between his loyalty as a son of the Church and his faith as a scientist: "I feel that you must resign yourself to taking me as I am, that is, with the congenital quality (or weakness) which ever since my childhood has caused my spiritual life to be completely dominated by a sort of profound 'feeling' for the organic realness of the World. At first it was an ill-defined feeling in my mind and heart, but as the years went by it gradually became a precise, compelling sense of the Universe's general convergence upon itself; a convergence which coincides with, and culminates at its zenith in, Him in whom all have their being, and whom the Society has taught me to love.

"In the consciousness of this progression and synthesis of all things in Christ, I have found an extraordinary rich and inexhaustible source of clarity and interior strength, and an atmosphere outside which it is now impossible for me to breathe, to worship, to believe. What might have been taken in my attitude during the last thirty years for obstinacy or disrespect is simply the result of my absolute inability to contain my own feeling of wonderment. Everything stems from that basic condition, and I can no more change it than I can change my age or the color of my eyes . . . the immediate effect of the interior attitude I have just described is to rivet me ever more firmly to three convictions which are the very marrow of Christianity.

"The unique significance of Man as the spearhead of Life; the position of Christianity as the central axis in the convergent bundle of human activities; and finally the essential function as consummator assumed by the Risen Christ at the center and peak of Creation: these three elements have driven (and continue to drive) roots so deep and so entangled in the whole fabric of my intellectual and religious perception that I could now tear them out only at the cost of destroying everything.

"I can truly say—and this in virtue of the whole structure of my thought—that I now feel more indissolubly bound to the hierarchical Church and the Christ of the Gospel than ever before in my life. Never has Christ seemed to me more personal or more immense.

"How, then, can I believe that there is any evil in the road that I am following?

"I truly recognize, of course, that Rome may have its reason for judging that, in its present form, my concept of Christianity may be premature or incomplete and that at the present moment its wider diffusion may therefore be inopportune.

"It is on this important point of formal loyalty and obedience that I am particularly anxious to assure you that, in spite of apparent evidence to the contrary, I am resolved to remain a 'child of obedience.'

"Obviously I cannot abandon my own personal search—that would involve me in an interior catastrophe and in disloyalty to my most cherished vocation . . . the Wenner-Gren Foundation which sent me here is already asking me to prolong my stay in America as long as I can: they want me to classify and develop the data obtained from my work in Africa. All this allows me a breathing spell and gives a purely scientific orientation to the end of my career—and of my life.

"This letter is simply an exposition of conscience and calls for no answer from you. Look on it simply as proof that you can count on me unreservedly to work for the kingdom of God, which is the one thing I keep before my eyes and the one goal to which science leads me."

He spent the last years of life peacefully resigned, it seemed, to his fate. He continued to write: *The Convergence of the Universe, Vision of the Past, The God of Evolution, The Appearance of Man, Le Christique*. He read the monographs of Julian Huxley, and the novels of the other Huxley, Aldous, and of Graham Greene, also a Catholic with a penchant for the unorthodox. His letters to friends were serene as always, with a radiant fidelity to his hopes for mankind. He spent long hours in the laboratory, as he had done in all the stations of his exile; his days were devoted to work and prayer. Each morning he celebrated his private Mass. In an order famed for its discipline as much as for its achievements, he was an exceptional follower of Ignatius. The older Jesuits are dispensed from the custom of a monthly spiritual consultation with their superiors—but Teilhard, said Father Robert Gannon, former rector of New York's St. Ignatius Loyola parish, "busy as he was, and living in rooms outside the parish," would come to him every month "as humbly as the youngest novice."

He often prayed, by his own account, for more than "a good death." He asked to be granted "something still more precious than the grace for which all the faithful pray. It is not enough that I should die while communicating. Teach me to communicate while dying."

It is perhaps in answer to Pierre Teilhard's prayer that the world has not been deprived of the body of his work. He would speak still, communicate his vision, though his own body be returned to dust; the endurance of his thought speaks well of the faith he served so well to the last. At the heart of that faith shines the same hope that another seer and champion of Christ, the apostle Paul, uttered centuries ago: that someday "God shall be in all": that despite all hardship, all pain and tribulation; despite hatred, terror and error, and all manner of cataclysm, ruin, disaster and evil, wars and rumors of wars, the ultimate destiny of the human race will be a convergence in unity, love and peace.

The human soul, said Tertullian, one of the early Fathers of the Church, is naturally Christian. In our time, with its ovens for genocide, its napalm and hydrogen bombs, when not just nations but the entire planet and its future are imperilled, is not any optimism about the development of mankind in peace and love naturally, inherently, most certainly Christian? Saintly priest, revolutionary prophet, brilliant scientist, "the Aquinas of modern thought," "a new Galileo," "one of the greatest minds of the century"—all these Teilhard de Chardin has been called; but perhaps his greatest distinction was that, heart, mind and soul, he was simply yet astonishingly and magnificently a Christian optimist.

(Free Press, 1967)

Christians for Revolution

IT IS SAID THAT WHEN POPE JOHN XXIII opened wide the windows of the Catholic Church, a pack of priests jumped out and landed on their heads.

In a daze, and who wouldn't be, some ran off to get married, to the consternation of their bishops and their parishioners, and have since sunk out of sight. Others equally restive and adventurous didn't drop out of the clergy altogether but have been acting rather oddly, even scandalously, just the same—their conduct strange and scandalous, the concerned Catholic might reply to the cynical, anticlerical jest, only to those who have no use for a progressive, revolutionary Church (as distinguished from the reactionary, institutional Church), an authentic and therefore radical Christianity.

The dramatic prototype, a sort of John the Baptist of the latter breed of unconventional priests, was Camilo Torres of Colombia.

When Father Camilo Torres announced that he could no longer celebrate Mass in an unjust society, he was branded a degenerate renegade by the ruling class. When he joined the Army of National Liberation, Communist-led guerrillas fighting a neocolonial and fascistic regime, not a few Christians in Latin America, including eminences and very reverend fathers, decided he had for all practical purposes lost his mind as well as his soul. When the 39-year-old university chaplain, sociology professor, labor leader and resistance fighter was killed in a clash with government troops in February 1966, just two months after joining the guerrillas, the church-going politicians and landlords of that underdeveloped, still unliberated Catholic country must have rejoiced to be rid at last of the troublesome rebel priest.

His fate recalls that of a contemporary and a mentor, Che Guevara: the enemies of the Colombian revolution buried the priest's body, but they could not destroy his ideas, the fire of his vision.

In Argentina, an underground group of priests and laymen calls itself the "Camilo Torres Commandos." In Guatemala, two Maryknoll priests and a nun left their missionary posts to join a band of guerrillas known as the "Camilo Torres Front." In Brazil, Bishop Jorge Marcos de Oliveira outraged the pious aristocracy when he declared that he would support a popular armed revolution, and that he believed Pope Paul would do likewise. In Peru, Cardinal Ricketts decreed that funds intended for the building of a basilica in honor of the country's patroness, St. Rose of Lima, be used instead for the poor in the slums. All through Latin America today, committed Christians—lay leaders, younger clergymen and the more enlightened hierarchy—invoke the memory of Camilo Torres in their struggle against an unjust and dehumanizing social order.

The Colombian priest and revolutionary was a writer of pamphlets, manifestoes and messages, and these continue to be circulated in his country, a testament to his faith, despite the efforts of the ruling dispensation to destroy all traces of his dangerous influence. In his "Message to Christians," Father Torres wrote: "It is necessary to take power away from the privileged minority and give it to the poor majority. This, if it is done quickly, is the heart of a revolution. The Revolution can be peaceful if the minority does not resist with violence. The Revolution is, therefore, the way to get a government that will feed the hungry, clothe the naked, teach the ignorant, comply with the demands of charity, and make possible a true love for our neighbors.

"This is why the Revolution is not only permitted but is obligatory for all Christians who see in it the most effective way of making possible a greater love for all men. . .

"I think I have given myself to the Revolution out of love for my neighbor," continued Father Torres. "I have stopped offering Mass to live out the love for my neighbor . . . When my neighbor no longer has anything against me, and when the Revolution has been completed, then will I offer Mass again if God so wills it.

"After the Revolution, we Christians will have the peace of mind which will come from knowing that we established a system which is grounded in the love of neighbor."

He was not nor would he ever be a Communist, he said; but he would fight with the Marxist-Leninists for "common objectives: against the oligarchy and the domination of the United States, and for the takeover of power by the people."

Camilo Torres, a Christian and a Catholic priest, died for the people of a country whose politics and economy had been monopolized by a powerful oligarchic class for well over a century. Then, as now, two political parties, the Liberals and the Conservatives, vied for power in Colombia, and partisan violence racked the country. With American encouragement and the blessings of a conservative hierarchy, the 25 or so families that composed the dominant elite led the resistance to radical social change.

A grim and not totally unfamiliar story . . .

FATHER SANTOS RABANG of Vigan is not likely to do a Camilo Torres—in ideology he is of a different mold and temper, and he has no plans at all of joining the New People's Army—but he is in his own way and in his own limited territory also a sower of rebellion, a subversive who would undermine the religious and political Establishment. Since he launched the Adventure for Christ, a youth movement, two years ago, he has been very busy making life rather dismal and uncomfortable for certain highly-placed Ilocanos, who, it goes without saying, would only be too glad to see him put away, permanently, if that should be possible.

But the prospect of an Armalite stitching his cassock and writing finis to his activism doesn't seem to worry him much. In Ilocos Sur, it's considered worse than bad luck to liquidate a priest. "A specially terrible curse, lunód, the Ilocanos call it," explains Father Rabang, "would strike the killer, his family and his children's children"—a popular superstition the 31-year-old assistant parish priest at the Vigan Cathedral has not, understandably enough, bothered to dispute in his intense, usually indignant sermons.

True enough, a priest has yet to be assassinated in that violent province, but Father Rabang's preoccupations still require a great deal of courage: goons in the grip of powerful spirits may forget about that lunód business, and as everyone knows, they have itchy trigger fingers.

Undaunted, cheerful, sporting Benjamin Franklin glasses and a modish hairstyle, the leader of the Adventurers, as his youthful followers are called, goes about Vigan conducting teach-ins on the Constitutional Convention, organizing peace and order rallies, lecturing at youth assemblies: a slim, earnest disturber of the status quo. When the barrios were burned in Bantay, he condemned the atrocity in a press statement, and mobilized his youth group to spearhead relief operations; in the same week, he was to be seen saying Mass for the homeless folk, in Ora East, only to be reprimanded by an older priest, who resented the "intrusion" into his spiritual backyard. Father Rabang continued nonetheless to bring aid and comfort to the Bantay victims, and went on from there to lead a demonstration of Ilocos Sur priests, seminarians and nuns against political terrorism, in front of Malacañang. In July last year, he spoke at the Kongreso ng Katarungan in Plaza Miranda, where he was warned not to stay too long on the platform since he offered a tempting target for those who would resent his account of the morbid goings-on in his home province.

Last November, during the Constitutional Convention polls in Vigan, Father Rabang was urged by nervous friends to stay indoors for his health. The chairman of the local CNEA, he dismissed their fears in lighthearted fashion, and made the rounds of the precincts, seeing to it that his young poll watchers were on the job. The CNEA volunteers managed somehow to keep out the usual goons, which is no mean feat in a place like Vigan.

"It was the best, the most peaceful ever held in Ilocos Sur," Father Rabang now says of that election.

At his daily 7 a.m. Mass at the Vigan Cathedral, Father Rabang usually gives a homily in Ilocano. Last February, the day after three blocks in the commercial section of Vigan went up in smoke, the young cleric, looking small and frail against the backdrop of the baroque altar, spoke of the disaster as a punishment for such crimes as the burning of Bantay. After his sermon, two of his parishioners got up and left—they were, he says, "close friends" of a provincial official and had presumably hurried off to report his latest heresy.

His most disturbing deviation from orthodoxy, in the view of the entrenched politicos, is his obsession to form "true Christian leaders, men and women who will not hesitate to speak up and condemn the evils in society." He deplores the fact that the "important citizens" of the town have remained passive and silent in the face of political terrorism, the killings, the suppression of justice. The Knights of Columbus, the Holy Name Society, the Catholic Women's League, the Vigan Rotary Club, the Vigan Consumers' Cooperative—these and other religious and civic organizations whose presidents sit on the Vigan Parish Council have shown no inclination for protest and mass action, according to Father Rabang.

"People are afraid," he says. "Or they owe political favors and so keep their peace." Thus he would repose his hopes in the young, the irrepressible Adventurers who will someday, he prays, take over the political and economic leadership of the province.

His concept of youth leadership stresses "Christian living, nationalism, social justice, and peace and order." The Adventure for Christ movement, he says, now has "hundreds of members," most of them in Ilocos Sur, the rest in Baguio City and Manila. The activities of the Vigan hard core, a rugged, long-haired group, range from "cultural presentations" (a special performer not so long ago was the violinist Gilopez Kabayao) to demos for land reform and clean elections. Considering their youth and their vitality, it shouldn't surprise anyone that the Adventurers would now and then embark on unauthorized expeditions, as when they marched by a provincial executive's mansion on the occasion of their second anniversary last January and exploded a string of firecrackers. The defiance of the Establishment was festive and symbolic, suggesting a style of courage that Father Rabang is striving to shape into the fortitude of "mature and militant citizens."

A manifesto Father Rabang issued at a Vigan peace rally led by the Adventurers last January sums up the ideals and objectives of his parish revolution:

"We are in a very critical situation. Every aspect of society is being challenged to change, or perish. . .

"Together, let us pray and work for love, not hate; for the rule of law, not anarchy; for understanding, not apathy; for peace, not violence. Involvement and commitment in a changing society is the only alternative to a bloody revolution."

The manifesto ends with Rizal's "Where are the youth who will consecrate their golden hours. . ."

Asked what his superiors—Monsignor Juan Sison lives next door to the cathedral convento—thought of his youth movement, the priest from Santa Catalina, Ilocos Sur, answers with a half-smile: "They haven't given me any encouragement, but they haven't stopped me, either."

FATHER BEN J. VILLOTE'S SUPERIORS tried to stop him—first at the UP, where he served as assistant chaplain from 1961 to 1966, and later at St. Rita's Parish, at Philamlife Homes, in Quezon City, where he was assistant parish priest for three years, until 1969, when he was "exiled" to his present post, the barrio of Tipas, in Taguig, Rizal.

Father Ben, as his friends call him, is a writer, an intellectual with a thin ascetic face and a driving energy that belies his fragile frame. He is 38, and comes from Gagalangin, Tondo; a graduate of Torres High School and the Jesuit's San Jose Seminary. After a brief stint helping out in the Jesuit mission in Cagayan de Oro, he spent two years working in a Mandaluyong parish "where nothing much happened." Assignment to the UP campus was a welcome change, and there he initiated what he calls "inter-sorority encounters," mainly to make the Catholic students, who clung fervently together in the UPSCA, "less ghetto-minded, and more open, more Christian." He met Nilo Tayag and Jose Ma. Sison, both of whom he admired, and still does, for their dedication and their integrity; he made friends with the campus writers brewing their own revolution; and he himself began to write those articles and deliver those sermons which were later published in a book entitled *Ferment*, brief essays and speeches "to correct the impression that nationalism at the UP is synonymous with communism."

The theme of Father Villote's *Ferment* is revolution. "What we need today," goes a typical article in the collection, "are spiritual revolutionaries who are willing to sparkplug a spiritual revolution that would radically change the spiritual status quo in the Philippines today. Oh yes, I admit that the Philippines is the only Catholic nation in the Far East. . . I admit our churches in the Philippines are always filled on Sundays. So what? . . . How often have you complained about the alleged commercial nature of religion in our country? How often have you complained about the hypocrisy of some of our prominent Catholics who make their religion a camouflage for their moral foulness? . . . We just cannot sit on our faith. We must stand on it, and prove to the world that our faith is a living

49

faith, a faith that is built on a living Church . . . We must go up with Christ to Jerusalem, and face Jerusalem with the boldness of a revolutionary. . . ."

The archdiocesan authorities heard of the Inter-Fraternity, Inter-Sorority Club Father Villote had organized, his cordial friendships with campus activists of various stripes, his dialogues with the professorial atheists in residence; and to isolate him from his UP friends, he was reassigned to the Philamlife parish, where "there was little sense of community," he now recalls, "what with people away in their offices most of the week and meeting only on Sundays, if at all." But the children and the youth made up for the indifference, the remoteness of their parents; Father Villote formed study groups, tutoring sessions, a combo, and the youngsters held many a lively session in the rectory, learning more about their Church and the problems of their country from the scholarly, soft-spoken priest. Some village elders frowned on the gentle youth agitator who went about his work often minus his cassock; the frowns turned into ferocious scowls when Father Villote said in a sermon that maids were human beings, too, and should not be paid inhuman wages. The pillars of suburbia dispatched a letter to Cardinal Santos, requesting Father Villote's removal from the parish.

But it was a *Free Press* article on the "Robot Church" that finally got Father Villote thrown out of Philamlife. In the Church today, he wrote in the article, there are "a growing number of disgruntled Catholics who are beginning to believe that they will never be able to find any meaning in Christianity at all if they remain part of the ossified structures of church politics. . .

"The choice . . . is no longer between remaining in the Church and abandoning the Church, but between 'sleeping with the Church and 'awakening the Church from within.' Those who prefer to awaken the Church from within have, of course, to run the risk of being branded 'disobedient' and 'insubordinate' by some of our churchmen. But these 'disobedient' and 'insubordinate' Catholics are not at all disturbed by such juridical verdicts because they honestly believe that mere juridical obedience does not necessarily invalidate before God their loyalty to the *Church as People*—even perhaps at the risk of appearing disloyal to the *Church as Establishment*. . .

"Faith today is no longer faith in a code of rules but faith in Christ-in-community."

Continued Father Villote: "Do our bishops have to live in palaces and ride in limousines and buy banks and wear precious stones and sit on thrones? Do our priests have to insist on demanding from their people a feudal respect for their priestly dignity to a point where priest and people are canonically made to occupy separate social spheres through the rigid discipline of clerical garb?

" . . . While it is true that our bishops and priests must remain leaders, their leadership must now begin to take another form. Gone are the days when the only form of leadership our churchmen knew was a leadership shared with kings who led simply because they had the power. It is about time we looked back farther than the days of kings and saw how the First Christian meant his leadership to be—a leadership through service, a leadership shared with the people."

In tone and direction, the article was a radical departure from the triumphant apologetics, the romantic rhetoric of *Ferment*: here was the new Villote speaking, questioning, criticizing the "Robot Church" of a rigid, tradition-encrusted hierarchy, and demanding a true and virile Christian leadership. The hierarchy responded quickly—a secret meeting of Quezon City priests was called; Father Villote was tried in absentia and condemned as imprudent, irresponsible and undisciplined; his mail was confiscated, his movements restricted; his parish priest ordered him to desist from conducting youth meetings and study sessions.

"It was a subtle Inquisition," says Father Villote, remembering his last year at the Philamlife parish. "I was never charged formally, but neither was I given a chance to defend myself. The Cardinal, the officials of the archdiocese never communicated with me."

Father Villote is happier now in barrio Tipas. He has not been excommunicated, and the punishment that is his "exile" to the Rizal barrio has given him the kind of apostolate he loves: a parish priest at last among farmers, laborers and fishermen. Tipas is the farthest barrio from the Taguig poblacion; the town ends there, the windy fields rolling away along the Pasig toward what looks very much like dissident country, the hills and mountains of Laguna. It represents the new frontier of the Church in the Philippines, this barrio far from the Archbishop's Palace and the commercial bustle of the metropolis.

The Taguig parish church has stone walls built in Spanish times, but the rest of the structure is native: the "Dambanang Kawayan," the "altar of the Filipino Christian where all are equal," is a backdrop of vertical bamboo poles. At their 8 a.m. Sunday Mass, Father Villote's people sing spirited Tagalog hymns yet to be heard in other parishes, the voices happy and full-throated, accompanied by a rondalla, the rhythms unmistakably Filipino; some of the hymns Father Villote composed himself. "We also sing Bandilang Mahal, the hymn of the New People's Army," says the priest who has begun to grow a goatee which, along with the thin Chinese cast of his face, reminds his visitors of Ho Chi Minh. Since his UP tour of duty, he has become more of an ideologue, more concerned with the "politicalization" of the masses.

The Tipas church Father Villote himself turns into a classroom for the political education of his flock, and during Mass yet—a radical innovation that's certain to merit the Inquisitors' ire, even as it has intensified the barrio folk's sense of "Christ-in-community." After the reading of the Gospel, he urges the congregation to comment on the scriptural passage. A man accepts the microphone and links the Gospel somehow to the need for irrigation and fertilizer; a woman discourses on the frivolousness of Filipinos even during Lent; a teenage boy talks of God and the Constitutional Convention. During Mass in Tipas all participate; now only the men sing, next only the women, then the children, finally all together, singing their Tagalog songs to the Lord.

The parish has begun what Father Villote calls "block multilogues," neighborhood teach-ins conducted by lay leaders. The teach-ins feature three topics, "discussion starters" which underscore Father Villote's current concerns: "the role of the masses in democracy and progress, the voice of the masses in the coming Convention, the voice of the masses in the coming local elections."

"We must learn what the people want for their community," says Father Villote. "We must mobilize them to form opinions on local and national issues. More than ever, we need to awaken people to their rights, to help them get ready for the time when they will have to decide for themselves.

"A revolution is probable but not inevitable. But if it's a revolution the people want, then the country will have a revolution. It will all be up to the people. The voice of a free, enlightened and politicalized people is the voice of God."

"A revolution," continues Father Villote, "may bring about a society that's free, socialistic, truly democratic. A society and a form of government incorporating some aspects of the systems in China, Cuba, Sweden, Chile and Canada. The system after the revolution may be hostile to an established Church, but not to Christianity, Gospel Christianity, the essence of which is love of neighbor. Christianity can and does exist without churches."

"If Jose Ma. Sison's revolution will bring about a society that will advance the total development of man as man," says Father Villote, "then I shall go along with him. To be free and human is to be Christian, not in the institutional sense with its built-in prejudices, but in the Gospel sense of commitment to and responsibility for fellow men."

ANOTHER CHRISTIAN LEADER for a revolution is Edmundo G. Garcia of the Society of Jesus.

"Father Ed" to the youngsters who look up to him as their leader, the eldest son of the late Secretary of Health Paulino J. Garcia is not an ordained priest, and the indecision of newspaper reports, whether to call him "Father" or "Brother" Garcia, prompted the then acting Jesuit Provincial, Hernando Maceda, to issue a statement last October clarifying the status of the 28-year-old activist:

"Edmundo Garcia is a Jesuit scholastic. With the permission of his religious superiors, he has interrupted the theological studies which immediately precede ordination to the priesthood in order to be engaged on a full-time basis in work among young people and in Christian social action. He is then on leave from his regular studies; he is not on leave of absence from the Society of Jesus; he remains a member of the Jesuit Order. . . . As to the title 'Father': in Jesuit schools in the Philippines it has become customary to give this title not to priests only, but also to the scholastics on the faculty."

Ed Garcia was then in jail, having been arrested along with leaders of the Federation of Free Farmers (FFF), students, some nuns and seminarians, for taking part in an "illegal" demonstration at the Department of Justice: they had occupied the office of Secretary Vicente Abad Santos, to dramatize their demand for action on more than a dozen land cases involving small farmers. Said Father Maceda, in the same statement: "In the Church today there is a growing number of men and women who desire to give of their time and energies to the struggle which the poor have to put up in order to bring about a society that is more just for today's and tomorrow's citizens. . .

"Obviously, even among Jesuits, not all will agree with the positions taken and the tactics used by Ed Garcia either alone or in conjunction with other Christian activists. But at a time when the Church is seeking ways of bringing the Gospel to man and his societies with greater authenticity, the efforts of our young Christian activists do indicate some ways in which the Gospel must speak to the Filipino and his society today."

Ed Garcia's compassion for the poor and the dispossessed took root in early boyhood: among those who first awakened his social awareness was his father, whom he remembers as "strong-willed yet gentle and loving, a man who loved life immensely and who loved people, a man of courage and integrity."

"When I was a kid, my father often took me and my brothers to our farm in barrio Sto. Cristo, in Gapan, Nueva Ecija, and there we spent long hours talking to the tenant farmers," says Father Ed. "Later he brought along my brother Pandy and myself on trips to the Visayas and Mindanao so that we could see for ourselves the conditions of poverty, the barrio people, the hospitals which got very little or no government support.

"I remember my father telling me once, when he was Secretary of Health, that the way the budget is apportioned by the government is a crime. He always had to fight in the congressional hearings for more appropriations for the Department of Health. But he very seldom got any increases because our leaders, so-called—they really aren't—think that national defense is top priority, along with the special funds of the presidential office, and of course their pork barrel. All these lessons deeply influenced me and my brothers. This concern for people which my father lived I cannot forget."

Father Ed and his four brothers refused to inherit the 40-hectare Garcia farm when their father died in 1968. "We believe that land belongs to the landless tiller and not to absentee landlords or inheritors," says Father Ed. "And we believe that tenancy, even leasehold, must go. The farmers banking on their self-reliance and initiative must own the land on which they have lived for so long. My mother accepted this decision. Some of our relatives and friends in the province were against it. The family still owes the GSIS, and there are difficulties, but my mother takes things in stride. OK, it hurts, but we must pay the price for our convictions."

The price has since included two weeks in jail last October, and the famous karate chop Gen. Gaudencio Garcia (absolutely no relation) dealt him last May when he and 86 other Lakasdiwa stalwarts were hauled off to Camp Crame after they disrupted a session of Congress by singing the national anthem in the gallery. For "Operasyon Tuligsa sa Kongreso," the Jesuit had drafted a manifesto:

"We act out of a sense of urgency. For so long, so little has been done. . . Our legislators have not sufficiently attacked the major problems that confront our people today. Our workers starve on wages that remain static. While prices soar, our farmers wait in vain for land reform that is both effective and substantial, our drivers pay prohibitive prices for gasoline to an unregulated oil industry . . . Congress must act now! Our suffering people can no longer wait!"

Ed Garcia heads Lakasdiwa—"strength of spirit"—the movement which he and his brothers, some Jesuit scholastics, students and labor leaders launched in February 1970, following the bloody demonstrations at Congress and Malacañang. "It's basically a vision of a way of life that is fully human and genuinely Filipino," says the Jesuit activist. "Lakasdiwa seeks the renewal of the values of the people. It is for the radical restructuring of our society—social, political, economic, spiritual."

Lakasdiwa members were in the forefront of Operation Bantay and took part in the student rallies in support of the jeepney strikes. They picketed the Asian Bishops Conference, the Cardinal's Palace and the Papal Nuncio's residence during Pope Paul's visit, brandishing placards demanding radical reforms in the Philippine Church. Plans for 1971 call for intensive ideological research, teach-ins for workers and peasants, and "mass actions for radical renewal."

The next massive demonstration Father Ed Garcia may not be able to attend: the exertions of the last two years have proved too much even for the hard-driving Jesuit rebel who was a track and football athlete in his Ateneo days and he is now confined in a hospital. He has barely recovered from surgery—the eighth operation in a row—but he just cannot remain still and idle in his hospital room; most of the day and far into the night he writes messages, strategic programs for Lakasdiwa, statements to the press.

In his "An Open Letter to the Filipino People," Ed Garcia writes: "We have a long journey that might last far into the night. But anything worthwhile has a price. And those of us who want our children to see the breaking of a new dawn must pay that price—in terms of time and talent, effort and energy, commitment and lives.

"This task, I realize, is far more difficult than most of us realize. To build the Filipino Social Democratic Front might, in the end, mean blood and the lives of men. But try we must, for the task of human liberation from the bondage of economic poverty, political tyranny and cultural deprivation is the task of every Filipino."

If all peaceful means should fail—"Then we will form guerrilla strike forces," says Edmundo Garcia, S.J. Revolution is a long arduous task, according to Mao Tsetung; and so could be a man's journey toward its trembling edge. Father Ed has come a long way from the boy visiting the farm in Gapan.

TO MANY OF THE RADICAL LEFT, the revolution is merely a matter of time, and it will be a revolution propelled by "Marxism-Leninism-Mao Tsetung Thought." Father Edicio de la Torre of the Society of the Divine Word is not one to discount the force of the gathering storm. Maoism in the Philippines is in fact his current field of study, and it is a rare day when he isn't asked to give a talk on the Maoist challenge.

Father de la Torre is, at 28, well equipped for the job. Both theoretician and activist—any revolution would do well to claim him for its own—he has had considerable exposure to the dynamics of organization, ideology and social reform, student and youth movements, and the psychology of the peasantry. The priest from Naujan, Oriental Mindoro, has served as chaplain of the FFF, is now chaplain of the Kilusang Khi Rho ng Pilipinas, a national youth organization as militant as Lakasdiwa. He teaches philosophy, theology and socio-economics at the SVD seminary in Tagaytay. Complementing these credentials is a fluent, quick-witted style at the podium, and the easy off-the-court manner of a basketball star, which he could have been, a casual charm which draws, besides solemn clergy and serious laity, crowds of colegialas and assorted long-haired rebels to his lectures.

But he is, like Father Villote, less than popular with Cardinal Santos, who has more than once asked the SVD Superior to keep the young priest within bounds. The Cardinal, presumably, was worried not only about Father de la Torre's preference for unclerical hairstyles and polo shirts, which could make it hard for a bishop to distinguish him from the Khi Rho radicals who follow him around. SVD conservatives, for their part, have reason to be wary of him: a manifesto he drafted together with like-minded priests in the religious order would have the Divine Word fathers give up all "exploitative assets" like agricultural lands and real estate held for speculation.

"There's a stretch of vacant land behind this building, for instance," says Father de la Torre in the parlor of the Christ the King Seminary in Quezon City, where he may be found if he is not teaching in Tagaytay. "As for the farms, tenancy has to go, and soon." Tacked on the wall is a poster pleading for vocations: "Until all men are free from all forms of enslavement, the apostolate of Christ is to free men from all idolatry and oppression."

Father de la Torre says of the role of the priest in the 1970s: "There are many styles and charisms, but if these years will be characterized by revolution, then the priest should be a servant of the revolution. His work for the revolution would be to humanize and revitalize ideologies, movements, organizations, programs and leaders, and to prevent men from being deceived into giving absolute worship to any man-made idol.

"A Filipino priest by his very office should also be involved in Filipinizing Christianity, which means purifying Christianity and going back to what's essential. As is his proper role, he should be concerned with building real communities of men. Hence, he must identify with those who are considered less than human—because silent, oppressed and powerless. This siding with the poor in their struggle for liberation is really also working for the liberation of the humanity of the oppressors who remain less than human as long as they oppress others."

Christians for a revolution will do well to read the Khi Rho literature on Christianity, imperialism and nationalism in the Philippines. Written by Father de la Torre, a mimeographed position paper makes these observations on imperialism and anti-imperialism:

"Imperialism is the main enemy of nationalism in any developing country. U.S. imperialism is the principal anti-nationalist force in the Philippines. Other totalitarian anti-nationalist forces are at most threats rather than actual 'omnipresent' and 'omnipotent' obstacles to Philippine nationalism . . .

"Anti-imperialism recognizes the historical and intrinsic connection of imperialism to unjust minority control of wealth, power and direction in the Philippines. Imperialism and social injustice are related . . . the alliances of feudal lord-bureaucrat capitalist-monopoly merchant remain the major native anti-nationalist force (despite their growing collection of native cultural items like santos and pottery)."

Christians must acknowledge "the role of Marxism-Leninism-Maoism" as the principal ideology of the militant movements for "national democracy." And Communists should not indiscriminately condemn Christian institutions and principles as "essentially reactionary," and discredit all efforts and groups operating within the Christian tradition as "clerico-fascist." Both groups stand to profit from dialogue, for neither Christianity nor communism can be denied their role in the development of Philippine nationalism. But more than dialogue, which can degenerate into futile angry debate, the need is "for both Christianity and communism to face up to the nationalist challenge"—which in the concrete means "identification with the oppressed people in their struggle for liberation."

The conclusions of a paper Father de la Torre read early last month as part of a Lenten lecture series at the Ateneo Law School Auditorium further define the correct Christian response, as he sees it, to the Maoist movement for national liberation. The paper quotes Nilo Tayag: "It need not be the Church as a particular institution but groups of Christians working with other radical movements who can undertake revolutionary changes."

Criticism and protest, no matter how passionate, are not enough: "The Christian must make a political choice," affirms Father de la Torre. "He cannot take refuge in a 'moral' pronouncement that has no political effectiveness." And to be able to make that choice, the Christian must examine present proposals, systems and methods. One such proposal is Maoism or the national democratic movement of the radical left.

"The Filipino Christian therefore cannot make a Christian political choice," declares Father de la Torre, "if he does not seriously examine the challenge of Maoism—not just as a stimulus to dedication, or as a co-critic of society, but even more as a concrete proposal for showing effective love to his fellow Filipinos.

"For in the final analysis, to take the challenge of Maoism seriously is for the Filipino Christian to take Incarnation in Philippine society seriously; to analyze concrete conditions and to side with the oppressed in their struggle for liberation, not as a self-appointed leader but as a servant of the revolution."

But what after the revolution? The question confronts Filipino Christians who hesitate to join the national democratic revolution, aware as they are of the more dogmatic aspects of Marxism-Leninism-Maoism, and the eventually repressive, anti-nationalist stance of certain Communist nations.

"Much depends on the participation of Christian groups in the revolution," says Father Edicio de la Torre in the parlor of the Christ the King Seminary, the quiet of the tree-shaded grounds outside broken only by the far voices of seminarians at a basketball game in the gym. "If they have served the revolution well, there will be a place, a role for them in the new society. And apart from the actual decisions of the party leadership, the proper role of the Church would be what it has always been—to be a critical witness to the fact that the perfect kingdom has not yet come."

The revolutionary and authentic Church is also the Pilgrim Church, not wedded to any political, social and economic system, never pausing too long by the wayside, always on the way to the Kingdom. In the words of the 15 Bishops of the Third World: "The moment a system fails to provide for the common good and shows favoritism to a particular few, the Church has the duty to cut free from that unjust system, seeking to collaborate with some other system more just and more likely to meet the necessity of the times."

The necessary struggle is here and now, and the Filipino Christian must make the choice while the light lasts.

(*Leader*, 1971)

Ferdinand E. Marcos: An Appreciation

CERTAIN LIBERALS AND NACIONALISTAS with presidential ambitions, and scores of other Filipinos, including many who once idolized him, will likely dispute it; but in our time, in our country, Ferdinand E. Marcos remains destiny's favorite son.

59

The trials he has had to endure, the fearsome obstacles he has encountered and overcome—tests of manhood which would have reduced lesser mortals to quivering blobs of jelly—have only added, it would seem, to the zest with which he has pursued, as the song puts it, his glorious quest. Charged with murder in his law student days, he defended himself with such flourish and skill as to win acquittal from the High Tribunal and went on from there to pass the bar exams with highest honors—a twin feat probably without parallel anywhere in the world. (It has been the tragic fate of other men as great and as brilliant to meet an early end, behind bars, on the gallows or before a firing squad, their full potential unrealized, the noble promise of their lives unfulfilled, mankind thus rendered so much the poorer.) From his daredevil exploits in the last war, he emerged with a chestful of Fil-American medals, the most decorated soldier of his country. The pride of his generation, he has since continued to win, with undiminished energy, the honors and prizes that the nation sees fit to offer only to the brave and the true, not the least of these rewards being the love of a fabulous lady. As everyone knows only too well, he became the first President of the Republic to be reelected, an awesome triumph which, true to form, he achieved with an unprecedented majority of two million votes over his LP rival, who, by the way, still thinks he wuz robbed.

That was but less than a year ago. Forward with Marcos and Lopez—the unbeatable Performance Team! Remember the tumult and the shouting, the sense of a vast master-plan carried out without a hitch, of irresistible destiny fulfilling itself? Remember J.V. Cruz on TV working suavely for his ambassadorship, explaining what "extrapolation" was all about, and Serging Osmeña hoarse and tired in defeat, and then the morning after, the outcries about goons and massive fraud and vote-buying all the rest of that exciting week? Barely ten months have passed—yet it seems like years ago. Was it only last November that the Second Mandate dawned upon an expectant land? So much has happened since then that it feels as though not months but years separate us now from President Marcos' day of victory. Propelled as it were by a combustible concentration of changes and events, the nation has moved forward, as President Marcos himself loved to predict, although he could not have guessed the precise direction—and such has been the distance we as a people have covered that Election Day 1969 now seems much more remote in time than it really is.

The President, of course, is not one to stand still or lag behind while history is in the making; and since the auspicious first month of Marcos II marked by unusually festive fireworks in the vicinity of Malacañang, he has been striding with the usual confidence and vigor toward more achievements, more honors and distinctions. The gods who watch over the Filipino race must have reserved their fondest benediction for the likes of him, for it seems there is nothing that he wills or does, nothing that he encourages or allows to happen which does not exalt him, does not distinguish him from the common run of men. His is a light that was never meant to be hidden under a bushel of mediocrity; his life indeed is the stuff of legend, and he can no more evade fame and distinction than he can renounce his sworn duty to his people, which is to serve them and make the country, if not "great again," at least not hostile to the idea of greatness. (He did say, after all: "This nation *can*"—not shall—"be great again.")

Thus to the scroll citing President Marcos' many achievements has been added some more honors earned in the six or seven months following the riotous celebrations of January. He has, for instance, in less than a year of the Second Mandate, merited the distinction of having the deepest and widest credibility gap ever to yawn at the feet of a Philippine president. ("If Marcos were to run today, Racuyal would beat him!" swears our barber from Pampanga.) Amazingly, for all the disgust and skepticism he has spawned, he has at the same time aroused the increasingly passionate attention of the populace, including even those citizens who normally pay no heed to politicians. ("What is Marcos up to? What will he do next?" wonder radicals and moderates, natives and aliens, labor and management, laymen and clergy.) Above all, his is the distinction of being held solely accountable, by more and more of the people, for the multitude of troubles that have of late descended upon the country.

Never before in our history have so many blamed so much on one man.

But so-called public opinion, the same history would testify, has not always been as enlightened as it should be; it has committed many gross and costly errors, and the living proofs of these blunders may be found today delivering privilege speeches in Congress. The voice of the people, in this country anyway, is seldom, alas, the voice of God; in the instances it has reflected divine wisdom, goons in the hire of the devil have been quick to silence it at the polls. Popular tastes and convictions are more often than not suspect, especially in so confused and clamorous an activity as politics, Philippine style. Public sentiment is rarely infallible, and as it applies now to the much-maligned President, it is wide off the mark, quite petty, misinformed, ungrateful, unjust, disproportionate, lacking in perspective. The accusation, spoken harshly where detractors of the President gather in rebellious array, as in Plaza Miranda or along Mendiola—the charge that he is a fascist, a fake patriot, a power-crazed, money-obsessed operator with the mentality of a small-town politico, is surely anything but a sane and reasonable conclusion. It is the emotional judgment of a people who believe, mistakenly, that they have been robbed of their faith and hopes in a man of destiny.

The course, the direction of Ferdinand E. Marcos' destiny belies the indictment of public opinion, his motives and ideals repudiate it, his actions disprove it. True, his greatness has dimmed somewhat, as if the general dissatisfaction with his regime had formed a smog that the radiance could scarcely penetrate—but the greatness is still there, in the man, for those who seek it, a guiding light for all seasons. Even the elect of God, we are told, don't arrive at divine knowledge without undergoing what mystics call the dark night of the soul; they must fast and pray for illumination. The perception of certain forms of greatness a notch or two below the Almighty's likewise calls for some effort, but the strain would be well worth it in terms of inspiration, splendor of vision and peace of soul. It goes without saying that such irreverent cynics as columnists Maximo V. Soliven and Amando Doronila—O ye of little faith!—are denied the spiritual rewards bestowed on the pure and humble of heart, like Teodoro Valencia and Emil Jurado, who are reportedly in constant communion with the power and the glory.

LET US THEN FOLLOW the example of the truly wise and contemplate, without partisan rancor, dispassionately but with all the powers of intellect and will, as Jesuit retreat masters are wont to remind us, the issues that the people's parliament has raised against President Marcos.

The President and his party, it is charged, spent P168 million in so-called barrio improvement funds and untold millions more in God knows what funds to "buy" his reelection, in the process of which he debauched the currency and brought down upon all our anxious heads a host of evils—ever-soaring prices, shrinking incomes, strikes, mass layoffs, business and industry in a state of suspended animation. Because of the economic dislocation—compound fractures is more like it, according to the President's more cantankerous critics—there is now an upsurge of graft and corruption, violence and gangsterism as the low- or no-income sectors of the population strive to cope criminally with the rising cost of living.

The President, it is further charged, is a champion of imperialism, feudalism and fascism. He has demonstrated nothing less than canine devotion to the imperialist cause in Asia, as witness the infamous Philcag deal and what Senator Aquino brands the "Americanization" of his regime. He has conspired with the rapacious landlord class to perpetuate feudalism, depriving the land reform program of needed funds, so his accusers say. He is a veritable Hitler who relishes the use of force to smash dissent in the streets and resistance to fascism in Central Luzon, charge student militants. At the same time, he has proved to be the *tuta* of a *tuta* with his Administration's brutal deportation of the embattled publishers, the Yuyitung brothers, to Taiwan.

The President, insist his persecutors, supports political warlordism—just think, they tell us, what a strong and moral President would have done after somebody's goons burned and shot up that barrio in Bantay! He has not acted to stop rampant deforestation, his critics claim, and at the rate our forests are being destroyed—three hectares a minute—this nation before long will be a desert, a wasteland! And how many of the promises he made way back in 1965 has he fulfilled? ("Bring down high prices . . . Rule of law . . . Economy in the government . . . Nationalistic policy . . . Heroic leadership," etc.) More savage questions are flung at us: Isn't he already the richest man in Asia, but still insatiable, wanting more loot, at least half of PLDT, shares in Benguet, a TV station, choice real estate in various parts of the country? When will he renounce his worldly possessions, as he promised, and set up *that* foundation? Isn't he just biding his time to impose martial law and install himself as the Great Dictator? Isn't he plotting to rig the

Constitutional Convention so he could run for a third term or become President for life? And so forth, and so on, a litany of outrage and apprehension.

Is President Marcos as detestable as these unkind critics, uncharitable detractors and irresponsible radicals have painted him out to be?

Could a man so favored by destiny and embodying a special greatness be such an abomination to his people?

One recoils from such malevolent thoughts. No! Impossible! Hindi! No puede!

It is time we put those wild-eyed and long-haired accusers of the President where they belong—in a padded cell and under sedation—and restored calmness and objectivity to the so-called public opinion of our disjointed times. This must be done in justice to the President, who has suffered enough in his mission to lead his people to peace and prosperity. The President is a man of heroic qualities, as we have seen; but he remains a man, vulnerable to the ailments that flesh is heir to. We gather from *Evening News'* Luis Beltran that the President suffers on occasion from a curious disease which "makes tears fall from his eyes, renders him deaf and makes his throat hurt." We could help ease the President's aches and pains, help lighten his grievous burdens by reassuring him of our loyalty and our faith.

Assuming, for the moment, that the malicious charges leveled against the President are true, men of good will and unflinching faith in the Marcos destiny—and this unfortunate country is not bereft of them—would still perceive that whatever harm might have been done is far outweighed, rendered insignificant, by the national blessings resulting from these presidential "crimes" rashly condemned by a disenchanted, short-sighted people. It is all a matter of point of view, of angle and depth (or shallowness) of vision: what is so outrageous from a certain vantage point is revealed, from another, as good and desirable in its true nature. Filipinos who now view President Marcos as a sort of calamity—not a few even blamed him for those earthquakes—should change the slant of their perspective, regard the object of their ire from a different plane.

Then will they understand what they in anger or prejudice or despair have failed to comprehend: that the President, even in committing what appear to be crimes against the people, or refusing to act for their benefit, has had only the people's welfare at heart. He knows that without the people, he would not be where he is today: at the seat of supreme power, his heart's desire, his destiny. It is simply inconceivable that a man of such charisma, sensitivity and intelligence should willfully deliver them to disaster; their doom would be his own as well, for is he not one with them? Did he not fight and bleed for them in the crucible that was Bataan? And despite the expense and the hazards, didn't he become congressman, senator and finally President the better to serve his beloved people and country?

NO FILIPINO LOVES HIS COUNTRY more than President Marcos—a truth that will reveal itself after the prescribed shift in viewpoint.

Consider anew the spending orgy during the last elections— was it not actually a laudable attempt to redistribute wealth and bridge the gap between the rich and the poor? As Senator Lagumbay, statesman and artist and one of the more perceptive of our solons, said recently concerning budgetary deficits caused by wanton election spending: "The father of children who are sick will not hesitate to go into debt to give them the medicines they need." The fiscal and economic consequences of the President's compassion for the electorate are not without their positive aspects—for has the price spiral not encouraged the people to give up vain material things and prodded them to practice austerity which, everyone will agree, is good for the soul and cuts down on cholesterol? "Do not lay up for yourselves treasures on earth, where rust and moth consume. . . " As for the President's alleged servility to imperialist America—is it not merely expressive of Filipino gratitude for American tutelage in the arts of democracy? And is not the "Americanization" of his Administration the next best thing to the statehood that most Filipinos still dream of? And regarding the Yuyitung case, for which certain benighted sectors of the press would consign the President to the innermost circle of hell, didn't the magnificent show of collaboration between Taipei and Malacañang further strengthen the ties that bind two "Free World" nations committed to the defense of freedom and democracy?

The President has a soft spot in his heart for the students, especially the nationalistic activists, and he has taken pains to provide them with issues to rouse them up and keep them from physical, mental and ideological stagnation. Suppose the President never bothered to give them cause for pickets and demonstrations—they would all be smoking pot and watching smut movies instead, languid preoccupations that would not predispose them to any politicalization. The rise of youth radicalism, which promises to restructure and revitalize our ailing society, the nation owes to President Marcos.

With regard to the Bantay case, the simple-minded had expected the President to do something dramatic, like helicoptering down on the burned barrio of Ora and poking among the ruins; but he wisely chose to maintain a statesmanlike distance from the protagonists, lest his presence be misconstrued as lending aid and comfort to one party or the other. It is true that he was photographed in a conspiratorial huddle with his old Ilocano friend, Congressman Floring Crisologo, but that was nothing but a pose arranged by a weekly magazine for a promotional gimmick. If he has shown little enthusiasm for land reform, as has been repeatedly charged, that could be due to his determination to spare long-suffering farm tenants the troublesome capitalistic burdens of ownership. As for the Philippines turning into a desert because of his alleged reluctance to stop illegal logging, has it not occurred to his simple-minded critics that rock and sand exports may yet resolve our balance of payments difficulties, and that as the Sahara of Asia, we shall probably strike oil and banish poverty for good from our underdeveloped shores?

True, he said he would renounce his worldly possessions and establish a foundation, but he didn't say when; great men have their own timetables, and will not be rushed by vile insinuations. Possibly the President has decided to postpone his philanthropic endeavors to a future term in office, a prospect that alarms his detractors, who have been issuing dire warnings that he will pack the Constitutional Convention with his men. But why should anyone be alarmed by his desire to be President longer than eight years or perhaps for life? Isn't it all of a pattern, the extension of the glorious quest, the irresistible command of that destiny which has brought us so many blessings?

If he wants to go on serving his people for as long as he can climb the grand stairway in Malacañang unassisted, the least a grateful nation can do is let him. Ten or 20 years more of nation-building may sap his strength and make climbing that stairway an ordeal, but neither age nor infirmity should deter him from his noble mission. Salazar of Portugal, one recalls, presided admirably over the affairs of his country from a wheelchair, if not a sick-bed, for the better part of his dictatorial reign.

"Politics galvanizes into action all the beautiful hopes that a man can nurture in his heart for his country and for his nation. Politics is my life," Hartzell Spence quotes Ferdinand E. Marcos in his biography of the President, *For Every Tear a Victory*, a book we keep on a special shelf of inspirational reading, along with the works of Norman Vincent Peale and S.J. Perelman (not a Jesuit).

No President has done more for his people. Never have a people owed so much to their President.

Tadhana, fate, has decreed it: Ferdinand E. Marcos, the sixth President of the Republic, will long be remembered for what he has done, and for what he will yet do.

(Free Press, 1970)

The Testimony of Ninoy Aquino

BENIGNO AQUINO, JR. would be turning a youthful and vigorous 52 next Tuesday had he not been shot dead on August 21, 1983.

He would be alive and well on the way—most of his countrymen, including those who wished to be forever rid of him, seemed to be quite sure of this—to realizing the goals that he had set for himself and our country. All this is to assume certain conditions, the grant of a presidential amnesty, for instance, that would have freed him to strive for "national reconciliation based on justice," as he put it in his arrival statement. So went one of the more optimistic scenarios that awaited him on his return from exile.

Was the presidency still the destiny he was compelled to pursue, despite assurances to the contrary given rather cheerfully to kin and friends? Was he resolved to remain the campaign manager, as he used to say with equal zest, in the Opposition's struggle to "restore" democracy in this decade, and once this was done, to retire from the political wars but still serve the nation from a statesmanlike distance? Whether one or the other, his decision, many of those who trusted in a beneficent fate were inclined to believe, would not but redound to the country's good.

As the nation is thrust from one crisis to another and moves deeper into a darkening future bereft of Ninoy and his leadership, the assassination at the airport should imprint itself more sharply in our people's memory. The man in white sprawled face down on the tarmac, in the bright sun: the scene as on a floodlit stage should become even more vivid and awesome, our comprehension of it more somber and penetrating, as a fuller measure of our country's loss shines steadily down upon it. Just as the dimming of the lights in an auditorium heightens the supreme moment, focuses our attention on the illuminated stage, so should this dark time that surrounds us render all the more stark, appalling and unforgettable that day and that moment they killed Ninoy Aquino.

If only Oplan Balikbayan had ensured his safety . . . if only his homecoming had not turned into the tragedy that has brought down on our country so much grief, wrath and turmoil . . . If, barring assassination plots, blood clots, terminal sickness and other disasters, Ninoy Aquino were with us today, as confident and irrepressible as ever, defying any calamity or danger. . . If, instead of the present dispensation, we lived under a regime of truth, justice, freedom and love of country; a democracy in which criticism and dissent are not only allowed but encouraged to flourish as the birthright of free men; in which it would be unthinkable, it would be impossible, for such leaders as Ninoy Aquino to suffer persecution, imprisonment and exile, not to say a brutal death at the hands of uniformed assailants, while the mastermind and the conspirators continue to lord it over the land as a matter of course. . . The "ifs" relating to Ninoy's life and death form a lengthening list: the what-could-or-might-have-beens that grow in number, like stars, even as they recede into history, into infinity.

For as long as there are Filipinos who seek a more just and humane society for themselves and their children, and honor the memory of Ninoy as one of the best and the brightest of the brave, so long will there be a sense at least of a better future obliterated as by a blind and evil force: a regretful musing over what precisely such a more hopeful prospect might be, had Ninoy lived to help construct it for our people. A single shot that black Sunday at the airport destroyed the hopes of Filipinos and their posterity of ever knowing what Ninoy, vindicated at the height of his powers, could have accomplished for our people's salvation.

Disregard, if you can, the manner of his death and its immediate consequences, the sorrow, shame and outrage at the murder, and all the troubles that have plagued us since the assassination. All this aside, the knowledge that the nation has been deprived irrevocably of the chance to test the mettle of Benigno Aquino's leadership in these last crucial years of our century, is enough to confirm the senseless monstrosity of what President Marcos himself has called this "dastardly crime." That vicious, corrupt and mediocre politicians should thrive and look forward to more rapacious days only reveals more piercingly the meaning of that death on the tarmac: the .38 or .45-caliber bullet shattering the brain of one of the most intelligent and talented leaders of our time, patriotic ambitions, heroic aspirations, and noble hopes and dreams all blasted away, the bloody waste of it all.

BUT SUCH WAS THE MAN, it scarcely needs to be said more than a year after his death and on the eve of his birth anniversary, that no power or agency could completely remove his remembrance and influence among the people he had come home to; in fact, Benigno Aquino, Jr., murdered, martyred, has become even more famous than when he out-talked and outpaced his fellow solons in happier days, before martial law. As a sophisticated lady, a consultant of sorts to the ruling elite, was heard to remark at a cocktail party the week Ninoy was buried: "Goddamit, they had to go out and shoot him— now the guy's doing a great deal more harm dead than when he was bouncing around in those silly boots of his," or slightly inebriated words to that effect.

Her chuckling audience of fellow loyalists have had good reason since to take her sardonic alarm more seriously. For while those who had plotted against Ninoy's life did put an end to his bouncing around, they succeeded too in having those boots, as it were, planted permanently where once the slightest mention of him would have been banned by the martial law regime. Now, for goodness sake, the fellow's being billed as the new national hero. . . All right, Jose Rizal shouldn't be moved down from his perch up there, and all Aquinoys ought to settle for Ninoy's being hailed as *a* national hero: not the greatest Filipino of them all, but only one of a company of heroes on a lower rung—which is more than you can say for some prominent figures who, it is said, do not intend to die and prematurely occupy their reserved niches in the pantheon of the immortals.

Ninoy Aquino as one of our national heroes, then—a Filipino hero for our time, an exalted status which, pending its formal proclamation, the majority of our people seem ready to affirm if a poll to that end, an honest one, not any of those rigged and ridiculous barangay exercises we have been treated to since 1972, were to be conducted from Batanes to Sulu. As a national hero, a hero of the people, Ninoy and all he stood for, his ideals, his words and deeds, would be held up for the veneration of Filipinos for ages to come. Contrariwise, wouldn't all this mean an implicit condemnation of those who had opposed and oppressed him? To honor Rizal is to consign to infernal depths the likes of Governor Polavieja and the friars who welcomed his execution.

It was probably to prevent this kind of indictment, indirect but no less ruinous and beyond appeal, that prompted those KBL assemblymen to block the Opposition proposal some months ago to proclaim Benigno Aquino, Jr. a national hero. For, indeed, if Ninoy were to be recognized as such, a patriot of exceptional courage and greatness of heart, mind and spirit, an inspiration to the generations, an exemplar of the Filipino race—if Ninoy were indeed all that, what would that make of *their* hero? The latter would shrink in the esteem of our people in inverse proportion to the increase in Ninoy's heroic stature. Some political historian or social scientist will do well someday to write a thesis, a paper, a book, on this law of diminishing heroes.

History will of course issue the final verdict, but already the undeniable signs, from popular movements to movable monuments, from yellow showers to chanting marchers, are that the Aquino cult is here to stay and will continue to grow, as did the Rizalian devotion at the turn of the century—with or without benefit of executive fiat, legislative sanction or official commission. Insistent public demand, one might say, has certified to Ninoy's worthiness as a hero in the classic mold: the man of dauntless courage who is the main actor in a recognizable rite or action performed for the good of others, at the cost of pain and grief, or even of life itself.

That one intense moment, lasting no longer than a held breath or two, when Ninoy was led out of the China Airlines plane and then down the service stairs to his martyrdom, is understandably what has transfixed the popular imagination. It is those fateful seconds ticking like magnified pulsebeats toward that single shot outside in the hot sun that have projected the most dramatic image we now have of Ninoy as hero: the voluntary sacrificial victim, or, to be military about it, as befits the martial emergency at Gate 8, the point man of a patrol who must go alone into enemy territory, and so is the first to fall. With its mythic power, this hypnotic visual record of the genial, bespectacled man in the white jacket who is about to die will long endure in the nation's memory, like that photograph of Rizal standing apart and alone, before the firing squad in Bagumbayan.

Yet, again as in the case of the hero from Calamba, that last portrait of the hero from Tarlac, for all its overpowering appeal, represents not an entire life, but only a fragment of it. Countless other moments, other episodes in Ninoy Aquino's life, led to the martyrdom at the airport, made it possible, even, as hindsight would now dictate, inescapable. It is in this light that we should begin to contemplate that life, by the grace of God 51 years of it lived in the present era, in our country; and thanks also to Providence (or perhaps the Avsecom, or other commands, as the Agrava Board has indicated), a hero's life now offered for our people's tribute and emulation.

To this end, biographies are being written, have been published, beginning with Nick Joaquin's *The Aquinos of Tarlac*. More such works will be written as scholars and historians examine a career that, by any account, responded to every major issue, problem and conflict of our time. The character of the man was such (and the nature of his oppressors as well) that, despite imposed silence and solitary confinement, he still found himself in the spotlight, as the foremost prisoner of the martial law regime. He will, in time, have his own Retana, Palma, Guerrero; and aside from the biographers, there will be others inspired variously by the Aquino phenomenon—the folklorists, the weavers of legends, sundry story tellers; maybe novelists, too, and filmmakers. And as those captivated by the life of Rizal have done, they will seek out for their instruction what Ninoy said and wrote, for he was fortunately in his own fashion also a diligent scribbler, a conjurer with words.

Already the Benigno Aquino, Jr. Foundation has put out four booklets of Ninoy's poems, letters and speeches. The list of projected publications grows apace as manuscripts are retrieved, files are collected, bits of correspondence come to light. From the years in college, and on the *Manila Times*, in Korea, in Tarlac, Congress and Fort Bonifacio, and finally Boston and Harvard, Ninoy's writings could fill quite a few hefty boxes. Among the projects he finished at Harvard was a book on models of government that can best preside over the transition from dictatorship to democracy; this too awaits publication.

An earlier book which Ninoy wrote has just been issued by the Foundation—an event of no little historical interest, for it is his first published book, and one that, apparently, could be published only posthumously, as if nothing less than the author's death by assassination could have released it from its own confinement. The three editions of the book, including a popular newsprint version, are now available at the Foundation's offices on De la Rosa St., in Legazpi Village, Makati.

NINOY BEGAN WRITING *Testament from a Prison Cell* in 1975 and finished it in 1977, two years under the most trying conditions in his maximum-security cell in Fort Bonifacio.

The New Society was at its zenith; for once, or so it seemed, rhetoric matched reality as the regime trumpeted its achievements, in diplomacy, the economy, land reform, peace and order. The people, cheering such extravaganzas as the Miss Universe Contest, the Thrilla in Manila and Kasaysayan ng Lahi seemed then to have forgotten Ninoy entirely, except when reports on his trial and impending judgment surfaced in the Manila press. As Ninoy hints on occasion in his book, he was not unaware that perhaps the people—"desensitized by the rule of fear"—no longer cared for his "fondest wish," which was to see "democracy restored in our benighted land." It was a time, he writes, when fear made "calm thought most difficult" and even a "whispered protest" called for "a measure of bravery."

A lesser man in the same circumstances would have surrendered by then either to apathy, despair or the demands of his persecutors; what Ninoy did was write a book. Outside of citations from authorities as ancient as Socrates and as contemporary as Amnesty International, the discourse that is the book is Ninoy's own, its tone and thrust and staccato style unmistakably his, which should at least recommend *Testament from a Prison Cell* to readers grown sick and wary of the ghostwritten literature of the New Republic.

As Cory Aquino tells it in her Foreword, she and her children managed "to smuggle out the manuscript, page by page" from the stockade—no mean feat, that, as her husband's jailers could not have been too eager to see such material circulated beyond the barbed-wire fence. Although "the charges against him were fabricated . . . Ninoy believed he should still present his side to the Filipino people"; and the result, a book of ten chapters, was intended to be his "closing statement" before Military Commission No. 2 and at the same time his credo, his testament, that Cory Aquino would now present, in Ninoy's name, to the Filipino people.

Testament's Introductory Note recalls that on the night of November 25, 1977, after being sentenced to death by the military commission and immediately returned to his cell, Benigno Aquino, Jr. wrote a letter to the justices of the Supreme Court. He had been "deceitfully silenced," Ninoy wrote the High Tribunal, by being locked up in his cell during the final eight hours of the trial. Specifically, he had not been allowed to read his closing statement before judgment—his right, he stressed, as provided by Section 76 of the Manual of Court Martial.

In any event, his testimony in his own behalf could not have made for pleasant reading or listening on the part of the military panel, for in it Ninoy sought to explain his struggle and his "proposed strategy for national survival," and "to focus the attention of the Filipino people and the world to wanton violations of human rights." It was so "explosive," in the words of the Introductory Note, that Military Commission No. 2 had no recourse but "to ignore the guarantees of due process and Aquino's constitutional rights" in order to stop him from reading it in open court.

Testament consists, for the most part, of Ninoy's detailed refutation of what he calls the "claims of Mr. Marcos' martial rule." He marshals his arguments with characteristic verve and urgency, bolstering his exposition with an array of quotations, capitalizations, underscorings, exclamation points. He devotes an entire chapter, the most lucid and closely argued in the book, to the distinctive features of a totalitarian government, a description influenced, no doubt, by his view of the first five years of the New Society from his detention cell. The longest chapter, "Evidence Tortured into Existence," contains extensive excerpts from the 1975 reports of Amnesty International and the International Court of Justice on the torture of political detainees; documented cases of grisly barbarities in which not only the victims but the torturers and their various methods are identified—"the martial law rack" of "this rule of injustice, brutality and falsehood."

TO RESIST AND REPLACE such a regime, Ninoy would place his trust and loyalty in a "Christian democratic socialist ideology." He tells us little, though, about his thoughts on this subject other than that it "flows from the mainstream of Christian democratic socialism as practiced in Austria, West Germany and the Scandinavian countries" and that it will "harmonize political freedoms and economic equality, taking and merging the best in the two conflicting systems—communism and capitalism."

Of communism he has more to say, partly because he had been charged—falsely, he insists most emphatically—with violations of the Anti-Subversion Law, and for his counter-arguments he needed a firmer grasp of the ideology he had allegedly made his own. His analysis and rejection of the Communist creed should be of special interest to both avowed Marxists and professional anti-Communists who, at this late date and for reasons of their own, might still associate Ninoy with that ideology.

"I am not a Communist, never was, and never will be!" writes Ninoy in his *Testament*. "These are my reasons:

"Communism calls for violence in the overthrow of existing institutions regardless of the cost in human lives . . .

"I believe in evolutionary reform and I regard all human life as equally priceless. I hold individual freedom most sacred, because it is God's gift. I cannot accept any form of dictatorship, whether of the Left, the Right or the Center . . .

"In communism the opposition is liquidated. I believe the opposition must be won over . . .

"Lenin argued that . . . a class war is a ruthless conflict, the Communist has no room for sentimentality, for romanticism, but must use all tactics and strategic means, whether legal or illegal, to reach his objectives. It is, said Lenin, the only way.

74

"I am a humanist, a democrat and a romantic," concludes Ninoy. "And that is where I part ways with the Communists."

THE SUMMATION OF HIS TESTIMONY, his testament, is Ninoy at his most eloquent. Here the words have a swing and resonance to them, a lyric ring and also a somber tolling as in an elegy. "My Duty," he has titled this last chapter; he may well have called it, with equal aptness, "My Last Farewell."

As he brings his brief, his testimony, to a close, he seems to be transported to some mystic height from which he can survey the whole panorama of his people's history: "an epic struggle to end oppression and to be free," a history "washed in the blood of our forebears, and sanctified, as we shall always recall proudly, with their lives, which gave it sterling nobility."

And then, as if reminded of his duty, he descends from that lofty region and returns with a resolute will to the reality of his cell, the military tribunal and his struggle—"against a system of injustice . . . that not only enslaves our people but compels them to declare themselves for tyranny and their oppressor . . . a system that pretends to save democracy while actually destroying it . . .

"My duty, as I see it, is to tell our people that we must not only dream of a good and just society. We must resolve to make this dream come true."

He prays that these "seeds of thought" that have germinated in him will "find fertile soil and bear fruit in the hearts and minds" of his countrymen.

"I wish I had more than one life to give, for even if I had a hundred lives, I would never be able to repay the love and affection bestowed upon me by our great people—to whom, when I was desperate, I confided my despair; and with whom, when I was hopeful, I shared my hopes."

Such sentiments can be regarded in either one of two ways: as nothing more than another politician's striving for some rhetorical effect, or the sincerest expression of a patriot's deepest convictions.

The folio of photographs in the midsection of *Testament from a Prison Cell* should persuade us, if we still need to be so prodded, that Ninoy Aquino in November 1977—and in August 1983—had absolutely no use for empty words and meaningless gestures. Ninoy, lean and haggard, arguing a point before Military Commission No. 2 in

1973; Ninoy looking faint and shockingly thin, during his 40-day hunger strike, in 1975; Ninoy, head bowed, in court for the reading of his death sentence, in 1977—the photographs are of a man whose life is in the balance and who can only mean what he does and declares as he has renounced all untruth, pretense and dissimulation.

The most moving picture of the lot is of course the one reproduced on the back of the book jacket showing Ninoy fallen on the tarmac. He ended his testament with the brave refrain from the National Anthem, about dying for one's country: *ang mamatay nang dahil sa iyo;* and here, for all to see, for all time, is the most graphic and indisputable proof that, by God, he meant every word of it. Slain, finally silenced, Ninoy lies utterly still in the square of light which the noise and commotion of the world cannot penetrate. His testimony is finished, verified and sealed in his blood. No retraction is possible now, nor any alteration of it, any more than the violent day can reverse itself and time stop and the homecoming exile turn away from his native land.

To perfect and then perpetuate the testimony that is his life by offering it up for his people and his country—that is what Ninoy Aquino did, that is what he lived and died for, why Filipinos may now commemorate him, the true, the brave and the martyr, as the pride of the nation, the hero for all generations.

(Panorama, 1984)

Scenes from the Life of a Cardinal

HIS CARDINAL SIN, his exasperated critics complain, is he talks too much.

He just can't keep his big mouth shut but must have his say about everything and everyone within earshot or not, sneer his disgusted detractors. Oh, if only His Eminence would shut up, they chorus crossly; if only he would learn to be more civil and circumspect, peaceable and quiet, and by his holy example show the sovereign people, the electorate especially, that silence is golden, they sniff piously—so their ambitions for country's sake and some *trapos'* profit would not turn to lead, their political dreams and martial schemes not be reduced to dross.

Slightly exaggerated, you might say—their sanctimonious outrage and Cardinal Sin's loquaciousness and all that.

True enough, His Eminence seems to relish every sociable chance that comes his way to sound off, to hold forth, to comment and counsel on matters great (freedom, democracy, free and honest elections) and small (condoms, the shrinking peso, Gloria Macapagal-Arroyo). And he likes doing all this in public forums and presscons, during demos against dictators or demagogues as well as at dinner parties for partisan dignitaries—always with evident sincerity, a cheerful openness, a kind of innocent candor; often with truthful byte and smart quote; sometimes with remarks to be later rued as more indiscreet and inane than profound, which only proves what the Cardinal himself well knows and admits with a humble chuckle: that he is not by any means human or divine, an infallible oracle, much less all-knowing and perfect, nor a saint (not yet canonized, anyway).

But people really close to him, longtime friends and associates—his late biographer Felix Bautista, for instance, or the businessman he calls Colonel Tony, and his secretary-spokesman, Father Ariston Sison, and the rector of the EDSA Shrine, his protegé Father Socrates Villegas—they would tell you that Cardinal Sin is one priest and prelate who, for all his publicized verbosity, his enjoyment of talk and company, values solitude and ever seeks silence as a pearl of great price.

It has been his practice, even before he was ordained priest in 1954, to rise at dawn and spend an hour or more in prayer and meditation before the Blessed Sacrament. He has been devoted, since his student days at the prewar Saint Vincent Ferrer Seminary in Jaro, Iloilo, to the Blessed Virgin—Our Lady and her rosary, which he loves to pray each day or night if not oftener, on his knees, in quiet church or chapel, away from TV eyes, cameras, loudspeakers and media folk.

OF LATE, HE SPENDS more time alone, in prayer, in contemplation, when the visitors are gone, when the day's duties are done, confides one of the Sisters on his staff. From the windows of Villa San Miguel, he would gaze out over the lawn at the trees and sky, in the sunset, in the last light—and in such peace and stillness, what would the Cardinal be praying for, what thoughts and reflections fill the silence?

Of such silence, Thomas Merton, the famous Trappist author who made it his vocation, has spoken: "If our life is poured out in useless words, we will never hear anything . . . and in the end, because we have said everything before we had anything to say, we shall be left speechless at the moment of our greatest decision.

"But silence is order to that final utterance. It is not an end in itself. Our whole life is a meditation of our last decision—the only decision that matters. And we meditate in silence.

"Yet we are bound, to some extent, to speak to others, to help them see their way to their own decision—to teach them Christ . . . so that they also may speak what they have heard."

Merton—Father Louis of the Order of the Carthusians of the Strict Observance—ends this particular meditation, in his *Thoughts in Solitude*, with the words of the Psalmist: "I have believed, therefore have I spoken."

Jaime Cardinal Sin (the Christian name precedes the title, to signify its worth and the baptism that conferred it as more precious and meaningful than any office or honor) rises from his meditations. He leaves the silence of the invisible cloister his faith has built around him even in the midst of his crowded and clamorous See. He girds himself for his mission, his battle, his crusade. Then, with a stout heart and a merry gleam in his eyes, for joy is the gigantic secret of the Christian, he goes forth to his flock, his people, and speaks to them what he has heard and learned, what he knows and believes.

As Archbishop of Manila, as Cardinal, as Prince (which means leader) of the Church, he has not taken a vow of silence, although he may choose to observe it in prayer at canonical hours like a Trappist or Benedictine. In the ceremonies at Saint Peter's Basilica that pronounced him a Cardinal, his mouth was ritually closed by the Pope, to symbolize the discretion he must observe, Nick Joaquin tells us in *The Book of Sin*, his classic life of the churchman from Aklan. Then his mouth was ritually opened again—to signify that he must not remain silent, that when speech is necessary he must speak out even at the cost of his life. For red is the color of the Cardinalate, red for "courage even unto death and the shedding of your blood," as Paul

VI intoned the ceremonial phrases on that May day in 1954, when Archbishop Jaime Sin received his Red Hat; courage "for the faith, the peace and the well-being of the Christian world."

Cardinal Sin must have taken that invocation and that commission most fervently to heart: to speak the speech when crisis and challenge and the well-being of his flock make it necessary, though not always trippingly or tremendously on the tongue. He has refused to be silent, to be silenced. He has not agreed with certain powers and principalities that the Church in the Philippines be a Church of Silence.

He has not been persecuted and punished as churchmen of courage had been in tyrannized countries where the Church was for long years silenced. He has so far received no letter-bombs, only hate mail delivered at Villa San Miguel. Words hurled at him, on the air waves, in print, have not broken a single bone of his substantial, towering frame. The explosive threat that he would be turned into a blasted martyr at the Quirino Grandstand last September 21 remained just that, an ominous warning crafted, it was said, by "spooks" in the hire of the Palace and Camp Aguinaldo.

Yet, in heroic faith and fortitude and fidelity to his Supreme Leader, Our Lord, he has more than proven himself as worthy of membership in the Sacred College of Cardinals as Mindzenty of Hungary, whom the Communists could subdue only by unrelenting torture and the ultimate inhumanity, the mind emptied, erased, by brainwashing; Stepinac of Yugoslavia and Wyszynski of Poland, who were imprisoned for resisting Marxist domination of their homelands and persecution of the Church; Tien of Beijing, who was spared the death he welcomed before being driven into exile; Gong of Shanghai who spent 30 years in Maoist labor camps and prisons.

Last year, as in the historic crisis year of 1986, Cardinal Sin spoke out, uttered what he had heard and believed in solitary prayer and elsewhere, to guide and inspire his people, to help them see their way to their own decision.

He affirmed, appealed, exhorted, commanded, warned, questioned, counseled, condemned (the fault or sin, never the sinner) and, as is his wont, cracked quite a few jokes on the side, including some excruciatingly unfunny tales—and in the process he made a lot of news and history in 1997, and more followers, too, as well as critics and adversaries.

All these have made him, in the verdict of the *Graphic*, our Man of the Year, together with his pet peeve, enduring friend, fellow mover and shaker of the times, and as he might call him with an impish twinkle, his favorite constitutionalist, President Fidel V. Ramos.

LAST AUGUST, on the eve of his 69th birthday, Cardinal Sin was reported to be ailing: high blood pressure, and a case of piss and disorder in his plumbing—prompting one cantankerous critic in the employ of our other Man of the Year to suggest that somebody who is that sick and maybe about to croak shouldn't get excited and yak too much.

To which taunt the Cardinal had a voluble answer, as recorded by *Graphic* senior writer, resident theologian and political pundit emeritus Quijano de Manila:

"I have to speak up. It's my duty, especially when I hear them claiming we are already a tiger economy but I don't see any wealth trickling down to the poor. Now they're saying our rice is not enough, we'll have to import rice—what will happen to our farmers? And they have devaluated the peso—won't the people be suffering? But they say we are making progress. If they are free to say those things, I am also free to say my say—this is a free country . . ."

There are certain grievous questions, problems, issues that the Church and the people have to contend with, he told Mr. de Manila:

"Family planning . . . they're going to teach grade-school children about masturbation. The condom is masturbation . . . I don't say we shouldn't have family planning, but it shouldn't be through abortion. The government says it is against abortion but foments it nevertheless . . . What you want to do, just do it. What will happen to this country if there's no more discipline and no more self-sacrifice? And they talk about progress. How about moral progress? Who are doing the kidnapping, who are collecting ransom? Members of the government—police, soldiers, officials.

"That's why I have to speak up," the Cardinal continued, "or nobody else will. Everybody will be saying yes to them. But it's necessary that somebody like me should speak up. When I am no longer Archbishop of Manila, I will not speak," etc.

Concerning the most crucial controversy, the projected amendments to the Constitution before the May 1998 elections—"I foresee trouble the moment the Constitution is touched and their tenures of office extended. Our country will become unstable. These politicians now in power will continue in power, when a purpose of this Constitution is to prevent dynasties. We are only ten years away from the EDSA revolution but again we would make possible a government controlled by only one person. If the Constitution is to be changed at all, it should be after the 1998 polls."

How about the charge, Señor de Manila asked, that he criticizes FVR because the President is a Protestant . . . The Cardinal sighed and chuckled: "I am not complaining about his religion, I am complaining about his regime. He says one thing and does another . . . Oh, I could go easy on him if I wanted favors—but that would be improper. When I end my work as Archbishop of Manila, I don't want it said that I failed in my duty to protect my flock from harm," etc.

But wouldn't he be meddling in politics, which was not his domain? "Politics is a human activity, and therefore involves every person," said Cardinal Sin. "So I have to speak. I would not speak if our laymen were not keeping so quiet. So who will speak on, say, those demolitions of squatter homes? They say it's none of my business. But who will protect these poor people if I don't who am of the Church of the Poor?"

But a Church that is rich in numbers, in grace, hope and strength—"The Church is very strong in the Philippines. You can see it with your eyes. Every Sunday, from four o'clock dawn to eight in the evening, Masses every hour—and every Mass crowded . . . This September I am ordaining eleven new priests. Last July I ordained three Chinese clerics to work with the Chinese community in Metro Manila. And the vocations among the women are even more profuse. Then we have the Couples for Christ, the Charismatics, the ministries for the laity . . . That's our main thrust now—to have lay people preaching the Gospel," etc.

TO PREACH THE GOSPEL is to live and abide by it, in the sacristy and in the streets, in the convent no less than in the home and the office, the marketplace, the court of law and the poll precinct. The Christian is a dual citizen, for he belongs, in Augustine's formulation, to both the City of God and the City of Man (not to be confused, of course, with Imelda's citadel of unhappy memory). Thus, the real, actual, practical blurring or dissolving of the "separation" (deemed so sacred by dogmatic secularists) of Church and State, as often happens in a predominantly Christian country like the Philippines.

"The cry of separation of Church and State is not something that can be tossed around without need for nuancing," the Jesuit barrister and constitutionalist Joaquin G. Bernas reminds us in a *Today* commentary. "Neither is it an all-purpose gag on the clergy. Frequently, however, those who cry 'Separate Church from State' really mean, 'Gag the clergy!' It is not our intention supinely to consent."

Quite the contrary, and far from supinely consenting—a posture it's hard to imagine him adopting, even if exhausted or ailing—Cardinal Sin voiced out loud and clear and repeatedly that he, and the priests and religious and lay people of his mega-archdiocese, and hopefully the rest of the nation, would not be stifled, would not be gagged. The word cardinal comes from the Latin *cardo*, hinge; and in 1997 His Eminence did provide the nation, the people, with a firm device, an indispensable joint, as it were, on which turned our history's door to the future. The hinge would not rust and fall. One Cardinal's voice would not be gagged, his flock would not be made *gago*.

Most certainly, mum's not the word for Cardinal Sin, neither is it nice passivity nor ass-licking-in-public relations nor any fake collaboration for national unity and progress and so on.

All this the Malacañang trio whom the excellent columnist Luis Mauricio not so fondly calls FVR's "TAE team"—Executive Secretary Ruben Torres, National Security Adviser Jose Almonte and Budget Secretary Salvador Enriquez—were compelled to acknowledge with extreme reluctance and dismay.

They, and Alberto and Carmen Pedrosa of PIRMA, and Lakas legislators like House Majority Leader Rodolfo Albano and Camiguin Congressman Pedro Romualdo, and their ilk and their clones and agents in the bureaucracy, the local governments and the media—they all were as pushers of the dangerous drug of power beyond constitutional limits, according to Cory Aquino and the Cardinal and, as it soon turned out, also in the judgment of millions of the citizenry and not just the massive crowd at the September 21 anti-Cha-cha rally at the Luneta. Even in the Palace-directed "consultations" following the mass protests, 12 out of 16 regions registered their opposition to Charter change before the elections.

Pushing Charter amendments to lift term limits on the President and not so incidentally some 87 three-term congressmen and a horde of governors and mayors before the 1998 elections—that's unconstitutional, illegal, immoral, for all practical purposes criminal and treasonous, and should be so exposed and opposed, and stopped in its tracks by the sovereign people. . . This was the alarm the Cardinal sounded, the warning he raised, the urgent message he began to broadcast as soon as the Palace and PIRMA and their fellow plotters in Congress made their first concerted moves to mangle the Constitution, in February of 1997—more than six months before the August anniversary of Ninoy Aquino's assassination and Mrs. Aquino's public declaration of reinforcing the Cardinal's good fight against Charter change and a second or extended term for Mr. Ramos.

The battle of words, speeches, homilies, press statements, court petitions, legal maneuvers, signature campaigns, filibusters, raged through most of the year. It was only toward September that bomb explosions recalling martial law '72 splattered the scene with blood or the prospect of it. And through it all, and at the high point of it, at the Luneta prayer rally which seeded clouds failed to rain out, and General Acedero's martial rumblings could not disperse, Cardinal Sin was in his best form, in fine fettle (leaner but not meaner, he had bounced back from whatever it was that had ailed and slowed him down)—calling for faith, courage and confidence even as he enjoined his flock not to believe, at the very least not to trust the political wolves, the Cha-cha thugs out to abduct and mutilate the Constitution and rob them of the '98 elections and their rights and their democratic treasure.

GISING BAYAN! Cardinal Sin roused the faithful last September 3, further annoying and discombobulating Cha-cha dunce instructors and pro-amendment pushers ranged against him and his legion of true Christian democrats—as distinguished from the Manglapus-led NUCD that had joined its negligible force to what the most credible and intelligent newspaper today likes to call the "party of thieves."

"On September 21, I am inviting all freedom-loving Filipinos to go to the Luneta and join me in praying for freedom in our country . . .

83

"We are not against improving the Charter. It's the timing that is very bad. It is very indecent for our government leaders to start this Charter change and allow themselves to be the first beneficiaries.

"Our common call is: Eleksyon Muna bago Cha-cha! No to Cha-cha now!"

Four days before the rally that was to coincide with the 25th anniversary of Ferdinand Marcos' declaration of martial law, the Cardinal opened up with one more canonical barrage:

"I am an optimist by nature. My optimism has grown even more in the last few days as I saw, heard and experienced the willingness of Filipinos to be heroes again for the cause of democracy. I am deeply touched by the numerous messages I have received from countless Filipinos all over the country urging me to carry on with our crusade for democracy this September 21 and beyond.

"Twenty-five years ago, we were deceived by orchestrated political turmoil and we were made to believe that martial law was the only answer . . . We are wiser now. Nobody can fool us anymore when it comes to the preservation of freedom, justice, truth and democracy . . . We will not allow dictatorship to return. Never again!

"If you are against military rule and authoritarianism, if you are for freedom and justice and peace, go to the Luneta on September 21. If you are afraid, do not go . . . Since Rizal died there more than a hundred years ago, Luneta's hallowed soil is reserved only for the brave and the patriotic.

"Only the brave have the right to be called heroes."

The people came, in the tens of thousands, in the hundreds of thousands, surging toward a million, and most assuredly more would have come had it been as bright and sunny as the afternoon of the pro-Ramos Jesus Is Lord assembly a week or so later. But the gatherer of heroes and patriots was anything but heroic and admirable, scoffed the budged chief, Salvador Enriquez, after the Luneta demo and similarly inspired protest rallies across the land derailed his Cha-cha train, routed his PIRMA caravan off the road and possibly wrote finis as well to his splendid dream of serving the nation in the Senate.

That vile meddler of a Cardinal, that horrid *pakialamero* and rabble-rouser, that abominable reincarnation of Padre Damaso, or epithets to that common effect, should stop generating vitriol and fomenting hate for our dear President Ramos, Cuya Badong fairly sputtered in a TV interview and in statements to the press. The Cardinal, moreover, was doing us faithful Catholics a lot of harm, cancelling afternoon Masses on September 21 to draw more people to the Luneta rally. Folks like Salvador E., who were trying their best to save their souls and Cha-cha at the same time, might have missed Mass then because of the Cardinal's devilish decree, and they now want to know—whose sin was it, theirs or Cardinal Sin's?

Why, oh why must the Cardinal do such things that harm "our Catholic sect?" He, the devout Salvador Enriquez, was bothered and bewildered, tried and tormented, by what the Cardinal-Archbishop of Manila was doing to what he called "our Catholic sect."

Now, professed Catholics, except maybe pre-schoolers with very short attention spans, who refer to the Holy Roman Catholic and Apostolic Church as a "sect" cannot in any council or congregation or publication be taken even half-seriously. Such religious ignoramuses, perhaps confused, titillated, by some sect's appeal (Ka Erdie's Iglesia believers and Brother Eddie Villanueva's evangelicals combined could add up to a humongous chunk of votes), maybe should just be laughed off the Catholic premises. But the Cardinal, compassionate shepherd and charitable pastor that he is, will most likely grant Cuya Badong unconditional absolution for dubbing him a dastardly Padre Damaso.

THE BUDGET CHIEF APPEARS to be only the most visible and vehement of the excremental advocates of Charter change, before and after those nationwide rallies that clobbered them.

There are the artful and practiced ones, inclined to prudence and restraint as the better part of disagreement, such as Palace assistant for political affairs Gabriel Claudio with his painstaking legalese and Sen. Juan Ponce Enrile, who tried to duplicate in the Senate the constituent assembly shindig organized by Albano & Co. in the House, all to no avail.

Against the Cardinal's stance on Charter amendments are also a number of columnists, radio commentators and PR pros. But they are reputedly no more than media racketeers on the take from the Malacañang budget office, so Father Ariston Sison shouldn't worry the least bit about the image and good name of his ecclesiastical boss.

Then, there's this new, or perhaps not so fresh, crop of the Cardinal's critics, who seem to be all from the Gabriela sisterhood, who have taken issue with His Eminence on birth control, women for the priesthood and such. Recently, they were all riled up over his comments—not on the Charter and the drug of power, but concerning Gloria Macapagal-Arroyo's presidential bid.

Gloria, the Cardinal had said to a roomful of reporters, is too young to be President, aside from the fact that she's, ah, well, hmmm, a woman, and the times call for a real, experienced, grownup man, somebody who won't run home crying to Mama when things get really tough, like in coup attempts, kidnappings, crime waves, which Gloria may be expected to do if and when she gets to be President, which prospect doesn't have my apostolic blessing and spiritual support, so I think it'd be a good idea if she would just give up the notion of running for President, etc.

Whereupon the feminists (and some queer fellows in league with them) jumped on the Cardinal and seemed all fired up to burn him at the stake for being so obnoxiously sexist, they fumed, making Gloria and her KAMPI campaigners very unhappy with his mindless chauvinist pronouncements on her age and gender.

An *Inquirer Magazine* lady editor's year-ender putdown of the chatty Cardinal summed it all up for Gloria's feminist battalions: Nuts to him for his "revealing sexist remarks and advice to Sen. Gloria Macapagal-Arroyo." These only "proved how the Catholic Church has remained pretty much in the Dark Ages." Worse, the Cardinal made "a lot of Catholics wish they were Buddhists and atheists whenever he dove into a political fray. Whatever happened to prayerful silence?"

By gawd and by gulay, as we used to say back in freshman college, there's that business again about being prayerfully, reverently and consistently silent. Are such dainty disdainers of the Cardinal and champions of Senator Arroyo also with PIRMA and for Cha-cha even now, after these have been dumped, or so it's made to appear, by Ramos and the LAKAS, to the relief and joy of anointed Joe de Venecia?

And, seriously now, should the Cardinal's "sexist remarks and advice" disqualify him from being named Man of the Year of *Philippine Graphic*, a democratic, non-gender-discriminating magazine published for the equal instruction and pleasure of both men and women?

NO, ABSOLUTELY NOT, those remarks notwithstanding, and we here hail Jaime Cardinal Sin all over again as our Man of the Year—for all the good things and the good news and history he made in 1997, for his heroic leadership and courage in the fight against the foes and would-be assassins of our democracy, for speaking out against the illegal, immoral, indecent and treasonous conspiracies against the Constitution and the people, for rejecting to be silent, for refusing to be silenced.

And, really, now, should he be faulted still for those things he said about Mrs. Arroyo? The Cardinal, kind and gallant as ever, didn't even so much as hint about what should really rid her of the notion that she ought to be made our President, and that's her lack of altitude and stature.

A tiny President elected to face the gigantic challenges of the 21st century might only demonstrate to the whole wired globe what Nick Joaquin has called our heritage of smallness. Besides, shorties generally sport, besides elevator boots or extra-high heels, an oversensitive arrogance. They tend to strut and puff out their pompous chests or bosoms, as the case may be; and such Napoleonic attitudes could turn off, tune out, lawmakers, generals, justices, investors, diplomats, foreign allies, the IMF, too, and the World Bank.

And how can the Armed Forces be loyal and obedient to a little Commander in Chief who has trouble trooping the line? And how would we citizens and civilians feel on seeing our Chief Executive looking diminutive and lost, and maybe even mistaken for a pubescent dependent in some leader's retinue, at a world summit of veritable giants? Like most people everywhere, those Presidents and Prime Ministers and Party Chairmen, the Clintons and Mahathirs and Mandelas and Kims, are getting taller, not the other way around. And last, from all accounts, Gloria seems to have paid heed to her wise Cardinal-pastor's advice and has given up being a presidential wannabe. She now just wants more humbly to be the anointed trapo's running mate.

So what's the beef? Are "lots of Catholics" still fed up with a Church stuck in the muck of the Dark Ages by a Cardinal's mere "advice" (for which he has apologized) to a lady politico? But the Dark Ages was when the Church and its bishops and its clergy and monasteries saved the light and knowledge and culture of the civilized world from the ravages of the barbarians storming the ramparts of Christian Europe.

Are they still going to be Buddhists, unbelievers or whatever just because the stubbornly "sinful" Cardinal-Archbishop of Manila has a duty and commitment and commission to speak out, and also this penchant, habit and "sin" to express his opinions on many things great and small as the Lord God made them all?

But the sort of Christians who will renounce the Faith just because they can't stomach what a priest or Bishop or Cardinal says somewhat in passing, not even a matter of doctrine or belief . . . Holy Maloney, they'll just as readily turn their backs on the Church of the Apostles, the Martyrs and the Saints, and of Cardinal Sin, just because the celebrant of the Mass doesn't resemble Richard Gomez or Brad Pitt, the homilist is stout, chinky and droll or dull, and the organist tends to strike the wrong notes, and the crowds, the choir, the wretched singing, the poor lighting. . . But the Church, said Chesterton, is first of all not a church . . .

Your Eminence—like that Badong Enriquez, they've got to be kidding!

(*Graphic*, 1998)

His Honor, Justice Puno

IT LOOKS LIKE IT'S GOING TO BE a long haul when you scan the country, or even just this part of town, from the corner of Taft and Padre Faura—a long dazed journey, not to "Philippines 2000," the splendiferous miracle promised the Fidel Ramos faithful a mere seven years from now, but to the reality of NIChood probably a century hence.

A wet afternoon the color of jeepney exhaust sets the tone for the dismal scene here on this block in Ermita that is one of the more entrancing sites around Metro Manila and which contains some of the most strategic and influential offices of the Republic. A mud-streaked sidewalk only less than a meter wide, it seems—"only in the Philippines," as they say—is crammed with damp commuters, ID photo stands and assorted vendors along the old Supreme Court side of Taft, from the congested NBI compound to the dilapidated corner

of Padre Faura. The jeepneys are doing what these wretched convey-
ances do best at street junctions, especially when the cops have gone
off for coffee and recreation, which is create a traffic gridlock—in this
instance, right below the LRT line, which in the first place must have
been designed to end such tormenting jams.

Plastered on the pillars of the LRT are signs protesting against
the anti-people orders of the education and labor departments, put
up no doubt by campus activists from the Manila Science High School
and the Emilio Aguinaldo College across Taft and the UP's Manila
College around the corner toward the "new" Supreme Court building.
More signs greet the pedestrian on Padre Faura: the street lighting
project, which only late-night strollers might appreciate, was under-
taken jointly by Mayor Alfredo Lim's administration and the "new"
Pagcor; litterbugs face a fine of P2,000 if not imprisonment. The warning is generally unheeded, to judge from so many Stork candy wrappers
like green leaves strewn about, together with *maruya* and fishball
sticks and other indigenous trash.

The Faura sidewalks are mercifully wider on either side, although one must still take care not to collide with the citizenry
taking merienda or reading about small-town warlords and rapist-
killers in the tabloids or just standing around, waiting for a dropped
billfold or an economic breakthrough. On either side, too, are cars
parked under the no-parking signs, including one rusty Toyota with
two wheels positioned obliquely on the sidewalk farther up the
street, between the Department of Justice and the UP Manila's College of Dentistry.

Toward Maria Orosa and where Mr. Gokongwei's domain begins, the noisy, crowded, impoverished shabbiness gives way to the
elegance of the Faura Café and similar establishments. Through a
coffee shop's misted window panes one glimpses strange circular ruins: the Ateneo chapel finally demolished despite the appeals and
injunctions invoked reportedly by a Catholic women's league from
the Supreme Court and adjacent institutions.

Back in the '70s, the Ateneo sold its College of Law building
beside the chapel to the owners of the Ramada Midtown and
Robinson's Department Store, and the huge statue of the canonized
lawyer Sir Thomas More atop the chapel moved with the law school
to Makati. "The King's good servant, but God's first" and the original "Man for All Seasons"—such was the lawyers' patron saint, the

great humanist and friend of the poor and martyr to the Faith, who defied the despotic will of Henry VIII and instead chose eternal loyalty to the Lord's Vicar on earth and as a result lost his head on the scaffold . . .

H. de la Costa Street in Salcedo Village, over which now broods the bronze figure of that most relevant 16th-century saint, is a long way, too, from Padre Faura—where More's spirit, some would say, not just his sculptured Renaissance likeness, has been absent for some time now. This legal premise, a lawyerly proposition, you might say, brings us back to the object of this gray afternoon's tour: the bulwark of our rights and liberties, the Supreme Court, which in this stormy month in the third quarter of 1993 is still under siege.

VISIBLY, PUBLICLY AGITATED as the visitor walks up the driveway of the High Tribunal is not some venerable jurist fuming over what Chief Justice Andres Narvasa calls the "polluted information environment," but a woman driver trying with the grimness of the besieged to back out from among the cars parked three deep on the front court. Besides the population explosion, the nation or at least this busy official section of Manila must endure prolific increase of vehicles, unless the government decides, as once planned, to transfer all its principal agencies to the outer limits of Quezon City.

To such a move, however, the justices are not likely to say aye, en banc or individually, since the Supreme Court building, renovated in 1991 under the auspices of then President Aquino and Chief Justice Marcelo Fernan, is surely one of the few truly stately and magnificent structures to house Filipino officialdom. The façade like a Roman temple's, with its white stone steps and classical columns, and within, the marbled corridors and walls, the tall paneled doors to the justices' chambers—all this suggests a world different from the rest of government; something invincible, traditional and timeless, more so in contrast to the sad untidiness and near anarchy outside.

The visitor goes up the broad stone steps aware that he is entering a world removed from the problems and perils that beset lower servants of the people. But a security guard keeps vigil behind one of the Greco-Roman pillars and he is holding a businesslike Uzi. Then one remembers there are a couple of sentries, soldiers in olive drab with slung M-16s, behind the wall by the shrunken sidewalk, on the Taft Avenue side.

Are the foes of the justice system—and there must be quite a few of these outside the law, outside the democratic fold in diverse ways—are they about to storm this citadel of the Constitution? Have those faceless poison-pen letter-writers a.k.a. "Concerned Practitioners" become so mad and desperate they might just take a sniper's shot at a *ponente* on a promenade or lob a grenade at the No. 9 Benzes clustered in the driveway?

Nothing of course in the order of a Bong Revilla or Robin Padilla flick is expected to disturb the solemn tenor of their days. But the justices these days, or so one gathers from that "polluted environment," are no longer as unperturbed in their remote niches as the people once perceived them to be, ages before the Supreme Court's present critics began besmirching the august walls.

The highest court in the land continues to be criticized, attacked, assailed. This state of affairs is a measure of, among other things, how both governors and governed have changed since the tenures of chief justices like Cesar Bengzon, Marceliano Montemayor, Roberto Concepcion—times when not the faintest breath of scandal threatened the composure of the Court, and no concerned rumor-monger dared question its integrity. As the supreme arbiter and exemplar of justice, the Court is expected to aspire to a kind of secular sacredness. If it won't or can't, to what, to whom, as the cry goes, will the aggrieved and oppressed people turn?

The *Philippine Daily Inquirer*, clearly not Chief Justice Narvasa's favorite paper, reports during the week the visitor goes to the Supreme Court, which is the third week of July: "Three new impeachment complaints were filed against Chief Justice Andres Narvasa and at least three other justices at the House of Representatives during Congress' two-month recess . . .

"The complaints were filed by ordinary citizens who claimed that the SC justices violated the Constitution and committed other 'impeachable acts' in the handling of their cases."

The first complainant, according to the *Inquirer*, claims that he was falsely charged by his employer with embezzlement during martial law and imprisoned unjustly. But the Fernan Court, including Narvasa as a respondent, rejected his petition for damages and other remedies on the grounds that it was filed in 1986, after the ten-year prescription period had lapsed. He was in prison during the Marcos regime, he said, and he could not file his petition then and expect the courts to be fair.

The second complainant, according to the *Inquirer*, alleges that the Supreme Court made a "sudden turnaround last year" in a P15-million land case her war widows' association was pursuing against a giant realty company. She earlier claimed that "a relative of a Supreme Court justice demanded P5 million from her to 'settle' the case in her favor . . ."

The third complainant accused the SC of "unduly delegating its power to decide on cases brought before it" and pointed to a resolution "signed by a mere clerk of court in the dismissal of a case he was pursuing in the SC."

The three complaints—coming after all those rumors and allegations of misconduct and corruption which have kept Chief Justice Narvasa and other top judicious honchos in robes busier and perhaps angry above and beyond the call of jury—have been referred by Speaker Jose de Venecia to the House Committee on Justice chaired by Representative Pablo Garcia. "[But like] past impeachment complaints filed against members of the Court, the new cases," the *Inquirer* noted, "lacked the necessary endorsement of at least one congressman," and it was doubted whether "the complaints would be taken up by the 41-member [justice] committee."

Also in Congress, the *Inquirer* tells us, the Committee on Economic Affairs headed by Representative Felicito Payumo has approved a resolution calling for the creation of a nine-man commission "to review possible 'defects' in the landmark decisions issued by the Supreme Court in the last 20 years."

Meanwhile, and to no one's real surprise, Atty. Miriam Defensor-Santiago jumped into the judicial ring and, as reported by the *Manila Standard*, "challenged President Ramos to name the persons behind an anonymous scandal sheet against Supreme Court justices, which she said is part of an effort to intimidate the justices and compel them to resign before they can reach a decision on her pending election protest."

And then, striking close to home, there's Associate Justice Teodoro Padilla's proposal for a commission to investigate complaints against members of the High Tribunal. The recent Multi-Sectoral Citizens' Forum endorsed Padilla's proposal to create "an independent probe body composed of two retired SC justices not engaged in the practice of law and the dean of a reputable law school."

Justice Padilla explains his proposal in this wise: If the investigation of administrative complaints against SC justices is conducted by the Court itself, "skepticism abounds, for . . . the ideal of the cold neutrality of an impartial judge may be far from attainable. When a justice of the Supreme Court has to look into the conduct of a brother justice with whom he meets almost daily and breaks bread almost as often, the chances are the cards will be loaded in favor of the brother justice under fire."

Chief Justice Narvasa has nixed Padilla's plan, saying it smacks of "experimentation" and, besides, there already exist "built-in mechanisms under the Constitution that vested the power to discipline with the Supreme Court."

In other words, 'tis salutary to sustain the status quo, lest the Rock of Law, as another prestigious publication once called the Court, crack further and possibly crumble.

MENTION OF SUCH TRAVAILS as currently rack the Supreme Court brings a wan smile to the rather boyish face of the newly appointed and, at 53, the youngest member of the High Tribunal.

"The Court does have an image problem," says soft-spoken Associate Justice Reynato S. Puno, who got his appointment papers only last June 28—one of the two newest members of the Court, the other being the equally accomplished scholar and educator, Dean Jose C. Vitug.

Observes Mr. Justice Puno as he sits in what looks like a brand-new leather chair behind a freshly varnished desk: "The judiciary as a whole is in a very peculiar position. It is very difficult for the judiciary to be defending itself against all these rumors and claims. For instance, on Chief Justice Narvasa's trying to defend the judiciary, we have two schools of thought here. One would say that it is not proper for him to be doing so, the other school of thought would say that he is not doing enough. It is very difficult for the judiciary to be engaging always in this kind of argument, especially with non-legal persons."

Would Vice President Estrada be one of these "non-legal persons?" Justice Puno would likewise agree, wouldn't he, that things were much quieter in this temple of justice on Padre Faura before the

Veep or one of his PACC agents or his ghost-writer added "hoodlums in robes" to the media's vocabulary?

"We have no data on the rating of the Supreme Court before this so-called Erap exposé," says the justice evenly, "so it is difficult to make a judgment, whether the Erap exposé has been responsible for the erosion of the image of the Supreme Court and the judiciary . . . But I tend to agree that a lot of these charges are disordered—disorderly . . .

"For instance," the justice continues, "I came from the Court of Appeals, there are at least 50 justices there and each has written a thousand or more decisions. The statistics will show that about 98 percent of these decisions have been affirmed by the Supreme Court. Now, for one or two decisions some people disapprove of, out of the thousands that have been written, they demand that all justices and judges resign . . .

"Again, some people are demanding resignations, but the truth is, the solution is not mass resignations, that has been done before, for example after EDSA. Resigning is not the key to the problem. Related to this is the problem of reorganization, a very complex and delicate problem. First, you must have the goods on the corrupt judges and justices before you can kick them out, then you have to face the next problem, looking for better replacements."

Be that as it may, it was one man's resignation that can be said to have helped Justice Puno move up and away from the Court of Appeals on the Maria Orosa side of the block to where he now sits in his newly decorated quarters (paintings in the styles of Amorsolo and Magsaysay-Ho hang on the beige lamplit walls). But no, he seems to smile with some relief, this office did not belong to former Justice Hugo Gutierrez. The latter resigned abruptly from the Court "out of delicadeza" after the publication of the *Inquirer*-Center for Investigative Journalism series claiming that it was not Gutierrez but the PLDT counsel who had written the decision favoring the PLDT over the British-affiliated Eastern Telecommunications Philippines, Inc. (ETPI). The case in point involved the use of a multi-billion peso "gateway" for overseas calls.

Justice Gutierrez's retirement, which was not due until 1996, and that of Justice Jose Campos, who had turned 70, created the two vacancies in the 15-member Court which President Ramos filled only weeks ago. In a real sense Gutierrez's replacement, Justice Puno has "inherited" the cases pending or on appeal in the resigned justice's division. One of these is the PLDT case, which the ETPI lawyers have brought back for reconsideration. Which means Justice Puno will have a lot of work, even homework, to do in the next few weeks and months, not to say the next 17 years, before his own retirement from the Bench.

But he is unfazed, and cheerfully he describes himself as an "early bird"—and, the visitor readily sees, a diligent one. "Before eight I arrive here, and I work usually till six or seven, and take home cases for decision, including Saturdays. Compared with the Court of Appeals, here the volume is greater, the cases more serious. Here the most important cases are decided, on top of all that the Supreme Court takes care of the administration, the control and supervision, of the lower courts. All of which is quite a load."

He tells of a typical working week: "Mondays and Wednesdays are devoted to division cases. We have three divisions, each with five justices. Tuesdays and Thursdays are devoted to en banc. And almost every day you have to tackle as many as 70 items on your agenda. Scores of judicial matters, cases filed either regionally or by appeal, coming from the lower courts, from various quasi-judicial agencies. Administrative matters such as complaints against judges, against employees of the lower courts like stenographers, clerks of court, sheriffs and others."

He agrees that reforms should be a priority in the judicial system: "There is the common observation—the observation, too, of Vice President Estrada—that we give too much due process to the accused. Our laws give litigants too many levels of appeal. Take, for instance, an ordinary ejectment order—this goes to the Municipal or City Court, then it is appealed to the Regional Court, then it is appealable to the Court of Appeals, then finally to the Supreme Court. All these steps and stages entail a lot of time, costs to the litigants and delayed justice.

"If you are a poor litigant, you get an unknown or ordinary lawyer who is pitted against a Makati-based practitioner. There, you see the difference between the legal combatants, that is why they say the rich and the poor can never be equal."

"In an underdeveloped country, there is always the problem of economics. An ordinary lawyer charges, I think, something like P1,000 per appearance in the lower courts. There are not enough free lawyers. There are not enough courts, or they are not available, even bond paper and certain papers, documents, are not available. Physical facilities are terrible."

Given these burdens and pitifully scarce resources, the imperative, says Justice Puno, is "to prioritize our cases." How to go about it? "Let us not, for example, treat a simple ejection case the way we should treat a case that involves millions of pesos."

"If you are a judge or justice trying a case involving millions of pesos and that case is not moving, you are tying up so much money that otherwise could go to economic development. That is what is happening. The 90-day trial—we aim for that, we are trying, but it is not easy. With respect to crimes, especially major crimes like kidnapping, rape, drug cases, my thinking is that these should undergo day to day trial. So that when the decision is handed down, whether conviction or acquittal, the public's memory of the crime is still fresh, people will remember and learn."

Another approach to "prioritization" is to revise some of the system's technical rules and procedures. In this regard, Justice Puno has in mind "murder cases like the Lenny Villa case" involving those Ateneo frat boys: "The procedure is for the judge to issue a ruling. Then the ruling is immediately challenged and brought before the appellate court. How many rulings will a judge make in the course of a trial? Not all our judges are bright, and criminals can have very smart lawyers. So why don't we change the rules and procedures as applied to these major crimes? Why not make it the rule that you cannot challenge every ruling?"

The setup, he concedes, has bedeviled the justice system from way back, and he thinks it's exactly the sort of problem that should be addressed by proper legislation. "Otherwise, people will always be complaining about delays in the administration of justice. You cannot just blame the judges because that is the law. The law that the judges have to interpret.

"The problem, then, cannot be solved by the judiciary alone. It has to remedied jointly with Congress and also with the Executive. Because the fiscals, the prosecutors, are under the Department of Justice, the police under the Department of Local Governments. They are under the Office of the President, not the Supreme Court. It is a problem of the whole government and the public, not just of the judiciary."

With such intense discernment and concern in the service of the highest, most decisive echelons of the judiciary, friends of the troubled Supreme Court may view with new hope and confidence its prospects both in the short term and on the advent of the Millennium.

THE APPROACH OF AUGUST calls to mind the Assassination at the Airport. Yes, Justice Puno would agree with the popular verdict, that justice has not been meted out to "all those who were suspected of being involved in the murder of Ninoy Aquino."

He would assume that Cory Aquino during the six years she was president "used all her powers to excavate more evidence." Apparently the excavation work was as unrewarding as that Fort Santiago dig. "It could be a very difficult job," the efforts to ferret out all the conspiratorial biggies, and what many believe was more than one mastermind.

Reopening the assassination case, which is after all the most momentous murder of a famous Filipino in this century, is essentially an executive task. Further investigative work, the gathering of additional witnesses and testimonies—"these are within the purview of the Department of Justice, under the Office of the President." He believes that if and when there are fresh leads, and even after the passage of years, "whoever is the incumbent President will not hesitate to reopen the case."

The assassination of Filipinos by their own countrymen, it turns out, is far from an impersonal, abstract subject, as far as Justice Puno is concerned. He tells why: one high noon in April 1977, his eldest brother was shot dead by an "NPA gunman" as he bowed his head in prayer before lunch, in a restaurant on the corner of Rizal Avenue and Lope de Vega. A .45-caliber slug blasted the skull of Manila CFI Judge Isaac Puno, Jr. even as his infant daughter, dead from a congenital illness, lay on a bier in the Knox United Methodist Church across the Avenida.

"That was the saddest day for our family. On the day we were to bury my brother's baby daughter was the time he was assassinated." Judge Isaac Puno, Jr. was the chairman of an ecumenical church-military liaison group. "He was apolitical, he was trying to help iron out differences, conflicts, between the church groups and the military which was arresting and detaining church people as subversives. Doing that work, dealing with the military, he became a target of Communist elements. They killed him with one shot to the back of the head, NPA style. There were two others with the gun-man—very young guys, 16, 17 years old. Later, the killers were apprehended and convicted.

"Then 1986 came, the EDSA Revolution. The new government and leadership decided on a policy of reconciliation, amnesty, and freed all those elements who were saying they were Communists. The killers of my brother—they were not in jail long enough, they were freed along with that batch led by Jose Ma. Sison. My sister-in-law and her three small children never got any help from the government. We felt we were the victims of those Communist elements, and the family was very unhappy to see the killers of my brother released, allowed to go scot-free.

"But what could we do? The government and leadership had made the decision that granting them amnesty was for the greater good of our people, our country."

What the heart sometimes protests, the intellect and will must accept for the greater good, if so decided by a legal, duly constituted government—a principle and conviction Justice Puno has made his own, at no little cost in blood and tears.

THIS QUALITY OF MIND, the willed focusing of the intellect on what best serves the law and the land, began to evolve, one gathers from Reynato Puno's own retelling, on Alvarez Extension where he grew up, near San Lazaro Hospital and practically on the boundary be-tween Santa Cruz and Tondo.

"I was born in Manila, in 1940, and I consider myself a Manileño. My late father, though, was from Pampanga, and my mother, a Serrano, is from Nueva Ecija. My father was a lawyer who was also in business, all sorts, like selling tools and eyeglasses. Yes, he was related, but distantly, very distant, to former Justice Secre-tary Ricardo Puno . . ."

The young Reynato was in Grade One at the Francisco Balagtas Elementary School, within walking distance from his childhood home, the year after the war, in 1946. It was another public school that he went to for his secondary course—the Arellano High School on Teodora Alonzo, which, "incidentally, was also the high school attended by Chief Justice Narvasa." His "first love" as a high-schooler was journalism and accordingly was on the staff of the school paper, *The Chronicler*.

For his university studies, his father's choice and his as well was the UP, first in the College of Liberal Arts for his two-year pre-law, where he met and shared classrooms with the likes of Heherson Alvarez, Ruben Ancheta, Haydee Yorac and Joma Sison. Then on to the UP College of Law, under the deanship of Justice Vicente Abad Santos and later of then Judge Irene Cortez.

In second year law, he became editor of the *Philippine Collegian*. A frequent contributor was a very serious fellow, Jose Ma. Sison, he recalls with a wry smile. His associate editor was Leo Quisumbing, now deputy executive secretary in Malacañang. As a *Collegian* editor in that heyday of youth activism, he had his first close encounter with Congress, when he was summoned to appear before the House Committee on Anti-Filipino Activities looking into "Communist infiltration" in the groves of Diliman. The radicals on campus envied him for being the only undergraduate called to the inquiry in the company of Cesar Majul, O.D. Corpuz, Ricardo Pascual and several other UP officials and professors.

UP Law's Class of '62 failed to produce a bar topnotcher, but he did hurdle the legal obstacle course with highly rated ease. He practiced for a while around Manila, before joining the law firm of then Congressman Gerry Roxas and future Justice Abraham Sarmiento as an assistant attorney. After that stint, he spent most of the '60s earning a number of master's and doctoral degrees, all on scholarship grants, from such institutions as the Southern Methodist University in Dallas, Texas; the University of California in Berkeley; the University of Illinois—along with prizes for the excellence of his treatises on Comparative Private International Law, Constitutional Structure and other such subjects. (His style, one is told, shows the influence of the great jurists he admires: Oliver Wendell Holmes, Benjamin Cardozo, J.B.L. Reyes, Roberto Concepcion.)

Back on native soil in 1970, he began his career service in the judiciary as Solicitor in the Office of the Solicitor General. He has since served in numerous judicial positions, all leading progressively upward: Quezon City Judge, Assistant Solicitor General, Appellate Justice of the Intermediate Appellate Court, Deputy Minister of Justice and acting chairman of the Board of Pardons and Parole, and after the EDSA uprising, in August 1986, Associate Justice, Court of Appeals. That was where he was when President Ramos picked him, from the final list of ten names submitted by the Judicial and Bar Council, as one of the brightest and most worthy nominees for appointment to the Supreme Court.

LOOKING BACK, JUSTICE PUNO can tell himself he has arrived exactly at the destination he had desired from the start: "What I really wanted, when I went abroad for postgraduate work and when I came back, was a career in the judiciary. I could have joined any one of the big law offices, no questions asked. If all I wanted was money, wealth, all I had to do was knock at the doors of the big law offices. I joined government when I came back from the U.S. and have stayed ever since. After 26 years in the government service, the last 13 in the Court of Appeals, I was appointed here. Every career justice or judge strives to be here, in the Supreme Court."

Now in the rare and infrequent hours when he is not pondering weighty matters of the law, Justice Puno devotes himself to three long-standing pursuits: chess, of which he is reputedly one of the judiciary's more brilliant players; tennis, which he plays usually at the Santa Lucia Realty gym near his home in Fairview, Quezon City; and preaching at Methodist services. As a lay preacher, he expounds on the Gospel occasionally at the Knox United Methodist Church on Rizal Avenue and more often at the Isaac Puno Memorial Methodist Church in Fairview, founded by the Punos as a memorial to their slain brother.

They are indeed a devout, dedicated clan, the Punos, whose Isaac Puno Memorial Foundation, assisted by evangelical churches in Germany, subsidizes the education of some 130 high school and college students in Metro Manila. The second eldest, Levin, is the legal counsel of the United Methodist Church. Another brother, Carlito, is president of the Philippine Christian University. Paul, a Ph.D. who used to run the memorial foundation, now works as secretary for his brother the jurist. Myrna Puno-Pelayo is director of Mary Johnston Hospital in Tondo, Isaac III is director of NEDA and the youngest, Marilyn Puno-Santiago, is confidential assistant to Associate Justice Isagani A. Cruz.

The justice's own young family beams from a framed portrait on the wall, above a Bible open on a stand. The eldest of his three children, Reynato, Jr., is 23 and finishing law at San Beda. Emmanuel, 19, is taking up business management at De La Salle. Marilyn, 12, is in Grade Six in Miriam College. His wife, the former Luzviminda Delgado, is Assistant Clerk of Court in the Supreme Court. When schedules permit, she joins him for lunch in his chambers, usually fish like *pesang dalag* and *kandule*. When he learned about his appointment, they celebrated with a thanksgiving service in the Puno Memorial Church and a family dinner at home. He is drawn to the simple life—austere, unadorned, contemplative.

Reflecting, finally, on what he considers his chief concern in the Court, he says it is "to keep the system of justice in our country strong, vigorous—and immaculate. The appearance of it should be presentable, admirable, to the people. You may be fair, you may be just, but if the people think otherwise, the kind of justice you dispense may not be credible and effective justice . . .

"If I have come to this Court with that kind of idealism, I suppose it is because I come from the poor sector of our society. From the grades to the university, I studied in the public schools. My orientation is toward the poor and I think I am of a liberal persuasion. So I specialized in labor and constitutional law. About 98 percent of labor cases wind up here in the Supreme Court. These cases concern the working class, the poor. That is why I am glad to be here."

The visitor is gladdened, too, by this enlightening talk with the justice who is, in more senses than one, the youngest hope of the tribunal still besieged, who as his guest takes his leave rises to shake hands—lean, small of frame, but with the wiriness of the tennis player that he is, and the chess adept's meditative gaze, and the humble yet confident voice and manner of the lay preacher who celebrates the promises of Christ.

The jurist in the City of Man is also a citizen of the City of God.

It is early evening outside on Padre Faura. The lamp-posts of Mayor Lim and the "new" Pagcor are alight, and a fine rain falls on the almost deserted street in the vicinity of which, in another age, the visitor sat in a shell-scarred classroom, and attended Marian devotions in the circular chapel dedicated to the sainted lawyer Thomas More, and listened to the Jesuits discoursing on the Law and the Scriptures, as the preacher of truth and justice Puno does on occasion in another chapel erected to commemorate a beloved brother.

The visitor drives away through the light, illuminated rain which, by some nostalgic alchemy, brings back a story first heard in those distant student days on Padre Faura.

Somebody, maybe a stranger or visiting alumnus newly arrived in town, was trying to call Loyola Heights for one reason or another, and by mistake dialed the switchboard number of another campus listed in the same section in the directory.

"Hello? Is this Loyola Heights?"

"No, this is Padre Faura."

"Oh, Father. Good evening, Father Faura."

Sorry, Ateneo joke only. But maybe worth one good laugh on the rainy, rut-infested road on the lap to NICdom, or just Buendia and Pasong Tamo.

(*Graphic*, 1993)

Interesting
Times

America, Amerika

ESCOLASTICO WAS BORN a couple of years before the Commonwealth—
that "instrumentality placed in our hands" by Messrs. Tydings and
McDuffie "to prepare ourselves," so Mr. Quezon said on that na-
ively happy day in 1935, "for the responsibilities of complete
independence."

The time and circumstances of his entry into this world (in a
provincial house on a street then called Washington) incline him
to think that he is sufficiently, even eminently, qualified to hold
forth on Philippine-American relations, a subject that, even now,
at once repels and attracts him. The mesh of contradictory sentiments no doubt suggests the extent, the complexity—the old colonial
syndrome, his more progressive confreres would say—the influence
which such relations have exerted on his Filipino psyche ever since
he first became conscious of American power and pelf, in the late
1930s.

In that decade and the next, which were consequential ones for
the Philippines and the U.S., he learned, along with his Catholic
catechism, to ask God to bless America. He has since realized that
his own country, long at the mercy of zealous Yanqui missionaries,
has more need of the Almighty's protection than the land of the prai-
ries across the ocean white with foam. Dawning on him as it did in
the early 1960s, and only after Mr. Carlos Garcia had declared that
Filipinos had every right to be "first" in their own country, his enlightenment has struck him as symbolic and reflective of the national
experience. The light from above was rather late in coming, but it's
growing ever stronger, suffusing the most benighted corners of the
archipelago.

This illuminating proposition Escolastico would qualify in his
cynical moments, for large numbers of his countrymen, years after
Mr. Romulo got rid of his stateside Oedipus complex, still look to the
U.S.A. as Mother America, benevolent bosom of democracy lavish
with milk and honey, in whose ample warmth Pinoy babes in the
underdeveloped woods would find relief from all their nightmares.
The appeal of that seemingly maternal refuge, encouraged by Wash-

ington and its local agents, is at best a dangerous illusion, Escolastico was to recognize more clearly at the height of the American war in Vietnam, when he resolved to be abreast of the times and took a long hard look at the American presence in Asia.

Uncle Sam dolled up to look like a young, extra-generous Mae West haunts the dreams of the Filipino lining up for his green card at the U.S. Embassy or working his ass off for a plaque and a wristwatch at a multinational firm in Makati—and it's all part of the long-playing con game introduced in these isles by Commodore Dewey at the turn of the century.

Imperialism is the name of the game, though apparently more gentle, more subtle, more PR-conscious now than when Douglas MacArthur's pater had to go chasing after General Aguinaldo all the way to Palanan; outwardly more civilized and humane, and thus made more palatable than the 19th-century European variety, which to this day exacts its toll in Africa, the Indian subcontinent and Indochina.

Innocent child of his time, Escolastico was handed his ticket and rooted for the winning team: Captain America and Bucky demolishing assorted Axis villains, John Wayne mowing down hordes of Apaches, and later, in the main event, General Kreuger's U.S. Sixth Army rolling down front Lingayen, for which he reserved his loudest cheers, in 1945, heedless of the price his country had already paid in a war not of its own making, would still pay for V-J Day. The exorbitant cost of being reclaimed by General MacArthur and the Democratic and Republican parties would entail such demonstrations of U.S. efficiency as the carpet bombing of Baguio after the Japanese had pulled out of that city, the artillery overkill that pulverized Intramuros, Ermita and Malate, and not long after, the economic coup de grace in the form of Parity and the Bell Trade Act.

IN THE FACE OF UNSPEAKABLE PRACTICES and dastardly acts, total, uncompromising denunciation is the minimal, all too common response. But Escolastico is not one to deny credit where it is due, no matter how infernal the wind may be from that direction; and so, despite nationalistic noises from the gallery, he would like at this juncture to acknowledge his debt to the language that Miss O'Connor and Mr. Dixon, Thomasites both, brought to Tarlac at the behest of Governor Taft, in 1905. The Philippine Commission employed English as an instrument of colonial policy, together with a system of education premised on the doctrines of the other Dewey, the professor from Columbia U; and the setup produced, as Escolastico is well aware, mixed-up, pseudo-literate Filipinos so susceptible to the charms of Jacqueline Susann, 20th Century-Fox and the remodeled imperialism. But the language is, among other things, a potent force for the authentic education of the Filipino, as Professors Agoncillo and Constantino and their disciples imply whenever they write their fervent tracts in English.

For his part, not having been born in Meycauayan or Maragondon, Escolastico has had no recourse but to pursue his political satori, as it were, through scriptures written in an imported tongue. Such indeed is the economy of salvation, secular or otherwise, that what is originally perceived as a scandal, a stumbling block, can sweep away the scales from neocolonial eyes and serve the ends of liberation.

What, in any case, has Escolastico got to say now about Philippine-American relations and all that? What truths has he who presumes to speak for his generation learned in the postgraduate reading room after his prolonged miseducation?

He has learned, to begin with, that America as an imperialist power was no stranger to Asia when it arrived in Manila Bay on the *USS Olympia* in 1898. Half a century earlier, the U.S. had already joined the European scramble for markets and raw materials for expanding industries, and wrested commercial, even extraterritorial, concessions from a beleaguered China. But it was its war with Spain that enabled the U.S. finally, by deceit and force of arms, to acquire an Asian colony it could call its own and thereby become a fullfledged member of the imperialist league.

The Philippines and its ten million inhabitants, including Escolastico's grandparents in Tarlac and Ilocandia, were relinquished by Spain for $20 million—or $2 per Filipino, which was a fantabulous bargain, compared, say, with what the U.S. had to pay per native capita in Vietnam, compelled by essentially the same "Manifest Destiny" which sent Krag riflemen floundering among the rice paddies of Caloocan or clambering up the cliffs of Tirad Pass.

Filipinos didn't much like the idea of being traded off in such fashion, and fought the Americans in a war that lasted three years and two months. The Philippine-American War—an "insurrection" to ignorant American authors and archivists—cost the U.S. 10,000 casualties and $600 million. More than 16,000 soldiers of the Republic died in battle, and 200,000 civilians perished from pestilence and disease in the course of the war. But the U.S. was merely "performing a great act of humanity," said Mr. McKinley in reply to American criticism of his imperialist adventure.

Imperialism is the ambition, policy and actual program of a dominant power to control lands, resources and peoples outside of its borders. Spurred by ideological or religious visions (the Protestant McKinley was bent on Christianizing the Filipino people all over again), or economic obsessions (U.S. trade and industry saw the islands as a gateway to the teeming markets of China), as well as by the momentum of its size and power (America's westward expansion had dealt with the Indians and Mexicans and impelled it beyond the gold mines of California), the aggressor nation proceeds to reduce the weaker country to a conquered territory, a colony, a client state.

In the thermonuclear age, Escolastico would add, imperialism seeks more than glory and riches: big-power hegemony wants overseas military bases to draw or parry hostile missiles that would otherwise vaporize the imperialist heartland. In the not unthinkable scenario of World War III, no MacArthur will return to liberate the Philippines from radioactivity.

OVER ITS TRUE FACE, which is violence, imperialism (capitalist no less than socialist) wears many masks, the expressions varying according to instructions from the home office. It can speak in kindly or convivial tones, especially when it's certain that it can get what it wants without using defoliants, cluster bombs and napalm.

The more refined aspects of American power as it operates in the Philippines have impressed many Filipinos, as witness the five million or so of Escolastico's countrymen who, before martial law, joined former Congressman Rufino Antonio's "Philippine Statehood" movement. Even more dismaying is the spectacle of Filipinos who, unable to wait for the honor of statehood to be conferred on these isles, emigrate to the U.S., bedazzled by the chrome and vinyl mirage conjured up by Hollywood, *Cosmopolitan* and such well-meaning folks as Rex Humbard & Co.

Both the "statehooders" and the fly-now-pay-later emigrants represent, almost in caricature, that despair which imperialism has every reason to encourage. The Filipino who has given up on his own people and native land will give in to and even endorse all manner of colonial enterprise. Outside of the hapless perimeter scavengers who have been mistaken for wild boar or dogmeat, the tendency is prevalent around Clark and Subic, though not by any means confined to these places. Even card-carrying leftists of Escolastico's acquaintance have not been spared the pathology, mumbling something about dollars and reality when pressed to explain their craving for U.S. citizenship. Since 1946, it scarcely needs to be said, many of those to whom Escolastico and his countrymen entrusted their political fate have exhibited the same subservience, and subversion of the national interest, notably in the era of the Magsaysay-Landsdale partnership.

There are, to be sure, all kinds of partnerships, collaborative efforts for the benefit of both nations, and Escolastico in all fairness won't make light of these. USAID, for instance, helps finance Philippine roadways so that the Ministry of Local Government and Community Development can bring more hope and cheer to depressed areas, and Ford and GM can sell more cars and trucks, and the oil companies can repatriate more profits, etc. Still, Escolastico would counsel everyone concerned, especially those important people who must deal with such institutions as the IMF, the World Bank and JUSMAG, to be on the lookout for booby-trap wires or strings attached to the U.S.-made package.

Philippine history, the sort that is not published by Ginn & Co., dictates and justifies such wariness, as General Aguinaldo was forcibly reminded after meeting with the commander of the Asiatic Squadron and the U.S. consuls of Singapore and Hong Kong, in 1899. Imperialist duplicity these days also goes about wearing *Gentlemen's Quarterly* suits and Dale Carnegie smiles. Pope Paul VI in his encyclical on the "development of peoples" has underscored the inherent lopsidedness in the relationship between the big, industrial nations and the countries of the Third World: unless moved by an access of justice and compassion, the superpower will in the natural course of things give the dirty end of the stick to the not so powerful, avowals of friendship and respect for human rights notwithstanding. Or to apply a law of physics to geopolitics: the bigger the mass, the more powerful its gravitational pull, the more pervasive and penetrating its influence on the smaller body.

For the interests and ambitions of countries or governments seldom if ever coincide. No matter how ostensibly considerate and magnanimous, the U.S. acts primarily, often exclusively, in what it considers its national interest—an elementary principle and fact of life obscured or concealed by propaganda, rhetoric about "Fil-American blood commingling on Philippine soil," and ritual invocations of "special relations." Contrary to what politician-orators are wont to proclaim on Philippine-American Friendship Day, there is no such animal as "friendship" between nation states: at the most they may agree, temporarily, as a matter of expediency, on certain political or economic interests.

But between peoples—as distinct from their governors and their governments—there can and should be an enduring friendship. At least twice Escolastico has been to the land of the free and the home of the brave, and is not unfamiliar with the finer aspects of' American civilization not to be found among the honky-tonks of Balibago. He has been captivated in more than one pleasant encounter by the immense and sincere capacity of Americans for friendship that's more meaningful than the jovial fellowship of Kiwanis or Rotarians. (The more captivating of those friendly Americans went by such names as Anne, Barbie and Janine.) So, then, on the Fourth of July, which his country also once celebrated as the day of its independence, he rises to offer a toast to a hope and a conviction: that in spite of American imperialism and its agencies, in spite of the arrogance of power and the ignorance and subservience that pay it tribute, it is both proper and necessary for the Filipino people and the American people to be friends.

Familiarity need not always and forever breed contempt; and, who knows, to be pragmatic about it the way the Gringos are, Filipinos could someday count on that friendship when it's needed most—as the people of Vietnam did, when millions of Americans marched and rallied to oppose and condemn what the White House and the Joint Chiefs of Staff and the Pentagon were doing to a small Asian country in the throes of liberation.

That massive anti-war movement, by the way, was not the first instance of American dissent to Washington policy. Some 65 years earlier, U.S. imperialism under the auspices of Mr. McKinley's covetous apostolate roused the more enlightened segments of American society to militant protest. Their moral outrage could not dissuade their government from imperialistic conquest, but they proved to all the world that not all Americans are prone to make a mockery of their noblest traditions.

The Fourth of July enshrines these traditions, which in sum are a declaration of the independence, the freedom of men and nations, from imperialism of any conglomerate, color, ideology or creed.

(Who, 1978)

The Imperialist, Anti-Filipino Puppet Show

"IMPERIALISM" is one of those emotionally charged words much in currency these days; like "tuta" or "fascism," it can arouse strong reactions akin to hysteria in both accuser and accused—frothing around the mouth, or seeing red, or the mind going blank, short-circuited by hatred and anger.

Perhaps much more dismaying is that reaction on another scale, which is apathy, or its twin, which is ignorance. Far too many Filipinos, for instance, just don't give a damn about imperialism: they aren't interested in finding out how it works, even as it continues to make them poorer and more wretched in their own country. Imperialism, ah, huh? It doesn't really exist, it's just something those long-haired youngsters blocking traffic in Quiapo invented to throw at President Marcos & Co. At best, an idea, an abstraction to be amused by; at worst, an imagined evil which drives misguided youth to smash windows or trample Ka Doroy's hedges at Luneta Park. Don't waste your time worrying about imperialism or neocolonialism or any other ism, *pare ko.* Think about something more real and concrete, like corrupt politicians, or rising prices, or that job you've been looking for in vain, or the income you'll never earn for your miserable family, or the house and lot you'll never have, and so forth and so on . . .

Which is what imperialism is all about—in addition to deprivations and impositions of greater, more injurious magnitude, including the perpetuation of an economic setup which frustrates all attempts at genuine development and progress, a servile foreign policy, and exposure to total devastation, not only fallout, in the event of a nuclear war.

Imperialism is the ambition and policy and actual program of a dominant power to control lands and peoples beyond its borders. For four centuries, imperial Spain held these islands as an outright colony; for four years, imperialist Japan tried to impose its own brand of colonialism upon our people. U.S. imperialism as it operates in the Philippines today, 26 years after "independence," wears the mask of neocolonialism: it keeps this country chained to the status of a colony, with the assistance of native allies, and without resorting to force of arms and blatant colonization, the techniques it employed to establish control over our land and people at the turn of the century.

Imperialism, American style, is very much a fact of life in this neocolony; but many are those who think U.S. imperialism a mere bogey, a figment of the anti-American imagination, or who don't think about it at all. It is to such Filipinos that Mr. Alejandro Lichauco, Constitutional Convention delegate from Rizal and one of the few perceptive and nationalistic economists left to challenge the still growing menace, would address his paper, "Imperialism and the Security of the State." To Filipinos who are blind to the workings of imperialism—and also, and more importantly, to those who are not unaware of the unrelenting subversion of the state by a "friendly nation," yet persist in abetting and collaborating with the very forces which are bent on exploiting the people, keeping them mired in poverty, maintaining the farce that is our "independence," and undermining the country's security.

In his 167-page study—which is comprehensive, cool and lucid, and anything but hysterical, certainly the most significant document so far to come out of the Constitutional Convention—Mr. Lichauco devotes an entire section to the role of certain highly placed Filipinos in the imperialist scheme to dominate the country:

"Over the last ten years, imperialism has found and developed in this country a new set of instruments for the achievement of its goals. I refer to the growing body of technocrats who have come to play a pivotal role in policy formulation and implementation, as well as in international negotiations. These technocrats have been effective in establishing, through their ideas and pronouncements, the general climate and intellectual atmosphere conducive to our government's acceptance of policies responsible for our continuing colonization.

"Today," continues Mr. Lichauco, "sensitive offices of the government charged with designing the country's economic policies are headed by technocrats whose views run parallel to, and coincide with, the policies espoused by imperialism. This explains the ease, and almost indecent haste, with which oppressive impositions are accepted by our government."

Delegate Lichauco pinpoints these offices and officials: "the Department of Finance, the National Economic Council, and the Board of Investments, headed, respectively, by Finance Secretary Cesar Virata, NEC Chairman Gerardo Sicat, and BOI Chairman Vicente Paterno."

But Mr. Lichauco might only be imagining unkind things about our so-called technocrats and seeing nonexistent "imperialist tools" hiding under every bed, as suggested by a columnist and would-be humorist in the employ of an American-owned newspaper.

In other words, the imperialist, anti-Filipino puppet show which in effect Mr. Lichauco says is being staged on the upper perches of officialdom amounts to no more than a bad superpatriot's dream. To demonstrate that it's no nightmare induced by a heavy nationalist dinner, Mr. Lichauco cites the following instances:

"In the case of Secretary Virata, one recalls that, as head of the technical panel which undertook preliminary discussions with its American counterpart in Baguio over a successor treaty to the Laurel-Langley Agreement, he committed our government to the position that the national treatment clause, which confers parity rights to Americans in all areas of business, will be incorporated into the new treaty to the fullest extent possible.

"Virata was recruited into the government service directly from the accounting firm of SyCip, Gorres and Velayo. Washington SyCip, who is the senior and managing partner of that firm, is an American citizen whose connections with the U.S. Embassy and the foreign community are extensive."

Secretary Virata, Mr. Lichauco goes on, has come out in defense of American businessmen "intervening in our process of Constitution making." In a recent talk before the Federation of Filipino-Chinese Chambers of Commerce, the finance secretary proposed "equal treatment" for aliens engaged in domestic trade. And as an officer of the SyCip accounting firm, Mr. Virata "actively promoted" the United Fruit project, which was "one of the biggest scandals of the Macapagal Administration."

For his part, NEC Chairman Sicat, says Mr. Lichauco, has written critically of "policies identified with economic nationalism," and has justified the practice of American and other foreign firms of borrowing working capital funds from Filipino banks. In an article attacking the nationalist policies proposed by the Congressional Economic Planning Office, Mr. Sicat "went so far as to suggest that, at this stage of our development, it really should not concern Filipinos who controls the resources and economy of their country." The same Sicat, Mr. Lichauco tells us, recently batted for foreign investment in the already nationalized rice and corn industry.

Also "aggressively promoting the economic interests of imperialism" is BOI Chairman Paterno, who is for removing "existing nationality restrictions in the Constitution, particularly those restrictions applicable to petroleum exploration and development."

Paterno's "pet project," according to Mr. Lichauco, is a bill which would allow foreign firms engaged in oil exploration and development to operate as "service contractors," thus exempting them from the nationality requirement. The bill, which sets down a liberalized oil exploration policy for the government, has just been approved by the House. The Paterno project, stresses Mr. Lichauco, was "actually suggested" by U.S. oil firms in the Philippines—and one Walter J. Levy, the "dean of American petroleum economists."

"Is this Walter J. Levy the same Walter J. Levy listed in the book, *Who's Who in the CIA?*" asks Delegate Lichauco. "And if so, was it wise of Finance Secretary Virata and BOI Chairman Paterno to have hired an agent of the Central Intelligence Agency to draft new oil exploration measures for the Philippine government?"

A CIA agent—who is sworn to work for American, not Filipino, interests—drafting policy for the Philippine government? And national policy concerned with oil, a strategic and politically volatile commodity? Good grief—or, rather, good night!

The Rizal delegate has asked the BOI in writing to clarify the identity of the "Walter J. Levy" hired to help out in the Paterno project. The BOI has yet to reply to Mr. Lichauco's query. Surely technocrats of Mr. Paterno's caliber must be familiar with the CIA book, which was available in Manila bookshops some years ago.

Mr. Lichauco also takes note of the Marcos technocrats' resistance to the idea of industrialization as the key to development, their enthusiasm for free trade, foreign investments, a foreign exchange system essentially free from restrictions, the IMF-dictated floating rate, and their "campaign to commit this country deeper into indebtedness with the World Bank"—which are all designed to strengthen the imperialist grip on the economy. To block full and real industrialization, for instance, by hampering the growth of such a basic and crucial industry as steel, is to maintain the agro-merchandising character of the economy and keep the country poor and underdeveloped, a primary objective of imperialist policy. A developed, industrialized nation, not a mere supplier of raw materials and consumer of imported goods, will scarcely suit the designs of an exploitative power. The floating rate and free trade, the absence of controls, are imperialist measures which have wreaked havoc on Filipino industries, while foreign firms, assisted by investment banking firms like Bancom (run likewise by solemn technocrats), extract from the host economy more capital than they invest, and remit huge profits abroad.

"Technocracy in the Philippines," declares Mr. Lichauco, "has come to function as the fifth column of contemporary imperialism and the technical efficiency of our technocrats, far from serving the ultimate interests of our country, has only contributed to the technical efficiency with which neocolonialism pursues its objectives."

Is this not tantamount to saying that Virata, Paterno & Co. work not for the Filipino people but for the CIA, USAID, the World Bank-International Monetary Fund complex, and other instrumentalities of U.S. imperialism?

Just asking.

WHAT WE KNOW FOR A FACT is that these gentlemen with their self-righteous air of infallibility, their pharisaical devotion to duty, are in the employ of Mr. Marcos, who is not exactly averse to the neocolonial status quo. Mr. Marcos is their boss. Who or what does their boss serve and represent? The best interests of the Filipino people? He and his favorite technocrats—what have they done to advance the liberation of the people from imperialist control and exploitation? Has imperialist domination been diminished under his administration? Has it not, on the contrary, grown more powerful and insidious and pervasive in the economic and political life of the nation? Have Mr. Marcos & Co. not proved to be willing instruments, if not puppets, of U.S. imperialism?

"Central to our national crisis is the problem of poverty," states Mr. Lichauco. "Imperialism and poverty are interrelated subjects because the former has institutionalized the latter." And this is precisely where the Convention can focus its energies and save itself from the judgment that it is an absurd and elaborate exercise in futility. For "unless this Convention comes to grips with imperialism, we shall be no different from our traditional political parties and our current politicians who . . . would explain our people's poverty in terms of such peripheral factors as graft and corruption, to which they both inevitably succumb, instead of its real and institutional cause, a force which they dare not confront."

The dehumanizing poverty of our people, rising unemployment, an inflation now out of control, a disoriented educational system, the exploitation of the economy, the social anarchy spawned by these conditions—these constitute the price the nation has to pay for neocolonialism and puppetry, and all are traceable, directly and ultimately, declares Mr. Lichauco, to "the imperialist phenomenon in this country."

Imperialism is therefore the prejudicial question before the Convention, Mr. Lichauco points out in a message to his fellow delegates. Poverty will not be abolished by the mere act of writing a new Constitution; but the Convention can, if it will, "dismantle the conditions responsible for the poverty of our people. And this we cannot accomplish if we do not dismantle imperialism as a phenomenon in this country."

This the Convention can make possible by making it the constitutional duty of both the government and the people to oppose and repel imperialism.

"Fail in this," concludes the delegate from Rizal, "and we become truly irrelevant."

Worse than irrelevant: the irrelevant are merely to be ignored, shunted aside on the road of history, and forgotten. Criminal would be more like it, and subversive—perhaps more subversive than any anti-Filipino puppet show staged by a foreign power. For the Convention then will have renounced its duty and turned its back on the people, without shame, without remorse, and made a mockery of their poverty, their anguish, and all their hopes. Imperialists and their puppets cannot be expected to promote Filipino interests: but what is one to think of Filipino delegates to a Filipino Constitutional Convention betraying the deepest aspirations of their own people?

Despair, the refusal to hope, is to the Christian the unforgivable sin. The refusal of the Convention, despite all appeal and warning, to recognize the instruments and techniques of imperialism, and to seize the chance to remove its stranglehold at last, would be the final subversion, the ultimate treason.

(*Leader*, 1972)

Human Rights, Inhuman Wrongs and Amnesty International

PRESIDENT MARCOS doesn't care for it.

To judge from his remarks on the subject, he doesn't think much of it, this London-based organization that has become identified in the minds of many people around the world with the defense of human rights.

Defense Minister Juan Ponce Enrile has likewise a very low opinion of it, and the same lack of enthusiasm is shared presumably by a whole panoply of generals and colonels in the Armed Forces of the Philippines.

They, and others mentioned or alluded to unflatteringly in Amnesty International reports, wouldn't be sorry if, first thing tomorrow morning, this contrary, meddlesome company were to announce that it was closing shop, and disbanding its 39 National Sections and its more than 2,500 Adoption Groups distributed among 140 countries.

But an organization that large and extensive, and depending on your view of the issues involved, that popular or notorious—valiant champion of mankind or vile conspirator in league with the devil—can be expected to resist all suggestions that it disappear permanently from the scene. By the nature of the work it does (or, as it has been charged, failed miserably to do), Amnesty International tends to remind people, including those who would have nothing to do with it, that it is going to be in business for a long while yet.

At this juncture, 21 years after its founding and with an array of National Sections firmly installed in Western Europe, the U.S., Canada, Mexico, Australia, Japan, India, Pakistan and several other countries great and small, it's no longer possible to pretend it doesn't exist, much less swat or smother it into oblivion.

A fact of international life that just won't go away, it is subject nonetheless to criticism, castigation, denouncement. Discredit Amnesty, expose its incompetence and hypocrisy, strip it of all credibility: then it won't matter if it refuses to be packed off to limbo; then will governments it has embarrassed and officials it has maligned be vindicated in the eyes of the international community. And such vindication is given very high priority, unless the aggrieved party is ready to reject the boon and blessings of the same world community: loans and other material aid, trade treaties, tourist dollars and such, aside from the more abstract rewards of prestige and friendship.

That, in sum, seems to have been the task President Marcos, cool and pragmatic as ever, chose to take up at the National Press Club forum (and on satellite TV) during his recent visit to Washington, DC, when he was tossed the old annoying questions about Amnesty International's claims of unjust detention, torture and "disappearances" of Filipinos opposed to his regime. No furious outburst, such as might have come from a lesser man sorely provoked, but a calm, civil reply, slightly dismayed and puzzled by the fault-finding injustice of it all. "It's not fair," Mr. Marcos said evenly, "to accuse the Philippines of violation of human rights when there has been no violation. If there has been any violation, we've punished those who have violated."

To be sure, the logic there is inviolable: if there have been no violations of human rights, why make such accusations, why fabricate such charges? Indeed, why the unfairness, and to what end? Those who pervert the truth, to the prejudice of a government, of an entire nation, must be blindly hostile, or grossly misguided, or sickeningly stupid. Amnesty International, alas, has shown itself to be all that, the President went on to imply in the Washington press forum as millions watched and listened:

"Well, I will tell you that Amnesty International has never come to the Philippines. That is why all they talk about is what they obtained as hearsay. Let us give one specific example. Father Abedicio, a famous case, is supposed to have disappeared. He is a member of the clergy in the Philippines, a Filipino. He disappeared and we couldn't locate him. And what did we discover after six months? We discovered that he had run away with somebody who claimed to be a nun. And that he was in Germany. How do you like that? And we got blamed for it. That's it. That's how Amnesty International has been reporting all these things."

That's it, all right, if indeed that's the way Amnesty goes about its work—and shame on those self-righteous busybodies for peddling hearsay as gospel truth and getting all muddled up over this tale of the padre who struck a blow for his all too human rights by taking off with a nun in tow. If the ignominious blunder is typical of Amnesty, which prides itself on a passion for truth and justice, it deserves at the very least to be laughed off stage.

And Amnesty is guilty of far more than fault-finding and false testimony: its avowed impartiality, President Marcos stressed before the editorial board of the *New York Times* later in the course of his U.S. visit, is but a cover for its Communist activities. More than just an unwitting tool of communism, it is in fact a conscious, industrious agent of the Marxist-Leninists in their campaign to subvert and topple the countries of the Free World, according to the president. While it assails these countries fighting for survival against communist subversion, it is lenient with the Communist bloc or merely goes through the motions to give itself an aura of credibility. The Philippines is witness to this duplicity, for in concert with "other leftist groups," Amnesty has been quick to protest against human rights abuses "whenever the government acts to protect citizens from subversion and violence."

The indictment strikes at the heart and integrity of Amnesty International, and calls into question not only its aims and methods, but its very reason for being. If it is not as impartial and independent as it has proclaimed itself to be, Amnesty forfeits that power of moral persuasion with which to sway world public opinion. If its human rights campaign is no more than a callous fraud designed to undermine the already embattled democracies, it richly deserves the harshest condemnation of the citizenry—unless, of course, you happen to be a member of those "leftist groups" which are said to be in cahoots with Amnesty.

The same assessment was underscored by Defense Minister Juan Ponce Enrile more recently, when he denounced Amnesty International for "distorting the facts on the so-called human rights violations in the country." On the eve of his Ministry's 43rd anniversary early last month, Mr. Enrile pointed out that "while we admit that there have been violations . . . these abuses have been thoroughly investigated and the perpetrators punished." Which should give the lie to allegations that the authorities concerned tolerate, if not sanction, such abuses. And Amnesty proved its partiality, its ideological bias, the defense minister said, when its representatives came "several years ago" to interview "members of the Marxist movement" on reported violations of human rights in the Philippines.

WHETHER BIASED OR NOT, the findings of those Amnesty representatives have since been published in the reports which the organization issues periodically and circulates worldwide.

Two of the more recent Amnesty publications, each a booklet of some 200 pages, focus on the Philippines: *Human Rights Violations in the Philippines*, put out in 1981 by the U.S. National Section (1304 West 58th St., New York, NY 10019), and *Report of an Amnesty International Mission to the Republic of the Philippines*, 11–28 November 1981, issued only last August by the organization's International Secretariat (10 Southampton St., London, England).

The first reviews accounts of reported human rights violations since 1972, including cases monitored by the first Amnesty International mission to visit the Philippines in November-December 1975. "Although the number of people believed to be detained fell from about 6000 in 1975 to fewer than 1000 by the end of 1980," notes the U.S. Amnesty publication, "reports in the same period indicated that more people were becoming victims of human rights violations of unusual brutality, including 'disappearances' and extrajudicial executions." The second report deals only with cases presented to the 1981 Amnesty mission, involving some 190 individuals ranging from the still detained Sixto Carlos, Jr. and the late Kalinga chieftain, Macli-ing Dulag, to anonymous barangay residents and unidentified members of minority groups in Mindanao.

Amnesty mission reports on particular countries supplement the group's annual reports. Issued last October, the 1982 report covers human rights violations last year in 121 countries. "Political killings, sometimes accompanied by mutilation and other forms of torture" were ordered or carried out, says the report, by government agents or security forces in, among other countries, El Salvador, Syria, Libya, Guatemala, Uganda, Pakistan, India and Iran. At least two Communist countries figure in the report: the Soviet Union, which "continued its drive against dissent," and Poland, where more than 5000 persons were detained by the martial law regime, most of them without charge or trial.

BUT WHAT, THE CURIOUS BYSTANDER may well wonder, are these human rights about which Amnesty International is so concerned, and which occasion so much controversy and contention, acrimony, anguish and agitation? What are these rights that are being violated, disputed, denied, defended, promoted, aspired for, in different countries and circumstances?

These are the rights enshrined in democratic constitutions, and preeminently in the Universal Declaration of Human Rights, which the UN General Assembly adopted in 1948. Behind them lie thousands of years of evolution, of defining and nurturing them, and gradually entrenching them in the universal conscience, as the human race, despite individual and mass savagery, brutal crusades and holocausts, pogroms and persecutions, developed a capacity for compassion, a desire to end or reduce oppression and suffering.

As crystallized and contained in the UN Declaration, these rights are: life, liberty and security of person; freedom from arbitrary arrest, detention or exile; the right to a fair hearing by an impartial court; and freedom of thought, conscience, religion, and peaceful assembly and association.

To these civil and political rights have been added economic and social rights, the right, for instance, to work or education. But it is the first and original category of rights that Amnesty and similar vigilantist groups worry about, since violations of these rights more directly imperil lives, or lead more immediately to grave consequences than, say, the denial of social security. And they are called human rights precisely because they are not conferred by society or high authority, but flow from man's nature as a human being, a human person.

That human rights are rooted in the very nature and dignity and infinite worth of the human person—created by God and reflecting His presence in history, as the theologians say—is a cardinal tenet of Catholicism. That is why the Catholic Church, we are told, will always protect the individual against the totalitarian tendencies of the state, a position affirmed of late by Pope John Paul II.

The Catholic connection may or may not have been present, but interestingly enough, the fact is that Amnesty International was founded by an English Catholic, Peter Benenson, who has been described by his colleagues as a "visionary" and a "saint."

HOW BENENSON, A FOUNDER-MEMBER of Justice, an association of British lawyers dedicated to the promotion of the UN Declaration of Human Rights, went about organizing Amnesty International, is narrated by British journalist, author and filmmaker Jonathan Power in his 1981 book, *Against Oblivion*.

The seed of Amnesty was planted in Benenson's mind by a newspaper report, in 1961, about two Portuguese students in Lisbon whom the Salazar dictatorship had sentenced to seven years' imprisonment— for the "crime" of "raising their glasses in a café in a toast to freedom." Benenson wondered if the Portuguese authorities could be persuaded to release the students with a bombardment of protest letters. From there the idea grew to encompass not only victims of political persecution in one country, but political as well as religious prisoners throughout the world.

Benenson enlisted the support of three friends, including David Astor, editor of the London newspaper, *Observer*, which published the new group's full-page statement calling for the release of eight

"Forgotten Prisoners" in as many countries. Among these were Dr. Agostino Neto, an Angolan poet, who later became president of his country; Romanian philosopher Constantin Noica, Greek Communist and trade unionist Tony Abiaticlos, Cardinal Mindzenty of Hungary and Archbishop Josef Beran of Prague. (There was only one Communist in the lineup, which might have prodded British leftists to cry "Unfair!") The article was carried simultaneously or in the next few days by the *New York Herald Tribune*, Germany's *Die Welt*, Switzerland's *Journal de Geneve*, and periodicals in Denmark, Sweden, Holland, Italy, South Africa, Belgium, Ireland and India. A Barcelona newspaper risked Franco's ire and gave the Amnesty message some column inches.

Amnesty's initial salvo, writes Power, hit several "political nerve centers." Donations and letters from several countries poured into Amnesty's cubicle of an office in London. Most of the letters sought assistance for political prisoners who had not resorted to violence in pursuit of their beliefs.

Benenson responded to this flood of appeals by urging schools and churches to set up groups of "sympathizers." These groups would "adopt" individual prisoners in other countries, write to them and to their governments and jailers, send money and other aid to their families. Thus began the Adoption Groups, Amnesty's basic action units in its worldwide campaign for human rights.

AMNESTY INTERNATIONAL TODAY has over 2500 Adoption Groups, a number of them based in countries even without National Sections. They vary in size and vitality: while some consist of only a dozen or two members, the notably active West German, French and Australian groups have thousands in their rank and file. Each group at a time is assigned at least two prisoners of different ideological, political or religious backgrounds; or three prisoners according to a scheme to encourage impartiality and an objective world view: one each from a Western country, a Communist state and a Third World nation.

No National Section or Adoption Group is allowed to work for prisoners arrested in its own country, nor is it obliged to report on local conditions. Thus the letters dispatched to a prisoner, and to relevant government and prison officials, embassies, media organizations and concerned groups, come from any number of countries except his own. Short of freeing him from captivity or saving him from torture and execution, the letter-writing campaign hopes to bring him a sense of the world's concern: in distant Denmark or Mexico or Japan, people are actually aware of his existence and working for his freedom. (There is no Amnesty agency in the Philippines, but the organization has contacts with groups like Task Force Detainees and the Civil Liberties Union.)

Most of the letters to government authorities are unanswered, reveal Amnesty officials, and Adoption Groups usually cannot tell whether their efforts, extending over a period of months or years, have achieved anything in a given country. But sometimes, "amazingly," reports Power, the letters alone—apart from other methods of bringing pressure to bear—produce "inspiring" results.

Power presents as a typical Amnesty success, documented and well-publicized, the case of Shahid Nadim, a Pakistani television producer and trade unionist. In 1978, Nadim was sentenced by a military court to one year's imprisonment and 15 lashes for organizing "a completely peaceful staff occupation" of four TV stations after management spurned a salary and working-conditions agreement. Next to Nadim's suffocating cell was an open toilet used by hundreds of other prisoners, and the stench often made sleep impossible. Then a fellow prisoner handed him a piece of paper, a copy of a letter that had been intercepted by the prison superintendent. Addressed to Nadim, the letter came from an Adoption Group in San Antonio, Texas, and said: "You are not alone. Don't lose heart. We are praying for you. If there's anything you need, don't hesitate to ask."

The Pakistani was to write Amnesty later: "Suddenly I felt as if the sweat all over my body were drops from a cool shower. The cell was no longer dark and suffocating . . . my colleagues were overjoyed . . ." The deputy superintendent summoned him to ask about the letter and was "so friendly and respectful . . ." Not long after, Nadim was released. He still often muses on "how a woman in Texas had written some kind words which proved to be a bombshell for the authorities and changed prisoners' conditions for the better."

Against Oblivion also quotes a letter to Amnesty International from an unnamed ex-detainee in the Philippines: "I was released from detention last December 14, 1976—thanks to the efforts of your organization. I was summoned to the office of Undersecretary Carmelo

Barbero where they showed me the folders of letters from Amnesty International pressing for the release of political prisoners . . ."

For broader, longer-term results, where its influence may be felt beyond the confines of cell blocks, Amnesty has recourse to publicity, lobbying campaigns in the UN and other world bodies, and special missions. Over 350 such missions have been sent to various countries in the last 20 years. These have taken up a variety of tasks: looking into "emergency" conditions in Indira Gandhi's India, visiting re-education camps in Vietnam, interceding for a death-row prisoner in the U.S., observing the trial of Basque separatists in Spain. Where the human rights group is barred, as in Russia, Amnesty workers have developed their own new techniques: appeals were made by overseas phone to the director of the mental hospital where their "adopted" prisoner was detained. Their efforts were of no avail, but they had registered their protest.

Where Amnesty missions go, and when, is decided by the nine-member International Executive Committee elected yearly by some 200 delegates from the National Sections. Missions are governed by a strict set of rules: they are not to enter a country without the express permission of a government, nor make statements to the press while still in the country. Only when a report has been made to the International Executive Committee is a memorandum on findings and recommendations sent to the government in question. Understandably enough, governments are most reluctant to admit that the reprieve or release of prisoners has been due to Amnesty efforts rather than official clemency.

Still, the organization claims that its missions and the attendant publicity, together with the "infuriating" cascade of letters, have not all been in vain. For instance, one of the highest ranking leaders of an East European country admitted, albeit unofficially, reports Power, that it was Amnesty work which led his government to release thousands of social democrats and other political dissidents who had been locked away for 14 years.

ALL THIS WORK ON BEHALF of prisoners is spurred by the organization's Statute or Mandate, which sets forth its objectives and the scope of its activities.

Amnesty has three fundamental concerns. These are, first, to seek the release of prisoners of conscience: as defined by Amnesty, these are men and women detained anywhere and under any political or ideological system for their beliefs, color, sex, ethnic origin, language or religion, provided they have not used or advocated violence. Secondly, to oppose the detention of prisoners of conscience, as well as political prisoners, deprived of a fair and public trial. Thirdly, to oppose, on behalf of all types of prisoners without reservation, the death penalty, torture and other "cruel, inhuman or degrading treatment."

Led by Sweden's Thomas Hammarberg, Amnesty's fourth and current secretary-general, officials of the human rights organization concede that the nature of Amnesty work allows only for a few and relatively modest victories. *Against Oblivion* cites some of these breakthroughs—in Uganda, Rhodesia, Nigeria; in Brazil and, rather dramatically, in Colombia, where the authorities opened prison gates to an Amnesty mission, the major newspapers of Bogota carried the full text of the delegates' findings, and following a national debate, the regime announced an amnesty. But in terms of the overall picture, Amnesty seems to be engaged only in scattered, desperate holding actions. The torturer is stopped from delivering more blows or applying the water cure. Some men are saved from execution or set free. But there is "for every release, another batch of prisoners; for every family reunited, another torn asunder; for every shout of exultation, a cry of suffering."

Yet the slow, difficult, troublous, often seemingly futile enterprise goes on—to defend and advance human rights, to try at least to give prisoners some hope and consolation, and spare them further torment and pain. In such countries as Guatemala, where, Hammarberg says, "there are no political prisoners, only political killings"; El Salvador, where thousands of peasants have "disappeared" or been massacred by rightist security forces; Nicaragua, where the Marxist-dominated junta has ordered the detention or execution of hundreds of the deposed Somoza's National Guardsmen; Tanzania, where "incredibly cruel torture" has decreased but not been eliminated; China, where the repression of "class enemies" and "foreign agents" is "often arbitrary and on occasion quite savage"; the Soviet Union, where, Amnesty reports, chemical and psychiatric techniques of torture are often used by a vast machinery of repression, and where "there has not been a single case (among tens of thousands of prisoners) in which a Soviet court has acquitted anyone charged with a political or religious offense."

From the looks of it, the overpowering odds ranged against it, it is a struggle that calls for immense reserves of faith, fortitude and dedication. Above all, perhaps, for that capacity for "radical hope" which, says the Jesuit theologian Ladislaus Boros, is at the core of the Christian vision—the same hope which the Church holds up to the faithful at the onset of Advent and the end of the liturgical year: that "God will bring to a good end all our stumbling efforts to bring a bit of love and justice in this world."

As Peter Benenson, echoing the ancient proverb, said of his newly born organization in December 1961: "Better to light a candle than curse the darkness." Especially if dawn has been postponed indefinitely.

Amnesty International promises to go on lighting those candles.

(Panorama, 1982)

Bataan: The Folly and the Fallout

ASIDE FROM FERDINAND E. MARCOS, now the Commander in Chief, and Carlos P. Romulo, now a major general, many other Filipinos fought in Bataan.

More than 60,000 of them, along with 15,000 American troops, fought the Japanese as well as hunger, malaria and dysentery for three months before Major Gen. Edward King finally surrendered the USAFFE forces on the hot, shell-scarred peninsula 42 years ago this week.

One of them was Antonio Aquino, eldest son of Benigno Aquino, Sr.

Ninoy Aquino's half-brother Tony was but a second lieutenant during the Battle of Bataan and won no medals for gallantry in action, nor was he chosen by destiny, as has been said of his most decorated comrade-in-arms, for feats of greatness after the war. Yet Tony Aquino has quite a few paragraphs devoted to him in John Toland's well-researched and immensely readable history of the Pacific War, *The Rising Sun*, which makes no mention of Ferdinand E.

Marcos at all. Apparently Toland, whose book was published in 1970, didn't see fit to include the daring exploits recorded in *For Every Tear a Victory*—which may or may not prove a certain disrespect on his part for Filipino war heroes; such cavalier treatment as some U.S. solons have exhibited, complain admirers of the incumbent president, with regard to the $180-million aid package to the New Republic this year...

One night in late February 1942, as Toland recounts it, Tony Aquino swam from Bataan to Corregidor with a bag of pingpong balls tied around him as a life preserver. He made the perilous crossing, braving sharks, shellfire and nervous trigger-fingers on the fortified island—"to warn Quezon of the increasing hostility between Filipinos and Americans at the front." The trouble had to do with dwindling food supplies, and Tony Aquino told the Commonwealth President: "We feel we should have the same rations as the Americans. We eat only salmon or sardines. One can a day for 30 men . . ."

Quezon was so enraged that "he summoned his Cabinet and said he would ask Roosevelt to let him issue a manifesto requesting the United States to grant at once absolute independence to the Philippines. Then he would demobilize the Philippine Army and declare the Philippines neutral. Consequently both America and Japan would have to withdraw their armies."

Quezon's message to the U.S. President had to pass through General MacArthur. The latter, reports Toland, not only cleared it for transmission; rankled by the suspicion that Washington had let him down, he added his own grim assessment of the situation. "There is no denying that we are nearly done," MacArthur wrote; Quezon's plan "might offer the best possible solution of what is about to be a disastrous debacle." MacArthur hoped that Quezon's "desperate proposal" would shock Washington into action and bring those long-awaited bombers and battleships from across the Pacific.

But Roosevelt and his Chief of Staff, General George Marshall, had already hammered out their grand strategy: Hitler should be defeated first, all available help should go to the British. No convoy had sailed out of San Francisco or Pearl Harbor to relieve the "Battling Bastards" of Bataan; the Philippines had been written off, and MacArthur's "last stand" was to serve merely as a symbol of resistance. Filipinos would go on fighting and dying in Bataan—for American propaganda.

Roosevelt rejected Quezon's proposal but managed in "masterful fashion," notes Toland, to convince the Commonwealth leader that America would never abandon the Philippines. "Whatever happens to the present American garrison," wired Roosevelt, "we shall not relax our efforts until the forces now marshalling outside the Philippines return and drive out the last remnants of the invaders from your soil."

The U.S. President's promise so overwhelmed Quezon that he "swore to himself and God that as long as he lived he would stand by America regardless of the consequences to his people or himself."

Quezon and then MacArthur fled Corregidor soon after. The fighting raged on in Bataan; successive defense lines were overrun by the Japanese in March, and on April 3, 1942, General Akira Nara launched his final offensive. Two days later his shock troops planted their flag on Mount Samat. A USAFFE counterattack quickly disintegrated into chaos and retreat.

When Bataan fell on April 9, Tony Aquino's company was ordered to assemble in Balanga, for the first lap of what would be called the Death March. On the dusty, unshaded road leading out of Bataan to Lubao, Pampanga, he marched for hours without rest or water, together with several thousand other prisoners. He had lost more than 50 pounds since he came to Bataan, but his legs were swollen. Men kept dropping out of the column, to be shot or bayonetted on the roadside.

In San Fernando, Tony Aquino's group was herded into an abandoned vinegar factory. The young lieutenant dropped exhausted on the floor. Fourteen hours later, he was awakened and taken to a schoolhouse where he found his father with a Japanese colonel. The colonel told Tony Aquino in a British accent: "Your father is a good friend. You can go home now."

Once alone with his son, Benigno Aquino, Sr. revealed that Quezon had ordered him and Laurel and other leaders "to pretend to collaborate with the Japanese: the first step would be to press for the early release of all Filipinos from prison camp."

Tony Aquino said: "Hurry, Papa, we are dying like flies."

Filipinos did die like flies—as many as 30,000 during the march and later at Camp O'Donnell, in Tarlac—and they died in a war that, President Quezon said, was not of their own making; a war, moreover, in which they were deceived, deluded, misled by their avowed

128

friends and champions in Washington. The terrible lesson of Bataan goes beyond the folly of inadequate planning, the lack of air cover, ammunition, food; the injustice of unequal rations. As Nick Joaquin expressed it in an article on the bitter, bloody futility of it all, written some years before Toland's history of the war:

"On every April 9, there are allusions to Bataan as a symbol and an inspiration. Bataan is a symbol of unspeakable things, and can be an inspiration only to dupes. But it should forever be a warning to this nation—the old warning that cries: 'Put not your trust in princes!'"

FORMER SENATOR JOSE W. DIOKNO raises the same alarm, and more: lordly princes they may not be, imperial overlords they must think they are; and to pay no heed to the warning, he is telling us in effect, would bring our people more pain, suffering and death than Bataan ever did, than any reprise of Bataan ever could. For imperialism—which is the policy of a nation-state to project its power and interests beyond its own borders—continues to maintain on Philippine soil military bases that are magnets for nuclear attack, he asserts; that expose our country more than ever to the Apocalypse of nuclear doom.

The steadfast nationalist and crusader against imperialism sounds the warning anew—first raised by the late Senator Claro M. Recto in the 1950s—in a primer issued barely a month ago by the movement of which he is the head and inspiration, the *Kilusan sa Kapangyarihan at Karapatan ng Bayan* (Kaakbay).

Filipino nationalism, the former solon defines as "the determination to uphold the sovereignty of the Filipino people—not of just a few and definitely not of foreigners—to freely decide the destiny of the nation: what kind of government we should have and who should run it, what is the common good and how to attain it, how our society should be structured, the wealth of our land and seas used, developed and shared, and how our culture should be preserved and enhanced . . . It is the firm resolve never to allow our people to be dominated or controlled by foreign powers or domestic tyrants . . ."

In our time, to be a Filipino nationalist, declares Diokno, is to be "anti-American"—because "it is American imperialism that is strangling the Filipino people. If it were Soviet or Chinese or Japanese imperialism exploiting our people, Filipino nationalists would be as 'anti-Russian,' 'anti Chinese' or 'anti-Japanese' as they are now 'anti-American.'"

The U.S. government—which is not the same as the American people, with many of whom Filipinos have warm, cordial relations—seeks as a general policy "to make the Philippines a bulwark of U.S. security." As a consequence, the U.S. government has adopted "specific anti-Filipino policies: maintaining military bases in our country; supporting the authoritarian Marcos government; demanding national treatment for U.S. investors; and imposing economic policies, through the IMF and the World Bank, which prevent the autonomous, authentic development of our economy by discouraging basic industries, aborting the growth of a domestic market, and deepening poverty."

.The bases, stresses Diokno, "seriously threaten our survival as a people." Clark Air Base is the largest U.S. Air Force base outside the continental United States; Subic Naval Base is the biggest U.S. naval installation after Pearl Harbor. These bases, Diokno points out, are not here to protect us—"They are here, first, to project U.S. power in Asia, the Indian Ocean and the Middle East; and second... to protect U.S. trade initiatives and economic interests."

Clark has nuclear-capable delivery systems, the fighter-bombers of the 13th Air Force. Subic is the homeport of 7th Fleet aircraft carriers with nuclear weapons and of Polaris submarines armed with nuclear ballistic missiles.

The Russians have more than 120 SS-20 missiles emplaced in the Lake Baikal region in Siberia. The SS-20 carries three independently targettable nuclear warheads; and each warhead packs the explosive force of 150 kilotons or seven Hiroshima bombs. Clark and Subic are within striking distance of these missiles with their 3,500-mile range. Soviet missile programmers have conceivably more than one SS-20 targeted on each of these U.S. bases.

In a nuclear war between the superpowers—the once unthinkable can happen without warning, by accident or design—Soviet nuclear missiles would surely be launched against Clark, Subic and other U.S. installations in the first few minutes of hostilities. A probable target would be Metro Manila, a vital communications and transport component of the U.S. Pacific war machine. A single SS-20 with its three nuclear warheads would kill 5.2 million Filipinos or 10 per cent of the population.

But the Philippines can escape the devastation of a nuclear Apocalypse, for Filipinos can get rid of the U.S. bases, says Diokno—"There are several ways of accomplishing this. One is by denouncing the R.P.-

U.S. Bases Agreement because it is illegal. They violate the Tydings-McDuffie Law which is part of our 1935 Constitution. If the U.S. then refuses to dismantle the bases, its refusal would be an act of aggression which we could bring before the United Nations. We could also quarantine the bases, deny entry and exit by land and water.

"Another way is to end the agreement by January 7, 1989, when the next review is scheduled, or by September 15, 1991, when the term of agreement ends."

All this would presuppose that the majority of the Filipino people, not to say their leaders, would become anti-imperialist and anti-American, as Diokno defines these terms in the Kaakbay primer. The demands of sovereignty and survival would leave them no other logical alternative—but why are Filipinos not all anti-American? Why, for instance, do only a few thousand militants, not tens of thousands or several millions of the citizenry, march and demonstrate against the bases?

"Partly out of self-interest," explains Diokno, "but mostly because of the myths perpetuated by the educational system established here by the U.S., and by the unabated inflow of American propaganda and cultural products. Such myths present the image of America as our benefactor and liberator . . . while that of Filipino nationalists as extremists and radicals, if not Communists. Yet the truth is that the U.S. has never done anything for us that has not been in its own interest, and most Filipino nationalists are not Communists or extremists but firm believers in liberal democracy."

The champions of the present order, those who would uphold it at any cost, improve it, make it more efficient and profitable, can only be disconcerted and alarmed by the truth as Jose W. Diokno perceives it. He disturbs their peace, threatens their self-esteem, their possessions which, they suspect, Diokno, once he has the chance, will give away to the poor. They must wish that he would just go away or at least shut up. Fiercely honest and uncompromising, he shows no signs of faltering in his nationalist campaign to set his people free—from the arrogance of American power; from neocolonial myths still prevalent long after the disastrous deception that was Bataan; from the dread prospect of nuclear devastation.

"I came through and I shall return," General MacArthur said as soon as he landed in Australia after his escape from Bataan—a solemn pledge that led to the slaughter of more Filipinos in the "Liberation" battles of 1944–45 than died in Bataan, in Capas and the Occupation.

When the missiles fall on the U.S. bases in our country, no American general will return to liberate us from radioactive fallout.

(*Veritas*, 1984)

A Portrait of Their Love

THE ELECTIONS WERE OVER—and what a victory for Ferdinand Marcos and the Nacionalistas! As NP standard bearer, he had crushed President Macapagal's reelection bid under an avalanche, the Comelec was to announce shortly, of more than 670,000 votes. The charismatic war hero who had assured his countrymen that "this nation can be great again" had swept to victory together with the majority of his party's congressional candidates.

It was the beginning of Ferdinand Marcos's "Mandate of Greatness" and/or "Covenant with the People," as his speech-writers wouldn't tire of reminding the nation in the ensuing decade, and beyond.

It was a Mandate and/or Covenant which Imelda Romualdez Marcos, even their bitterest political foes would concede, had to a great extent made possible.

She had been his personal campaign manager no less, and in that role, rhapsodized a weekly magazine, "she scintillates; she outshines everybody . . . she has learned the art of making the audience sigh, cry and laugh with her." Another publication was equally enthusiastic: in every city, town and barrio all over the country, "it was not enough that she blessed these places with the radiance of her beauty and the sunshine of her smile; she had to be in a perpetual motion of speaking, handshaking and oftentimes singing during public rallies . . . ."

The elections were over, and the "perpetual motion" of the attractive, dynamic duo had paused and come to a stop—temporarily, of course—at the Marcos home on Ortega Street, in San Juan, Rizal. It was November 1965, some days after the thrilling (to Marcos partisans) electoral contest, and Ferdinand and Imelda could sit back and relax, already confident of victory, as they waited for the final tallies.

After the sound and the fury, the speeches, the renditions of *Dahil sa Iyo* and *Pamulinawen* from Aparri to Jolo, all the tasks and tensions that an election campaign imposed on a presidential candidate and his campaign manager, they could at last pose, rested and refreshed, for a tranquil photograph together. Which they did, in the house on Ortega Street.

Bob Razon took their picture, and the result, as you can see, is a touching portrait of an utterly charming fellow and an irresistibly lovely lady who are deeply in love—with each other, it scarcely needs to be said, as well as with the nation, the electorate, the triumph of the moment, the promise of the future, greatness, nobility, truth, goodness, beauty and other exalted things that stir heart and soul . . .

He gives the photographer his best smile, and the effect is gentle, ingenuous, almost collegiate and boyish, at age 48. She is 12 years younger, and the camera has captured what one smitten writer has called "the dusk-haunted glow of her loveliness." She inclines her head with a sweet, deferential affection toward her husband. After the picture-taking, one easily imagines, she will excuse herself and with wifely devotion finish the cooking that the photo session has interrupted—*pinakbet*, perhaps, or some Waray dish, fish most probably, for she has learned how conscientious he can be about fats, calories and such. She won't be rushing out of the kitchen to supervise the construction of some huge monument or brief AFP generals on something like "national economic liberation" or jet off on an urgent mission to New York, Moscow or Beijing. They have been married 11 years; their eldest child is nine. The children perhaps have come in from their play, to watch, together with the more fervent Blue Ladies who are always hanging around, their parents sitting so handsomely, so unforgettably, for the photographer. And are those the songs from Camelot playing softly in the background?

The photograph could well have been inscribed: *To our Valentine, the Filipino nation . . .*

Among other things, a romantic relic, a poignant memento from a time and season the nation would never know again—for it was taken 18 years ago . . .

Four years before President Marcos obtained his second "Mandate of Greatness" through "guns, goons and gold," in the view of practically the entire media—which would later prompt a sulky Mr. Macapagal to remark: "If I had spent but ten per cent of the public funds President Marcos used for his election campaign in 1969, I could have beaten him hands down."

Five years before the massive student demo in front of Congress, the Siege of Malacañang, the First Quarter Storm.

Six years before the Bombing of Plaza Miranda and the Suspension of the Writ.

Seven years before martial law, "constitutional authoritarianism" and the "New Society."

Sixteen years before President Marcos received his third "Mandate of Greatness," by defeating one Alejo Santos at the polls.

Eighteen years before the murder of Benigno Aquino, Jr., the cries of "Marcos, Resign!," calamitous devaluation and a near-bankrupt economy; Imelda Marcos announcing her resignation from the Executive Committee, and a distressed nation still wondering whether her time in public office would indeed be "co-terminous," as she has said, with the President's . . .

Happy Valentine to all of you out there who voted for FM, the photograph seems to be saying, even now, today, 18 years after Bob Razon clicked his shutter, in the house on Ortega Street, in San Juan. Which is maybe as it should be, for Valentine's Day also brings memories that break the heart, wringing from it a cry of regret, protest and pain, as those who have loved much and lost more know only too well, and too late.

(Veritas, 1984)

Thinking Not So Brightly,
Feeling More than a Bit Stupid

IT'S AS IF THE PLANE HAD CHANGED GEARS, and your insides along with it. The drowsy, aircon-like purr of the engines in the morning high above the Pacific has been replaced by what sounds like a reluctant growl. Now the big bird descends through the cloud cover and crosses over the Quezon coastline, lowering its flaps for the glide down to native land.

Even before the first green outlines of Luzon can slide into view beneath the slanting wing, compatriots around you in the cabin all seem to strain forward against their seat belts, and peer excitedly, ardently, not a few of them noisily, through the ports for a glimpse of our Bayang Magiliw. This time, you just can't bring yourself to join in their fervor burning for the land of the sun returning. These fortunate souls look like they can hardly wait to disembark at the Ninoy Aquino International Airport and maybe kiss the tarmac or the floor of the passenger tube before rushing out to the abrazos of family, kin, friends, neighbors, townmates, officemates, prayer group brods and sisters, fellow barangayistas and other associates ready to make merry at a beer-and-crispy-pata bienvenida.

But shame on you . . . As the plane banks slower now over the Bay and those anomalous reclamation areas and the squalid sprawl of Parañaque and Pasay harboring drug dealers and shabu addicts, you don't feel like cheering at all or bursting into song, not even the softest humming of a bar or two from the Pambansang Awit, as you were somewhat inclined to do in homecomings a people power's revolution and more than one administration ago.

If loving spouse and devoted children were not there waiting to reclaim you and bring you home safe though not too sound. . . it occurs to you—another guilty sigh and twitch of your aged frame—that if the immigration people and your dollar reserves allowed it, you might just go hop aboard the next plane out and prolong your sabbatical abroad, anywhere but in the land of your birth and the home of your people. Yup, even some place where you don't know the language and anyone, like Srinagar or Krasnoyark, so long as it's at least a few thousand miles from outta here.

It also occurs to you the next minute and as the jumbo jet shudders to a stop that you are not thinking so brightly, entertaining and being entertained by such unpatriotic thoughts, which makes you feel more than a bit stupid. You can only envy your fellow countrypersons fairly bouncing up from their seats and collecting their duty-free packages and assorted Pinoy baggage from the overhead racks, chatting happily and maybe on the verge of singing, if not Julian Felipe's anthem, folk-danceable tunes like *"Manang Biday"* and *"Sarung Banggi,"* while you take your time getting ready to step out wearily and proceed not too briskly to the passport counters and the authorities checking on whether you've brought in AK-47 parts, prohibited substances and other contraband.

Why so? Why your different scenario from the glad one followed by noble and ever loyal citizens out there, whether arriving or departing or simply staying put? Happy, contented folks who can warble those sprightly ditties, wave the flag or give the thumbs-up sign, maybe capable of all three at one and the same time, and in any kind of weather, felicitous, frightful or foul . . . An impressive nationalistic feat, that, and surely an uplifting spectacle just perfect for a Philippines 2000 commercial if not a People's Initiative for Reform, Morality and Action (PIRMA) recruitment poster—smiling mouth in song, waving the colors with one hand and up-thumbing or is it thumb-upping with the other (just with a single thumb, silly, unless we're speaking here of an extraterrestrial hand with one such digit too many), and keeping it up despite tropical depression, typhoon, flood, lahar, garbage, gridlock, graft, police criminality, military mayhem, political pandemonium and other indigenous calamities.

When you set foot again on terra all too cognita, why can't you wave and cheer or at least produce some sounds that could mean the Filipino can always go, go, go? You suppose, age, metabolism, lack of certain vitamins, hormonal deficiency and all that have got a lot to do with it. That's to say, being a sexagenarian—a nice, peppy, intriguing word that rarely matches how you feel—must account for not thinking so brightly and so on about the Philippine condition once more demanding your devout attention. That, and jet lag, of course, and without a doubt the state of the nation itself, beginning with the state of the airport.

THE NAIA, you've always thought, is certainly not the kind of international airport Ninoy Aquino would have found worth dying for, though he was killed there, murdered by Marcos' minions, violently, horribly, stupidly, 14 years ago this month.

No Filipino, for that matter, ought to suffer and die for it, or be sacrificed to it, except, you've likewise always believed, the people who designed and built it, probably the ugliest, most idiotic and wretched international airport this side of the planet if not the galaxy. Its architects and builders, dear cronies, one is told, of Ferdinand and Imelda, deserve not an instant assassin's bullet to the head, but a slow, more agonizing termination such as that brought about by the unholy torments Padre Torquemada devised especially for heretics in the dungeons of Sevilla.

The NAIA—one winces at having to associate Ninoy's name with it—must have been built precisely to make the few hours that air travelers have to spend in there an occasion for misery, torture and nausea. For starters, whereas airports in London, Washington, Chicago, San Francisco, Houston, Madrid, Amsterdam, Mexico, Bangkok, Singapore, Tokyo, Seoul and other cities of the civilized world are built wide and low and with practically all sections on one broad level for easy access and transit, the NAIA is constructed like a dismal, three or four-tiered cake, with a maze of dim passageways around and between floors. (The better, observes a colleague, the astute editor Willie Baun, to conceal customs rackets and assassination plots.)

One approach ramp leads to the departure area, another goes to the arrival zone, a third seems to go nowhere. Stupid ramp designs, moronic drivers and imbecilic (sometimes homicidal) airport guards conspire every day and night to create a chaos of traffic around the terminal. One vicious rainstorm can turn the usual chaos into a gargantuan traffic Inferno stretching from those congested ramps all the way to Roxas Blvd., as happened at the start of this typhoon season a couple of months ago.

On the sunny day you fly home from San Francisco, conditions at the airport are nothing unusual, meaning, you should have drunk more than your customary Budweiser intake on the long flight or otherwise become a stoic sexagenarian able to handle the hassles of arrival without giving in to rage, despair or a blood clot.

The corridor from the tube exit to Immigration is bright and attractive enough, with real plants along the walls and lovely diorama-style scenes, Rizal Park and Mount Mayon and the Banaue Rice Terraces and such, intended to boost the spirits and spending capacity of the first-time tourist. These postcard-pretty panoramas, courtesy of Mina Gabor's department, only work the opposite effect on you, annoying and depressing you instead. Because you know strollers are likely to be mugged and mutilated at the Luneta, poverty and unrest simmer around the Perfect Cone, the once fabulous terraces are desolate and crumbling.

Behind the holiday smiles, the festive facade, lurk kidnappers, rapists, pedophiles, holdup men, crooks in uniform or not, all sorts of public and private sewage, coliform germs swimming among the blissful blondes at Boracay. (So what else is new? Waiting for you at home is nearly two months' worth of newspapers bearing mostly dreary disastrous tidings, from the Monte de Piedad fiasco to the latest resurrection of PIRMA.)

The tiny, bespectacled lady in her passport booth is bored and distracted, and hardly glancing at your likeness and identification waves you on as obviously you are neither Libyan terrorist nor Laotian heroin smuggler. She is about the only uniformed person in the entire airport complex you consider hugging in gratitude. It's not so easy to take as kindly to the characters presiding over Baggage Claim and Customs. A huge scowling individual like a PNP director who has gone AWOL grabs your dollar fee and with a grunt releases to you a dirty baggage cart with handles so sticky your fingers almost get glued to them. Around the baggage carousel mill what seem to be at least a thousand Balikbayan arrivals, each collecting about a dozen Balikbayan boxes. At no other airport anywhere in the world, you are sure, do so many traveling citizens return with so many crates requiring so much time and muscle to retrieve, check and haul out. And the airport layout itself, you glumly note again, doesn't help matters any, putting up a virtual obstacle course between customs and your family waiting somewhere outside to drive you home.

Perhaps because the books and magazines you accumulated abroad make suspicious bulges on your suitcase, a customs man who looks like a moonlighting AFP colonel on forced leave insists on your zipping it open for his authoritarian inspection. He regards the Barnes & Noble bargain hardcovers (Mailer, Burgess, Naipaul, et al.) and the *Esquire*, *Atlantic* and *Harper's Magazine* copies with something like disgust, and turns his back to attend to perhaps more lucrative luggage.

You push the cart with the bags out the door, and a horde of porters blocks your path. But for a globe-trotting sexagenarian you are no pushover, not yet anyway—you paid a dollar for the use of the cart, ha—and you fend off their clutches, break free and roll your cart out onto the ramp.

ACROSS THE RAMP-DRIVEWAY welcomers are standing packed behind a wall of iron grilles, disheveled and forlorn as prisoners of some genocidal dictator waiting to be shipped to an extermination camp. The more desperate among them are shouting out names like cries for help.

People who come to meet people at the airport are treated more humanely now, as they can gather thus in a more or less open space, unlike in years past, you recall with a shudder, when they had to do their waiting inside the terminal, in a hot, smokefilled cavern overlooking the hall through which arrivals passed on their way out.

Twice, in the '80s, you had stood vigil there for incoming friends, managing not to collapse from the heat and the sweating press of the crowd and the cigarette smoke, before catching the attention of your special arrivals and hollering to them to wait outside by the exit and then rushing across the ramp and down a couple of stairways and out to the parking lot and then driving around and up the same stupid ramp to pick up your passengers. At other airports in the civilized world, at Barajas, Changi, Chiang Mai, De Gaulle, Heathrow, Kennedy, Narita, O'Hare, Schipol, there's absolutely no need for anyone to do all that standing and sweating and running up and down and about.

So, if those taipans and other folks who are set, you've heard, to improve the old airport and build two other terminals for the NAIA—if they are thinking brightly, which you suppose they must do to remain taipans, and they want to stop thousands of plane passengers (and their welcomers) from feeling more than a bit stupid as well as aggravated, they can study the designs and operations of these world-class airports if they haven't done so yet, and adopt, copy, reproduce, recreate what makes these air terminals the world-class facilities that they are: intelligent, rational, efficient, secure, comfortable, attractive, worthy of the global citizens of the Third Millennium.

You are at last out of that dingy, discombobulating cake of a terminal, but you are not yet free of its malignancies. The family car is not among the haphazard file of vehicles on the ramp so you cross over to a relatively new architectural feature of the airport: a concrete passage sloping down to a second arrival area, so steep that a runaway baggage cart hurtling down could break people's backs. The architect and engineer responsible for this confusing anomaly and peril also richly deserve the rack, the wheel, the spikes and other death-dealing instruments of Padre Torquemada.

Your sexagenarian legs don't buckle and you tackle the descent with the loaded cart successfully to the second arrivals zone. The steep incline aside, why another and lower level for arrivals and their welcomers? It's not possible to think this out brightly, the question only makes you feel more than a bit stupid.

Further aggravation is supplied by another pack of hustlers more pushy than the porters. These look like the women's auxiliary of the Kuratong Baleleng, taxicab touts for the franchise operators sanctioned by the airport authorities.

From one of the more pleasant taxi agents—she wears a gold-toothed smile and hoop earrings—you learn that the fare to your place in Quezon City would come up to something like four times as much as the properly metered amount, a sum that at once repels the sensible Ilocano in you. The investigative reporter in you then asks her where you might find a taxi not of their line, some bus or other vehicle to get your tired carcass out of there. The lady snorts disdainfully and points beyond the lights of the parking lot to the outer darkness, where remnants of the Baleleng gang could be lying in wait for stupid locals and unwary tourists.

As a result of all this, you are thinking not so brightly and are sorely tempted to lecture this taxi solicitor, vainly, ridiculously, on how nice and easy it is to push your baggage cart out to the parking lot or to a taxi stand or bus stop at airports in truly civilized cities of the world, and so forth and so on. Before you can think some more dimwitted and distressing thoughts about the NAIA and airport-sanctioned taxis, your spouse, daughter and son-in-law drive up in the car, and one of the first things your much better half has to say, after the osculations and embraces, is what kind of stupefying idiocy is this, an airport with two drives or ramps for arrivals so people coming over to fetch people have to drive about and up and down and guess which is the right level to wait on, *que barbaridad*!

FINALLY YOU ARE SETTLED snugly in the back seat, the car at last driving away from the accursed airport, but not speeding home, inching along is more like it, for what seems like half of the day, on EDSA and through Makati and then South Super toward Quirino Avenue and Nagtahan. The traffic, too, doesn't encourage you to think brightly and succeeds even more than conditions at the airport to make you feel stupid.

Here we all are, 70 million Filipinos just two years away from the 21st century and the Third Millennium, with Fidel V. Ramos cheering and prodding us all to ride on the peppery tiger of his own making so we can really get going to Philippines 2000, and all the while more than slyly hinting that he is bent on leading us all the way there as President still or Premier somehow or something. But we have yet to resolve the horrendous traffic mess, we can't even do the simplest thing taken as a matter of course in a civilized and progressive country, which is to be able to drive from one place to another without the risk of running out of time, patience and sanity.

Except for Fidel V. Ramos and other VIPs, mostly politicians and generals with their siren-equipped escorts, and absurdly, tricycle drivers invincibly ignorant of traffic rules, we are all caught in the great democratic Filipino traffic jam that entraps private cars, vans, buses, pickups, jeepneys, cargo trucks, container haulers, tankers, even calesas straying into the pestilential gridlock.

The stupid traffic monstrosity that the ill-starred Romeo Maganto could not slay, and that his successor as Metro Manila traffic director, Florencio Fianza, is attempting to tame, futilely so far and, it appears, hopelessly to the end of the century—after all is said, tried and undone, you are persuaded to ask if it's not the metaphor, the mirror image, the reflection and spawn and consequence of the pandemonium that is our politics. There are just too many vehicles on the road (100,000 cars added to the melee every year, and how many more jeepneys and buses?) as there are far too many politicians all over, with the barangays breeding more of the same with every local election. (How about a Politician Reduction Scheme? And why not ban all types of vehicles made and sold before 1990, except M-Benzes, and henceforth allow car sales only in selected provinces in the Visayas and Mindanao? Is anyone listening? Is there hope . . . ?)

Look at the jeepney and bus drivers violating all the traffic laws in the book, getting passengers on and off in the middle of the street while the bribe-fattened police play blind and dumb, in the process snarling up traffic some more—don't they call to mind, you are impelled to ask, trapos running rampant, violating the laws of the land with impunity, spending billions of the people's money in so-called countryside development funds for their very own development projects, including various profitable enterprises and their reelection? Consider the arrogance of these drivers, the motorists stubbornly changing lanes and blocking others, their persistence in mocking all that makes for reason, law and order in the streets—shouldn't these remind the sane and sober in our society, you are compelled to say, of the unrelenting drive for a "people's initiative," which is in truth merely the initiative of some unsavory political types and their barangay lackeys, to turn Fidel V. Ramos into our PIRMAnent president?

Democracy and the Constitution, and reason and sobriety and decency, enjoin them to desist from perpetuating and enthroning power, and to wait till after the '98 elections only ten months away to amend the Charter, to change supposedly deficient, irrelevant and obsolete provisions in a true and valid Constitutional Convention, not a phoney plebiscite or a trapo Constituent Assembly. But you suspect they won't ever yield, they must have their way in the matter of term limits, by hook as well as by crook, and at any cost, from twisted constitutional bumpers to smashed democratic fenders and any number of passengers and bystanders landing in the emergency ward.

Even after the Supreme Court issued them a traffic ticket twice, the self-anointed champions of "Reforms, Modernization and Action" and their clones, encouraged by the likes of anti-democrat turncoat Lakas-NUCD president Raul Manglapus, refuse to get off the road. You wonder with no little alarm: what ploy, what alternative route or argument will the Almontes, the Pedrosas and the Pagdanganans of the present regime use next? That FVR should stay on in the Palace (along with 87 three-term congressmen in the House and a host of provincial governors and mayors) as he and he alone can stop the peso from further plunging?

YOU ASK YOURSELF at this point: Is it the system that is to blame? The overall setup, avowedly liberal democratic as well as uniquely Filipino—ultimately, might it not account for the political chaos and the partisan mess, just as the state of the road system, the network of streets, the infrastructure, would explain the traffic tribulations of the metropolis?

A distressing case in point, you'll tell all who care to listen, is Mayon Street some blocks from where you live in Quezon City—the street that starts off from the Welcome Rotonda (renamed quite recently after San Juan de la Cruz, the Spanish mystic, who must now intercede for the desperate motorists of Quezon City) and ends after some 15 blocks at Del Monte Avenue. If there's one thoroughfare that's perfect as an abject study for a symposium on the link between streets and traffic problems, that should be Mayon, the whole pitifully devastated length of it, in particular the three-block portion along which repose La Loma Precinct No. 1 of the Central Police Command, the La Loma Post Office, a branch of Land Bank, the QC Treasurer's Office, a public market, a Land Transportation Office branch and the Eulogio Rodriguez High School.

Concentrated in this part of the street in front of these institutions are exhibits of all possible types of potholes, cracks, furrows, indentations and surfaces to be found on roads in the Philippines if not the whole underdeveloped world. There are craters as deep as carabao wallows, cracks and slabs of a bewildering variety, troughs of sand and pebbles, mounds of clay, ridges of rock or hardened mud—all forcing traffic to a stupid wobbling crawl, including the freight trucks, the ten-wheelers that intelligent and forceful traffic directors should have ordered rerouted to a highway outside the city but now continue to churn up the street into an abominable mess.

What are Mayor Mel Mathay & Co. doing about it? Shouldn't the QC mayor and the city engineer and whoever represents the district in Congress be made to ride up and down the street nonstop in a jeepney for a whole day or until they are reduced to whimpering wrecks begging the people for forgiveness and mercy? How many times has Mayon Street been dug up, asphalted, cemented, then dug up and repaired again, off and on and here and there, from the Marcos-KBL regime to the Ramos-Lakas-NUCD era? How long will Mayon remain in this woebegone state—a few more years, a decade or more into the next century? How many streets in all the towns and cities of the country en route to Philippines 2000 resemble wretched, devastated Mayon?

How many millions in public works money and some congressman's CDF have gone down the drain or into a disreputable contractor's time deposit and the pockets of barangay agents?

On the corner of Amoranto Avenue and Mayon Street stands one of the proud signs of the times—a steel and aluminum stand memorializing the names of Barangay Norberto Amoranto officials elected only last May, headed by Punong Barangay Exequiel Libon. What, you ask yourself as you walk by their displayed names one drizzly, polluted morning soon after your return from another clime, are Mr. Libon and his honorable councilors, his *kagawad*, doing about the terrible state of the streets in their barangay? Shouldn't they take time out from gathering people's signatures for some initiative or other, and petition Mayor Mathay and the congressman concerned, Belmonte, Yap, Aquino, whoever, and the public works department and the city engineer as well, to please have the blighted, blasted street repaired and rebuilt once and for all before it disintegrates into a rotten swamp?

Mr. Libon and his councilors—are they not a bunch of Lakas-NUCD trapos, too?

Aren't they also capable of singing the anthem, waving the flag and giving the thumbs-up sign all at the same time, and then capping the performance with a lusty cry: "The Filipino can go, go, go"?

Thinking not so brightly and feeling more than a bit stupid, you have to answer yes, and with that you know you've really come home.

(Graphic, 1997)

Driving Us Nuts

THE MERRY MONTH OF MAY must be pork-barrel bonanza time in our district of Quezon City. From the chaotic and tormenting, not a few would say cataclysmic evidence, the same goes for the rest of Metro Manila, except for some isolated neighborhoods like those in La Loma and off Rizal Avenue, between Bambang, say, and Blumentritt, where backwater isn't just a fancy metaphor but the black, foul, stagnant pools that people living there have to wade through even during the dry season. (When the rains come, these hapless folk, whom their congressman and City Hall don't rate much as faithful fans and voters, have to wade through dark, malodorous streams.)

It's when the countryside or citywide or whatever-wide development funds are funneled down to the local government units, the LGUs.

Around the middle of May, or between the hottest days of the year and the year's first deluge, is when the development funds are doled out—from the Budget Office in the Palace through our honorable legislators and then what's left of the loot to the LGUs, the district engineers and the public works contractors.

The windfall for the latter beneficiaries may not be that cyclonic, but the contracts blown down must be real fat and juicy, again to judge from all the frenzied digging and earth-moving and bulldozing going on around Metro Manila, to the discomfiture, to say the least, of us motorists. And all this is aside from the traffic anarchy and agony brought on by the construction of the LRT line from Cubao to Baclaran, and the Skyways projects that the previous administration started and that we motorists pray will be finished well before the end of the Erap era.

Anyway, it's that time of the year in our part of Mayor Mathay's Quezon City, and they've dug up three-fourths of D. Tuason as they've begun to excavate half of Banaue and at least a third of several adjacent streets. Not only for the resurfacing and recementing of these streets, which they did last year, if not the year before. Also to replace the drainage, if we are to go by those portable concrete culverts and pipes stacked along the devastated streets.

All this public works activity all over town is stupid and distressing enough for people who drive. Why the digging and building and repairing have to start a few short weeks before the rains is bound to be idiotic and calamitous for the populace, beginning with Metro Manila's daily commuters.

When the first real tropical disturbance descends on the city of our afflictions, these streets will still look like they've just been worked over by Chinese Silkworm missiles, with the jeepneys crawling and sloshing over the muddy troughs and flooded craters, the traffic going from merely excremental to intolerably excruciating, especially if it's past lunch-time or you have a lousy bladder or radiator.

The most appalling prospect the Metro Manila motorist can contemplate on this fine May morning is exactly this—that the production the pork-barrel-and-public-works directors have just put on the road will still be showing, running or more likely stupidly bogged down, when the school year opens in June and education adds to the general congestion.

Why the idiotic scheduling of these projects? The simple answer, *gago*, is that what's moronic and irrational is also, for the company behind the roadshow, very profitable business.

Typhoons, floods, excavations, half-finished projects, impassable streets, impossible traffic—these, you ought to know by now, scarcely disturb the flow of those developments funds, also called pork, which is larded with fat greasy stuff, which is bad for the system—any system, that is, but the lucrative setup long the bane of society and the boon of legislative crooks and their business associates . . .

BUT SUFFICIENT ON THIS FINE DAY are the evils thereof. Forget what you are going to run into and get stuck in this June. Getting to Makati City before noon is trouble enough, as I'm further persuaded when I find myself smack in the middle of what's now practically no man's land—D. Tuason Street, a major thoroughfare.

The morose idea comes to me as I stop and go, stop and go forward somehow in a creeping column of vehicles, on a rutted, potholed strip along the rain-filled trench that was, only last week, the middle two lanes of the avenue.

For an infrastructure job like this one now being inflicted on the citizenry, why not set up a giant billboard with the name and more-than-life-size likeness of the offending contractor—the president or CEO of the firm—along with his office location, home address, phone and fax numbers? Also his favorite golf club, karaoke joint or parish organization, as the case may be?

And not just those modest little signboards saying this is another street rehabilitation project courtesy of your generous representative and kind-hearted mayor, but billboards of King Kongan proportions that you can read a demolished block away. So the more excitable motorists will know just where to send their letter-bombs when, six months after the job is supposedly finished, the concrete paving has cracked in 369 places, the street has blistered and buckled in half as many spots, and the new drainage is all clogged up, flooding stretches of the avenue with rainwater and sewage. All of which, of course, would call for another barrel of pork, another contract to dig up and replace the concrete surface that's been programmed to last only for five and a half months . . .

Will some congressman of exceptional intelligence, conscience and integrity (Joker Arroyo? Roilo Golez?) consider filing a bill making these contractors' billboards mandatory, and a fake, botched-up public works job more or less a heinous crime?

Frank Sinatra is crooning "Embraceable You" soothingly on tape as I try to drive out of D. Tuason by turning right into Dapitan. But the corner traffic lights have conked out—the engineered result, rumor has it, of an impending multimillion-dollar deal with a foreign firm to replace the traffic-signal system in Metro Manila. It's more than ten minutes before I can get clear of the bottleneck. Only to come upon more of the same, and though varying in volume, duration and idiocy, all accounting for the manic depression that must affect enough motorists in the metropolis.

There's a nasty traffic jam building up on the corner of Dapitan and Mayon. For at least three reasons, as far as I can see—the traffic lights here are likewise on the blink, the usual jeepneys are hogging the intersection, and assorted vehicles are parked in front of the Santa Teresita Barangay Hall on the corner.

This last phenomenon, custom or whatever, of privileged local biggies using half of the street in front of the barangay office is, you'll have noticed, the established, sanctified practice all over, in every town and city. Street obstacles and hazards, along with those fancy racks with the names of barangay officials and those corner guardposts like outdoor toilets blocking the driver's view—all due to the Code of Local Governments authored by Senator Pimentel, whose political intentions and ambitions have spawned these stupid and costly monstrosities.

Among other things, it's the price people have to pay for residing in a democracy, one is told—the more local government, the more exorbitant crap and imbecility, and you'll just have to groan and bear it. And there's nothing and nowhere more democratic, indeed, than the streets of Metro Manila this May morning, as I learn all over again, escaping finally from the gridlock on Mayon-Dapitan and proceeding at last toward Forbes (not Makati but Sampaloc).

Democratically, obtusely, absurdly, both streetside lanes of Dapitan are occupied by parked vehicles of every imaginable kind, leaving only the patched-up, potholed middle lane for traffic.

I decide to spare myself any extended masochistic reflections on the whys and wherefores, except to remind myself that this business of street parking uses well over 60 percent of road space in Metro Manila. And that it's absolute cretinism for the PNP, the MMDA, the Department of Transportation, and other authorities and agencies concerned, not to see the connection between stupid gridlocked traffic and streets crowded with parked vehicles all over Metro Manila.

How to clear the streets of these parked vehicles and open them up to more and smoother traffic—can it still be done short of declaring martial law and employing the Army and the Marines to tow off these vehicles and their owners to detention camps? Is that the one final solution, given the irredeemable idiocy of the traffic powers that be, beginning with the MMDA? (Politicos like Jejomar Binay only use the Authority to project themselves for a reelection bid, so why not hire non-political managers for a change, huh?)

Mercifully, Dapitan is one-way and one can still cruise down its congested length without risking a head-on collision, only a chancey bump from a stray tricycle or a truck suddenly backing out from its slot.

What if it were two-way, with all these cars, jeepneys and trucks parked on two sides? It would take motorists thrice the time to drive down it. Whoever decreed that it be one-way must have been the rare genius extant in City Hall or some traffic agency. Or was Dapitan made one-way to make room for all the vehicles that have to use it for a parking lot. Huh?

This profound Filipino puzzle I leave for the nonce to the proper authorities. What I allow to exercise me as Frank Sinatra sings a jaunty "You Make Me Feel So Young" and I turn left into Blumentritt, which is two-way and also cluttered with parked transport, including several units under repair, is why more streets aren't made one-way, for easier traffic.

Now it happens that over the last quarter of a century, I've had the chance to observe traffic conditions close up in Hong Kong, Bangkok, Rome, Paris, Tel Aviv, Athens, Amsterdam, Madrid, Barcelona, London, New York, Houston, San Francisco, Los Angeles, Mexico City, Havana. And this much I've learned—the people who run these places are bright and sensible enough to make main avenues and most alternate streets one-way.

Despite the density, the street loads, their system helps get the traffic going faster than could a whole regiment of zealous traffic cops.

Sure, they still have their bottlenecks, but none as long and dense and outrageous and stupid as ours. And in less crowded cities like Havana and Managua, you can go from one end of the city to the other fast on one-way streets without a hitch, which you'd think commuters should at least be able to do in a developing country.

At this juncture, which is before the extinct traffic lights on Padre Florentino cor. Forbes, I indulge for a minute in my usual driver's fantasy—thoroughfares like Forbes and España, Rizal Avenue and Quezon Boulevard, Taft and Buendia and several others are all one-way, with the traffic going zoom-zoom and away . . . Well, not exactly like in Houston, where cars can go up to 70 on the freeways and flyovers that crisscross the city, but maybe more like in Bangkok and Mexico, where the traffic gets moving briskly despite the massive total of vehicles on the road.

But, no, only a few miserable streets like Dapitan and Padre Florentino are one-way in these parts, while most other avenues like Buendia and Pasong Tamo, where I'm headed, are two-way, even three-way, hahahaha, despite the traffic density, which rhymes with insanity. Because, one is forced to surmise once more, stupid idiocy prevails at the MMDA, the Department of Transportation, etc. And also because too many people, city voters all, won't go for the one-way solution, as it would make them use their legs, which are used to being folded up inside jeepneys instead of for locomotion from a bus stop, say, in Quiapo to the house and primetime soap in Santa Cruz.

Political, economic and cultural factors, in other words, make that one-way dream just that—a motorist's utopian fantasy, impossible to translate into reality, till perhaps a more authoritarian dispensation imposes the one-way grid to help unclog streets in the next century.

Meanwhile, instead of a rational reign of grids, it's two-way, even three-way, hahaha, for most of the narrow streets and the wider avenues as well—like Forbes (now Antonio Mendoza, but not even the stupid idiots in City Hall call it that), which goes from Tayuman to Nagtahan Bridge and so carries a great deal of freight. Producing, predictably, an enormous traffic buildup between Dapitan and España, especially between nine and 12 noon. That's when every other delivery truck and gasoline tanker and pedalling vendor in Metro Manila join the melee, the traffic lights are off, and so are the traffic cops intent on an early lunch.

SO IT GOES, ALL THE WAY over Nagtahan and on Quirino Avenue and South Super—the crowded, variegated, anarchic, free-wheeling democracy on the road that can drive a motorist nuts. From pushcarts and tricycles, even carretelas, to Pajeros and Benzes and trucks straight out of "Mad Max." Only in the Philippines . . . Only in Metro Manila . . . the incredible number and variety of vehicles that pack every square yard of street space, flouting all traffic laws and regulations in the book and getting away with it, and more amazingly, with hardly a scratched fender, a busted bumper.

A blue Mercedes (NAK-252) nearly sideswipes me. A maroon Suzuki Samurai (TPL-631) brakes abruptly before my chariot, missing my bumper by inches. A sleek black Honda (16-H—hey, didn't low elitist numbers go out of fashion years ago?) dashes into a momentarily free lane, cutting off a Toyota van. A huge extra-long San Miguel delivery truck (NZA-398) fills up three lanes, threatening to squash any imprudent motorist in the way.

Why do these enormous, ponderous cargo trucks compete for road space during the busiest hours? Because, for the most part, the country doesn't have a decent railroad system to speak of, let alone use, to transport goods, produce, heavy machinery, equipment, people. And so all these freight trucks, even six-wheelers, whole rumbling fleets of them, crowding roads where they shouldn't be. Because, instead of building up and expanding and improving a rail network for Metro Manila and outlying provinces and ports, the Ramos government or, rather, profit-crazy official crooks and thugs, construct flimsy, stupid apartment buildings for mass housing right next to the rotten railroad tracks.

Frank Sinatra belts out "New York, New York" as I get to the Buendia-South Super crossing, and the railway bar isn't working. But a fellow in shorts and sando is, waving a red flag to indicate that a "Metro Tren," as this string of dilapidated coaches is called, is negotiating the junction and all are well advised not to delay its creaking passage. The coaches appear empty—people would rather take those wretched jeepneys and buses than commute with hoodlums and drug addicts, whom the PNR and the PNP don't believe like riding on trains.

Tamaraw taxis (UGX-322, PVL-727, UDZ-645) make like drunken jeepneys, weaving in and out, and only a motorist with the reflexes of an F-16 fighter pilot can swerve out of harm's way. And what's this gigantic Hyundai container truck (PXU-239) doing late in the morning in the middle of busy Buendia? Ditto this Gold Line Tourist Bus (NXM-104), belching out black clouds of diesel exhaust and taking up space good for half a dozen cars?

A gray box-type Lancer (PEK-158), the guy at the wheel probably driven really nuts by the abominable traffic, spurts into an opening and nearly rams a jeepney that has stopped obliquely to load passengers (these contraptions are not to be dignified with plate numbers). Closer to the usual lunatic gridlock on Buendia-Pasong Tamo, a black Isuzu Trooper (BTR-888) has accomplished a feat other drivers have tried doing but couldn't—crumpled the rear end of an old red Corolla.

The turgid traffic slows down some more, curving around the two entangled vehicles, inching on to the corner, where the stop lights have of course blinked out and another jeepney is parked within whistling distance of the traffic cop and aides on duty, blocking cars going into Pasong Tamo.

So what else is new?

An hour and 23 minutes after setting out from QC, I finally get to park inside the compound that Divine Providence and the head honcho of a Makati group of companies permit me to share with the newly assembled units of a car dealer.

After about nine hours, during which I take care not to give the slightest thought to the bumper-to-bumper traffic around Ayala, the horrid gridlock farther down on Pasong Tamo and the catastrophic digging and earth-moving on nearby Amorsolo (for the Skyways), I'm back on the road—retracing practically the same discombobulating route, back on Pasong Tamo and Buendia after eight p.m. and on to South Super, Quirino, Nagtahan, España.

It's the same arduous, distressful drive, aggravated by a whole stupid set of different traffic quirks, puzzles, perils and atrocities—like unlighted PLDT and waterworks excavations, oncoming cars not dimming their lights, trucks and taxis without tail lights, jeepneys running without any lights at all, to save on batteries, and not a single mobile patrol or motorcycle cop to ticket these barbarians abroad in the night.

About these motorcycle policemen—how come they are always out in full force for funerals, but are nowhere around to check on errant drivers? Wouldn't stationing one or two of these goggled characters on every busy avenue help ensure a safer, smoother traffic flow? Has that elementary mission ever occurred to their superintendent and his chief?

Or are these but senseless, useless, stupid questions a Metro Manila motorist would be saner and better off not asking?

But all in all, it's been a fine day's driving, more pleasant than most. The odd-even scheme has allowed me to drive my odd-numbered car instead of submitting to the mercies of homicidal bus and taxi drivers. It didn't rain to flood half of the streets of Quezon City, Manila and Makati. Some traffic lights still worked. There were no multi-car smashups, nor buses and freight trucks turning turtle atop cars, houses and people.

And one may still hope that in the first decade of the new century, the next millennium, they'll finish building the new LRTs and Skyways. The traffic then in Metro Manila is bound to improve— unless the MMDA, the LTO and stupid idiocy allow 10,000 more jeepneys and 8,500 more tricycles to mess up traffic some more.

I get home before 9:30 p.m. without running out of gas and the consolations of philosophy, and with nary a scratch on the carriage I washed and waxed only the other day.

One of the nicer days for driving, all right—but no thanks to the mayors, the police, the MMDA, the Department of Transportation, the public works contractors and the rest of the gang, and people trying their damnedest to drive themselves and everyone else nuts.

(*Graphic*, 1999)

Ancient and Ever New

Growing Up with the Santo Niño

IN A WAY, AN ITALIAN STARTED IT ALL, which was just as well, for the folk devotion to the Santo Niño is joyful, innocent, irrepressible and Roman, as in Roman Catholic.

When Rajah Humabon of Cebu had been baptized, wrote Pigafetta, the chronicler of Magellan's expedition, his wife expressed her desire to become the second Catholic of these islands:

"After the dinner, the chaplain, with many of us, went ashore to baptize the native queen. While the priest was getting ready for the ceremony, I showed her a little statue of the Child Jesus. When she saw it she was deeply moved and, crying, asked to be baptized. She received the name of Juana. The queen wanted the image, to take the place of her idols; so I gave it to her."

The Santo Niño has been with us ever since, the crowned Little Prince of wood and ivory carved by a Flemish artist, robed in the splendor of medieval royalty or in familiar baro and bakya, cross and orb in his hands, borne in spirited procession or just standing still and smiling down on the happy multitudes from many an altar.

January is the month of the Holy Child, and the Sunday following the Solemnity of the Epiphany, or the revelation of the Infant Jesus to the Wise Men who came to worship him, is his festival in our country. History and culture manifest his gentle, lovable yet mysterious and enigmatic ways that surely neither the Spaniards who brought him to this land, nor the Cebuanos who welcomed him, could have dreamed of in their first encounter, almost 500 years ago.

It seems only yesterday that the cult of the Santo Niño inspired, in Manila, yet another distinct demonstration of fealty—actually the revival of an old ritual for an advanced celebration, as if the wise men of this secular city sunk in squalor, disorder and decay wished to prove a more fervent devotion than that which the Church would sanction.

"Buling-Buling," a "street dance and parade" to honor the Santo Niño, was to be held starting from Liwasang Balagtas and winding up at the Shrine of Zamora in Pandacan. Officials of the once Loyal and Ever Noble City, delegations from various schools, organizations and barangays, as well as "selected beauty titlists and others"—all dressed in "Filipino costumes approximating those of the period," the early 1880s, when the "Buling-Buling" was born—were to go "dancing and singing through the streets accompanied by guitars, rondallas, brass bands, drum and bugle corps." The revelers would serenade, said the fiesta publicists, "selected Hermanos and Hermanas" gathered on their balconies, and "entice" them to join in the flower offering to the Santo Niño at "the climax of the program."

We didn't have the chance to watch and cheer along with the hardy tourists then in town, but it must have been a glorious, rousing affair to rival the festivities in Tondo, Cebu, Aklan and a score of other devout places.

A report from the Santo Niño's own city revealed that an even earlier fiesta was celebrated in his name—when "almost something mysterious," as one priest put it, ended the "Mactan coup" without a single M-16 being fired, four years ago.

The news that a crack Marine battalion was coming to retake the air base may have encouraged the "stubborn rebels" to give up; but most Cebuanos seemed convinced that the novena to their powerful infant patron in the "churches, private chapels, homes and even along the roadsides," together with the processions and Cardinal Vidal's own prayerful appeals, were what moved heaven to intervene and put a peaceful end to the siege. The Visayas Command chief himself, Brig. Gen. Renato Palma, who throughout the crisis wore a medallion of the Holy Child, said that he "prayed long and hard"; and so too did the renegade Brig. Gen. Jose Comendador, for a peaceful way out, no doubt. Their fervent entreaties were promptly answered, the rebels surrendered and a "fiesta atmosphere prevailed in Cebu . . ."

And so it goes, and so it has been—that confident, childlike, some would say childish faith in divine deliverance shared by cardinals, generals and the general public and producing happy signs and wonders—including quite a few that the Church might frown upon, since Pigafetta gave his treasured gift to the Reina Juana.

THE SPANISH COLONIZERS knew their business, and the people they had come to conquer and convert to the Christian faith.

Suppose they had shown up bearing not a pretty doll-like image of the Infant Jesus, but a black and lacerated Christ with contorted face and gaping wounds—the figure of a man of sorrows such as about to expire from the exquisite tortures of the Spanish Inquisition? The friendly natives with their gentle anitos would all have fled in alarm and terror—or the more warlike among them, like their neighbor in old Mactan, would have speared the Portuguese captain-general and his chaplain and companions off to their eternal reward.

Our history then would have taken other directions under the aegis of less benevolent deities and far from solicitous kings, and our country deprived of the honor and glory of being the only Christian nation in Asia, the light of the heathen Orient.

Providence and Carlos Primero (who would be associated with other potent spirits) were kindly disposed to their unbaptized children in the newly discovered lands beyond the Spanish Main; and it was the benign aspects of Christendom that our Cebuano brethren saw and readily embraced.

Their descendants and fellow countrymen were subsequently treated with less concern and courtesy than their baptismal sponsors had pledged. But even their alien, unchristian subjugation would be to their benefit and enlightenment, so that by the time of the Revolution (whose centenary, by the way, we commemorate in this decade), the truly illumined ones among them could distinguish between the Church and churchmen, between Christianity and the baroque superstitions spawned by Spanish Catholicism, and as Rizal, del Pilar, Mabini and Aglipay did, bestow on the latter their most profound disrespect.

The Spanish friars but for a few holdouts in the vicinity of España and P. Noval, in Sampaloc, and, it is alleged, on the board of San Miguel, have long since vanished from our schools and parishes; the faith that they brought us remains, that and the Cult of the Child. Nothing strange, for this particular devotion has grown deep roots in Filipino soil nurtured by elements older, stronger and more enduring than imported ivory and golden vestments.

THE MIRACLES, the prodigies and favors attributed to the Santo Niño have occasioned, understandably enough, no little amount of doubt and dismay.

One recalls how, after the furious floods of July 1972 and the Weather Bureau had confirmed the arrival of better weather, the Lord and Lady of Malacañang claimed credit for the finding of the stolen Santo Niño of Tondo—whose disappearance, it was said, had caused the skies to weep so much destructive rain. Amazing reappearances, nocturnal wanderings, icons that vibrate and sway and speak in supernatural voices, and the host of alleged miracles wrought by the Child through the centuries—these have provoked as much assent perhaps as derision and amusement.

But devotees disturbed by such displays of unbelief may derive comfort from the counsel of the French Jesuit scholar, Charles Miel: "We must acknowledge that as really believing Catholics we appear to those outside, today no less than in the past, as people who accept strange, even monstrous beliefs. We must not be astonished, much less worried. St. Paul realized that from the beginning. Because what was folly to man was at the same time the wisdom of God . . ."

Father Miel, whom the eminent theologian Henri de Lubac quotes in his classic study of Catholicism, was speaking of "Man as Adult," and continued thus: "In Paul's eyes, the people will listen to the Good News. Why? Because the world is no longer in its infancy. At what moment in the destiny of an individual does the child become a man? . . . the precise moment at which we become adult is that in which, after some tragedy or failure, struck by the sense of our own helplessness, we at last exclaim: 'Lord, deliver me from myself, a poor and wretched man.' It is only at that moment of honest humility that childhood comes to an end."

The Child may yet deliver us all, as individuals and as a nation, from our proud, weak, dishonest infancies.

HOW CUTE, how charming and lovable and loving is the Santo Niño enshrined in cathedral, chapel, home altar, bedroom, boardroom, office, department store, corner tienda and jeepney. He is doubtless the representation of the same child or, rather, the boy Jesus of whom the Gospel speaks:

"And it came to pass after three days, that they found him in the temple, sitting in the midst of the teachers . . . And his mother said to him, 'Son, why have you done this to us? In sorrow, your father and I have been searching for you.' And he said to them, 'How is that you sought me? Did you not know that I must be about my Father's business . . .' And he went down with them and came to Nazareth . . . And Jesus advanced in wisdom and age and grace before God and men."

The Child grew up to manhood, became the Christ who was to proclaim: "Seek first the kingdom of heaven" and "I bring not peace, but a sword" and "What does it profit a man . . ." Not the sweet, mild, sentimental plaster Jesus adored by the pious rich, but the Lord who came to shake the world to its foundations and turn its values upside down, who was neither all meekness nor gentility, who drove the profiteers and money-lenders out of the temple—a dangerous man whom the political leaders and the high priests of Jerusalem condemned to death, an intense gatherer of crowds speaking words of wrath:

"But woe to you scribes, and Pharisees, hypocrites!—for you have neglected the weightier matters of law, justice, mercy and faith . . . for you are all whitewashed tombs which outwardly appear beautiful, but within are full of dead men's bones and all corruptions . . ."

The Infant tender and mild, sleeping in heavenly peace when the shepherds and the Magi came, and the Boy whom his mother found in the temple, did not remain a child forever but grew in wisdom and age and grace—as we also grow, advance to maturity, and work and strive for the fullness of our vocations and our nationhood, even as we hail the Santo Niño and offer him the gift of our childlike faith.

(Times-Journal, 1995)

San Jose

THE FIGURE OF THE CATHOLIC PRIEST looms large in our history, as it does in the annals of other Christian lands: Dominic—as well as Torquemada—in Spain, Patrick in Ireland, Becket in England, Marquette and Junipero Serra in America. It was a priest, Andres de Urdaneta, and his four Augustinian companions, who brought the Faith and, with it, the diverse arts of civilization to our country 400 years ago this week. Typical of the missionaries who arrived by galleon in the 16th century was Father Antonio Sedeño, superior of the first Jesuits from Spain, who taught the people "to bake bricks, carve stones, make lime . . . he obtained seeds without number, taught the cultivation of silk; he planted mulberry trees, made looms; he was responsible for the coming of painters from China . . ." After the pioneer priests who baptized our forefathers and laid out the roads and founded the towns—and to them surely we owe much of infinite value— came the friar of unhappy memory, the landlord-cleric whose identification, and even active role in a colonial regime, contributed to the general unrest that finally flamed into revolution; thus he, too, though in a manner he could not have envisioned, helped create the dream of one nation. The execution of Fathers Gomez, Burgos and Zamora led directly to 1896 and gave us a national hero: had they not been garroted in 1872, Rizal would have become a Jesuit, said Rizal, who found his vocation in exile and martyrdom. A particularly intense revolucionario was in fact a priest, Gregorio Aglipay, who would defy both Madrid and Rome; his schism earned him excommunication, but there was no mistaking his love of country.

Today our nationalistic aspirations have found fulfillment in the clergy: Cardinal Santos and the bishops, and de la Costa of the Society of Jesus, Katigbak of the Dominicans, and the growing number of Filipino priests, both secular and religious. Even the political vision of extending the influence of Filipino leadership abroad in Asia has its counterpart in the Church: the Catholic hierarchy has plans for the establishment of a Philippine Foreign Mission Society: in the spirit of Urdaneta, Filipino priests would cross the seas to plant the seeds of the Faith, to fulfill "the apostolic responsibility" of "the only Christian nation in Asia."

As one set apart to perform, on behalf of the community, public ritual acts, particularly sacrifices to a supernatural power, the priest belongs to an office as old as mankind. Primitive man revered him as soothsayer, healer, exorcist: the shamans of Siberia, the diviners of the Bantus. Long before Christ, temple ministers, such as those of Assyria and Egypt and the Aztecs of Central America, interpreted the will of the gods, appeased them with ritual sacrifices; and before the coming of Spain, the *sonat* of the Tagalogs presided at rites to placate the local deities.

In the order of Christianity, the closest precursor of the Catholic priesthood was the high priest of the Old Testament, who alone could enter the inner sanctum without profanation, to offer the blood and ashes of atonement—a foreshadowing of Christ's supreme sacrifice on the cross. The chief function of the Catholic priest is also to offer sacrifice, that of the Mass: Calvary renewed in an unbloody manner. Religion is his reason for being; the altar, his domain. But like his predecessors before the Christian dispensation, his influence, for good or ill, has not been confined to the sanctuary.

In affairs not formally religious or ecclesiastical, in areas of human activity and knowledge the layman claims his own, one encounters cassock and tonsure: Copernicus expounding on the laws of planetary motion, Bellarmine formulating the principles of democratic government, Faura tracking a typhoon, Hogan in the midst of a labor strike. The centuries since Christ testify to the presence of the priest in a multitude of roles, as adviser to kings, confidant of presidents, explorer, scientist, artist, writer, physician, social worker, soldier, builder of cities; and his involvement in events outside convent and sacristy— for it is among men that he lives and works, not among disembodied spirits—has by turn been praised or bitterly condemned, blessed or fiercely reviled, or simply accepted as customary, according to the prevailing fashion and doctrine. In various climes and ages, he has been called friend of mankind, champion of progress, defender of liberties; and also despot, obscurantist, enslaver of minds, enemy of the state.

In one country he may be a prisoner bearing the marks of torture, saying Mass secretly in his cell, or Graham Greene's fugitive in disguise, starved and friendless, hunted by the secret police. In another he is invited to deliver an invocation at the opening of the legislature; he serves on a government committee on education, and sits at the head table of a wedding feast; no building or factory may be inaugurated without his benediction. If he is a parish priest, the living and the dead keep him busy, but somehow he finds time to trade banter with the ruling junta and play basketball with the boys: a regular fellow, no more mysterious and controversial than the school principal, it would seem, though the misinformed may think him somewhat of an oddball, having renounced swearing and matrimony.

But wherever he is, and no matter what he does, whether measuring the galaxies or advising a troop of Boy Scouts or drawing up a drainage ditch, and even should his superiors declare him an apostate, a renegade outside the communion of the faithful, he does not cease to be a priest. Even if stripped of his priestly functions, he never loses his spiritual powers, according to the Church; a Catholic priest, once validly ordained, is "a priest forever."

SUCH IS THE NATURE OF THE PRIESTHOOD to the Church: a man "taken from among men and ordained for men in the things that pertain to God," as St. Paul defined him, remains a priest forever, "according to the order of Melchisedech." The theologians speak of a "character" imprinted permanently on the soul of the priest by the sacrament of holy orders; a mark, a quality that cannot be erased or removed from the recipient, though he may lose his own faith. He possesses for life, the Church teaches, the powers that are the essence of his calling: the power to forgive sins ("Whose sins you shall forgive, they are forgiven," said Christ), and the power to consecrate bread and wine into the body and blood of Christ ("Do this in remembrance of me . . ."). These powers, we are told, flow from the fact that the priest shares in the priesthood of his Lord; he traces the authority bestowed on him through an unbroken line of bishops to the apostles, whom Jesus ordained at the Last Supper to celebrate the Eucharistic Sacrifice in his name.

"The ministers of Christ and the dispensers of the mysteries of God" whom St. Paul speaks of were the bishops and deacons and elders or presbyters (from which the word "priest" is derived) of the early Church; to perpetuate the priesthood, they were empowered to transmit it to other men. In the bishop the priesthood is said to reside in its fullness, for he alone can consecrate another bishop and ordain other priests by the sacrament whose external symbol is the imposition of hands, a rite mentioned in the Acts of the Apostles and the Epistles of Paul. That the Catholic priesthood is "of divine origin" the Church has pronounced a dogma, a "revealed truth," final, unchangeable: "If anyone says that Christ did not constitute the apostles priests, or did not ordain that they and their successors in the priesthood offer his body and blood," declared the Council of Trent in the 16th century, "let him be anathema."

In the Church then, pope and cardinal-archbishop and humble pastor belong to one priesthood, trace their authority to a common source, claim the same spiritual ancestry. By the same token, an absolution given by an anonymous missioner on a remote Pacific isle is no less valid to the faithful than one granted by the Pope; and the vernacular Mass in a makeshift barrio chapel is essentially no different from the Sacrifice at St. Peter's. It is these powers—to absolve, bless, consecrate—that in the eyes of faith set a priest apart from other men, though he may resemble them in everything else. His mere presence would proclaim to the world the existence of a realm of invisible and supernatural values, though the world may only scoff at his claims as the relics of a less enlightened age.

As one who would speak and act in the name of Christ, he inspires aversion or love; the most persuasive lesson he can hope to teach is the lesson of his own life. The late Cardinal Suhard, founder of the priest-worker movement in France, described him as "a sign of contradiction, the disturber of consciences, continually fostering a higher goal . . . there is something in him which ultimately escapes men, a secret which familiarity does not enable them to grasp . . . his role is a strange one. He is of heaven without being in it. He is pledged to celibacy, but he is called 'Father' because he generates and sustains children in the spirit. He belongs to human society precisely because he is not of it. In relation to society he must somehow or other be its adversary, even as he builds a bridge between it and God. Always there will be men who will never forgive him for recalling and perpetuating Him Whom they thought they had suppressed. To them he is no artisan of peace but a minister of unrest, a scandal, incomprehensible . . . But to the end of time he will endeavor to save society from becoming self-contained, to remind it of the promises of Christ, the reality of transcendent values, the tremendous fire that is the love and the mercy and the justice of God."

Pursuing their avowed mission of perpetuating Christ in the world are close to 400,000 Catholic priests from every race and nation, some 4,000 of them in our country, preaching, counseling, conducting missions and retreats, engaged in myriad tasks; ordained men of varying degrees of virtue, zeal, responsibility, talent and temper, but all bound to the service of the Church. A vast number belong to religious orders with specific duties, from education to publications to parish work: Benedictines, Franciscans, Salesians, Columbans, Redemptorists. Others drawn to the contemplative life live in isolated monastic communities, such as the Cistercians or Trappists; theirs is not an active apostolate, but by prayer and penance they would gain spiritual favors for the Church and mankind.

The majority belong to the secular clergy: the diocesan priests from whose ranks come most of the prelates who govern the Church: the Pope, the cardinals, the bishops throughout the world. As pastors of parishes, they are the front-line priests who have the most to do with the laity and the world at large; and the success or failure of the Church in a particular diocese depends mainly on their ministry. Barring the direct intervention of the Almighty, their competence and efficiency to a great extent depend, in turn, on the training they have undergone in the seminaries, which are charged, as Pius XI affirmed in his encyclical on the Catholic priesthood, with "the formation of holy, dedicated and learned priests."

IN THE PHILIPPINES TODAY some 3,500 seminarians study in 60 seminaries for the diocesan clergy, including 22 administered by religious orders. Among the larger ones, in point of enrollment, are the Metropolitan Seminary of St. Vincent Ferrer in Jaro, Iloilo, with over 200 seminarians; the Mary Help of Christians Seminary in Binmaley, Pangasinan, with 169; the Seminario Concillar de San Carlos in Makati, Rizal, with 158; and the University of Santo Tomás Central Seminary, with 136.

As a continuing institution, the oldest and perhaps the one with the strictest standards is the Jesuit-administered San Jose Seminary, off E. de los Santos Avenue in Quezon City. San Jose, which antedates UST by ten years, has an enrollment of 174 seminarians, including 56 majors (those in the higher grades of philosophy and theology) and 118 minors (high school up to third year of college). One of the two interdiocesan seminaries in the country (the other is Santo Tomás), it is for clerical students from any diocese and also for candidates in various religious orders; almost all the provinces are represented this year in its roster of students, a number of whom are non-residents from the neighboring Oblates of Mary Novitiate, and from the Franciscan Minor Seminary in San Francisco del Monte.

From the highway dusty with the traffic of freight trucks and buses, past the outposts of commerce—a mini-golf club, a dairy plant, a display of farm machines—a concrete road leads to the seminary's gray-walled, red-roofed, three-story building, with acacias shading the front drive and the statues of St. Joseph and the Christ Child set on a massive pedestal. From the visitors' parlor, a door opens on a courtyard, and a cemented walk to the chapel, in front of which stand the carved likenesses of St. Ignatius of Loyola, and Pius X, who in 1915 commissioned the "new" San Jose as an interdiocesan seminary. Beyond the chapel is a cluster of wooden structures: additional classrooms, the auditorium, the refectory, the minors' library.

Farther back are a row of basketball courts and a sloping field of brown grass: nothing else will thrive there, for adobe lies beneath the thin soil. But the seminary, as the term denotes, cultivates seedlings not in the earth but in the soul: the vocations of young aspirants to the priesthood. Every aspect of life at San Jose is so directed to this end that the unfit are soon weeded out, or finding the regimen stale, flat and intolerable, leave of their own accord. These are a tiny fraction in any given year; for instance, in 1964, only two out of some 150 left the seminary; the rest, knowing full well the demands and the disciplines of the priestly life, strive on toward their chosen goal. Many a priest, by his own testimony, remembers as the happiest and most rewarding phase of his life the years of prayer and study and companionship he spent in his seminary-home.

The building in Quezon City is actually one of several homes San Jose has occupied since its establishment; its long journey, which began in old Manila, reflects the fortunes of its Jesuit administrators, and of the country as well, in the intervening centuries. From 1601, when it was founded as the Colegio de San Jose by Father Diego Garcia, S.J., a scant 30 years after Legazpi established the seat of government in Manila, to 1817, long after the Jesuits had been expelled from the colony, San Jose was housed in a building near the Royal Gate of the Walled City. The colegio changed its location twice inside Intramuros in the period from 1817 to 1915, when, again in the custody of the Jesuits, it opened classes at the Ateneo compound on Padre Faura. After the 1932 fire that gutted the Ateneo, San Jose found itself back in Intramuros, remaining there until 1936, when it moved out to its new building in Balintawak. The Japanese took over the Balintawak site in 1942, but the seminarians, those who remained, managed to continue their studies in three or four different places, including La Ignaciana on Herran. After Liberation, San Jose remained on Herran, in three rented houses, until 1951, the year it transferred to its present building.

But its odyssey is by no means over: already a building to house the major seminarians is nearing completion at Loyola Heights. The projected transfer appears to be dictated by a kind of *aggiornamento*: the seminarians would have more campus facilities at their disposal, and their proximity to the Ateneo, where a number of their professors reside, should enhance a dialogue with the modern world. When the seminarians move to the Loyola campus, San Jose, too, will have come full circle, tradition-wise, for in 1601 it stood next to the Jesuit Colegio de Manila and its students attended classes at the latter until the Society of Jesus was banished from the Islands in 1768.

San Jose during those years was not devoted exclusively to the training of the clergy, although the large bequest it received from

Esteban Rodriguez de Figueroa, a wealthy Spaniard who perished in an expedition to Cotabato, was used mainly for the education of secular priests. As a boarding school for both lay and clerical students, it had a limited enrollment, and in the 167 years before the expulsion of the Jesuits (the handiwork of the Bourbon kings, who resented their power and influence), San Jose graduated no fewer than a thousand students. These included lay alumni who held high positions in the government, and one archbishop, eight bishops, 79 members of religious orders and 40 secular priests, among whom were some of the first Filipinos admitted to the college.

The administration of San Jose was transferred to the archbishop of Manila after the departure of the Jesuits; in 1875 a royal decree channeled San Jose funds to the support of the schools of medicine and pharmacy of Santo Tomas. The Americans in 1899 claimed the college endowment on the grounds that it was Spanish crown property—the issue was disputed between Taft and Archbishop Harty, who maintained that the institution was an *obra pia*, a religious work of the Church and never the property of the king. The matter was settled amicably, San Jose reverted to the archbishop, Santo Tomas retained use of the colegio building then on Padre Faura; and it was not until 1915 that the Jesuits, by the express wish of the Holy See, regained the administration of San Jose "in order that they may use its revenue for the education of Filipino youth aspiring to the priesthood."

AS AN INTERDIOCESAN SEMINARY, San Jose will celebrate its golden jubilee this June. In the last 50 years, it has had 10 Jesuit rectors, and the succession of nationalities mirrors the epochal changes in our history: the first four were Spaniards, followed by four Americans; the first Filipino rector, Father Antonio Leetai, assumed office in 1957. He was succeeded last year by Father Jesus Diaz, brother of Malacañang Executive Secretary Ramon Diaz, and whose previous assignment was with the Jesuit Generalate in Rome. Most of the 36-man faculty are American Jesuits, but Filipinos hold a number of key positions: Father Catalino Arevalo is dean of theology; Father Eduardo Hontiveros, who teaches dogmatic theology, is moderator of publications; Father Vicente San Juan is prefect of the major department.

They and 23 others on the faculty—one of them, incidentally, is Father Jose A. Cruz, uncle of Gemma—are Ph.D.'s, as are the visiting professors: de la Costa, Bulatao, Cullum, Wiley. In proportion to the size of the student body, San Jose has perhaps the largest concentration of doctorates among schools in the country: academic excellence is one of its major objectives. "This objective," reads a description of the course of studies for the major seminarians, "should determine our admissions policy, the quality of our teaching, and the strictness of our marking . . . our standard (should) at least equal the higher level of education in the Philippines." To qualify for the "honors course" in either philosophy or theology, the seminarian must have a grade of 2 in certain subjects, no lower than 2.5 in others; in the higher classes emphasis is on individual oral examinations in Latin or English or both.

San Jose awards two civil degrees, A.B. and M.A., both in philosophy. There are no tuition fees; the seminary charges only for board and lodging (P90 a month) and for the use of textbooks and the library (P30 annually): a total of P1,020 for the school year. "This has been made possible by our generous patrons, and by the earnings of seminary stocks in certain corporations," explains the rector, Father Diaz. A number of the seminarians are supported by sacerdotal burses, donations given in a lump sum or in installments; among San Jose donors are Cardinal Santos and Catholic families here and in the United States.

After high school and the necessary Latin, the future priest at San Jose undergoes 10 years of earnest study: three years of liberal arts, after which he is invested with a soutane in a solemn ceremony; another three years devoted mainly to philosophy, and four more to theology. He is ordained to the priesthood during his last year of theology, usually in the diocese to which he belongs, returns to the seminary to complete his studies, before setting out finally for his assigned post in obedience to his bishop. More than piety will be required of him in his life's work; to prepare him adequately for the tremendous tasks ahead, the seminarian must spend the greater part of his waking hours in classroom and study hall; his day is governed around the clock by a host of rules (a booklet lists 117 for the major seminarians). But life at San Jose for those who accept it is by no means a stiff, morose round of book learning and grim disciplinary measures.

The student-priest is up by 5:30, attends the daily 6:30 Mass with the entire community, lunches at 12 after a couple of classes, then takes an hour off for siesta or recreation; by 4:30, he is husking the floor or tidying up the grounds on days of *manualia*, or dribbling a ball on one of the outdoor courts; he is in bed by 9:45. As in other schools, there are extra-curricular clubs; the seminarians put out three publications, a quarterly literary magazine, a monthly newssheet sent to San Jose alumni, and a scholarly journal, *Studium*, a recent issue of which suggests the range of intellectual pursuits at the seminary: *The Thought of Teilhard de Chardin; Emil Brunner: A Protestant Viewpoint; A Look at Existentialism*. Twice a week, the majors teach catechism in four high schools in the vicinity; once a month they have a special day off when they can go in twos anywhere within prescribed bounds; visitors are allowed two Sundays a month. There are annual retreats and novenas, monthly devotions to the Sacred Heart and St. Joseph, and about a dozen spiritual exercises through the week, from "meditation" to the chanted litany of the Blessed Virgin—and also occasional movies at the auditorium, plays and operettas staged by the students themselves, symposiums, debates, choral concerts, lectures (Prof. Benito Reyes gave a talk recently on Indian philosophy, and a CFM group came to discuss "matrimonial problems"). Every other month, classes go out on excursions; there are sports tournaments, holidays, semestral vacations.

AND THE SEASONS PASS, and each year new hopeful faces arrive to take the week-long entrance tests (last year, San Jose accepted 16 out of 40 applicants in the minor department). The dust blows on the highway and the rains fall on the grounds streaked with adobe, and in November the alumni (more than 200 since 1915, ranging from archbishop to missionary) come for a day of remembering and merriment.

The years pass, and the seminarian, like the young Christ in the hidden time of Nazareth, grows in grace and wisdom before God and men; his class advances steadily from the minor level to philosophy to theology—and the day of ordination.

"Looking back, it doesn't seem like a long time at all," muses Father Angel Lagdameo, an ascetic-looking, bespectacled Josefino from the diocese of Quezon. The 24-year-old priest was ordained last December in Lucban, where he was born: he is back at San Jose, to complete his theological studies. As far as he can recall, he had "always wanted to be a priest—a secular priest in order to reach more people." The "cura" in his home town, a close friend of the family, was one of his childhood heroes—"a saintly, humorous man"—and quietly, insistently, the dream grew of someday "becoming like him." His sense of vocation, the conviction that God was calling him to the priesthood, became stronger, clearer, he says, with each year at the seminary, which he entered 12 years ago as a high school student.

As a young boy in Lucban, he was not unusually pious—"Sunday Mass, at the most"—but even then he sensed that "the most important thing is to serve God." His desire to be a priest was not attended by visions or angelic voices, nor did it occasion any anguish of choice or doubt: "It was as though everything was pointing in that direction. I couldn't imagine myself studying for anything else, pursuing some other career. My mother was all for it, and of course that helped a lot . . ." He is grateful to his professors at San Jose for helping him "realize" his "dream," and he looks forward to "working with and for people" in Quezon—"most probably in my home town."

By his own account, the course of Father Lagdameo's vocation has been a placid, uncomplicated one, and in that respect he resembles most seminarians who were drawn to the priesthood early in life: from the beginning there was no question of taking any other road. Others traveled a longer route involving not a few detours before they found themselves at San Jose. One such fellow with a "delayed" vocation is crewcut, boyish-looking Nicolas Mesa, Jr., of the archdiocese of Manila, who at 26 is in his first year of A.B. as a minor seminarian.

Mesa graduated from La Salle with a commerce degree, major in accounting, in 1960, and worked for Philamlife until the middle of last year, when he decided to enter the seminary. Behind that decision, he says, were years of "wrestling" with his vocation; he had begun "thinking about the priesthood" when he was in kindergarten at the Holy Ghost Institute run by sisters in Tarlac, where his father, an army officer, was then assigned. After high school at Mapua Tech, he enrolled at La Salle, and there became good friends with the college chaplain, Father Felix Perez, an alumnus of San Jose. "During college and after graduation," says Mesa, "there was always the idea of the priesthood at the back of my mind somehow, but I couldn't come to a decision, and I let things slide. I went around, had fun, parties, the usual things, but I couldn't get rid of the thought that I wasn't doing what I was meant to do . . ." He began seeing Father Perez again, and going to the sacraments more frequently than he was wont to do, and reading about the Faith—"Sheen, Sheed, *The Imitation of Christ.*"

Last July, he made up his mind "to give San Jose a try." He appears quite happy about the turn of events; his father, who tried to dissuade him from entering, "now thinks it was a great idea." Still two years from his first *sotana*, Mesa seems undaunted by the prospect of being in his mid-thirties when he finishes his seminary training. He hopes someday "to serve God more fully as a missionary priest."

Another latecomer who is certain that the priesthood is his real vocation is Jose Silverio, Jr., of the diocese of Bacolod, brother of Luis, the famous golfer. He is 30, finished architecture at UST in 1956, is now in his final year of theology. Like Mesa, he started thinking early about becoming a priest; in Bacolod City, where he grew up, he often served Mass—"but through high school and later at UST, I'd tell myself, whenever the idea came to mind, that the priesthood wasn't for me. It was for others so disposed, others more worthy. It wasn't until after graduation, when I was working for an architectural firm in Bacolod, that I began to see things in a different light. I realized that if everyone who felt drawn to the priesthood thought like me, there would never be any priests. I guess that was the turning point. I began seeing the Redemptorist Fathers—they have a monastery in Bacolod, St. Mary's. The folks weren't exactly unanimous in their approval when they learned about my decision, but before long I was on my way to San Jose."

That was in 1957, and the architect-turned-seminarian is scheduled to be ordained this June. A lean, intense, outgoing type, Silverio looks like a natural for parish work: he speaks enthusiastically of the "wonders one can do for young people." At barrio Bago Bantay in Quezon City, where he teaches catechism, he has befriended the neighborhood toughs who barred his way the first time he showed up for his religious instruction class.

"I talked to them," says Silverio. "They gave way. I haven't had trouble from them since. The important thing is to reach them, talk to them, as individuals. In a group they tend to be cocksure, reckless. But when you get to talk to them one at a time, you find they can be nice and friendly. They have problems, like most people, and they seem glad to have someone to tell their troubles to. And I listen, and I talk to them . . . What counts is a dialogue, a personal dialogue, a two-way arrangement. In the liturgy—the Mass, the sacraments, the ceremonies and hymns—the Church seeks the participation, the active sharing of people. The more they understand what it is all about, the stronger, the more joyful will be their faith.

One may know all the doctrines and theories but they won't work, really work with people, unless one can touch their hearts and minds, and get them to stop and listen."

Which about sums up the mission of San Jose: the training of priests the eloquence of whose lives and speech, like Paul's at Athens and Ephesus, would make men pause from their occupations, and listen to the good news of the Resurrection, the glad tidings of their redemption. It is a tradition that spans the centuries since Christ commissioned his apostles to be "fishers of men"; and a spirit as young and vital and hopeful as that of the Church, in the new Pentecost proclaimed by Pope John, opening wide her windows the better to engage in a dialogue with the modern world.

(Free Press, 1965)

The Church and One
Not So Holy Roman Catholic

TO START OFF ON THE PROPER theological note, you could say quite reasonably, in the spirit of the patriarchs and the prophets and in the words of the Nicene Creed, that the whole thing began in the mind of God, "the Father Almighty, maker of heaven and earth, and of all things visible and invisible." If you prefer a less cosmic, a more down-to-earth and human genesis, you could trace it all back to the stable-cave in the little town of a minor colony of the Roman Empire where Jesus was born, he who "became flesh by the Holy Spirit of the Virgin Mary; and was made man."

If you accept the claims of the Roman Catholic Church, you could say it all began atop a mountain in Galilee, with Christ, risen from the dead, telling his followers: "Go, therefore, and make disciples of all nations, baptizing them in the name of the Father, and of the Son, and of the Holy Spirit . . ."

Or you could move up and away, in time, from those events recorded in the Gospels and cite some date when the early Church, persecuted and threatened with extinction under the Roman Empire for over three centuries, survived and found new life and strength—say, 313 A.D., when the Emperor Constantine and his counterpart in the East, Licinius, decreed an end to the ban on Christianity, and legalized the worship of the Man whom a Roman governor had condemned to death. You could single out one of the General Councils early in the Christian era, when the Catholic Church vanquished a clutch of heresies and grew in might and splendor—as at Chalcedon in 451, with the assembled bishops pledging their loyalty to Pope Leo I and declaring: "That is the Faith of the Apostles! All the orthodox among us believe it to be so!"

Or to choose more martial, cataclysmic beginnings, you could point to the Battle of Lepanto in 1571, when an armada under John of Austria (*White founts falling in the court of the sun/ The Zoldan of Byzantium is smiling as they run*) smashed an invading Turkish fleet and saved Europe, and the colonies of Europe, for the Christian faith—a victory ascribed to the intercession of the Virgin of the Holy Rosary, an exalted lady who continues to inspire the rapturous devotion of Catholics to this day, particularly in this country among folk identified in one way or another with the Dominicans of UST.

In the same year as Lepanto, Miguel Lopez de Legazpi took possession of Manila and thus tightened the hold of Catholic Spain on the Philippines, which had been "discovered" a scant 50 years earlier by Magellan, a Portuguese who was no less militantly Catholic than the Spanish sovereign under whom he served. Magellan's landing on Homonhon in 1521, Legazpi's arrival in Cebu in 1565, his formal conquest of Manila in 1571—you could trace the coming of Catholicism in the Philippines back to any of these colonial milestones, for beyond each one unfolded vistas of evangelization for the Spanish missionaries who were to set sail from San Lucar and La Coruña in Spain, and later, from Acapulco in Mexico.

Their Catholic venture, spanning more than three centuries, was fraught with uncertainties and perils, was besieged by sea and by land, assaulted by zealous warriors of hostile creeds; but Sword and Cross would stand fast at the ramparts, aided, it was to be claimed more than once, by the hosts of heaven. Instances of divine intervention could only cheer Catholic hearts, for the Almighty appeared ill-disposed toward other Christians if they were not Catholic, no matter how pure and fervent their own designs on these islands—

as witness what the Dominicans now in Quezon City celebrate each October as *La Naval de Manila*.

In a series of naval battles around Luzon, the outnumbered, outgunned galleons of His Catholic Majesty routed the warships of the Protestant Dutch; never again, goes a Dominican chronicle of the La Naval victories, would "the Dutch . . . disturb the peace and faith of the Islands." In 1652, the Cathedral-Chapter of the Noble and Ever Loyal City of Manila declared that the "victories achieved by Catholic arms . . . must be considered miracles, vouchsafed by God through the intercession of the Blessed Virgin." It was the triumph of Lepanto all over again, the power of the rosary unconfined by time and geography, the Catholic Church rescued from her enemies and receiving a new mandate, as it were, to proceed with its sublime mission. (The more restless natives, it has been noted, regarded that mission with hostile suspicion, but even revolutionary violence could not destroy a faith that had gone native.)

Such then were the fortunes of the friars who labored to Christianize these islands, and by 1800, they were to be found preaching the Good News and supervising the building of churches by forced labor even in the remotest corners of Luzon which earlier missionaries had failed to reach. One such community, in the fastnesses of southern Pangasinan, was the *visita* of San Miguel, which was to become the pueblo of San Miguel de Camiling, and eventually, just Camiling, the name it bears today as a municipality of Tarlac province.

In the 1830s, when it was made a town, Padre Juan Alvarez de Manzano and Padre Benito Fontcuberta, both of the *Sagrado Orden de Predicadores*, came to Camiling, to build a church and minister to the spiritual needs of the Ilocano migrants, refugees from a northern revolt, who had settled on the riverbanks dense with the *kamiring* trees from which the settlement derived its name. Despite the convulsions of the Revolution, and the passage of a world war, the church built by those intrepid Dominicans stands today as sturdy and massive as ever, the town's largest, tallest structure, baroque façade, high dome, soaring pillars and all, a provincial bastion of Catholicism and a monument to its dominant influence: a Fil-Hispanic church of the Roman Catholic Church.

For the Catholic-born subject of this magazine chronicle—let us call him Escolastico, which is as good a Christian name as any—this is where you might say it all began, here in the sanctuary of this parish church where sacred mysteries as old as Christendom have been celebrated each day without fail, for well over 160 years.

YOU COULD, AGAIN, be strictly theological and say that Escolastico was baptized into the Roman Catholic Church because God, who knows and ordains all things, so willed it. But proximately, contingently, as the scholastic philosophers might say, he was received thus into the Church because his parents happened to be Catholic, and the society in which they moved and breathed and had their being expected no less: infants who remained unbaptized for weeks after birth represented at the very least a kind of scandal, an ignorant denial of custom, distressing evidence of parental neglect. The Sacrament of Baptism administered as soon as the baby could be transported to church without risk of damage to its tender tissues—this was both traditional and necessary in Catholic families, which knew that the unbaptized suddenly taken away from what was at best a precarious existence would spend eternity in Limbo, forever banished from the face of God.

So it came to pass that on a January morning in 1933, Escolastico or rather the two-week infant boy who would be christened with a properly Hispanic Christian name, made his first appearance before the high altar of the church in Camiling—not in the baptistry to one side of the nave, but right in the sacristy, for this was a first-class ceremony, complete with a joyful pealing of the smaller bells in the belfry. Escolastico's father was not without ecclesiastical connections, to begin with, and for this jubilant occasion, the baptism of a first-born son, the proud paterfamilias had invited his grand-uncle, a monsignor no less from the archdiocese of Vigan, to preside at the liturgical rites.

Escolastico does not recall the touch of the water by which the Holy Spirit washed away the stain of Original Sin from his infant soul, nor the pinch of salt rubbed into his as yet toothless mouth to indicate that "by the doctrine of faith and the gift of grace, (he) should be delivered from the corruption of sin, experience a relish for good works, and be delighted with the food of divine wisdom." Even if Escolastico as a baby had heard the words being intoned over his tiny head, he would have had to know enough Latin to appreciate the proceedings in the course of which he became a member of the Mystical Body of Christ, a vessel of sanctifying grace, an heir of heaven.

Catholics barely a month old, it has been widely observed, lack the proper response to such solemn ceremonials, usually exhibiting either total indifference or total annoyance. Escolastico in his christening robe and bonnet, formally attired for the first time in his life, probably slept through it all, or got red in the face, kicking and squalling in protest, his furious crying sounding small and strange and faintly echoing between the adobe walls soaring up to the baroque dome where sparrows nested, as the cries of little children sound, frail and fading in the shadowy recesses of a church.

In any event, Escolastico was now a member of the Roman Catholic Church in the Philippines, much like most of the inhabitants of this "the only Christian country in Asia" born since that blessed day in March 1521, when Rajah Humabon and 800 other Cebuanos were baptized, with Magellan as their godfather. One's *ninong* is duty-bound to look after the spiritual if not the physical well-being of his godchild: Escolastico had for baptismal sponsor an uncle who, to put it charitably, was distinguished by an unyielding adherence to Ilocano frugality, and Escolastico grew up without the largess enjoyed by children supplied by Providence with free-spending godfathers. His Tio Ponsong must have assumed that his sister and brother-in-law were sufficient for the job, and so for Escolastico childhood Christmases and birthdays went by with nary a catechetical lesson, much less a silver coin, from his resolutely frugal ninong.

Tio Ponsong was not entirely wrong in his assumption, though, for Escolastico's mother was as devout as any true daughter of the Church you can hope to find in this country. She went to Mass, if not daily, three or four times a week, and among Escolastico's earliest memories of her are of early mornings sweet with the warmth of fresh-baked pan de sal and the gentle fragrance from her brown San Antonio devotional dress when she came home from church and gave him her hand to be kissed. She was always praying a novena to some saint or other; San Antonio was a favorite along with San Vicente Ferrer, and there must have been a dozen other saintly champions to whom she addressed her endless petitions—for peace, for joy and good health, for upright children and whatever else good Christian mothers ask for—to judge from the collection of novena pamphlets she invariably carried to church or kept under the altar at home.

Along a wall of the bedroom where Escolastico slept when a young boy were ranged plaster statues, each about two feet high, of the Sacred Heart, the Immaculate Conception, San Antonio, San Vicente Ferrer and one or two other saints, in rectangular glass cases set on a cloth-covered shelf. Before the images his mother would gather the family for the recitation of the rosary, and quite early in childhood, Escolastico learned to kneel for long minutes without cushions on a hard floor, while his father and mother took turns leading in the prayers and the tiny plaster faces inside the glass cases wavered ever so slightly in the candlelight. *"Preforus . . . preforus . . ."* Escolastico and his younger brother recited in a soothing, somewhat vacant rhythm, while the smoke from the candles plumed thinly toward the ceiling and evening rain or wind rustled acacia leaves on the roof. His mother knew the Litany of Loreto by heart, and Escolastico would listen with a kind of awe to the sighing voice imploring:

Mother most admirable . . .

Virgin most faithful . . .

Seat of wisdom . . .

Cause of our joy . . .

Gate of heaven . . .

Morning star . . .

It was Escolastico's introduction to what may be called the poetry of faith, and in a town still without a parochial school, without nuns to shepherd children to their prayers, the nightly rosary at home constituted his first lessons in religion: the Sorrowful and Joyful and Glorious Mysteries. Supplementing these were a catechism given by an aunt, with line drawings depicting a boy flanked by a devil and an angel, the latter turning away in tears whenever the boy besmirched his heart with mortal sin; and a book of biblical stories, also a gift from some solicitous relation, of which Escolastico now remembers nothing except for a sepia illustration showing St. Peter being led out of prison by an archangel.

WHEN ESCOLASTICO FINALLY had his First Communion, he was way past the age of reason and going on ten; the war was on, and its outbreak must have delayed his reception of the Eucharist. By far the most important event in his young Catholic life, Escolastico's First Communion was by outward standards a lonely, even forlorn affair, for unlike his cousins in the provincial capital with its Holy Ghost Institute run by nuns, he was the lone child communicant that chill dark morning in 1943 or 1944.

The previous day, he had gone to confession, nervously half-whispering to Padre Ablang in the dusty dilapidated booth what boyish faults he could dredge up from his mind. Under a sky still dark with night and powdered with stars, in the silent town, he walked to church with his mother down the main street, past the elementary school building turned Japanese garrison, the shadows of the soldiers keeping watch on the lamplit school porch slanting menacingly on the wall behind them.

It must have been around December, for it was cold, and he shivered both from the chill and the tremendous prospect of swallowing the Body and the Blood of Our Lord Jesus Christ. Sharing with his mother a pew set specially for the two of them within the enclosure formed by the curve of the communion rails, a pew right in front of the altar, Escolastico knelt for the day's first Mass in the flickering dark, his eyes sandpaper-rough from having risen so early, his mouth dry, his knees quivering. Then Padre Ablang was coming toward him bearing a golden ciborium filled with communion wafers, and in a moment it was over, the cardboard taste of God sticking for a numb second or two in his mouth before he could swallow and the dissolving host slid down his throat.

Perhaps that First Communion should have marked an access of piety, of sanctity and heroic virtue and apostolic zeal; but Escolastico after that first nourishment with the Bread of Life seemed, curiously, gradually, to withdraw from the embrace of Holy Mother Church instead of burrowing deeper into her bosom. Whatever the reason—a reaction to the coddlings of childhood, the religious indifference of his closest friends, the upsurge of new energies, the clamor of newly discovered interests, not the least of which was the profound mystery of the female anatomy—whatever it was, Ticong, as he was now called by the equally restless companions with whom he roamed the town and swam in the river and ogled the girls, soon stopped going to confession and communion and forgot about praying altogether. Where before he had run home on hearing the first tentative strokes of the Angelus—in full tone the church bell had a massive somber clang that hovered reverberating over the town— now he lingered long after dusk in the plaza, in the company of degenerate and blasphemous elements, the very same characters whom his mother and aunts and spinster cousins tended to dismiss as being beyond salvation.

Spiritually, Ticong made little or no progress in high school, although on Sundays and feast days he managed to make it to church, and then only out of a vague sense of obligation. So deplorable was his Catholic conduct at this stage that, on a Good Friday, even as the townsfolk commemorated the Passion and Death with a somber procession, he together with some friends saw fit to spy on a barrio couple locked in passionate rapture in the shadows under the bridge. The private nonsectarian high school, which had unceremoniously absorbed him after the primary grades, made no provisions for the religious welfare of students, a state of affairs no one bothered to question. It was just the way things were, in that town and in that time not long after the Liberation. In his frame of mind Ticong found the secular setup quite natural and acceptable, except perhaps for the fact that the principal happened to be his father, a situation which strained their relations somewhat.

Now a staunch Catholic in his own fashion, a stolid believer in fidelity, honor, industry, and not sparing the rod, Ticong's father had, by his own admission, been a bit of an anticlerical in his UP student days, an irreverent critic of the clergy. A number of uncles and cousins in Abra and Ilocos Sur were ordained priests, and as a young man it seems he had been urged no end to follow in their clerical footsteps; but he had other plans and consequently developed an allergy to anything remotely resembling a cassock. But by the time Ticong was a gangling lad in high school, his father had long discarded his disdain for men of the cloth, and got along famously with the new parish priest, a tall, bulky, rather swarthy veteran of the archdiocese, a quietly efficient man with pensive bloodshot eyes and an odor of cigars about him.

The *cura parroco* bore the name Francisco Gago, a name that could not but startle Ticong when he first heard it; he wonders about it still, years after the priest suffered a heart attack and went to his heavenly reward. The name, so bluntly unflattering, to say the least, must have been a cross that the priest had to carry through life, Ticong used to think; but after the first incredulous response, the Catholics of Camiling got used to it: "Father Gago," the name pronounced with respect and affection. Perhaps it was one more proof of the supernatural qualities of the Roman Catholic Church: that so stupid and abusive-sounding a name could not detract from the worth of the man nor the cause that he served so gallantly to the end.

The priest was not without detractors, to be sure: the town drunk whom Ticong heard one evening shouting out the Padre's name clear across the plaza, and the local gossips who insisted that the cleric from Pangasinan was father not only to spiritual children, that the lovely girl and her brother who occasionally visited with him in the *convento* were actually of his flesh and blood. This was not exactly appalling news to the elite of the elect, as far as Ticong could tell: they must have revered the vocation if not the man inside the cassock, and such fealty Ticong was to discover, years later, in himself and in other Filipinos, even among avowed skeptics. A certain deference toward priests seems an ineradicable part of the culture, so that even the crudest jokes about the clergy convey a kind of inverted awe.

Surely no joking matter was the faith and its ceremonials to Father Gago's ardent disciples: Catholics like Doña Salud, who had much to thank the Lord for, including the town's biggest rice mill; and Mr. Galang, who suffered from diabetes and rheumatism but, like Job, still found ample reason to thank God. Mr. Galang, who lived across the street from Ticong's house, was probably the most devout of the lot, being not only a daily communicant but a tireless Bible reader and quoter as well, particularly of the Apocalypse of Saint John. Ever anxious about the good of his neighbor, he came to inform Ticong's father one afternoon, when the sky had assumed an ominous reddish tint, that the end of the world was coming that weekend or the next few days. The world did not end, neither did Mr. Galang's afflictions, some of which were of an intriguing nature, if Ticong's more adventurous friends were to be believed. As they related it, they had climbed the santol tree in Mr. Galang's backyard one night and from their illegal perch had seen the old man prompting, by candlelight, a female member of his household to do penance: which was not too unusual, except that the poor woman was tied by the wrists to a huge wooden cross.

But in the light of day, Mr. Galang looked anything but mysterious and inquisitorial, just another *catolico cerrado* with a mild frown, a shade too intense in his devotions perhaps, but in demeanor hinting of no nocturnal demons to exorcise. The same could be said of the rest of Father Gago's placid practicing Catholics, undisturbed by the unbelieving and the indifferent, or by stigmata and such Catholic signs and wonders. The parish priest did not levitate while celebrating Mass, no peasant girl saw apparitions of the Blessed Virgin, no heretic bothered to nail his thesis on the church door. The closest to a disruption of the church calendar was when the Bishop, in town for the fiesta's *misa cantada*, refused communion to some women in sleeveless dresses. Through the liturgical seasons the same tiny spinster went on playing the organ in the choir loft, and the three old *cantores* like frail stragglers from the Revolution failed to discourage the faithful, no matter how earnestly they mangled the Latin responses.

Vatican II and the hopping *cursillistas* and the "liberation" priests were still a long way off in the future, and Father Gago celebrated Mass facing the high altar, his back to the people, as his predecessors had done since the founding of the Parish of San Miguel Arcangel. The rites within reflected the sameness of the limestone façade, the sheer bulk of which made the church appear to Ticong as being much older and more immovable than the Zambales mountains looming beyond the long roof of the convento. Sometimes, in the plaza at sunset, Ticong would happen to glance at the church dome, high and pale in the last light: above it billows of luminous clouds filled the western sky. The montage of dome, clouds and sundown suggested immense, unknown distances.

SO THEN, THE CATHOLIC CHURCH for Ticong when he was twelve or thirteen was, among other personages and things, Father Gago vigorously sprinkling holy water up and down the aisles before the start of Mass, Father Gago preaching the Sunday sermon from the pulpit adorned with floral curlicues and the faces of angels.

At the main entrance to the church stood a wooden screen on which was painted a local artist's uninspired concept of Saint Peter's Basilica atop a hill, with streams of grace flowing down to the multitudes below; in the pale blue sky hung a triangle framing the Eye of God staring in baleful welcome at parishioners coming in from the warm dusty street. Behind this screen and on the very last bench from the altar, Ticong sat listening to snatches of Father Gago's homilies. More often than not Ticong's mind and eyes wandered during Mass, his fancy flitting among a stupendous variety of subjects such as only a crowded Catholic church contains: latecomers searching for seats, trends in local fashion and footwear, the ponytail of a girl some pews away, Tio Gilber's thinning hair, Tia Luring's diamond earrings, the pillars made out of kamiring trunks (eight on either side), the rafters of the high unceilinged roof from which droplets of bat urine sometimes sprayed down like unholy water on the hapless congregation.

The idle contemplation of church art helped pass the time: San Antonio and San Martin de Porres and Santa Teresita in their respective side niches, the *carrozas* parked in the corridor leading off to the convento, the left side altar with San Roque perched on top, with a dog that seemed to be lapping up the wound on his leg, and most imposing of all, the retable like some Renaissance vision of heaven, populated by a galaxy of *santos* led by Saint Michael the Archangel, the town's patron, enshrined above the altar thrusting a spear into fallen Lucifer's neck.

The churchgoers, for their part, provided a budding sociologist with ample material for analysis, representing as they did a cross-section of the town's populace. Often would Ticong find his curiosity drawn, even as the Holy Sacrifice proceeded at the altar, to a large family ranged in a pew, or to a barrio couple shuffling barefoot down a side aisle, or an old woman in rumpled *baro't saya* draped with scapulars, or one of the town's rich, broad-rumped matrons fingering a gleaming rosary. The holy water font where parishioners blessed themselves was the scene of diverting mini-rites, men and women executing the sign of the cross in diverse ways, patting their heads and chests with more than the prescribed gestures, their genuflections likewise following no set pattern, some making a profound bow toward the altar, others settling for a kind of one-step hop.

But what was more revealing was the ranking of pews: the landed families had the more handsome and cushioned pews out front, with their names on the backrests, "Familia Bengzon," "Familia Kipping," and so on, while the less affluent invariably occupied the middle rows, and the lower middle class and the proletariat chose to crowd into the rear benches. The stratification of society seemed then to be a natural, inevitable process in the sight of God if not in the eyes of rebels, of whom the rice-rich province was to spawn quite a few.

But at the communion rail, class divisions dissolved into egalitarian ranks: without push or pull, everyone waited for his turn to receive the Bread of Life. Contrary to what the unbelievers preached, you were saved or condemned regardless of your social status, sartorial style and capacity to contribute to the coffers of the Church.

FOR ALL HIS INATTENTION, the teenage Ticong sometimes found himself listening earnestly to Father Gago pontificating from the pulpit. One sermon he remembers following in its entirety, a discourse in impassioned Ilocano on the Gospel for the First Sunday of Advent: "At that time Jesus said to his disciples: 'There will be signs in the sun, the moon, and the stars. On the earth nations will be in anguish, distraught at the roaring of the sea and the waves. Men will die of fright in anticipation of what is coming over the earth . . . ' " Judgment Day: *Ukum* in Ilocano, as dreadful a word as doom, with a final, irrevocable sound to it. Ticong imagined the earth writhing and shattering in the fire of God's wrath, and the souls of the damned cascading like coals into the blazing pits of hell.

At the Consecration he knelt with sweating hands clasped tightly, gazed fervently at the Body of Christ in an anguish of faith, love and penitence, asking the Trinity, the Blessed Virgin, Saint Michael and other saints who cared to listen, to deliver him from eternal damnation. Chastened, he emerged into the same everyday world outside; the sun shone on the same plaza and streets and houses he had always known, but he felt, perhaps for the first time in his life, the inherent impermanence of all created things, the transitoriness of the visible world and all that it promised or contained.

How long this somber mood, this consciousness of the Last Things possessed him, Escolastico cannot recall; most likely no more than a couple of days, such were the fluctuations of thought and feeling in a boy so immersed in the life flowing ceaselessly about him. If he had heard voices or seen visions . . . But the passage of time, the sense of motion and change and the end as well as the beginning of things, and almost always, an intimation of a wisdom and a love and a power in but not of this world—these would visit him again, returning even after long lapses from grace, after extended wanderings from the heart of his childhood faith in pursuit of some happiness outside the religious truths he had first learned as a young boy.

At the Ateneo de Manila, the college founded by the Jesuits in 1859—alma mater of many distinguished Filipinos from Jose Rizal to Emil Jurado, from Gregorio del Pilar to Reli German—Esky, as the provinciano Ticong came to be addressed in acknowledgment of his status as a Manila college freshman: Esky was to learn more about that faith into which he had been born. He was fifteen, a boarder in a dormitory in Ermita, feeling quite alone and homesick, not yet at home in the new world in which he must find himself: the Quonset huts and acacias on Padre Faura and a whole unexplored city waiting at the junctions of unfamiliar streets, that first month of the rainy season of his first year in the city. Closer than he thought but still ahead were a myriad experiences and revelations of an entirely different order from anything he had known. Yet in the deepest center of it all, in the core of all the new knowledge that came rushing at his heart, intellect and will, there shone still, as he was to reflect years later, the same faith that had claimed him as a child.

The accidents of a thing change, but not its essence, as his Jesuit philosophy professors would say; and Escolastico or Ticong or Esky, in some wordless way, knew this to be true of the Christian faith as proclaimed by the Catholic Church, when he knelt in the college chapel to pray to the same Christ he had first received in communion, a long time ago, it seemed, in the old church in his hometown, in Tarlac. (About the essence, the fundamentals of the faith—what would baffle and bother Escolastico was some baptized Catholic's rejection, renouncement, of what the Church taught and stood for without first knowing what these were, as found in books written, say, in the last 1000 years. More understandable was a non-Catholic's unfamiliarity with the works of Augustine, Aquinas, Maritain, Chesterton, Merton, Sheen, Sheed, de la Costa, Arevalo, Bernad, Rahner and John Paul II.)

He was a Catholic growing up, still to encounter the full force of the hungers and afflictions that are the lot of every man born into the world. He was fifteen and still growing, and beginning at last to learn about the life and history and nature and vision of the Catholic Church, in a deeper, more reflective way; a seeking and a learning that he in the future might grow weary of or be discouraged from or even pretend to spurn but could never really disown or abandon, any more than he could deny his own name, ancestry and birthrights—which include, he would someday come to believe with the full assent of heart and intellect, a claim on the legacy of the Faith that flamed to life from an empty tomb 2000 years ago: the inheritance of the Resurrection accepted, acclaimed, celebrated through the centuries, from Peter to the present Pope, from Stephen to the other day's martyrs at the gates of cruel cities, from Paul to the missionaries laboring now in the Global Village, the Patricks and Francis Xaviers of our time, Mother Teresa and her nuns serving the poorest of the poor, the sick and the dying, for love of the Risen Lord. All of them, the famous and the exalted, and the vast majority of the faithful, the humble, obscure multitudes such as Jesus gathered on the roads and hillsides of Galilee and Judea— with everyone of them, in the ultimate democracy that is Christianity,

Escolastico would be persuaded to think, he shares the same hopes, favors and gifts. The spiritual citizenship makes all equal in the truest sense, with pontiff and peasant, cardinal and clerk and housemaid entitled to common privileges and rewards, and subject to the greatest of the commandments, which is to love and serve God and fellowmen.

"Pray for us, O Holy Mother of God"—Mother of Our Savior, Virgin Most Powerful, Refuge of Sinners, Queen of All Saints; the same most gracious Blessed Virgin of Bethlehem and Nazareth, and of Guadalupe, Walshingham, Czestochowa, Manaoag, Lourdes and Fatima—"pray for us, that we may be made worthy of the promises of Christ."

So then, in spite of what he might become or what he might do or fail to do, he would with God's grace, God's graciousness, and the intercession of Mary, be found worthy of the assurances of the Resurrection.

That hope, Escolastico would tell you if you should ask him today, many years away from that boy kneeling in the chapel on Padre Faura—that hope is what being a Christian means.

(Sunburst, 1974)

For Love of Lourdes

BECAUSE OF WHAT HAPPENED THERE 141 years ago this month, a town in the southwest of France has become one of the most famous places in the world. As many as five million people from different lands go there each year, making it more popular and busier than Jerusalem or Fatima or even Rome as a center of Christian pilgrimage.

Because something most unusual and marvelous happened there on February 11, 1858, a lot of the women in our country will put on their best white dress, with a blue sash around the waist, and go to church on this day with more than the customary fervor of Sunday. Many of the menfolk too, minus that dress and sash, of course, but most likely with the rosaries they may not usually have in their pockets.

For it's the great feast of the Virgin Mary as Our Lady of Lourdes—a grand fiesta that's certainly not just for the girls, as you'll very well see if you join the crowds in our parish church on Kanlaon, in Quezon City. Lourdes Church is the principal shrine in the country of the Blessed Virgin Mary under that title, as was the original church of the Capuchins in prewar Intramuros. Dedicated to her, it bears as well the name of that town in France where it all began that February, when the Mother of God appeared to a 14-year-old peasant girl named Bernadette Soubirous.

One of the first things we learned about the town of Bernadette, on our first visit there back in the '60s, was that the townsfolk pronounce its name as a single syllable: "Loord," which rhymes with "moored"—an intriguing phonetic touch, one thought, stirring ancient echoes. For as the guidebooks tell us, the Moors captured the town when it was a Roman outpost 2,000 years ago, and an Arab chief converted to Christianity was its first elected mayor after it was in turn conquered by Charlemagne.

From the 19th century on, French and English fought over Lourdes, until 1406, when the French took over for good. Its central hilltop fortress made it the most strategic bastion in that mountainous region near the border with Spain.

Old prints show Lourdes as no more than that medieval fort and a cluster of stone houses in the time of the Apparitions. The town has since acquired a huge railway station, over 300 hotels, entire blocks of shops offering religious articles and souvenirs, and at all hours a swarming, clamorous, commercial bustle—but not on the other side of the river Gave, the Domain of Our Lady. To the believer, that is hallowed ground, the site of the Visions, the Grotto and the healing spring; the public rituals, the candle processions—and the miracles.

On afternoons when the rain lifts and the sun floods the great square before the Rosary Basilica, a multitude gathers for the blessing of the sick, the invalids and the crippled in wheelchairs or on wheeled stretchers.

The officiating Bishop raises the Blessed Sacrament in the bright air and with the monstrance traces the sign of the cross over the suffering faces. From the kneeling throng rises the thundering roll of the invocations, in Latin, French, English and other languages: "Lord, if Thou wilt, Thou canst make us whole . . . Mary, Mother of God, pray for us! Saint Bernadette, pray for us!"

It is in such moments, we are told, that the miracles happen.

Suddenly, the "lightning of the supernatural" would strike a man, woman or child in the last stages of some terminal disease. The chosen one would be made whole, cured, completely, instantaneously—by the power of God, it is believed, and through the intercession of the Immaculate Virgin, whose name is invoked.

Thousands of such instant cures have been reported in the more than 140 years of the Shrine. But the nonsectarian Medical Bureau, established in Lourdes in 1884 and under the supervision of an international association of 5,000 doctors, has recognized fewer than 2,000 of these cures as "inexplicable by medical science."

The bishops commissioned to review the "inexplicable" cures have proved to be even more rigorous than the physicians—the Church has pronounced only 67 cases as "miraculous." The vast majority of those who have gone to Lourdes in hopes of a cure have left unhealed—but, as many have testified, they were granted another "miracle," the gift of fortitude, even joy, in their suffering.

THE WISE OF THIS WORLD will smile at such faith. Emile Zola wrote a novel that dismissed the wonders of Lourdes as "human credulity, the need to believe in the Lie." The determined rationalist would explain away the Lourdes miracles as the workings of hysteria or mass hypnosis or "still unknown forces of mind and energy."

As Cardinal Newman said, "A miracle is no argument to one who is, on principle, an atheist." Still, there has been no lack of able defenders of Lourdes even outside Catholic bishopric and pulpit, as witness the scientist and Nobel laureate Alexis Carrel's *Voyage to Lourdes*, Protestant Ruth Cranston's widely translated *The Miracle of Lourdes*, and the works of the English journalists Alan Neame and Patrick Marnham.

Franze Werfel wrote *The Song of Bernadette* in thanksgiving after the people of Lourdes gave him refuge from the Jew-hunting Nazis in 1940. "For those who believe," he counseled his readers (and those who would see the film based on his book that starred Jennifer Jones as Bernadette), "no explanation is necessary . . ."

That may be so—but there is, one is led to think, an "explanation." And that is the love of Our Lady—such a love for all men and women redeemed by her Son, such an abiding concern for humankind, that she won't confine herself to a distant heaven or, on earth, to Nativity scenes, pious images and religious pageantry. She refuses to be made mythical, unreal, unreachable, and so appears and speaks to those whom she chooses to be her messengers, as she did at Lourdes—to give assurance of her compassion, which reflects the love of Christ, for the poor, the sick, the afflicted, the oppressed, as well as those who cannot bring themselves to believe in her.

The February feast of Our Lady of Lourdes celebrates the compassion of the woman who has been called (because God chose her from the beginning) "the world's First Love."

(Graphic, 1999)

The Day the Sun Danced for Our Lady of Fatima

"LOOK AT THE SUN!" the little girl cried out to the crowd.

She was ten years old, and her name was Lucia dos Santos. A child with "a happy disposition, very playful and affectionate," recalled her eldest sister, Maria; and "a chatterbox, never still for a moment," as described by her uncle, Manuel Marto.

But now she was standing quite still, face to the sky with an expectant intensity far beyond that of children at play.

Together with her even younger cousins, Francisco and Jacinta Marto, she stood beside a small oak tree in the middle of a vast crowd—as many as 70,000 people, most accounts of that October day 77 years ago in Portugal would agree, gathered in the hollow of rock-strewn field and pastureland called Cova da Iria.

The people had started arriving in that remote and desolate spot since early the previous day, despite continuous rain from a storm sweeping across the country. From around the Serra de Aire, the mountainous central region, and from Coimbra, and the capital, Lisbon, and Setutal and Sines farther south, they had come on foot or in carts and cars over the muddy roads, converging in the rain on the long, oval depression like a natural amphitheater about a mile from the village of Aljustrel, the birthplace of Lucia dos Santos and her cousins, in the town of Fatima—for word had spread that a "great miracle" would take place there at noon of October 13, 1917.

It had continued to rain all morning. At noon it was still raining, when suddenly Lucia cried, "The Lady is here! Put down your umbrellas!"

One after another the umbrellas came down. The people waited in the rain, praying the rosary, singing their ancient hymns to the Blessed Virgin. But some now began to murmur in disappointment, others cursed aloud and bewailed their futile, miserable vigil, for the multitude was as human, diverse and restless as any drawn by the promise of the marvelous since the time of Christ.

The people closest to Lucia by the *azinheira* tree saw her uplifted face turn rapturous, radiant—as if reflecting, one witness was to say later, "a white light shining from an invisible source." Then: "Look at the sun!"

What happened next, men and women of this earth had never seen before and may never see again: an astounding spectacle that burst forth with an awesome, almost apocalyptic power witnessed, not by a few favored individuals in an exclusive trance, but by tens of thousands of people.

Whatever it was in the verdict of believer or unbeliever, there is no denying that something most unusual and astonishing occurred that noonday at Fatima, in that country on the western rim of Europe seven decades and seven years ago this week; an event, moreover, that remains one of the most documented in our insatiably curious and crowded century . . .

The rain stopped. The clouds parted and the sun appeared. The people looked up and were amazed. For the sun, as recounted by several hundred eye-witnesses, had become like a pale, metallic disc that everyone could gaze at without being blinded.

One account which can hardly be called an effusion of hysterical piety was written by a journalist at the scene, Avelino de Almeida, and published in the anticlerical government newspaper, *O Seculo*, "without comment":

"From the road, where the vehicles were parked . . . one could see the immense multitude turn toward the sun. . . . It looked like a plaque of dull silver, and it was possible to look at it without the least discomfort. It might have been an eclipse which was taking place. But at that moment a great shout went up, and one could hear the specta-tors nearest at hand shouting, 'A miracle! A miracle!'

"Before the astonished eyes of the crowd . . . the sun trembled, made sudden incredible movements outside all cosmic laws—the sun 'danced,' in the typical expression of the people . . .

"People then began to ask one another what they had seen. The great majority admitted to having seen the trembling and the danc-ing of the sun; others affirmed that they saw the face of the Blessed Virgin; others, again, swore that the sun whirled on itself like a giant Catherine wheel and that it lowered itself to the earth as if to burn it in its rays . . . they saw it change color successively. . . ."

Another correspondent's account, in the Lisbon paper, *O Dia*, told of how the sky "illuminated the vast landscape with a strange light . . . The grey mother-of-pearl tone turned to silver as the clouds were torn apart and the silver sun, enveloped in the same grey light, was seen to whirl and turn in the circle of broken clouds. A cry went up from everyone and people fell on their knees on the muddy ground . . .

"The streaks of light turned blue as if coming through the stained-glass windows of a cathedral and spread over the people who knelt with outstretched hands. The blue faded and then the light seemed to pass through yellow glass. Yellow stains fell on white handker-chiefs, against the dark skirts of the women . . . People wept and prayed and uncovered heads . . ."

Dr. Domingos Pinto Coelho, an eye specialist, wrote in the news-paper *Ordem:* "The sun, at one moment surrounded with scarlet flame, at another aureoled in yellow and deep purple, seemed to be moving, whirling rapidly, at times appearing to be loosened from the sky and to be approaching the earth, strongly radiating heat."

Dr. Almedia Garrett, a professor at the University of Coimbra, saw "the sun's disc spinning round on itself in a mad whirl. Then, suddenly, one heard a clamor, cries of anguish rising from all the people. The sun, whirling wildly, seemed to break loose from the fir-mament and advance threateningly upon the earth as if to crush us with its huge and fiery weight . . ."

Said Maria da Capelinha, a devout woman from Aljustrel: "The sun turned everything into different colors . . . Then it shook and trembled. It looked like a wheel of fire that was going to fall on the people. They began to cry out, 'We shall all be killed!' Others called to Our Lady to save them . . ."

Manuel Marto, father of Francisco and Jacinta, declared in his testimony: "What was most extraordinary was that the sun did not hurt our eyes . . . Then, the sun appeared to stop spinning. It began to move and dance in the sky until it seemed to detach itself from the sky and fall upon us. It was such a terrible moment."

Wrote Father Manuel Pereira da Silva: "The sun appeared with its circumference well-defined. It came down as if to the height of the clouds and began to whirl giddily upon itself like a captive ball of fire. With some interruptions, this lasted for about eight minutes . . ."

In a pastoral letter, Dom Jose Alves Correia da Silva, Bishop of the Diocese of Leiria, which included the parish of Fatima, remarked on "the most marvelous nature of the solar phenomenon of October 13":

"The children had foretold the day and the hour at which it would occur . . . in spite of bad weather, several thousands congregated at the spot . . . they witnessed all the manifestations of the sun which paid homage to the Queen of heaven and earth . . .

"This phenomenon, which was not registered in any astronomical observatory, and could not, therefore, have been of natural origin, was witnessed by people of every category and class, by believers as well as by unbelievers, journalists of the principal newspapers and even by people miles away, a fact which destroys any theory of collective hallucination."

In October 1930, after eight years of study by a canonical commission, the Bishop of Leiria pronounced the visions of the children "worthy of belief" and officially permitted the cult of Our Lady of Fatima.

Lucia dos Santos had said that during one of the apparitions at Fatima, the "Lady of the Rosary" had told her: "In October I will perform a miracle so that everyone can believe."

AN ELOQUENT ADVOCATE of Our Lady of Fatima was the late Father Horacio de la Costa. In an address delivered November 3, 1950, before the First Friday Club in Boston, and later published in the journal, *Catholic Mind*, the Jesuit scholar, historian and future Provincial of the Society of Jesus in the Philippines dwelt on three aspects of the apparitions at Fatima which struck him as particularly significant.

The first, said Father de la Costa, is that "the Mother of God revealed herself to the three children, Lucia, Jacinta and Francisco, as a Lady of Light."

Lucia described Our Lady, he said, as "all of light," as wearing a tunic and mantle that were like "waves of light." The folds of her dress were "not really folds" but "undulated light," and what appeared to be the gold edging of her mantle was an "intenser light."

Each of the monthly apparitions—six in all, from May to October 1917—was "announced by a flash of light" and accompanied by "unusual changes in the color of sunlight." Such was the brightness of the apparition that Jacinta and Francisco at times could not look directly on the face of the Blessed Virgin. And "the multitude present at the last apparition at Fatima, freethinkers and skeptics as well as the devout, saw with their own eyes the great miracle of the sun"—a prodigy of whirling, streaming light which, according to some interpreters, signified Our Lady's "power over the fiery portents of the atomic age."

Said Father de la Costa in his lucid discourse: "Light, then dazzling light, would seem to be one of the dominant themes of Fatima; and it may not altogether be a coincidence that the one to whom Our Lady principally addressed herself was christened Lucia: a derivative of the Latin word for light."

The second significant element is that Our Lady mentioned in all her messages communicated to the three children "the fact of sin; our need to realize the gravity of sin; our need to make reparation for our sin and the sins of others."

The Immaculate Virgin asked the children to accept the suffering that God would send them "in reparation for sins" and "for the conversion of sinners." She commanded them to pray the rosary daily, to help bring peace to the world—it was the third year of the First World War—"thus suggesting that there exists an essential connection between avoidance of sin, between reparation for sin, and the establishment of world peace."

In the final apparition at Fatima, Our Lady's message, said Father de la Costa, was clear and explicit: "People must amend their lives. They must not offend God any more. He is already much offended." She insisted on conversion as "an urgent and immediate need . . . because upon it depends not only the salvation of souls but the peace of the world."

It is but presumptuous folly, a vain and perilous delusion, then, to believe that the issue of peace or war is resolved only in the councils of the powerful and the wise of this world. God's justice and mercy have much to do with it, and the intercession of the Blessed Mother, the prayers and penance of the humble and contrite, and the petitions of little children can save us all (as they already have, many now believe) from falling into the abyss of global war—for many years until the collapse of communism in the Soviet Union in 1991, the threat of a nuclear doomsday for the planet.

The third important aspect of Fatima concerns Russia.

"In 1929 Lucia, already by that time a lay sister, wrote to the Holy Father asking him to consecrate Russia to the Immaculate Heart of Mary. There is some doubt as to whether the Pope received the message in the form she drafted it. At any rate nothing was done about it until 1943, when Pope Pius XII consecrated the whole world, with special mention of Russia, to the Immaculate Heart. A year previously Lucia wrote that Our Lady, at her second apparition in July 1917, had said: 'If my demands are listened to, Russia will be converted and there will be a period of peace. Otherwise Russia will spread her errors throughout the world, stirring up wars and persecutions of the Church.'"

There has been "some hesitation," Father de la Costa took care to note, about accepting this part of the message as authentic. Those who doubt or object to it allege that Lucia made mention of it, not at the time of the apparitions nor in the course of the canonical inquiry, but only at the "very late date" of 1942. Moreover, unlike the other Fatima messages, this communication does not have the "corroborative evidence" of the other children, both dead, and "rests entirely on Lucia's bare assertion."

This detail of a private revelation (as distinct from the declared, definitive creed of the Church, to which she demands assent) today invites conjecture at least, in this era of Gorbachev and Yeltsin many years removed from the cold war tremors of the 1950s.

While a novice of the Sisters of Santa Dorotea in Tuy, Spain, had Lucia dos Santos come under the influence of an emigré-confessor who had suffered under the Bolsheviks? Had Sister Maria das Dores perhaps been persuaded to help in an anti-Communist crusade by some ultraconservative superior who saw Stalin's Soviet Union as the archfoe of Christianity and who was even then alarmed by leftwing agitation in Portugal and Spain?

On the other hand, said Father de la Costa, there is the draft of Lucia's letter to Pius XI about the consecration of Russia, written in

1929—"fully seven years before the Communist attempt to seize power in Spain." Furthermore, "Lucia, in spite of the difficulties and doubts, has stuck firmly to her statement . . . we may, I think, consider at least as solidly probable that Lucia did receive some communication from Our Lady regarding Russia, even if we cannot be quite sure . . . of the terms of the message."

Lucia herself has explained that she "sensed rather than heard Our Lady speaking to her in so many words"—saints and mystics of the Church have had the same "ineffable experience." But the substance of "what Lucia understood from Our Lady we can all by this time understand: that the peace of the world depends to a great extent on Russia . . ."

Indeed, to reflect on the messages of Fatima, Father de la Costa declared, is to be reminded that "the various manifestations of Our Lady, of which we have historical record, have invariably taken place at the frontiers of Christendom, and precisely at that frontier which is most in danger."

The threatened frontiers were geographical during the Middle Ages, in Spain, Portugal, England and Poland—thus, the apparitions and the great historic shrines of the Blessed Virgin in Zaragoza, Alcobaca, Walshingham and Czestochowa.

The frontiers under siege have also been of the mind and the spirit—thus, the visions of Juan Diego in Guadalupe, during the Spanish conquest of Mexico, to bring enlightenment to the arrogant colonizer and assure a conquered people of Our Lady's care and protection; and in France, the Immaculate Conception revealing herself to Bernadette at Lourdes, when the "devastating rationalism" of the 19th century mocked the Christian faith, and miracles of healing soon "brought many a skeptic to the feet of the Mother of God."

In 1917, when the Communists seized power in Russia, in the very month of the "miracle of the sun" at Fatima, the frontiers were "more than geographical or economic or social or political" and have remained so in our time—for Our Lady, said Father de la Costa, made it clear that peace in the world, peace in the nuclear age, is "above all a moral problem, the problem of sin."

Not the sin alone of those who would wage war on "Christian men and Christian things" to advance the Marxist-Leninist millennium: "*Our* sin, too . . . for heavy though the guilt of the Communist leaders may be, we are in part responsible. Through our social injustices, through the heartless exploitation of the workingman and of colonial peoples, through the mad pursuit of sinful pleasure while the less fortunate die of hunger and disease . . .

"For the heart of our crucial problem, the problem of peace, is the fact of sin; and to dispel the darkness of that dark and disobedient heart it is to Our Lady of Light that we must go."

Light: to cast out the dark idolatry of our pride, hypocrisy, greed, lust, falsehood, hatred, violence and indifference to the sufferings of others; light such as that supernatural radiance in which the shepherd children beheld the Blessed Virgin at Fatima, where now stands her resplendent Sanctuary on hallowed ground once bathed in the rays of a whirling sun; such light as suffused and surrounded the figure of the Mother of God at the Cova da Iria, the same Virgin Mary, Mother of Christ, whose power comes from her Son to whom she seeks to draw all men; the same Virgin most renowned, Nuestra Señora, she of the innumerable titles and devotions, salutations and shrines from Nazareth to Montserrat, from Manaoag to Medjugorje; Ang Mahal na Birhen, Help of Christians, Queen of Peace, Our Lady of the Most Holy Rosary who is hailed and honored in our country in the luminous splendor of her festival of La Naval de Manila in October.

(Sunday Inquirer, 1988)

Love According to Therese

WHO IS THIS THERESE, and why are they saying all these things about her? And this month, and through March, and on to the last week of April, why all the hustle and bustle, the commotion and clamor, the fervor and rapture of crowds throughout the country over what's called a reliquary, something like a treasure chest containing, of all things, bits of bone from the mortal remains of this Therese, for heaven's sake?

She was French and a Carmelite nun who lived and died in the 19th century.

She was born Marie Francoise Therese Martin on January 2, 1873, in Alencon, a little town in the verdant, tranquil region of Normandy in northwestern France (the setting some 70 years later of "The Longest Day" of a violent century).

Therese Martin was 15 when, like her three elder sisters before her, she entered the Carmelite convent in the nearby town of Lisieux. As Sister Therese of the Child Jesus and of the Holy Face, she lived for nine years within the walls of the contemplative Carmel, not ever leaving the monastery until her death on September 30, 1897, at age 24, when her small, frail body wasted by tuberculosis was taken out for burial.

Long, long ago and far, far away, as tales of magic kingdoms and star wars and adventures might begin or end. . . . Over a century ago, in the time of Rizal and the Revolution in our country; more than a hundred years before the turn of the Millennium and our time, since the death of Sister Therese. Millions less silent, simple or obscure in life; countless men and women more renowned, a host once acclaimed as great and famous—all have become as forgotten dust and gravestones in the wake of history. And yet . . . The little nun's story has proved to be far more real, to say the least, more powerful, beautiful and enduring than any tale from fairyland and the realm of stars, or in the proud and mighty annals of this world.

As Saint Therese of the Child Jesus, Santa Teresita (the little Teresa, not the "bigger" Teresa of Avila) to her Filipino devotees, she has become and remains an "inspiration to millions of 20th century Christians"—make that the 21st century faithful, too—"and her life is known throughout the world," says Father Michael Hollings of the Catholic Institute of International Relations in London, in his popular 1980 biography, *Therese of Lisieux*. It was the life, as faithful, intense and courageous as it was short, of a young woman whose "vocation and mission and reason for being," as she herself exulted, was love.

All this one learns from Father Hollings and John Beevers, author of *Storm of Glory,* and others who have written about "The Little Flower of Jesus" (as the teenage, sentimental novice called herself) and her "Little Way" to holiness and perfection, which is the path accessible to every man, of everyday simplicity, obedience, dutifulness and, always, love.

But what was this love that Therese often spoke and wrote about?

SHE EXPLAINS THIS LOVE, she celebrates and rhapsodizes on it, as a lover will, in *The Story of a Soul*, her spirited autobiography that the Prioress of Our Lady of Mount Carmel, her own sister, Mother Agnes, made her write as a matter of duty, with which she complied with obedient humility and, it seemed, some amusement.

Would anyone find any use, Sister Therese had mused, for these jottings of hers in an exercise book? Early in her novitiate, she had wondered, too, as she would confide in her journal, about her real and ultimate vocation.

For an answer, she read chapters 12 and 13 of St. Paul's Letter to the Corinthians. She meditated on a passage from St. John of the Cross, on "the depths of my nothingness"—and finally she saw, she understood that "since the Church is a body composed of different members, she could not lack the most necessary and most nobly endowed of all the bodily organs. I understood, therefore, that the Church has a heart—a heart on fire with love. I saw too that love alone imparts life to all the members so that should love ever fail, apostles would no longer preach the Gospel and martyrs would refuse to shed their blood.

"Finally, I realized that love includes every vocation, that love is all things, that love is eternal, reaching down through the ages and reaching out to the uttermost limits of the earth.

"Beside myself with joy, I cried out, 'O Jesus, my love, my vocation is found at last—*my vocation is love.* I have found my place in the bosom of the Church, and this place, O my God, Thou hast given me in the Heart of the Church . . . *I will be love* . . .

"I am but a weak and helpless child, but my very weakness makes me dare to offer myself, O Jesus, as a victim of Thy love, I have been chosen, though a weak and imperfect creature, as Love's victim . . . in order that Love may be wholly satisfied, it must stoop even into nothingness and transform that nothingness into fire.

"Love is repaid by Love alone . . . I have sought and found a way to ease my heart by giving Thee love for love."

That sure beats all the longings of love songs, all the sweet throb, pain and passion of love poems, of any time and all times, coming from the pure heart and soul of a saint and mystic, from a divine and deathless fire sparked from mortal nothingness by the Eternal. And that wasn't all. Perhaps the most amazing grace and marvel this side of time was that *The Story of Soul* was only the prelude to a greater life, fuller, more abundant, generous beyond earthly measure, beneficent beyond all worldly treasure. For on the night before she died, as she entered into her final agony, she exclaimed, "I could never have believed it possible to suffer so intensely. I can explain it only as my great longing to save souls . . . I have no regret for having surrendered myself to Love." And, at the last: "I feel my mission is about to begin . . . to make others love God as I have loved Him . . . to teach souls *my little way* . . . I will spend my heaven doing good on earth."

And in the hundred years after what the Church commemorates joyously as her *natalitas*, her birthday in everlasting life, countless have been the miracles attributed to her intercession—miracles of grace, of conversion; prodigies of the spirit and marvels of healing; temporal favors, protection from disaster, distress and the shocks that flesh is heir to, blessings of health, peace, joy and peace of soul.

Hers must be a busy heaven, all right. What she so longed and worked and prayed for in Love's name, she got.

On the first anniversary of her death, in September 1898, 2,000 copies of *The Story of a Soul* were printed, recalls another enamoured biographer, Jean Chalon. The book has since been published in scores of editions. It has been translated into nearly 50 languages, and copies by the millions have been circulated in almost all countries.

Beginning in 1899, records Chalon, pilgrims have been visiting the tomb of Therese in Lisieux. Pilgrimages from various nations come every year, and abound with claims of cures and favors.

In 1907, Pope Pius X initiated her formal glorification by the Church, calling her "the greatest saint of modern times."

In 1921, Pope Benedict XV dedicated to her his "Decree on the Heroism of the Virtues of the Venerable Servant of God."

In 1923, Sister Therese of the Child Jesus was beatified and in 1925 was canonized by Pius XI.

In 1927, she was proclaimed by Pius XI the principal patron, equal to the Jesuit St. Francis Xavier, of all Catholic missionaries.

In 1944, St. Therese was proclaimed by Pius XII a patron of France, equal to St. Joan of Arc.

In the centenary of her death, on Mission Sunday, October 19, 1997, Pope John Paul II elevated St. Therese of the Child Jesus, the Little Flower, to the highest place of honor in the Church. John Paul proclaimed her a Doctor of the Church—the 33rd of the canonized elect so honored, and only the third woman hailed as Doctor by the Vatican, after Teresa of Avila and Catherine of Siena.

Pope John Paul declared in his homily at the proclamation rites in St. Peter's Square: "Among the Doctors of the Church, Therese of the Child Jesus and of the Holy Face is the youngest, but her spiritual itinerary shows such maturity, the intuitions of her faith expressed in her writings are so vast and so profound that they merit a place among the great spiritual masters."

THE RELICS OF ST. THERESE, fragments of bone in a gold urn, had been brought to the Rome ceremonies from the Carmelite Convent in Lisieux. Priests, nuns and a multitude of devotees followed the urn in procession, and after John Paul declared her a Doctor of the Church showered the urn with red and white rose petals, recalling her promise that after her death she would let fall on earth "a shower of roses"—her favors and gifts of love, her bounty and blessings.

The relics—in Catholic tradition and practice they are revered as symbolic touchstones for the greater glory of God, the bestowal of His benefits, and the strengthening of the faith, embracing in this instance the veneration of St. Therese—arrived in the country last January 30 in the course of a round-the-world pilgrim tour that began in Brazil in December 1977.

Throngs of the faithful have already gathered and prayed before the relics of Therese who has come to be called the Millennium Saint, in Quezon City, Muntinlupa, Ayala-Alabang, Pasay City and Manila. Huge crowds of devotees have venerated the pilgrim relics in Angeles City, San Fernando, Cabanatuan City, San Jose City, Aritao and Bayombong in Nueva Vizcaya, Ilagan, Tuguegarao and Laoag City.

This Valentine week, the holy relics go to Baguio City and Tuba, Benguet; to Vigan and San Fernando, La Union, and Dagupan City; to Iba, Subic and Olongapo City, and then to Balanga, Bataan.

From Sunday, February 20, to the end of the month, the sanctified remains of St. Therese will visit Tagaytay, Lipa, Batangas City, UP Los Baños, Tayabas, Lucena and then Gumaca, Quezon. In the itinerary for March, the destinations are in this order: Lopez, Quezon; Daet, Camarines Norte; Naga City, Legazpi City, Tacloban City, Palo; then Cebu City, Dumaguete, Bacolod, Iloilo City, Jaro; then Zamboanga City and Jolo, Sulu; Ozamis City, Cagayan de Oro City and Malaybalay, Bukidnon; Davao City and Tagum and last to Puerto Princesa, Palawan.

In the first week of April, the relics visit Camp Crame and Camp Aguinaldo, before being flown to Taiwan and Hong Kong. They will come back for Holy Week, when the faithful may venerate them at the Carmel of St. Therese on Gilmore, Quezon City, and in the convent of the Carmelite Sisters in New Manila. From there they go to Novaliches, then to Dipaculao, Maria Aurora, San Luis and Baler, all in Aurora province; then to Infanta, Quezon, before returning to the Church of St. Therese of the Child Jesus at Villamor Airbase and departing for Paris on April 28.

By then, several million Filipinos will have been drawn to view and touch and pray before the reliquary, in remembrance and veneration of St. Therese of Lisieux, Santa Teresita del Niño Jesus.

The showers of roses she had promised, blooms of faith, hope and love—love of God, and love of neighbor and fellow pilgrim for love of Him—flowers, too, of God's favor and mercy in this year of the Great Jubilee, might have fallen by then upon our nation and our people, especially the poor, the humble and the obscure, like the widowed nursemaid and *labandera* Adela Quindiagan, formerly of Barangay Sinilian, Camiling, Tarlac, now of Barangay St. Peter, La Loma, Quezon City, who came with her two children and her sister and brother-in-law to line up for hours on Mayon Street in front of the Capuchins' Santa Teresita Church on the night of February 2 even if only for a fleeting glimpse of the relics of the Little Flower of Jesus.

The small, simple, smiling woman said, in what seemed an instinctive reply to a neighbor's unspoken query:

"Because we love her."

(Graphic, 2000)

The Not So Joyful Mysteries of Agoo

THE VIRGIN OF AGOO, more solemnly known as the Immaculate Queen of Heaven and Earth, has changed her mind about going on with her regular apparitions atop that guava tree on that hill in Barangay San Antonio, because some people have been pestering her to please say a few kind words about their own glorious vision in her messages to Judiel Nieva.

She refused to have anything to do with this grandiose plan of theirs, although its advocates, she assured Judiel in her final appearance, may continue to expect the maternal love and guidance of her compassionate heart.

It seems her more prominent devotees, in particular some devout politicians from La Union and Pangasinan, have been asking the Blessed Virgin to include in her messages even just a line or two in favor of the parliamentary system and maybe a fourth term for certain incumbent congressmen. From which prospect the Immaculate Queen of Agoo could only turn away in sorrow—or so the tale went, more or less, as told by one radio commentator who is apparently in thrall to the presidential, as most people in this predominantly Christian country still are, a proposition that can be checked out by research groups, investigative agencies or commissions on inquiry, if they haven't done so already.

Such probe bodies could likewise demonstrate and establish that the Blessed Virgin in her alleged messages delivered in Agoo over the last few years has not once mentioned so secular a subject as local politics, let alone a change in the form of government, much as our pious politicos might wish to hear heaven's endorsement. On the contrary, her supposed statements and instructions—addressed presumably not just to Judiel Nieva but to all Filipinos and the rest of humankind—have been about more profound and exalted things, more tremendous themes: prophetic, millennial, cosmic, cataclysmic, eschatological, this last in reference to "final matters" like death and the afterlife, the eternal destiny of individuals, entire nations, humanity, the whole world.

In this regard, precisely the character, scope and intent of the Blessed Mother's purported messages to Judiel—their content as well as their style, tone and rhythm, their idiom and syntax or arrangement of words—have been what an ecclesiastical probe body studied and analyzed over the last two years.

The Virgin of Agoo allegedly gave Judiel more than 250 messages—a few in Ilocano if it was a "private" apparition, he said, the majority in English during "public" visions. It seemed the Virgin preferred an "international language" when there was a large crowd.

THE COMMISSION ON INQUIRY of the Diocese of San Fernando, La Union, was convened by Bishop Antonio Tobias to look into the truth or falsity of the Agoo apparitions. It subjected to the most conscientious scrutiny—words claimed to have been spoken by the Mother of God surely demand no less—such Marian memos as the following allegedly given to and dutifully written down by Judiel Nieva (misspellings and other earthly lapses have been corrected for clarity's sake in this article), beginning when he was around fifteen, which was more than a couple of years ago:

From the moment of my conception, I was singled out with an infinite dignity, because God destined me as the Mother of the Word Incarnate . . . God bestowed upon me all the graces and beauty of holiness, so that I will be fit to be the Mother of His Only Begotten Son who is equal to Him in all things.

* * *

I am your Mother, the Stella Maris. My light beckons to you, for I am the Star of Salvation and Hope who will bring you to the Port of Eternal Bliss . . . So many of my children do not want to listen to me. They do not want to hear me, and it makes me shed tears of blood. My love for them is immeasurable.

* * *

The world goes toward its ruin while Satan deploys his power to destroy it. This is very close now. You are about to reach the most painful and bloody conclusion of the Purification. This will take place in these years. I wish to save the world by the victory of my mercy and love. That is why my Immaculate Heart will triumph.

* * *

I will always ask you to consecrate yourselves to my Immaculate Heart and the Sacred Heart of my Divine Son for world peace. But it seems that your response has been very, very, very slow. Why, my children? Why? Let my Immaculate Heart reign side by side with the Sacred Heart of Jesus in every place, from the church to the chapel, from palace to the poorest hut.

* * *

Oh my dear children, pray and forgive the people because they don't know what they are doing and saying. Pray for the people who are lying, injuring the good name of others by slander, tale bearing, rash judgments, contemporary speech and the violation of secrecy. My children, pray for them . . .

200

The last cited and quite recent injunction allegedly from Judiel's heavenly visitor might strike the now controversial seer's followers as referring to his critics and detractors, especially the skeptical members of the church commission that conducted the inquiry into the Agoo visions.

The four-member Commission on Inquiry of the Diocese of San Fernando, La Union, chaired by Father Samuel Banayat, declared in a report issued last September 6 that the messages supposedly received by Judiel Nieva from the Blessed Virgin Mary had been "plagiarized," copied and repeated practically verbatim, except in places where they were garbled or incorrectly reproduced, from published accounts of Marian visions in other countries. The foreign sources of the texts in question included Fatima, Medjugorje and Akita.

The famous, canonically approved Fatima apparitions occurred in Portugal in 1917. Medjugorje, in what is now embattled Bosnia-Herzegovina in the former Yugoslavia, was the scene in the 1980s of a long series of the Blessed Virgin's apparitions to six youths that reportedly have been "privately accepted" by Pope John Paul II. Akita, near Tokyo, is where Sister Agnes Sasagawa's visions in her convent chapel beginning in 1973 and the image of a "weeping" Virgin have been "approved" by Bishop John Ito of the Diocese of Niigata.

In the judgment of the commission, the Agoo affair was more than a case of what might be called visionary plagiarism exhibiting, in the unedited versions, "incoherence and inconsistency of style and expression." The commission pointed to the "doubtful state" of the image of the Immaculate Queen of Heaven and Earth that the followers of Judiel Nieva had enshrined on Apparition Hill.

A Manila sculptor and the commission members had examined the image and discovered "canals in the inner sides of the eyes and a hole with a copper tube in the crown"—features not normally found in carved religious icons, leading the priest-investigators to deduce that these details had much to do with the profuse "tears of blood" staining the Virgin's face and dress. The "miraculous" blood could not be examined, though, as all traces of it had since been wiped away.

Furthermore, although the alleged apparitions led to "conversion of hearts and renewal of faith," they also brought about "division, hostility and disobedience" to the Church. There was the rift between "traditionalists" and "modernists" among the clergy and the faithful inflamed by the mysteries of Agoo, and the conflict between Father

Roger Cortez, a Charismatic Movement preacher based in Quiapo, who was accused of pocketing donations for the Agoo shrine (a "smear drive," he said) and fellow priests who disbelieved in the apparitions. There was the squabble between the Nievas and their relatives and neighbors, the Demetrio Sisons, over ownership of Apparition Hill and adjacent plots, the real estate value of which must have risen fantastically in the calculations of local entrepreneurs entranced by their vision of a Lourdes-like pilgrimage center flourishing alongside the tourist playgrounds of a Philippine Riviera or Costa del Sol— Agoo's prosperous contribution to the greater glory of Philippines 2000.

And finally there was the matter of Judiel's "lifestyle," which the commissioned noted had become "materialistic and worldly." The alleged visionary had either declined invitations to appear before the panel or proved too evasive in his answers. In any case, he had shown himself to be anything but a "model of simplicity" associated with those visionaries who had communed with the truly miraculous.

In view of the available evidence, and in a sense also the lack of it, the Commission of Inquiry had to conclude that the supposed apparitions of the Blessed Virgin Mary to Judiel Nieva were "far from being supernatural," that Judiel acted in all these not so joyful manifestations of the supposedly miraculous with "grave dishonesty" and "apparent will to deceive." In sum, a trick show, a hoax perpetrated by a fake visionary.

The findings of the commission were announced at a press conference conducted by Father James Reuter, S.J. in the diocesan office in San Fernando.

The commission's report, said Father Reuter, will be forwarded to the Catholic Bishops Conference of the Philippines (CBCP) and the Vatican.

BUT TRUE BELIEVERS in Judiel's alleged visions are not inclined to give credence to the church commission and its conclusions. Quite a few of them, in fact, are indignant and will not forgive, one gathers, the clerics whose "rash judgments" have injured the "good name" of their sainted seer.

One of the more outspoken of the Agoo pilgrims is former Bangko Sentral external debt analyst Flora Gisbert, who together with a group of retired executives and employees made the trip to Apparition Hill on September 8, "to honor the Blessed Virgin on her birthday." A

Manila Times feature quoted Flora as saying, "I actually expected the findings. If the Church could discredit something as big as Medjugorje, why not Agoo?"

She was a witness, as so many others were, Ms. Gisbert said, to wondrous sights and happenings in Agoo, on that unforgettable first Saturday of March 1993. At around 4:30 in the morning, she and her daughter had seen "stars" coming out of the ground and "silver and golden lights" streaking above the crowd of thousands gathered on the hill. The streaks of light, she said, were "angels" come to signal the start of the day's apparition. "It was like New Year," and what they saw and felt had "positive results" in their lives . . . "All these things happened through Judiel, so he must be for real."

Engr. Bruno Panes, Jr., former president of the Immaculate Queen of Heaven and Earth Foundation which oversees the Apparition Hill shrine and Judiel's affairs, has likewise remained steadfast in his belief in the Agoo phenomena, in particular the Virgin's "tears of blood." Said Panes, in the same *Times* story: "The image was being carried in public when I first saw it shed tears of blood." Several times he had seen it happen—"all in public." It was impossible for people to have "manipulated such an event in full view of hundreds of people."

Jenny Estrada, also from the Bangko Sentral, said it all for the group: the commission's verdict of deception and fakery was nothing but "their opinion" which could "not take away what we experienced in Agoo . . . Nothing will change my belief."

Indeed, even if church authorities have declared it as nothing supernatural, the Agoo event has for a pious hoax proved to be rather durable, and has cast a stronger spell than could be banished over-night by a probe commission. Its power—a fusion of the people's devotion to the Blessed Virgin, the hunger for divine revelation, the multitude's yearning for heavenly intercession amid so much anguish, misery and poverty, the anticipation of another Lourdes or Fatima bestowed on a faithful land, the impulses of folk Catholicism, various fanaticisms, curiosity, publicity, showbiz and other elements, sociopolitical, anthropological, mysterious or otherwise—was vividly demonstrated on March 6, 1993, when more than a million people converged on the town in La Union, drawn by Judiel Nieva's announcement that the Virgin of his visions would appear and perform great wonders on that glorious day.

203

We had waited for an inner voice to tell us to arise and drive all the way to Agoo. We heard no such voice and so, foregoing the penance of a horrid, penitential journey and maybe the spectacle of the dancing sun, stayed home that March weekend and forever missed the chance, assuming we could have managed to come close enough in that immense crowd, of seeing Judiel Nieva, not in the aspect of the awesome and dazzling archangel whose name he bears, but in the flesh, human and for real, kneeling in front of the microphones with lambent eyes gazing up at the top of the guava tree or the clouds in the bright sky while Joe de Venecia, Joe Aspiras, Danding Cojuangco and their spouses stood by with prayerful expressions and eyes also turned heavenward, the ever solicitous Father Cortez kneeling beside his ward or pupil or protegé who seemed to be listening to words from an invisible presence and then writing them down in a notebook, the messages to be typed later and xeroxed and printed for dissemination to the faithful by the Immaculate Queen of Heaven and Earth Foundation, Judiel listening supposedly to the Mother of God and looking calm, normal, unflustered, unchanged—this to us is the real prodigy, the wonder, the marvel, the virtual miracle—Judiel carrying on without the slightest sign of going into a trance or trying to, as people around could see and as recorded by all the TV and still cameras on the scene, without showing any indication of an altered state of consciousness, unlike the visionaries of Lourdes, Fatima, Garabandal and Medjugorje observed and tested by doctors, psychologists, scientists, Judiel going about it with eyes wide open, fully awake, nothing extraordinary, not missing a beat nor ruffling a ringlet, writing down the Virgin's messages in his notebook with Father Cortez looking on in solemn approval, all in a day's work, for God's sake . . .

So, now, what next in the annals of Agoo?

A balanced, thoughtful, dispassionate view of the Agoo phenomena as judged by the Commission on Inquiry is offered us by UP professor and TV host Randy David—somewhat surprisingly as he is known to be more familiar with Marxist dialectics than Catholic apologetics.

"To disbelieve the apparition at Agoo," observes Professor David in his *Inquirer* column, "is not to disbelieve in Mary. And to distrust Judiel is not the same as distrusting the three children of Fatima or Bernadette of Lourdes."

To the church commission, "what was under question is not the devotion to Mary, but her reported apparition in Agoo . . . the Church will have nothing to do with what is not true. Faith does not mean the suspension of our natural standards for validating experience; it only means the readiness to look beyond the natural frame of experience when it can no longer furnish the answers . . .

"The commission's declaration of a non-miracle at Agoo may have cost the Church a million potential returnees to the faith as well as a chance to establish a pilgrimage center in the country. But, on the other hand, I am sure it has bolstered the Catholic Church's standing as a community of sensible human beings who do not require miracles to establish the truth of their faith."

True—yet miracles, we are just as sure, have happened and will happen again, in other times and other places, out of God's graciousness and mercy.

(Graphic, 1995)

An Easter Prayer

LORD JESUS CHRIST, who suffered and died and was buried, and on the third day rose from the dead, according to the Scriptures, and who will come again at the end of time to judge the world and of whose kingdom there will be no end; Lord Jesus, whose rising from the tomb on the first Easter is the cornerstone, the center and heart of our faith, as first proclaimed to all of God's children by the men and women of Galilee whom you had called to be your disciples, and by Paul the Apostle who, in his Letter to the Christians of Corinth, declared that if you had not truly risen, then that same faith was vain, foolish, and those who believed in you would be of all men the most to be pitied; Lord Jesus, who, on the evening of the Day of the Resurrection came into the Upper Room in Jerusalem though the doors were shut, to greet your followers gathered there with the words: "Peace be with you"—Lord, on this Easter of the year 1990, we beseech you grant us in this country that peace you brought with your most gracious and joyful greeting to your Mother and Peter, John, James, Andrew, Mary Magdalene and the others; the peace that the world by its nature cannot give and that you alone can give, as the last 20 centuries have witnessed and testified since that early morning when the three women went to anoint you with perfumed oils and found the huge stone rolled back from the entrance to the tomb and the tomb itself empty, for you had been raised, just as you promised, your victory foreshadowed by your raising of Lazarus in Bethany four days after he had died, your conquest forever of sin and death and its dark empire, which is also the sign and assurance of the resurrection of all who believe in you, commemorated again this day as the greatest feast in Christendom, the very same message announced once more on the front page of this and other journals today, by the President of the Republic and the Cardinal-Archbishop of Manila and the Papal Nuncio from Rome, all three dignitaries sounding the same traditional note of Christian hope and rejoicing in the midst of adversity, conflict, misfortune, etc., as did their exalted predecessors in years past, and which sentiments are dutifully read or at least glanced at and then forgotten, if not on the same day, then the day after, lasting no longer in our distracted secular minds than the latest news about politicians and crooks and violence and crime and the inauguration of some club or boutique, which is all the more reason, Lord Jesus Christ, for our people's need of that peace you gave to your disciples when you appeared to them still bearing the marks of the nails and the centurion's spear on your body, for there is little or no peace in the corridors of government and in the streets of our cities and in the slums of the wretched of this corner of the earth and in the towns and villages in the countryside, where the poorest of our people live out their lives if they are not being cut down by Armalites and driven from their huts and fields and fishing grounds by the war that rages on between brother Filipinos in this the only Christian nation in Asia, etc.; the 30 percent of the population that our prayerful President and, we suppose, also the pious politicos in the LDP, LP, NP or whatever, not to mention the bishops and businessmen breaking bread in breakfast prayer meetings, as well as the revolutionaries who worship not you, the Risen Lord, but the gods of history, scientific socialism and the class struggle, say they want liberated from poverty and every man-made oppression, stark evidence of which confronts all with eyes to see in the ruined barangays and mass graves and evacuation centers in Quezon and Camarines Norte, in Samar and Negros Occidental and Lanao and Davao del Sur, and right here in Metro Manila, a reality stacked up literally against the back wall of the Archbishop's Palace in the neighborhood of the National Mental Hospital, a dense decaying concentration of hovels prevented only by the sheer height and thickness of the wall itself from crowding and spilling over onto the neat, spacious lawns, where our National Artist, Nick Joaquin, remembers savoring what he calls by far the tastiest, crispiest lechon he had ever chewed on in his celebrated sociable life, during some bright elegant affair attended by the best and the brightest doers and thinkers in our society, which happily bountiful bash somehow calls to mind other societies in crisis, in other lands also predominantly Roman Catholic, like Brazil, with its poor multitudes and affluent few and its famed archbishop, Dom Helder Camara, living and working among the poorest of the poor to make your peace visible and present among them, and El Salvador, with its appalling gap between the many who are hungry and landless and the few who are rich, and with its own renowned and saintly pastor, the martyred Bishop Oscar Romero, killed for his solidarity with the dispossessed and suffering poor, whose cause, which is the struggle against all the powers and principalities that oppress and repress them from the fullness of their humanity and dignity, probably demands too in our country the compassion and selflessness and sacrifice of Camaras and Romeros who care not for golden ornaments and chauffeured limousines and elegant banquets as ludicrous and scandalous as the pompous luxuries of the wealthy in an impoverished, embattled country, before peace, that joyous peace you gave to your disciples on the night of the first Easter, can begin at last to be seen and known and really loved in our nation, as you, Lord Jesus, are said to want to be seen and known and loved in the lives of those who profess to believe in you; for we are a people who for good or ill ever seek to follow the ones ordained by church and state to lead and guide us, which may account for the sorry state we are in that many think calls for nothing less than divine intervention here and now; but if that be not your will, at least, we implore you, help us to find and possess the peace of your Resurrection, by calling forth in our time, if not by 1992, before the end of the decade, the end of the millennium, the brave and noble leaders to reconcile our people with one another and unite all, in truth and justice, which is the foundation of all peace, your peace and that which even unredeemed human love might give; and pending that blessed and longed for consummation we hope too that you bestow on our land graces more modest and immediate, such as the strength of will for the rich to give up that extra Pajero or condo or real estate or plantation and give the money to the poor, and for the rest of us common folk who are in the majority, the clarity of vision and strength of spirit to be worthy of our vocations to serve and uplift our brothers and sisters in every appointed task during this our journey, our pilgrimage to what Father Andrew Greeley, one of your wisest and most eloquent modern disciples, a sociologist and author and by the way bestselling novelist, has described as most certainly not like the sunset dimming, fading into the night at the end of those old Western movies that starred Roy Rogers or John Wayne, but Alleluia, praise be to you forever, as the unutterably beautiful sunrise that is our Christian destiny: all this we ask you, Lord Jesus Christ, who by your suffering and death and the power and glory of your Resurrection brought new and more abundant life into the world. Amen.

(Times-Journal, 1990)

Critical
Conditions

Nick Joaquin/Quijano de Manila
and Other Anomalies

The modern world seems to have no notion of preserving
different things side by side . . . of saving the whole varied
heritage of culture. It has no notion except that of
simplifying something by destroying everything.
—G. K. Chesterton

The underlying motive . . . is simply a hypertrophied sense
of order. The present state of affairs offends them not
because it causes misery, still less because it makes freedom
impossible; what they desire, basically, is to reduce the
world to something resembling a chessboard.
—George Orwell

Si Nick Joaquin, Nationalist Artist na, pa inglis-inglis pa.
—A Not So Literary Critic

AS WE ALL KNOW, THE OLD SOCIETY came to a bad end. One night in
September 1972, the O.S. was rolled up like a stained, stinking, dis-
integrating carpet and carted away to the furnace or dustbin or
wherever history dumps such rubbish. Bright and early the following
morning, we Filipinos found ourselves milling around in a different
corridor, straight and gleaming, down which we were enjoined to
proceed in orderly ranks toward our true destiny.

Its final fate, its ignominious termination, even the circumstances,
the hour and the setting of its formal abolition, have been properly
recorded, and the graphic chronicle of the times the O.S. encompassed
will doubtless provide many a moral lesson to all Filipinos and their
posterity. We are more or less agreed on the manner and moment of
its dissolution, and the event has since been commemorated annually, with solemn as well as joyful rites, as befits the close of one era
and the start of another. Christians in this season of the year, regardless of their doctrinal differences, are mindful of a similar sense: of

an entire mass of time split by the death of the old dispensation and the birth of the new.

We all know what happened to the O.S., as Christians know what superseded the Old Testament. Of the Christian anomaly, that scandalous offense to the neatness and order of human reason, Graham Greene has remarked: that, along with the absurdity of believing that life should exist by God's will on one minute speck in the universe, we are asked to believe in a parallel absurdity: "that God chose a tiny colony of a Roman empire to be born." Strangely enough, he adds, "two absurdities seem easier to believe than one." There was, 20 centuries ago, a Birth and a Death, certainly, as there was a definable end and beginning in the sociopolitical order, in the small hours of a September night, five years ago. But if we are familiar with the fate that befell the O.S., we are, come to think of it, not so certain about its beginnings.

When did that Old Society beast come slouching toward this archipelago to be born? What signs in the sky heralded its coming, who or what presided over its birth? Should we trace the advent of the O.S. back to the Luneta on July 4, 1946, or did it perchance debark from Commodore Dewey's flagship one morning in May 1898? Was it installed in some earlier, benighted century—on June 24, 1571, perhaps, when Legazpi organized the Ayuntamiento de Manila—so that it can be said that what was dismantled by martial decree consisted of nothing less than an entire history? Or must one reckon its arrival by a more recent date, say, the first congressional elections of the 1960s? These are not idle queries, for those of us who rejoice over the passing away of the O.S. owe it to ourselves and our children to know the precise nature and quantity of the foul garbage that was sent to the incinerator that fateful night in '72. Whether Christian, Muslim, agnostic or unbeliever, or simply retarded, adult Filipinos ought to know just what in heaven's name they are celebrating.

In any event, the O.S. lasted long enough to earn its despicable label. It was, we are often reminded, the basest of times, the worst of times: such is the verdict one would think no good could have come out of it. Yet, that vile, horrid, corrupt, cantankerous, anarchic, revolting time, clime and state of the nation—from which, by the way, we all should acknowledge our ancestry—did spawn quite a few good things. If by O.S. we mean the decade or two before martial law, then assuredly it left us certain legacies we ought not to consign to oblivion.

The ten or 20 years before Proclamation 1081 were surely not without some redeeming, beneficent qualities—shafts of light against the howling dark, if you wish to be melodramatic—and only the over-zealous New Filipino would paint it all black. It was, among other things, and despite the general malaise, a creative, innovative time, a period of ferment and growth in various sectors; and the activity in these areas produced a heritage of diverse arts and artifacts that the nation will do well to preserve.

A goodly number of the items in this legacy can be listed down, according to one's values or inclinations, to wit: Teodoro Valencia's passion for people's parks, Kerima Polotan's pungent prose, Julie Y. Daza's sparkling social criticism, E. Aguilar Cruz's explorations of the Manila of his affections—preoccupations which were conceived or sustained in the bosom of the Bad Old Days and which continue to flourish in this happy hour. Jose Joya, Aguilar-Alcuaz and Malang, to name but three of our foremost painters, antedated the current renaissance in the visual arts like so many John the Baptists, though they refused to subsist solely on locusts and honey. In their turn like prophets and precursors, such writers as Nick Joaquin, N.V.M. Gonzalez, Bienvenido Santos, Alejandro Abadilla and Lazaro Francisco composed their books, to add to the native canon. Ignoring partisan protests, the Cultural Center rose almost as if by miracle from the bay, radiating light and energy, and a proud consciousness of the artistic resources of the race. In a decidedly lower order one may include in our O.S. inheritance such institutions as the beerhouse and the massage parlor, both of which are said to promote domestic trade, employment, mental health and national well-being—the last two, it should be noted, unsupported by statistics and still subject to controversy and debate.

SURELY NOT TO BE DISPUTED or denied—except perhaps by our more-Pinoy-than-thou brethren who wish the English language had disappeared by martial decree along with the English-orating congressmen, and the warlords, and the private armies—is the treasure trove that Nick Joaquin/Quijano de Manila, together with Filipinas Foundation and National Book Store, has of late rescued, as it were, from those who would induce in us a kind of national amnesia.

With the recent publication of Nick Joaquin's *A Question of Heroes*, subtitled "Essays in Criticism on Ten Key Figures in Philippine

History," and Quijano de Manila's *Amalia Fuentes & Other Etchings* and *Doveglion & Other Cameos* (the fifth and sixth collections of his journalism), it's superfluous to state what his more intelligent readers have long known: that his essays and articles—originally published in the *Philippines Free Press*, the O.S.'s most famous weekly until it went out of business in '72—comprise a pleasurable, enriching loot, scooped out from years past and preserved now in attractive packages, to the gratification of everyone with a fine greed for such riches. Not so evident, perhaps because they are casually assumed by most of Nick Joaquin/Quijano de Manila's readers, are the implications of the enterprise on which he and his publishers have embarked. That folks abound who seek and delight in such bounty as Filipinas Foundation and National Book Store have helped provide, seems to be further proof, if this be necessary, that Nick Joaquin/Quijano de Manila's medium, not to mention his message, is alive and, well, still kicking ass. It is not yet about to be snatched from us by the undertakers, even now, on the threshold of the 1980s, when both official and private ministries would, if they could, gladly garrote that tongue the terrible Thomasites brought to these shores more than 70 years ago.

In this light, *A Question of Heroes* by Nick Joaquin, and the latest tandem volumes by Quijano de Manila, amount to an anomaly, as do the National Artist's four other compilations of articles, his plays, his poems and short stories, and his novel about a woman in an anomalous condition, *The Woman Who Had Two Navels*. Here is the spectacle, and also the archetype, the exemplar, the portrait of the Filipino as writer and journalist persisting in the use, and what splendid use, of this alien language! What nerve, what verve, what treasonous ignominy is this, writing in a language that is not and can never be that of the broad masses, while the truly wise and progressive struggle for complete, total if not immediate national liberation—which includes our liberation of course from the English of the imperialists and their degenerate lackeys, the socio-economic elite . . . The rhetoric is fashionable, compelling, soul-stirring; it is, also, quite ironically, inspired to a great extent by a dialectics of foreign origin. As only to be expected of such fervor, it is either blind or indifferent to large areas of the truth and reality (a continuously evolving complex) it claims to serve as invincible, infallible interpreter.

213

THERE IS A TENDENCY, in hard-breathing, brow-knitted circles, whether these be in theology, science, politics or literature, to deny or distort contrary data, and construct whole systems of thought and action immunized to reject anything that disagrees with the proclaimed doctrine. The consequences, more often than not, are awkward and distressing. Such was the credibility gap that once stretched as wide as the Atlantic from the sandaled feet of allegedly God-appointed seers who insisted the world wasn't round. Around the revered delusion baring its teeth as dogma, the annoying facts will gather sooner or later and chase it away into the outer darkness, where there is whipping and groaning of treatises. The subsequent enlightenment may take all of an epoch, as happened after Copernicus, or a generation, as in the matter of Philippine-American relations, or two and a half hours on a Saturday afternoon, as in the case of some scholars who, in the face of incontrovertible data, are able to overhaul their decrepit premises and prescribe a more realistic response to reality.

This much appears to have been recognized by some of the ardent souls who would erase all vestiges of English-for-and-by-Filipinos. Confronted with the fact of Nick Joaquin/Quijano de Manila, they have managed, to their credit, to suspend their own logic and surmount their antipathy, at least for the time it takes to type out a short essay, in order to pay tribute to the man and his works. Instructive, indeed, is the case of the critics who, for reasons solemnly proclaimed, consider English an abomination second only to radioactive fallout or falling hair, yet feel obliged to praise—in correct collegiate English, to be sure—the Filipino writer and journalist who has done and is doing more than any other in our country to advance the cause of this accursed colonial language. If medium is message, a proposition demonstrated most vividly in the works of the gifted artist, the phenomenon of Nick Joaquin/Quijano de Manila cannot but invite respectful, if sometimes begrudging, attention.

His class of anomaly is occasion for at least some reflection, some rethinking, on the part of the patriotic language technicians: he cannot be argued away, as an observable fact or event cannot be argued away. In the laboratory that is our living, growing art and culture, he happens to be a most observable fact—all too often a loud audiovisual performance, some fans and friends who don't drink beer have been heard to complain—and as such may yet succeed in overcoming any prejudice against his medium and his message.

The point, perhaps much too sharp for comfort to those who can hardly wait to serve as pall-bearers for a language that in this corner of the Global Village may be in *rigor* but not yet in *mortis*, is that the language Nick Joaquin uses to express his and his people's genius may not be an accursed affliction after all. On the contrary . . . This is bad news in certain quarters, the sort of dark tidings which once cost foolhardy messengers their heads. For the Filipino future has been mapped out, or so we are told, and it would not do to revise the brave new charts, which allow no latitude for the English language. But, again, the facts, the data, if we would but allow them, argue otherwise.

HISTORY, IT IS CONTENDED, is on the side of the language dogmatists: but history, including that which has yet to be written, responds to the gravity of what is objective and real—such as the fact that English today is anything but a dead or esoteric language like Latin or Sanskrit or Swahili, as any Filipino well knows who keeps tabs on what's going on in the world outside of his barangay. Moreover, the accidents of history, which will not lend themselves to revision, have formed an inclination for the language in the Filipino—the Filipino, to be more specific, who takes his schooling seriously and whose literate tribe has increased, the oft-repeated lament to the contrary. Regardless of the condemnable colonial motives which, at the turn of the century, prompted the imposition of the language on the educational system, the capacity for it exists: a capability increasingly recognized as an asset, incidentally, in the developing countries of Asia and Africa. Every schoolhouse in the country testifies to that potential; what the teachers make of it is another story, a dismal one for some time now, but not hopeless. To write off the "masses" as incapable of learning even basic English is to regard them with that feudalistic snobbery which the doctrinaires themselves should be the first to denounce.

There also exists the enormous temptation to judge the validity, the viability of English by the way the language is maltreated and mangled in these isles. True enough, its weird manifestations, with which college deans, editors and radio-TV station managers are painfully familiar, could prod even the sympathetic to call for its immediate banishment. The spoken varieties of it, with their mystifying accents bred from Aparri to Jolo, can curl the hair of the speech-and-drama professor with an M.A. from Yale or Stanford; and the anomalous compositions penned by the studentry as well as the faculty can bring tears to the eyes of the devout grammarian (who usually can't write a passable paragraph to save his life, but that is another story). But the question of English-for-and-by-Filipinos is an issue that transcends the anxieties of freshman-English teachers or American-trained speech instructors.

For one, if standards have to be invoked, we are well-advised to pass judgment, not according to the least or the worst denominators, but by the better and the best, of which we have an impressive supply, in government and in the universities, in the arts, and the media, too. For another, over and above the absurd, appalling varieties that the language has inspired in our country (and in the U.S., England and other countries), there exists a broad, multi-layered area where English functions as an effective tool, an instrument of communication. From local government to diplomacy, from the classified ads to trade and industry, from agricultural research to computer technology, the language can and does serve the ends of Filipino development, the fulfillment of which, all men of faith and good will in this developing country will agree, is a consummation devoutly to be wished. (Spare our countrymen *naman* the prolonged adolescence of poverty.) Thirdly, there is a species of Filipino English, including Taglish or Engalog, the sort Nonoy Marcelo writes, which is not to be sniffed at, being, again, for the mod, mobile Filipino, an aid to knowledge and communication.

So let the thousand obnoxious English-grafted flowers bloom, to paraphrase a great Asian leader (who, late in life, endeavored to learn the language). Be not scandalized nor driven to despair by the linguistic anomalies that are inflicted on and by the mass media. Take it away! the language dogmatists cry as they wince and shudder at the sight and sounds of this imperialist, neocolonial medium which Filipinos continue to use, or try to, as do millions of non-Americans and non-Englishmen around the world. But for now and, in all likelihood, for a long while yet, it won't be taken away from Joe Quirino and Joe Guevarra, Leah Navarro and Basil Valdez; from your favorite emcee and your candidate to the Batasang Pambansa and every other letter-to-the-editor writer in town; from Filipinos who want to know more, not less, of the world they live in, and the Filipino poets, essayists and novelists who happen to write in the English language.

THE FILIPINO WRITER who uses a non-indigenous language is not by any means a recent anomaly, as he can invoke a tradition that goes back to Jose Rizal. There were earlier exemplars, but Rizal the poet and novelist embodied most profoundly the problems of language, national identity and consciousness as these relate to the Filipino artist. To the Spaniards an insolent, intolerable deviation from the norm set for the Indio, he not only learned but mastered the colonizer's tongue, and the results of that temerity we proudly commemorate every December 30.

But to the pure of art Rizal must ever remain an anomaly—for from their point of view, isn't it curious and puzzling, to say the least, that the same Rizal who said, *"Ang hindi magmahal ng sariling wika, ay higit pa sa hayop at malansang isda"*—isn't it foul and fishy that the national hero chose to write in the language of the conquistador? Why, in the name of Lapu-lapu and Balagtas, did Rizal write his "Last Farewell" in Spanish? A patriot, a martyr who would pierce the veil of the future, shouldn't he have written his last testament, addressed to all generations of Filipinos, in the language of the Tagalogs? Does the apparent anomaly lie perhaps in the fact that Rizal, on the eve of his execution, on the last night of his life, a time for any mortal man to shed all pretense, all dissimulation, knew more than ever in the depths of his being that Spanish and not Tagalog was his *sariling wika*? Assuming that the answer is yes, did Rizal's use of the language of the colonizer to advance the cause of Filipino liberation and freedom make him any less Filipino in the eyes of his contemporaries and in the judgment of posterity?

Isn't it not only possible then, but most advantageous and even imperative, in certain conditions and circumstances, for a Filipino writer to use a language dictated by his *sarili*, not necessarily the *sariling wika* dictated by birth or racial identity or party membership, to advance the cause of Filipino liberation and freedom? Assuming, again, that the answer is yes, does not this confirm, in the context of the Filipino struggle for authentic liberation and development, what George Orwell has propounded in his classic essay on politics and language: that language is not just a natural growth but an instrument which men shape for special purposes and definite objectives?

217

In our day, and from the viewpoint, once more, of the language doctrinaires, doesn't Nick Joaquin/Quijano de Manila's writing in English make him less Filipino than he would otherwise be if he wrote in Pilipino? Since, from the evidence, he is no less enlightened and devoted to his country than his detractors, can we not assume, rather, that his use of the language is not a misguided and futile preoccupation? Suppose the young Nick Joaquin had paid heed to the so-called proletarian critics of the 1930s, and proceeded to write, not of the Noble and Ever Loyal City and the Cycle of the Revolution as he understood it, but of the peasantry and the social unrest in Pampanga and Tarlac, would he not have betrayed his own past, and violated his own identity, his own integrity? Suppose, further, that he had allowed himself to be persuaded, by the same proletarian critics (who had succeeded to some extent with Manuel Arguilla), to write in Tagalog, could he have produced a work as sincere and true and enduring as, say, *Mga Ibong Mandaragit* or *Isang Dipang Langit* by Amado Hernandez? Given Nick Joaquin/Quijano de Manila's Catholic, middle-class background, and the shape and thrust of his genius, wouldn't we have been deprived of *A Portrait of the Artist as Filipino, A Question of Heroes,* his incomparable fiction and his superb journalism, and been given instead a pile of dreary and unreadable socialist propaganda? Doesn't all this suggest that a Filipino writer's identity and integrity should not be tampered with, either by the state or those who strive to supplant the state, so that whether Tagalog, Ilocano, Cebuano, Ilonggo, Maranaw, or multiple mestizo, he can contribute his fullest share to the struggle for Filipino liberation and freedom?

If, as predicted by those doctrinaires who fear or despise the English language, the use of this vital, international medium of knowledge and culture is reduced, limited, by legislation or popular will, to a narrower segment of our society than is conversant with it today, wouldn't such a turn of events produce the grossest anomaly: an even more favored elite—an elite with almost exclusive access to a valuable instrument for economic, cultural and political progress? Wouldn't the creation of this more entrenched and powerful elitist class, in place of the democratization that the various regions and language groups have been undergoing partly with the assistance of English, set back the struggle for authentic freedom and liberation?

HOWEVER, SUCH IS THE DETERMINATION as well as determinism of the campaign to rid this country in the 20th century of the benefits to be derived from learning and using the language, that it's not at all inconceivable for the book-burners to prevail someday and build a ferocious bonfire out of all the English books, periodicals and other publications Filipinos have turned out since Camilo Osias came back from Columbia with the draft of his *Philippine Readers*. But pending the ascendancy of the incendiary commissars—kin to the brainwashing specialists, the historical revisionists and other dogmatic reformers, whose industry the historians have amply recorded—such books as Nick Joaquin's *A Question of Heroes* and Quijano de Manila's *Amalia Fuentes* and *Doveglion* offer pleasure and profit to Filipinos who can read superb writing in English without going into ideological convulsions.

The appeal of journalism-as-narrative, the dense yet lucid clusters of ideas, insights and details, the sheer readability—these qualities, obviously enough, are what make reading Nick Joaquin/ Quijano de Manila the rewarding experience that it is, and comprise a virtual graduate course for the writer or journalist who wishes to advance in his craft. Less obvious are certain considerations which the articles and essays imply—conclusions suggested, for instance, by the fact that he writes the way he does, faithful to his own angels and demons, and unwilling to employ his art in the service of this or that current, duly-authenticated revolution.

Consider the implications inherent in the matter of identity, of identification—the pseudonym Nick Joaquin has been using since the early 1950s to byline his journalism. Why the rather fictional, fanciful nom de plume for reportage which, more than can be said for the efforts of other journalists before or since, plumb the depths of the Filipino experience? Quijano de Manila—Quijano being both an anagram for Joaquin and a synonym for "caballero"—doesn't the mere sound of it conjure up the colonial centuries, in particular the Castilian aristocracy, the European opulence and arrogance of Felipe II's Noble and Ever Loyal? Why not Kihano or, better yet, Ginoo ng Maynila, instead—wouldn't that be more Filipino, more in the spirit of the Filipinism that this Manila-born magus, this worthy son of a colonel of the Revolution, should espouse? A writer enamoured not only of Spain and things Spanish, but also of the English language, and Dickens, Melville, Evelyn Waugh, Cole Porter, Frank Sinatra: an anomaly more than thrice compounded. . . .

If all that sounds facetious, which it indubitably is, it's because it reflects the absurdity of that kind of nationalism which, in effect, projects the Filipino as a creature bereft of any history or, at best, possessing only the disjointed, select portions of one. Pursued to its logical conclusion, such chauvinism, outbreaks of which sometimes gallop through the groves of Diliman, would remove all traces of the Spanish and American influence in our art and culture, our literature and journalism, our mass media and cinema, not to mention our religion, our martyrology, our folklore, and Mike Hanopol's *Jeprox* vibes, and Aling Yoling's *adobo* and hamburger (though it's time we forgot about those boys in the Broadway band and kept the military-industrial complex 7,000 miles away). The result, presumably, would be, not just the New Filipino, but the Pure Filipino, freed from all malign, corrupting powers and faculties, including the capacity to remember the past, the better to deal with the challenges of the present and the future.

A laudable enterprise, if one is a true believer in that kind of purity; unadulterated fantasy, if one is of a more sober persuasion, as happens to be the case with most Filipinos who are old enough to vote in a referendum. Besides involving an overnight feat of genetic mass engineering, the project calls for the annihilation of whole regions of our national history. A parallel, on the individual level, would be to pretend that the years of one's childhood and youth had never been, and that one has arrived in the present moment, like Athena springing from the brow of Zeus, sans the bother of growing up and learning and maturing. Now, such make-believe can lead to ludicrous complications if you aren't a Greek goddess. The whole venture belongs more to the realm of mythology or science fiction than to life as it is lived in the real world, which is composed, most people are agreed, of nations with histories, each nation in turn composed of individuals, human persons with their own genealogies and biographies.

THE FILIPINO NATION did not emerge full-blown from the night of time. There was, and continues to be, a growth, a development proceeding from all that composed the past and making use of it, incorporating it, as cell builds on vital cell, tissue on living bone. A still uncollected essay by Nick Joaquin, "Apologia Pro Triba Sua" (shades of Cicero and Cardinal Newman—non-Filipinos both!), celebrates this growth, this dynamic and irresistible evolution as it concerns the modern Christian Filipino, the descendant of several generations. The same sense of a continuous history, of biography, of character evolving from a particular past, in fact forms the thematic strand that binds together the "etchings" and "cameos" of Quijano de Manila. Character as destiny, character shaped by the sum of a man's past actions, and leading up to that "mortal moment" when "event turns into epiphany, interview into evangel," is the burden of his latest journalistic collections: Amalia Fuentes' rebellious coming of age, Anding Roces impelled by a sentimental courage to hunt for the stolen Rizal manuscripts, the career and capture of the dedicated Dr. Lava, the aging Jose Garcia Villa still playing the young rogue.

On a far larger stage, and limned by the same strange fateful light that touched the tragic characters of Euripides and Shakespeare, each of the major figures of the Revolution acts out his character and destiny in *A Question of Heroes*: " . . . in the dusk glimmering into half-light the faces slowly become clearer, here a Mariano Gomez riding off to meet the Cavite outlaws, there a Pedro Pelaez hurrying to early Mass at the Cathedral, and at the University are students gathered in angry protest when the dawn breaks with a cry, a crash, a clamor, abruptly wakened people rushing about in panic to see the coil of smoke over the fort in Cavite, to see smoke in the mist through which the sun cleaves, the first long shaft of sunlight falling on a stoic Padre Gomez, a crazed Padre Zamora, a raging Padre Burgos being led to the scaffold, the mist shredding about them in the sunshine till the haze blurs the air and it's morning, morning in Paris for Juan Luna in his busy studio, morning in Ghent for Rizal bent over his manuscripts, morning in Manila for the concealed Marcelo del Pilar directing the marchers in the Great Manifestation, and late morning in Madrid for Lopez Jaena, at a sidewalk café, having the first cup of his bohemian day, waiting, as the sun climbs, for less hardy expatriates to stagger up from bed and hangover, but waiting in vain, for the heat of the day has drawn them back to its orient, their fires have lit a red noon, and the blaze of noon is Katipunan red, is Bonifacio at Balintawak, the Magdiwang in Noveleta, Aguinaldo in Kawit, Rizal whirling around in Bagumbayan. . . ."

They were not conventional heroes, not the "standard warriors of legend" nor "champions of unequivocal qualities." The two greatest heroes of our history—Rizal and Aguinaldo—resisted heroism, were in fact anti-heroic, writes Nick Joaquin; and the further anomaly was that they were *ilustrados*, members of that contemptible class with a Pavlovian propensity to egotism, thievery and treason, if one is to believe the historians of the nationalistic orthodoxy. Yet it is the anomaly, the scandal, the deviation from the sacrosanct standards and credos that, in the end, makes and transfigures history: in religion and science, in revolution, in art and literature.

Anyway, the two events which we commemorate this month—the Birth of the Saviour and the Martyrdom of the First Filipino—would suggest to seekers of the light that what is condemned as an anomaly by the high priests, the military prosecutors and the cultural commissars usually outlives its executioners. Unlike the Old Society, the language—and with it, certain values and visions—that Nick Joaquin/Quijano de Manila has made his own, and for which, by force of example, he invites a decent respect, will most probably not come to a bad end.

(*Panorama*, 1978)

Nihil Obstat

1.

OR *AYOS LANG*, IN MANILA SLANG. But why the Latin, man? Because—henceforth and forthwith and with malice toward some, this department will be dispensing the required whys and wherefores to the inquisitive as well as the inquisitorial—because a touch of this great *mater* and *magistra* of languages, this venerable tongue of Catullus and Virgil and the *Ecclesia*, and in italics yet, can in certain instances today, especially this day, cause the eyebrows to rise a fraction of an inch, a facial movement with a salutary effect on the psyche, the *anima* or *spiritu*, whatever it is that informs the being of man and

---

Excerpts from the Editor's Notes in *The Manila Review*, 1974–1978.

enables him to reflect on his existence and compose verses and create patterns of sound, color and movement, among other things. Eyebrow-lifting (not the cosmetic kind) is to be preferred, the mental hygienists assure us, to its opposite, which wrinkles the brow and narrows the eyes and tightens the line of the mouth, not to mention assorted blood vessels, as happens when the old migraine starts acting up or one is visited by solemn, sobering thoughts about the nation and the human condition. On the human condition we all now and then have solemn thoughts; life is generally a serious business (*And all our yesterdays have lighted fools/The way to dusty death* . . .), no matter what the public-relations people say. Knitted eyebrows, it can be confidently argued, attended the making of the Eroica, of *The Brothers Karamazov* (especially that one) and *El Filibusterismo*. The contents of most journals, this quarterly not excluded, tend to prove that cheerless reflections are the rule rather than the exception. All the more reason, we should think, to indulge—occasionally—in the exercise endorsed above. At the very least, it makes for the easy removal of the mote in one's eye: counsel from Scripture which, by the way, sounds properly intimidating in Latin.

The matter of language: once more, and with feeling, an implicit, inevitable issue for Filipinos writing in English, for a new publication in English; more accurately perhaps, a distressing issue to Filipino writers who resist English (and not just the American variety) as an alien medium, the mere mention of which mocks their sense of nationhood. Such hostility, we have always believed since Grade 3 or 4, is not only misplaced, but futile; it rejects so much of Filipino reality, including the role that popular Tagalog culture has assigned to the language, a function daily evident in the ease, for instance, with which our TV singers shift from a *kundiman* to the latest from The Lettermen. For those who insist that only those Filipinos who write in Pilipino are capable of producing works of enduring merit, the contemplation of the careers of such novelists as Conrad and Nabokov should be most enlightening. In a small, obscure town at this moment, who knows, a schoolboy has just discovered in himself a special sensitivity to the English language. Perhaps he will in his manhood write the Greatest Filipino Novel, to be read wherever English is not an unfamiliar medium, which means not only in his own land, but in many countries (the Russians and the Chinese are even now busy learning it). Or perhaps he will be struck by supernationalistic lightning on the road to his Damascus, and this Filipino genius of literature from Laguna or Ilocos Sur or Negros Oriental or Lanao del Sur, despite his early devotion to English, will end up writing his masterpiece in Tagalog or Ilocano, or Cebuano. In that event, let us hope that he will find an English translator worthy of his greatness, lest the world be deprived of his art. For the world has been generous, has provided us with the riches in Tolstoy, Mann, Camus, Kawabata, Borges, and a legion of others— in English. *Utang na loob* should operate in the realm of art and culture no less than in economics, say, or foreign relations. But here in our Bayang Magiliw, English is dying, or haven't you heard, *'pare ko?* The language as we know it may be black and blue, pummeled all these years by our peculiar usage or non-usage; but the pall-bearers have a long wait ahead of them. The transfusions continue via the world media—we are not about to drop out from the Hollywood trade and the satellite networks; and the President of the Republic, to cite but one Filipino author, writes his books, and quite happily, from reports, in English. Yes, Viring, there's such a thing as Filipino writing in English; a growing, evolving, improving literature, which we on *The Manila Review* salute with affection and respect. (Dissenting opinions—typed double-spaced, please—are hereby solicited; we'll accommodate them in this department or some other corner, and perhaps be spared a few long hard nights of solemn cogitation.)

But don't be misled by the foregoing: *The Manila Review* as a matter of policy favors the creative over the critical; the accent will be on fiction, poetry, drama, painting, photography—creative work, while only a charitable tolerance might be granted ponderous treatises bristling with footnotes and out to prove some Byzantine proposition or other. If we had to choose, for reasons of space, between a less than memorable short story and an inspired critical essay, it would take just a millisecond for us to select the former; the latter can wait, criticism can wait. The artist takes precedence over the critic, who would be out of business if the poets and fictionists didn't first do their work. But the artist-critic, as distinguished from the merely critical, the uncreative critic, will always be accorded due honor, and space; we'll be glad and privileged, indeed, to be able to publish critical articles by N.V.M. Gonzalez, the Tiempos and the Caspers, Ricaredo Demetillo,

Emmanuel Torres, Leonidas Benesa, and others who can write of their craft as only the true artist can. All this would sum up what we have set out to do in this journal: to provide a home and a forum for the creative imagination. That's our one unchanging commitment, and for once we must disagree with Graham Greene (our own personal candidate for the Nobel Prize), who says he would like to have "a new commitment every day of the week." And the name given this quarterly—chosen from a list with Filipino reso-nances: *Molave, Pasig, Intramuros*—is to our mind singularly apt, identifying at once the quality, the flavor, of our tasks: Manila as a byword here and abroad, as the magnetic north of writers in the archipelago, and the remembered touchstone of the Filipino artist-in-exile. (The rest is silence—or the dismal sounds and furies of the seminar-workshop.)

The Manila Review welcomes contributions from writers young and old, active or retired, male, female, or of indeterminate sex; but not political transmissions of any persuasion or tracts in de-fense of sodomy and same-sex marriage, whether these come with a note of endorsement from the budget department and stamped, self-addressed envelopes or not. Payment is usually after publica-tion, but writers in very desperate straits may collect earlier, we have been told, upon presentation of relevant documents to the proper authorities. If *The Manila Review* must come up with a slogan, it might as well be: "Down with tripe and red tape!" Such distressing products of the blighted, benighted imagination will never earn our *Imprimatur.*

(1974)

2.

THE SPECTACLE OF WRITERS in solemn assembly never fails to amaze, amuse, intrigue and intimidate us—not always in that order, though—and the prospect of the Afro-Asian Writers Conference scheduled for late this month at a plush suburban hotel moves us to what the in and chic would call Maoist self-criticism: what is it anyway about the concrete reality of writers' conferences that bothers and bewil-ders us?

Is it the tension between secret, sullen art and open forum; the contradiction between solitary poet and pundit on the podium? Is our sometimes mirthful bafflement—or heresy or prejudice or ignorance—based on the unsound proposition that writers are always better endured in print than over a loudspeaker system? Is it our traumatic failure to win, for our sophomore class in college, not even the bronze medal in the annual oratorical contest that now makes us wince at the sight of a panel of speakers about to deliver us from long-held misapprehensions? Is it simply a case of sheer sloth, or a congenital inability to sit still for longer than half an hour (except at the movies), a liability which has prevented us from learning poker, Scrabble and other civilized diversions? Or is it all due to the benighted suspicion that anyone above the age of reason can just stay home and watch TV and still not miss anything—by reading the transcripts, the conference proceedings which some industrious committee will put out anyway sooner than later? Is it about time, then, that we got rid of the notion that writers should only be read and never heard?

For these are the times, we are often painstakingly reminded, that try writers' souls. The somber solver and the sanctioned patriarch will not shrink from the service of their country's literature; and he that stands it now, deserves not the tongs of future critics and governors. No novelist is an island; every artist makes his peace with the contingent; let the dull clods be washed away by the sea. Any man's debt diminishes us. Never send to know for whom the tolls bill. And he is a scoundrel who does not take refuge in patriotism. In a word, the message is commitment, and not only to your barangay— and what better medium in the Global Village, the evolving Noosphere, than the audio-visual? Dylan Thomas and Brendan Behan went about it their own way, merrily performing before many an entranced audience; Norman Mailer and Yevgeny Yevtushenko don't mind doing their thing in the spotlight. One can reel off a list of lesser lights whose vocation seemingly is to labor at the lectern rather than in the solitude of a night-bound room.

Surely no dim-watted source of illumination was William Faulkner, who came to these parts years ago on a lecture tour sponsored by a friendly government. Mr. Faulkner looked forlorn, bemused, reduced, as he spoke wearily, haltingly, in an almost inaudible voice that didn't belong to the Compsons and the

Snopeses, about the heart of man, the soul of man, that part of him that will endure and prevail, in a sweltering auditorium packed with UP students who then and there decided to have nothing to do with Contemporary Lit. beyond what was necessary to survive the semestrals. The great writer's insomniac eyes wandered disconsolately about the hall as if searching for the nearest bar, or the far sanctuary of his book-filled study in Oxford, Mississippi; and one wonders again what uncharacteristic impulse had led the Nobel creator of Yoknapatawpha County to travel so far only to disenchant his listeners.

A Dale Carnegie seminar or one of those creative-dynamics courses much favored by idle subdebs, account executives and assistant bureau directors, might have done wonders for old Bill Faulkner the lecturer—but to judge from the record, which will be found in the libraries of future centuries, he like Mary chose the better part. To the writer, the "terrifying whiteness," as Graham Greene put it, of a blank sheet of paper waiting to be filled, can be more kind, more gratifying and immensely profitable, than rows of avid faces expecting a performance as scintillating, say, as Van Cliburn's or Sinatra's. One Sinatra fan who appears to agree with the aforesaid dictum is Nick Joaquin, the country's foremost fictionist, who, for all his sociable boisterousness, is exceedingly stage-shy. So is the brilliant novelist Wilfrido D. Nolledo, a person so private that a teaching stint at Santo Tomas became a virtual agony. Would all this prove Cyril Connolly's contention that the true function of a writer is to produce a masterpiece? And that the other functions he is made to bear—as panelist, as manifesto-maker, as activist—are less than true; are at best incidental and expendable?

The writer John Updike is one of the more famous Americans the Writers Union of the Philippines has invited to this month's conference. We haven't had the pleasure of listening to Mr. Updike holding forth from the podium, but we happen to be one of the many Asians—a considerable number in Japan, *Time* tells us—who admire the man's work, and we've read practically every crafted word he has written, including his "Talk of the Town" notes in *The New Yorker*. In its unfading green jacket, a copy of *The Centaur,* properly inscribed, stands in the center of our Updike collection like a trophy—which in a sense it is, for we acquired it in the course of a visit with the writer in Ipswich, Massachusetts, some ten years ago.

227

In the brown-golden light of that New England fall, we drank Budweiser beer from frosted cans and watched his children wrestling on the lawn and talked of nonliterary things, planes and airports and distant islands and tennis—he wore his playing togs, having just come in from a doubles match a couple of leaf-strewn blocks down the street. Tall, gangling, crew-cut, he was the relaxed, casual host and immediately impressed us as a wry sort of guy who would much rather write than talk about literary society. Has the decade since wrought a radical change in his manner and turned him like Norman Mailer into a vocal dispenser of weighty pronouncements about the fate of the planet and the vicissitudes of the inhuman condition? Or will he sulk and survey the hall seeking escape, the tennis court in Ipswich, the imagined streets and steeples of Tarbox, and in the process disappoint, as Mr. Faulkner once let down his hosts, the organizing committee of the historic enterprise?

In any event, *The Manila Review* will, as a matter of duty and service to the common good, follow the proceedings—taped and typed, if not live—and will publish in forthcoming issues the timeless, relevant, memorable pronouncements emanating therefrom.

Now emanating from the pages of this issue are the vibrations from various bright talents—namely, to start off with the fictionists, Linda Ty Casper, who has published two short story collections and a novel (*The Peninsulars*), and is currently on a Radcliffe writing fellowship to research on the Philippine-American War (the "Philippine Insurrection," in textbooks still to be revised); N.V.M. Gonzalez, one of the country's leading novelists, whose awards span the Commonwealth and the present Republic, and who now teaches English and writing in Hayward, California; Cirilo Bautista, Palanca Award poet, *Free Press* short story prize-winner and professor of literature at De La Salle College, in Manila; and Ibrahim Jubaira, of Zamboanga City, now Philippine cultural attaché stationed in Colombo, Sri Lanka. The poets form an equally formidable group: Edith L. Tiempo, a Ph.D. (English) from the University of Denver and chairman of the English department of Silliman University since 1969, has won several fiction and poetry awards, and published a novel, a collection of short stories and a book of poems, selections from which have been anthologized extensively here and abroad; Emmanuel Torres, the author of two volumes of poetry, is liberal arts professor at the Ateneo de Manila, where he is curator of the university art gallery; Federico

Licsi Espino writes fiction and poetry in English, Spanish and Tagalog, for which he has received a stack of prizes; both Marra Pl. Lanot, an editor in a Quezon City publishing house, and Tita L. Ayala, who keeps house on a Davao banana plantation, have been writing poetry of consistent distinction since their undergraduate days at the University of the Philippines.

Providing the nonfiction vibrations are Ricaredo Demetillo, poet and professor, whose criticism of Philippine criticism has already brought us at least two offers of a spirited rejoinder from his colleagues at the state university; E. Aguilar Cruz, painter and journalist, whose "autochthonous" article, though written 30 years ago, remains a strikingly valid document on art trends in the country; Wilfrido D. Nolledo, who has added to his achievements (*But for the Lovers*, a novel published by E.P. Dutton; prize-winning plays and short stories) some of Philippine cinema's more memorable screenplays, and whose article in this number first appeared in the journal *Unitas* of the University of Santo Tomas; Cristina Pantoja Hidalgo of the UP English faculty, as lucid and perceptive a critic as any literary quarterly can hope to find in this part of the world; and Franklin A. Morales, who teaches literature at the Lyceum of the Philippines and serves as consultant to the Board of Censors for Motion Pictures. The visual vibrations are the handiwork of journalist-painter-critic and *Filipino Heritage* editor in chief Alfredo R. Roces, whose drawings were recently on exhibit at the Cultural Center of the Philippines.

A number of prospective contributors have promised to deliver their manuscripts before the next quarter—Henry Francia, for one, who is putting the final touches to the script of the English-Tagalog rock-opera, *Mahal*, which we look forward to publishing; Alberto Florentino, for another, who reports he has just written two new plays; and Ninotchka Rosca, who has set aside for *The Manila Review* "at least two stories" from a collection of unpublished fiction. Nick Joaquin is coming up with "a new essay on history and culture"—surely a treat not to be missed by Joaquin fans, who comprise the majority of the more literate folk hereabouts. Sheaves of poems, and admirable stuff, too, have arrived by car or courier from Rita Gadi Baltazar, Gemino Abad, C.V. Pedroche, Cirilo Bautista and Gilbert Luis Centina. Jose Carreon is working on the Tagalog translations of his Palanca poems, for

The Manila Review; Ninotchka Rosca and Ma. Luisa Torres hope to complete "in a month or two" their translations of the Tagalog poetry of Amado V. Hernandez, Alejandro Abadilla and Virgilio Almario—bilingual works on facing pages should inspire quite a few master's theses from literature majors, aside from introducing Filipino bards of the same feather to English readers abroad.

Meanwhile, the mails have deposited in our P.O. box a load of excellent material, including a longish excerpt from Bienvenido N. Santos' latest novel, *The Man Who Looked Like Robert Taylor*, which came all the way from Wichita State University in Kansas, where Ben S. is writer-in-residence; and N.V.M. Gonzalez's article on English Literatures in the Third World—more specifically, on English as "a tool of de-colonization"—which he read as a paper at an international conference in Arkansas. Which concerns us neocolonized Filipinos indeed, and which is where we came in—the conference bit, that is.

Despite our misgivings, the *escritorium concilium* is maybe as important and valuable and necessary after all as the *Literaturae Anglicae in Mundo Tertio*. But that's enough Latin for the nonce; more would strain the little we know of the lingo, and even open us perhaps to the charge of literary obscurantism.

We are for the spread of knowledge, for light and for others having it more abundantly; we refuse to peruse the deliberately abstruse, verily a most pestiferous form of abuse. Happily, so far we on *The Manila Review* haven't prompted anyone to cry obscurantist; but pained cries raised by altogether different grievances have reached us following the release of the maiden issue. Complaints made in all sincerity, as far as we can tell, like the burden of the note, written on scented stationery yet, from an anonymous lady saying the glossy coated paper of the magazine made for difficult reading, a verdict since confirmed by myopic friends who apparently compounded their difficulties by reading under a hard bright light. Her wish therefore is our command, as some forgotten wise man once phrased it; the paper we're using this time doesn't shine like tinfoil and won't bother tender, sensitive eyes. A reader in Cebu City expressed dismay over the "unimaginative literalness" of a short story illustration: a valid vexation perhaps, but expressed without the boorish acrimony which iconoclastic ignorance takes delight in employing against the serious artist. Such

pestilential coarseness spawns—to revise Hemingway somewhat—
the lies that crawl on the skin of literature. To delouse the latter, if
it should be so infested, is the task of the intelligent, sober and
honest critic, the only kind worth printing and reading. *The Manila Review* stands ready to help qualified sprayers make good use
of their literary DDT. The agnostic, the pessimistic and the indifferent will say the temple of the Word will not be cleansed, but we
believe, yea, in the power of the sprayer.

(1975)

3.

IS THERE LIFE AFTER the writers' conference?

After the Afro-Asian Writers Symposium hosted by the Philippine Writers Union last January—yes, but maybe it's not yet time to
break out into full-throated alleluias, though it's Eastertide in The
Only Christian Nation in Asia.

Imperilled, in paralysis, was the literary life in the first two
years of martial law. But the thaw has begun, is under way. The
goods, hopefully, are about to be delivered; the buds are discernible
on the greening branches. Signs of growth, of renewal, have been posted
at the crossroads being cemented and spruced up by the present
dispensation. Where the writers go from here, and how far, will depend in large measure on the writers themselves. Authentic talent
seldom if ever consults official roadmaps and manifestos; legislation,
as the history of all the world's literature would testify, does not
produce talent and genius.

But the state can make the trip less hazardous, and more secure, more profitable to all concerned, beginning with the patrons of
the arts now entrenched in government, and whom the Lord, praise
be to Him, has seen fit to raise up in our time, to resurrect and renew
the cultural life of the Republic whether New, Mothballed or About to
Be Born.

"The Filipino imagination," the President has said, "should
not be exercised exclusively in the political and economic realms.
We Filipinos value the spirit as much as we aspire to material
advancement . . . This is the essential project of art and politics:

the liberation of the creative genius of our people." To liberate and celebrate that creative genius, the Cultural Center of the Philippines and the Folk Arts Theater were built; the National Artist Awards were created to express the nation's "gratitude and appreciation." The writers of the land, we are assured, have the best wishes of our governors and may look forward to Pentecost. We are witness to the spirit if not the body of the resurrection, and among the signs of life that are cause for rejoicing is the proposed establishment of a writing center at the University of the Philippines, a project that should hasten "the liberation of the creative genius of our people."

We have yet to see the brochure of this writing institute, but if and when it is set up, the center can be expected to be an entity of, by, and for the writers, precisely to enhance the writing life in this country. That, it scarcely needs to be said, should be its sole reason for being; funds for development are not unlimited, and these, the national leadership would remind us, are to be applied judiciously, where most needed. A writing center, of the proportions envisioned, is of course premised on the proposition that the making of novels and plays and poems is no less important to the life of the nation than the manufacture of fertilizer or the discovery of a cure for the coconut-killing *cadang-cadang*. Impatient thinkers of a heretical bent would argue that, in the larger perspective, the development of the national literature is the more important business.

More often than not, impatient heresy defeats itself, achieves nothing—until a century or two afterwards. When so much is at stake, do not light your pyre, but let your heart burn within you, as did the disciples on the road to Emmaus. The art of the possible and the proximate should encourage us to accept a more modest decree: that the arts be given as much assistance as is now bestowed on the irrigation program. *Sursum corda*: the national leadership recognizes the role and value of writers as the country's more precious resources, not depleted but rather augmented, enriched and refined by use, their intrinsic worth unaffected by debauched currencies and fluctuations on the stock market.

Like the Great Filipino Novel that remains to be written, the projected writing center teases the mind with a host of possibilities. What will be the shape, the visage of this creature that draws closer to Diliman to be born? Given its essence, how will it demonstrate its nature? How will it operate in its time and place in our society? How will it resolve the tensions between politics and literature, an issue that, not a few would contend, is very much at the heart of the matter, from Cervantes to Rizal to Solzhenitsyn? Or will it view the matter differently and declare that the conflict is only apparent, that literature *is* politics, that the writer can no more disengage himself from the sociopolitical fact than the human organism can subsist without air and water? Will it take more kindly to the "committed" than to the "nonpartisan"—or will it promote the development of both, its solicitude extended equally to the poet tormented by a private Inferno and the novelist aflame with visions of national liberation? Will its curriculum accommodate cantos of outraged conscience as well as lyrics celebrating nothing more tremendous than the love of man for woman?

So much for the broad considerations. As for the narrower, though no less vexing, questions: how will such a writing center cause literature to be created, to be written, not just discussed, analyzed, studied, as is already being done even in the Quiapo-Sampaloc universities? Will it try to "teach" writing, as the fraudulent or the misguided profess to do—or, more wisely, will it gather the creative, the actual as well as the potential ones, and provide whatever help is needed, moral and material, for each writer's unique and fullest development? The latter approach opens up many avenues of assistance to both active practitioner and would-be writer: in the form of fellowships, grants and pensions; the time and the freedom to reflect, to create, or simply to roam about and do "nothing." Even in idleness, that strange sloth which the world finds hard to understand, the truly creative writer, the gifted writer, does not cease to do his work.

The proposed writing center should be able to correct an anomaly which, again, is brought to mind by all the lofty rhetoric reverberating from the usual commencement exercises this April. What have our universities, self-styled dynamos of art and culture, vaunted havens of the humanities, done to strengthen and promote the writing life? Some of our best writers, the country's pride, have fled to more hospitable campuses abroad, while virtual illiterates stay on as college deans, or heads of literature and language departments: the one-eyed charlatan is lord of the blind. A Catholic university, run by an order famous for its centuries-old fidelity to the humanities—*Lux in Domino,* and *Eloquentia et Sapientia,* as well—appears to have exchanged its commitment to the liberal arts for an obsession with business education, which, concededly, produces graduates who are generally simple and tractable, unlike those troublesome alumni who ended up at the wrong end of a firing squad at Bagumbayan. Endowments to institutes of management and golf tournaments and pelota courts for bankers and advertising executives are given priority—while nary a centavo from the reverend treasurer goes to the publication, say, of a collection of poems. By definition, a university values its poets more than its golf or pelota players; and until the poets on the faculty and in the alumni association come up with their own sports league, the situation at the very least calls for an administrative examination of conscience. The Exercises of St. Ignatius would be most useful in this regard, stressing as they do the primacy of the spiritual, the mental and intangible (and, by extension, the artistic) over the allurements of Beelzebub and the imperatives of Mammon.

Among our colleges and universities, one counts on the fingers of one hand the institutions which are not bereft of a certain affectionate regard for artists and writers. The University of the Philippines, Santo Tomas, Silliman and, of late, De La Salle (long a bastion of the business mind)—the writer may seek and find shelter on their premises. Still, the hospitality granted the creative sensibility would seem to be more the child of tolerance than enthusiastic policy. The writer-professor is expected to perform in the classroom as industriously as his nonwriting colleague (with lamentable results on the former's creativity), else he risks losing his quota of classes come next school year. Perhaps only a presidential decree can inspire university administrators to be more generous to the writers in their employ. Despite inflation and all, the gross of academe can support a few cultural endeavors, to help liberate the creative genius of the race. For instance, a university-funded foundation for writers would do more for the life of the mind and the spirit—the life which the schools are vowed to nurture, and which will long endure after the GNP technicians have crawled to their rest—than another gym or tennis court or one more airconditioned wing for the college of commerce, which will only add to the horde of unemployed banking and finance majors.

A major obstacle to the fuller development of literature in our country is the publisher who, like the business-minded "educator," is incapable of treating the writer as more than a product to exploit, to sell, to "maximize" profitability, as the management boys like to say. The Writers Union of the Philippines is well aware of the problem and is considering filing a suit against a large publishing firm, a printing and book-distributing outfit that has made it a habit of using the works of Filipino writers and giving them little if any compensation.

Among the numerous titles which this Quezon City-based publishing company issues annually if not semestrally (the student population explosion echoes merrily in the board room) is an anthology of short stories, the long-suffering authors of which were paid the princely sum of 30 pesos each about 15 years ago, when the book was introduced by its enterprising editors in an overcrowded diploma mill. The book has since gone into several editions, to the delight of the anthologists and their employer, and to the dismay of the writers who never again heard from the publisher after the first form letter soliciting their "permission to reprint."

An official of the Writers Union—a spirited lady whose elegant essays are much favored by pirate-editors—talks over her gin and tonic not only of halting the further printing of such books, but of impounding all copies in stock, and having the culprits hauled off to Camp Crame. All of which the Writers Union could well bring off, for aside from the government's sympathy, it has received a formal pledge of assistance from the Integrated Bar of the Philippines. Indeed it is time our writers were treated less cavalierly by the book-merchants. One test case, and the ensuing bad publicity, should suffice to make the book-businessmen and their agents think long and hard before using "approved reading materials" without permission, or under patently unjust terms, or, as has happened once too often, without any compensation.

But what if these publishers then ban Philippine literature from their presses and just stick to cookbooks, tourism brochures, and manuals on animal husbandry? It would be a consummation they themselves devoutly do not wish, for the audience, the market, if you will, for Philippine writing, in English and Pilipino and other Filipino languages, is not diminishing, is in fact growing, despite some morose obituaries to the contrary. Government policy, the focus on the indigenous, ongoing programs to make the Filipino more conscious and proud of his heritage, his culture, his art, his literature—profit-oriented pragmatists that they are, the booksellers dare not disregard all this, even as their cash registers ring in the day's loot from *The Joy of Sex*, not to mention Mills & Boon.

And if the powers now resplendent and regnant should decide to underwrite, on a large and meaningful scale, the creation and publishing and reprinting of literature. . . conceivably, in such beneficent circumstances, more works will be written, the abusive publishers can close shop for all the writers care, and time will bring about the rest, including the responsive readership the lack of which Mr. Nolledo decried in the January issue of this journal.

As in other vital areas in our developing society, production must rate highly on the agenda. The contractor for parade floats, according to current professional rates, gets something like six figures. Now the nation certainly can do with fewer parades and floats, which only the childish and mesocephalic care to remember the weekend after. But the nation, the true life of the nation, today and tomorrow, needs to be infused with a flow of literature: novels, plays, books of short stories, poems and essays, the most deplorable of which can outlast the monumental efforts of the propagandists and the PR operators. Suppose the allocation for one parade float were to be awarded, instead, to some deserving playwright or novelist . . . that kind of bread, spread often enough, could kick off the literary renaissance that's always around the corner.

Of course, manna from literature-loving patrons is no guarantee of excellence, greatness. Sponsors of awards and contest judges do make gross mistakes, and prizes sometimes merely honor the supine and the ridiculous. But in themselves literary awards, fellowships and such, in the context especially of a growing, developing literature, do draw out a tremendous amount of ambition, energy and talent that otherwise would be claimed by more pressing, immediately rewarding ventures. After a brief brilliant season many a writer of promise has disappeared into the maw of matrimony or business or the bureaucracy, never to be heard from again by humankind—because, unless endowed with superhuman qualities, he simply could not function as a writer and at the same time appease his mother-in-law and other authorities he as a member of civil society cannot defy with impunity. (A single book in more

236

enlightened communities can take care of the mortgage and the groceries, and leave enough to spare for holiday cruises and other amenities.)

The portrait of the artist as a starved young man working on his masterpiece in a dusty garret is as false and silly as the notion that there exist in the Philippines such Victorian nooks and crannies for the artist to starve in (though there are other corners in the house where he may languish away from malnutrition). Hunger may induce visions; to translate these visions into stanzas, paragraphs, chapters, pages of print, the writer has need of adequate nourishment (some would prefer a liquid diet, courtesy of San Miguel or La Tondeña), lest he lapse into a cataleptic fit.

If not yet so instructed, the budget disbursers should be reminded that a patriotic compassion on their part can help Filipino writers in desperate straits escape that cataleptic fate, that sterile and almost inanimate trance, which is the opposite of the creative life. To produce, perhaps to earn a pension . . . "Why should we honor those that die upon the field of battle," said Yeats, "a man may show as reckless a courage in entering into the abyss of himself." From the mine, the deep creative shaft, the writer emerges with his treasure—whether of great price or small, triumphant or most plain and humble, it goes into the building of the edifice that is our national literature.

Stone upon stone, year after year, the structure broadens its base, grows, and rises. The architecture would reflect the evolving richness and variety and density of the surrounding terrain. A country's literature is not just one or two or three masterworks, as England's is not only the works of Shakespeare and Bernard Shaw, and Russia's, not only *War and Peace* and the stories of Pushkin and Chekhov. The national literature is the accumulated weight and depth and breadth of a multitude of efforts, major, minor, and in between; and acclaimed or accursed, decorated or denounced, every writer who is worthy of the name and is not silenced, contributes his share to the vast and noble enterprise, the construction of a home for the heartbeat and soul, the memories, dreams and visions of the nation.

Recently returned from their quarry with building blocks for the edifice are this quarter's writers led by Nick Joaquin, whose eminence in Philippine letters is disputed only by the ingrate and the ignorant. The first piece he has written since his abrupt unemployment in September 1972, his essay in this issue, according to one who should know—the occasionally modest Joaquin himself—"will change the way history is being written in this country," a view with which we heartily agree, having had to plow through the witless prose and the constricted perspectives of our professional historians, or historiographers, as these be-degreed scholars like to call themselves. Without even a secondary degree to his name (he rejected an honorary doctorate from a Jesuit university, perhaps to affirm his loyalty to the Dominicans, whose seminarian he once was), Joaquin the novelist, short story writer, poet, playwright and journalist is the nation's premier writer, the most profound and eloquent artist of our time.

As dedicated to the craft, and one of our ablest prose stylists and poets, Bienvenido N. Santos is professor and writer-in-residence at Wichita State University in Wichita, Kansas, whence came the novella-length excerpt from his unpublished novel, *The Man Who (Thought He) Looked Like Robert Taylor*. A recipient of the Republic Cultural Heritage Award and other honors, Ben Santos has written some of the best short stories in our literature; one of these, "The Day the Dancers Came," about the Filipino as exile, *The Manila Review* intends to reprint, in tribute to one of the country's finest writers.

To complete the trio at the spear-point, as it were, of our literature's forward thrust, the excellent novelist, critic and fisherman, N.V.M. Gonzalez, appears in this number with an article on the English Literatures of the Third World, originally a paper delivered at an international teachers' symposium in Little Rock. Arkansas. His perceptions of English as a tool of de-colonization should give pause to the vociferous patriots in our midst who have no use for the language brought to our sacred shores by George Dewey and the Thomasites.

To all appearances not only at ease in the language but employing it with precise grace and passion are Antonio Enriquez and Benjamin S. Bautista, fiction awardees both, the former a government information officer based in Zamboanga City, the latter a department head of an agro-business firm in Makati. Even more committed to the same tradition—poetry after all is nothing if not a pure intensity of language—are the poets featured in this issue, a whole phalanx of them: Gemino H. Abad, a Palanca Award winner who teaches at the UP; Emmanuel Lacaba, who is also a short story writer, stage actor, lyricist and critic; Rita Gadi Baltazar, an attractive official of the Department of Labor, which position has not aborted her poetic labors; Guillermo C. de Vega, an artist currently in twin disguise, as Special Assistant to the President and chairman of the Board of Censors for Motion Pictures; Mauro Avena, formerly with an investment bank and now happily free-lancing; Conrado V. Pedroche, who since pre-war days has been writing memorable fiction and poetry; and Celestino M. Vega, likewise a competent veteran, after long years of service on the verge of retirement from a government agency, but never, he assures us, from the art of poetry.

Mr. Vega's vigorous confidence, shared by fellow artists young, middle-aged and ancient, is one more unmistakable sign of life, of renewed hope in the future of the national literature. The sap rises; the green breaks out smiling on the face of the land. The writers are writing, the critics are criticizing, the editors are editing—an anthology of poems was published recently, edited by the distinguished poet and critic Emmanuel Torres; and any day now, the Writers Union will issue a volume of new writing in commemoration of the Afro-Asian Writers Symposium. As though prompted by the energy generated by the Symposium, a number of workshop conferences have been held in the past few weeks, the most notable being the seminar on "Afro-Asian Literary Awakening" at De La Salle College and the conference on ways to promote the creation and quality of literature, at the Development Academy of the Philippines.

The workers are busy in the quarry, or the mine, or the vineyard, or at the building site, or wherever our rather peripatetic metaphors have taken them; anywhere but in limbo or hell. It looks like it's going to be a great building. It looks like a great harvest. Alleluia? Well, OK, Alleluia, just once, but with feeling.

(1975)

4.

THE VIEW FROM THE ORCHESTRA, the movie critics assure us, is getting better all the time. They don't mean the Hollywood and Cinecitta imports, but Filipino films, Tagalog pictures, which the local cognoscenti used to flog out of a sense of duty. Since the state of film criticism has generally been healthier than the state of homegrown films, it behooves every movie addict capable of a minute or two of sustained thought to pay solemn heed to the glad tidings.

The skeptic whose neocolonial precedents have conditioned him to swear by the likes of Antonioni, Truffaut, Kubrick and Polanski (as well as critics like Sontag and Kael) is urged to hurry over to his friendly neighborhood theater and see for himself: Filipino films are not what they used to be, when the simple, unadorned, unambitious *bakya* clattered down the aisle on Saturday afternoons. Our films are now more serious, more intelligent, more profound, goes the refrain. Not that the industry never before desisted from insulting the movie-going intelligentsia—it did come up with some classics, as the aficionados are quick to remind us: *Badjao, Anak Dalita, Biyaya ng Lupa.* But what's really cause for celebration now, we are told, is that this season's new wave appears to have all the features of a long high tide broad and strong enough to wash away once and for all the flotsam and jetsam, and a jumble of curious artifacts besides, that have for so long clogged our movie screens.

A most disturbing claim, fraught with revolutionary implications. Before all that garbage, if it be such, is flushed away to oblivion, perhaps we should give it one last sympathetic, even loving sniff, on behalf of the multitudes who never regarded it as a condemnable mess. For the species of Filipino film that, from reports, is about to become extinct, is not without some redeeming value, a necessary social function: which is, quite simply, to distract the people from the burdens of their condition. (Marx had it all wrong: it is not religion that is the opium of the people.) From the first bucolic tear-jerkers to the recent bomba-karate productions, Philippine cinema has succeeded exceedingly well in subverting reality, disarming it, making it more attractive, more agreeable: fantasy as national liberation.

But to judge from the trend typified by the works of Lino Brocka, the new Filipino film would promote another mode of subversion, that which Rizal the novelist introduced in our literature. A major function of this movement and this discipline is the demolition of myths, none of which, in our society, is more insidious perhaps than the happy ending. Illusions explode in the pages of our fiction. The unhappy Maria Clara stands petrified on the convent roof, a ghostly figure framed by thunder and lightning. Simoun commits suicide in the desolate house by the sea. A bullet kills Concha Vidal, Tony Samson dies on the railway tracks, in the hopeless dawn. An abyss separates the popular dream (the *contrabida* knocked out cold, the lovers singing happily ever after) from Julio Madiaga, in *Maynila: Sa Mga Kuko ng Liwanag,* trapped in a dead-end alley, the blood-stained ice pick still in his hand, death in the black form of a mob rushing toward him and blasting from out of his throat a long soundless scream.

Julio Madiaga's cry of protest, terror and despair, so deep as to transcend all sound and utterance, rends the veil behind which many of us are not prepared to look. Artists of a somber disposition, of an absolute honesty and integrity, call our attention to what lies beyond the screen, even as most of the world's business, its rites, codes, games and entertainments, strive to deny it. Not too many moviegoers care to look in that direction, just as few readers are inclined to contemplate the bleak vision of a Kafka or a Beckett. Wars, massacres, murders and various other horrors treated according to the proper commercial formulas provide the harmless pleasures of vicarious experience; but for the uncompromising filmmaker to define, in starkly convincing terms, the shape of human destiny as he sees it, unredeemed and inescapable, is something else, an anomaly, a heresy that appeals only to a certain quality of imagination and courage.

Films like *Maynila* will, in all probability, remain the bold exceptions to the rule, contrary currents in the still prevalent wave on whose crest bobs the cheerful troupe of Chiquito and Dolphy. Unless popular tastes have been transformed overnight by some miracle or decree, Grade-B movies and the other films pegged lower down the alphabet will continue to draw and mesmerize the majority of the populace. Which is just as well—for if cinema creators like Brocka had their way and filled all our screens, and TV too, with all sorts of existential agonies and heaven knows what forms of neo-realist wisdom besides, what is to become of all those movie fans, and they are legion, who are devoted to *Darna* and are consoled by *John & Marsha*? Since the state is duty-bound, especially in times of crisis, to bring comfort to the commonalty, think of the enormous resources and energies it will have to expend, to replace all that cinematic balm now still accessible, happily, in our movie theaters.

Still dispensing, when we visited it last, the same romance and derring-do to what seemed like the same audiences, was the moviehouse where, countless reels and scores of theaters ago, we saw our first film. Much like its double programs, the Cine Oriente appeared to have changed little, except for superficial touches on the façade, and some concessions to technology, the most evident one being a wider screen.

The hard wooden benches still creaked and harbored bedbugs; electric fans rattled in the warm urine-smelling dark; the lights during intermission revealed the same sheet-iron roof and sawali walls—no matter, we remember the place with an affection such as one reserves for an address where one was perfectly happy. It contained a universe compared with which the world inhabited by parents, siblings, schoolmates, teachers and assorted authorities was drab and tame, indeed; its revelations were of the same order as landfall to the first ocean mariners, or the unfolding of an uncatalogued galaxy to the astronomers on Mount Palomar. Night after night, the handsome, the beautiful and the virtuous triumphed over monsters, wild beasts, tyrants, criminals, calamities and heartbreak.

Night pervades our memory of the place. A blaze of yellow bulbs illuminated the front of the theater: from across the plaza the low, square building looked like a solitary funhouse left at the edge of a dark plain. Puffs of winged insects blew in from the dark and pulsed among the bulbs, above the thin woman in rags selling peanuts, the dusty apron of cement, the torn photo stills on the stained wall. Before it acquired its own power plant, the town where the Cine Oriente cast its spell received its nightly quota of electricity from a neighboring province; the lights came on only at dusk. While the day had an exclusive claim on reality, night and the cinema enjoyed a certain affinity, as though one could not have an existence without the other. The sense of that nighttime air sometimes touches us still, as we sit in the airconditioned dark of a city theater many years away from that provincial moviehouse coming to life in the twilight. . .

Lights at dusk, a flickering screen, sounds and images in a shadow-filled, circumscribed space—something tribal, secret and instinctive in the memory of those nights has been transposed, one feels, into Beatriz Romualdez Francia's *Mahal*, the script of which is featured in this issue. Los Indios Bravos, the gallery-

242

theater-café in Ermita commemorated, three years after it closed shop, by the first "electro-mechanical, mystical Filipino rock musical," had its own nocturnal aura, a confined lamplit quality that was hospitable to a breed of writers, artists, visionaries and related mystics intent on one kind of trip or another. More often than not the trips led somewhere—euphoria, ecstasy, nausea, nirvana, karma, a diminishing or heightening of reality, which is what art, and *Mahal*, are all about.

Some of the Indios faithful may find fault with the characters and configurations of the musical's Kosmik Kafe; others in the congregation may quarrel with the order and pacing of the episodes, as these were initially presented at the Cultural Center earlier this year. (A shorter version is forthcoming, according to the producers.) But only the most fastidious among the elect will dispute the vitality, the irrepressible force, the unprecedented concentration of talent, energy and nostalgia that went into the making of *Mahal*. Read in the proper spirit, the script more than suggests the rock opera's unique thrust and power; it should also provide the cultural historian with material for a chapter dealing with the Manila art scene of the 1960s. That chapter will not be complete without a roster of the Indios initiates, among whom were some of the country's finest painters and poets.

Among the latter would be Cesar Ruiz Aquino, five of whose recent poems appear in this issue. Formerly of Zamboanga City and Silliman, he is now resident guru in Baguio City, where he teaches at the UP College. Likewise a poet in academe is Luis Cabalquinto, who studied writing at Cornell University, taught at Los Baños, has been published in poetry anthologies in the U.S. and Australia, and is at present taking graduate studies in English at the University of the Philippines. Perhaps never an Indios habitue but in spirit and style identifiable with that now dispersed fraternity, Arnold Molina Azurin is as versatile and restless as they come, commuting between Manila and his native town, Vigan, on various cultural errands, and still finding time to write feature articles for the weeklies and dispatches for a news agency. From farther north is Edilberto M. Guerrero of San Nicolas, Ilocos Norte; a University of the East alumnus and a public relations man with Great Wall Advertising, he hopes to come out soon with his second collection of poems, to be called "Full Circle," which is the title of his cycle of 12 poems in this issue. Ricardo de Ungria, a Manileño, studied at De La Salle and the UP, and before his present teaching job was a lead singer, for "three rocking years," of the disco-playing Finnegans Wake Band, which may or may not account for his somewhat Joycean flair for words.

Wordsmiths with familiar bylines are this issue's nonfiction contributors: Petronilo Bn. Daroy, a literary critic and essayist with the UP English Department, and Loretta Lichauco, a literature and art history graduate of the University of Edinburgh who wrote reviews for the *Manila Chronicle* between teaching sessions at Assumption and De La Salle, and now runs the Kalinangan ng Lahi theater-gallery in Quezon City, which appears to be gaining a following as motley and talented as the old Indios crowd. Familiar names, too, and doubtless with their own following, are the painter and art theoretician Esquivel Embuscado, who writes on the aesthetics of dissection; Ninotchka Rosca, winner of Palanca and *Free Press* fiction awards and a magazine journalist of note; E.P. Patanñe, former magazine editor and now publicist for a bank, whose "The Bomb" is one of the three Philippine short stories included in a PEN anthology published in Korea; Norma Miraflor, a prize-winning fictionist now editing a Singapore-based monthly; and C.V. Pedroche, who started writing in earnest back in the good old 1930s—when, by the way, LVN Pictures, Premiere Productions and the Cine Oriente came into being, and Ely Ramos, Rudy Concepcion, Jose Padilla, Jr., Rogelio de la Rosa, Carmen Rosales, Rosa del Rosario, Norma Blancaflor, Tita Duran, Paul Muni, Clark Gable, James Cagney, Errol Flynn, Olivia de Havilland, Joan Crawford, Barbara Stanwyk, Marlene Dietrich, Charlie Chaplin, the Marx Brothers, Johnny Weismuller, Tim McCoy and Rin-tin-tin beckoned to the multitudes and offered them surcease from boredom, loneliness, melancholia, neuralgia, heartburn and the thousand shocks that flesh is heir to, as their successors continue to do, in our day, and will keep on doing, subverting reality, altering it, making it less bitter and abrasive, more kind, malleable and enthralling, offering a glimpse of that paradise man lost by his original sin and would ever try to regain despite the gut-wrenching, heart-tearing final terror of Julio Madiaga's scream.

To help man forget, if only for a while, the consequences (now showing or coming soon) of his primal fault, or to remind him of his fate—either enterprise is not opposed to the highest art. For this, we have the testimony of the supreme dramatist, no less: the bard and playwright who wrote *King Lear* as well as *A Midsummer Night's Dream*.

(1975)

5.

THE ART OF THE STORYTELLER bids fair to be the world's oldest profession. While evidence for the antiquity of the other commerce amounts to folklore or fiction, literary scholars point to the great number of tales, delightful pieces that entertained our shaggy ancestors in the flickering night, conceivably before they went off to hunt for other nocturnal pleasures in the dawn of history.

One of the finest extant examples of the short story, for instance, is the Egyptian "Anpu and Bata," which dates back to around 1500 B.C. and suggests, we are told, an even earlier ancestry, a more ancient literary tradition that spanned the reigns of several Pharaohs. "Once there were two brothers, of the same father and the same mother, and the older of the two was married"—variations on the theme of Potiphar's wife have since been recounted in narratives as different and far apart as *The Arabian Nights*, *The Divine Comedy*, and last Sunday's episode of the season's top-rated TV serial. The ancient Chinese and Hindus, the shepherds and warriors in the days of Homer and the Hebrew prophets, the first Malay settlers on the nilad banks of the river Pasig—all had their stories to relate and remember, responding to the same impulse of the heart and imagination that today creates fiction in its multimedia forms; the same summons in our time to comprehend, through the art of the novelist, the playwright and the screenwriter, what it means for men and women to be born into the world.

If not the oldest, it's certainly one of the most durable and pervasive of man's preoccupations, so that even fictionists whose fancies no longer turn lightly to springy lasses continue to be prolific in their labors. Tolstoy was a venerable patriarch of prose when he produced his huge fertile novels; Kawabata was no strapping young man when he penned his masterful portrait of the Master of Go; and Graham Greene in his seventies has not ceased to add "new territory," in the words of the critic Alfred Kazin, "to the distinguished continent of his fiction," the latest such conquest being yet another novel on betrayal and salvation set in the humid geography of Africa.

245

The list is long—of writers, many Nobel laureates among them, whose devotion to their art neither debts nor taxes, arthritis nor arbitrary censors could diminish or destroy.

That time and age should make them more deeply committed to an enterprise begun in early youth is cause indeed for amazement—on the part of those tough old realists who insist they have no use for fiction as they go about imposing their economic or political order on the chaos in their neighborhoods. These practical fellows live their fictions without knowing it, and very likely are avid fans of television and the movies, which modern-day storytellers have made their domain. The irony cannot but delight fictionists like the Argentinian Borges, with his somber yet playful obsession with labyrinths, mirrors and disguises.

For the fact is that the race wouldn't be human, it might as well go to the rats, if by some dictator's decree fiction in all its forms were banished from the earth as inimical to the New Sanity. A remote possibility, though, for most human beings at this stage of their evolution, including those empowered to proscribe all literature that disagrees with their grand designs, do enjoy stories, in print or pictures, on stage or screen. Future ages may see the development of fictional forms such as only science-fantasy writers now dare dream of—the universe of a 23rd-century Shakespeare, for instance, distilled in a dream-producing pill to be taken at bedtime. The essence of the art, however, will ever remain the same: the communication of an artist's personal, individual vision that's more significant and appealing (and quite often more disturbing) than the communiques of pedagogues, pundits and politicians.

But to come down to the here and now that we inhabit: the Filipino's fascination with fiction antedates the novels of Jose Rizal, and has become so ingrained a habit, an attribute of his personality, that any dissection of what's called the National Identity would be grossly incomplete unless it examined this particular alchemy. To be sure, imported fiction, much of it maudlin trash, is favored by an alarmingly high percentage of the populace, as confirmed by the sales charts of the Avenida Rizal bookstands; and those kinky *komiks* being sold or rented out all over town draw far more readers than Nick Joaquin, Florentino Dauz and Efren Abueg put together. Many a promising writer, too, has given up the dream of writing that great Filipino novel for some other easier, more lucrative trade. But despite all this,

246

the vital signs are again on the upswing in the intensive care ward, which is occasion enough for at least two cheers.

The novel and the short story in these parts simply refuse to expire and be interred, the usual morose diagnoses notwithstanding. In fact, Filipino fictionists, particularly those who write in Pilipino, have never been busier; what will all those komiks and films trying to keep pace with a galloping population, no weaver of local illusions need languish in the stalls of abject poverty. Meanwhile, for those with literary sights trained not exactly dead-center on the mass-market, there are the annual Palanca and *Focus* awards; the recently announced Regal Press contest for the best novels in Pilipino and English; and the Cultural Center of the Philippines' forthcoming competition for the best novels, also in the two languages, to mark its 10th anniversary late next year. Fictionists too but of a different genre, the playwrights are as active and militant and relevant as ever, as befits those who proudly invoke the name of Pampango dramatist Aurelio Tolentino. And convinced perhaps that publishers in a compassionate society shouldn't live by high-priced textbooks alone, some booksellers have begun seeking out Filipino fiction for priority listing in their catalogues.

But whether the prospects are economically encouraging or not, there's a breed of writers for whom the writing of fiction is nothing less than a vocation demanding a constant striving for excellence, a quality of technique to bear the weight of deeper perceptions; and it is more such writers, and less their critics or readers, that Nick Joaquin and N.V.M. Gonzalez, two of our foremost fictionists, must have had in mind when they wrote the critical essays which are featured in this issue. Joaquin's "The Filipino as English Fictionist" raised Tagalog hackles when it was delivered as a lecture earlier this year; but the intention clearly was to clarify certain aspects of the art for the benefit of homegrown fictionists in either language. The renowned oracle may be less than fallible when discussing Tagalog literary traditions; but the spirit of truth can be seen hovering over his lectern when he holds forth on what fiction is or should be, in the Philippine setting. At the very least, the piece in question offers certain observations, insights into the craft and its language, that the Filipino fictionist might ponder to his advantage.

The same applies to Gonzalez's "Notes on a Culture and a Method," which tells of how the author went about writing "On the

Ferry." The latter is not Gonzalez's latest short story, having been written in 1963, but it happens to be one of his finest, and reprinting it here together with the writer's own discussion of his work should provide a critical stimulus, we thought, to faltering fictionists in need of such stimuli. For all their carefully nurtured individualism, the solitary nature of their art (stories and poems after all are not written by committees), writers do teach and learn from one another, and the process doesn't require enrollment in a summer workshop, either. Reading what a conscientious fictionist like Gonzalez has written on the making of one excellent story can be much more enlightening than attendance in a literary seminar combining tedious lectures, bizarre accents and doctrinaire egos, and redeemed only by the presence of poetic beauties.

No less illuminating are the two other articles in this issue—*"Florante at Laura* as Allegory of Protest" by Lucilla Hosillos, a Ph.D. from Wisconsin who is with the UP English Department; and "Religion and Nationalism in Rizal" by Father Raul J. Bonoan of the Ateneo de Manila and the Loyola House of Studies. Competent explorations, among other things, into the sensibilities of two great figures in Filipino literature, these articles, on Balagtas and Rizal, should appeal not only to the literati but to everyone with a more than casual interest in Philippine art and culture.

No casual dabbler in matters historical is Lilia Ramos-de Leon, staff writer and secretary to the board of the National Historical Institute of the Philippines, whose short story, "One Day in Jerusalem," marks her first appearance in this journal. She has published fiction and essays in various national publications, as has Amadis Ma. Guerrero, the author of two fiction collections and a staff member of the publications section of the Population Center Foundation. An Ateneo alumnus, Guerrero in his "Retreat" deals with a time and temper quite removed from the skeptical seventies, which fact should provide historians with a footnote or two. More explicit data the art historian or biographer will find in "The Gallant and Graceful Art of Abueva," an interview with the distinguished sculptor and National Artist by Eric S. Caruncho, a journalism graduate of the UP Institute of Mass Communication.

Also a UP Masscom graduate is this issue's lead poet, Luis Cabalquinto, who sent over his poems from New York City, where he is writing more poetry and finishing a first novel. About the other poets in this issue (storytellers, too, in their own passion, a flock of

248

the same species as the bards who sang of legends and omens around the first camp fires): Ernesto Superal Yee is a graduate student in creative writing at Silliman University; Jose F. Lacaba, former magazine journalist, is working on a couple of screenplays; Melito Baclay is about to get his MBA at the University of San Carlos in Cebu City; C. Meng Magno, from Dagupan City, is on the editorial staff of *Focus* magazine; Elsa Martinez-Coscolluela, a Palanca and Cultural Center of the Philippines awardee for fiction and drama, holds an M.A. in Creative Writing from Silliman and is currently academic dean at Our Lady of Mercy College in Bacolod City; Santo Tomas Philosophy and Letters graduate Ricardo A. Trinidad is the sports-writing Recah Trinidad of *Expressweek* magazine; Carlos G. Novenario is with the Presidential Press Staff in Malacañang.

This issue's playwright, Mig Alvarez Enriquez, earned his MFA in Creative Writing at Iowa University in 1957, and teaches at the University of the East in Manila, which recently staged "The Other Maria Clara," a zarzuela based on his novel, *The Devil Flower*, at the Cultural Center of the Philippines. His three-act "A Tale of Two Houses" demonstrates, vividly, the wide reach and timber, the power of fiction in the dramatic mode: it is as resonant with history as the works of Joaquin, with whom he shares a nostalgic affection for those customs and ceremonies in which art and beauty are born.

"To remember and to sing . . ." Thus wrote Virgil or Tolstoy or Joaquin. Such is the vocation of the storyteller: the lonely voice raised in remembrance and celebration, solitary, sometimes scorned, often unrewarded, yet persisting in drawing us closer to the firelight, the warmth of our common humanity—an art as old as man, and as new as the young unknown teller of tales who comes forward, hopefully, to offer us his gifts.

(1978)

6.

WE HOLD THESE TRUTHS to be self-evident (sometimes) in certain scholarly circles: that historians are not created equal, that they don't all endow their creations with the same admirable qualities, that among these are life, liberty from error and prejudice, and the pursuit of excellence.

There are historians who are born writers, and there are historians who, it seems, would rather suffer a myocardial infarction than write interestingly and well. There are historians whose popularity and influence, especially among would-be revolutionaries on excitable campuses, are inversely proportional to the narrowness of their vision, the limitations of their scholarship; and there are historians who measure up to the highest standards of the profession, yet are relatively unhonored and unsung, not to say unread, because they have no enthusiasm for that romantic, absolute, wipe-the-slate-clean kind of nationalism so irresistible to the more vocal and ambitious among the undergraduate masses. Some historians, assisted by a ghostly horde of researchers and writers, bestow on mankind works so monumental they might as well be cast in bronze and erected at the Cultural Center; while other historians, utterly lacking in resources and resourcefulness, have had to pawn their last historical relic or historic heirloom to pay for the mimeographing of their badly typed monographs.

Some historians set out to write a history of a people's consciousness and end up writing what amounts to a history of *some* people's un-consciousness—that peculiar state of the "modern mind" still to be liberated from the old secular myths about the inevitable progress and perfectibility of man: a rigid frame of mind to which the final dogmas on human existence have been proclaimed by Hegel, Freud, Marx and Lenin (and, in some quarters, Mao): a doctrinaire viewpoint that calls itself materialist, yet would expound on something so spiritual as consciousness; a parochial perspective which, even as it entrenches itself, profitably so, in an institutional base made possible by the value system drawn from the Judeo-Christian tradition, cannot distinguish between the Christian faith and the Christian world, and will not consider, at the very least, the testimony of those who call themselves Christian, from Paul of Tarsus to Ignatius of Antioch some 20 centuries ago to men in our time like Christopher Dawson, Reinhold Niebuhr, Jacques Maritain, Teilhard de Chardin, Arnold Toynbee, Thomas Merton, Horacio de la Costa—historians and philosophers and scholars who have written of the leaven that is Christianity operating, despite every contradiction and hostility, in human history, which includes, it is safe to say, the history of the Filipino people.

Other historians likewise set out to write a people's history but do not fall prey to that arrogant and destructive partisanship (called nationalism by fervent sophomores) which ignores evidence not stamped with the prescribed ideological imprimatur; that presumptuousness which, as the eloquent Christian writer C.S. Lewis once described it, "claims to see fern-seed but can't see an elephant ten yards away in broad daylight." (Some historians, it is true, come close enough to the elephant to smell and massage choice portions of its anatomy, but like the six blind men in the nursery rhyme mistake the doggone animal for some other blasted thing.)

Historians whose fidelity to their vocation and sense of scholarship won't allow them to turn propagandist and disregard elephants and other realities, whether these are ten yards away or just a couple of inches in front of their noses, aren't very fashionable these days, when it is argued loudly and sometimes convincingly that socio-historical criticism, to be valid and consequential, must be so "committed" as to see only one side or end of the menagerie. But those historians who are all for recognizing elephants, lions, cows, carabaos and other beasts in the landscape, regardless of passionate opinions to the contrary, can derive some reassurance from the observations of the sociologist Andrew M. Greeley, who states, in his *A Future to Hope In,* that historical writing proceeding from a profound respect for facts will endure and in the long run prove to be far more effective and salutary than the outpourings of Mr. Goebbels' present-day counterparts, "not merely because it is balanced, but also because it is true." Eventually, "accuracy triumphs over militant propaganda, though the militants may sell a lot of books and newspapers in the process." In the Philippine situation, eventually, the cause of the people, which is not necessarily the cause of some prominent patriots, will be better served by historians who remain steadfast in the pursuit of truth, honesty and justice, and thus appeal, not to angry adolescents (most of whom forget about their revolutions when they grow up and work for a living), but to the deepest loyalties of a mature, strong, and responsible citizenry. Maybe.

These reflections on historians and their works came to us as we reread in galley proof late one night Father John N. Schumacher's piece in this issue. The review article is, among other things, an excellent antidote to the superficial, mindlessly laudatory, public-relations jobs that pass for book reviews in the Manila press. Father Schumacher's study of Renato Constantino's *A Past Revisited* should help liberate some historians and their disciples from the myths that have enchained them, so that, in the words of Mr. Constantino himself, "historical reality may be correctly perceived, the present understood, and the future envisioned."

Originally from Buffalo, New York, U.S.A., Father Schumacher entered the Society of Jesus in 1944, and came to the Philippines in 1948 to study philosophy at the Sacred Heart Novitiate in Novaliches, Quezon City; he did graduate studies in history at Georgetown University in Washington, where he obtained his Ph.D. in 1965. Since 1965 he has been professor of church history at San Jose Seminary and the Loyola School of Theology, and of Philippine history at the Ateneo de Manila University. The Jesuit historian's published works include *Father Jose Burgos: Priest and Nationalist, The Propaganda Movement, The Catholic Church in the Philippines* and *Church and State: The Philippine Experience*. A nationalistic footnote for all concerned: John N. Schumacher, S.J., is now a Filipino citizen.

Three other articles deal with the historical, which may well make history the theme of this issue, except that we didn't intend it that way: material made to order, manuscripts produced according to editorial Letters of Instructions almost always tend to be stale, flat and unreadable. Not prompted by directives of any sort other than their professional preferences, Eric Casiño, who holds a Ph.D. in Anthropology from the University of Melbourne and who's now in Honolulu as a visiting professor at the East-West Center, writes on Manila before the arrival of Legazpi; Carlos Quirino, noted historian and former director of the National Library, recalls the nationalism of Commonwealth President Manuel L. Quezon; and Elizabeth V. Reyes, versatile magazine journalist and scuba diver, presents an affectionate portrait of a museum that would preserve the culture of the lowland Christian Filipino, "the spirit and substance of our history and our heritage."

Part of that heritage, a vital aspect though not usually exhibited in museums, has to do with literature, the writing and publishing and reading of it; and each in his unique and original way, the fictionists, poets and critics in this issue add their contributions to the living, growing, evolving culture. Poet Gemino H. Abad replies to crucial questions concerning the criticism of poetry posed by his fellow University of the Philippines professor and literary critic, Isagani R. Cruz. Historians in their own fashion—of nostalgias, predicaments, conflicts and celebrations—are short story writers Tomas N. Santos, from Legaspi City, who teaches English at the University of Northern Colorado and whose fiction has appeared in *The Greenfield Review, The North American Review* and other U.S. journals; F. Sionil Jose, novelist, editor-publisher of *Solidarity*, founder and secretary of the Philippine Chapter of PEN International, and this year's Palanca first prize-winner for fiction; Antonio Reyes Enriquez, another award-winning writer, whose second collection, *Dance a White Horse to Sleep and Other Stories*, was published in Queensland, Australia, in 1977; and Jose Y. Dalisay, Jr., a staff economist at the National Economic Development Authority, and the winner of several awards for fiction, drama, and radio-TV and screenwriting.

Likewise an award winner, and explicitly historical in the poetry he has contributed to this issue, is former Development Academy of the Philippines consultant Edel E. Garcellano, whose "Conjectural Poems" project an energy and resonance worthy of the heroic figures they celebrate. More muted and private but nonetheless as intense in their histories of dreams, visions and interior journeys are the verses of the other poets in this quarter: Lilia Lopez-Chua, a graduate of the University of San Carlos in Cebu City and a business executive in Davao City; Vicente Bandillo, still at San Carlos U as a liberal arts student, and a painter who exhibits at Gallery 90, in Cebu City; Alfredo O. Cuenca, Jr., political theoretician, journalist and consultant to the Bureau of Broadcasts; Francis C. Macansantos, who has taught at Silliman University in Dumaguete City, where he recently earned an M.A. in English Literature; Simeon Dumdum, Jr., formerly with the Cebu regional office of the Ministry of Public Information and now a practicing lawyer; Baboo Mondoñedo, a well-traveled Assumption College alumna, newspaper columnist, and former hotel and advertising official; and Bienvenido N. Flores, Jr., who has an M.A. in Sociology from the University of Louvain in Belgium and is now on the faculty of St. Louis University, in Baguio City.

History as literature, literature as history: they are such close kin it's not always possible to tell one from the other. Which is just as well, for history and literature may be said to be inspired by the same muse, called forth by the same summons to write down, now that it's still day, the story of man's fate, the record of his passage.

Mindful of this, we are privileged, indeed, to be able to gather in these pages some of the country's finest historians, poets and writers of fiction, and to listen to the wisdom of their common discourse— not all the time so earth-shaking, to be sure, but all adding up to one more step, we like to think, one more paragraph if not a page or maybe two, in a chapter in the history of a people aspiring, through their art and craft, to be more human, humane, devoted, dauntless, and heroic; to be more Filipino.

(1978)

Full of Sound and Fury, Signifying Ateneo Dramatics

PRODDED BY ANXIOUS PARENTS and an uncle-alumnus who loved to declaim in Ciceronian accents, I arrived at the Ateneo de Manila in 1948 with my Tarlac transcript of records and a freshman's awe of its venerable traditions, its famous institutions. These had been restored and revitalized following the war that had reduced the Ateneo's Padre Faura campus to a desolation of shrapnel-pocked ruins; and infused with that single-minded vigor for which the Jesuits are famous, and a sort of post-Liberation exuberance, they thrived and resounded among the Quonset hut-classrooms beside the demolished buildings.

There was, first of all, the Ratio Studiorum, forged by Ignatius of Loyola and his first disciples in the University of Paris; a system of education that was at once Catholic, classical and contemporary, and one of its more audible expressions was the oratorical contest which reputedly spawned future politicos and statesmen. There was the Sodality of Mary, the Chesterton Evidence Guild, *The Guidon* and the basketball team captained by a non-Muslim called Moro Lorenzo and which bore the name "Blue Eagle," the mere utterance of which sowed fear and trembling in the heathen bleachers of De La Salle and San Beda. And there was Father Henry Lee Irwin, S.J., who taught philosophy, literature and rhetoric. Then already in his white-haired sixties, he was an institution who in a more than figurative sense embodied an Ateneo tradition—dramatics, an activity almost as old as Jose Rizal's alma mater itself, the Jesuit author and historian Miguel A. Bernad notes in his *Dramatics at the Ateneo de Manila* (Ateneo Alumni Association, Manila, 1977).

Subtitled "A History of Three Decades, 1921–1952," Father Bernad's handsomely printed book records "The Reign of Henry Lee" and several other episodes, major and minor, which made the Ateneo stage a byword in both student and professional dramatics during those years. Its focus on Father Irwin's role, his brilliant if tempestuous ways, the length and breadth of his influence, may incline one to conclude that the book is addressed exclusively to Ateneo alumni, particularly those whom he directly coached and molded on the campus. The impression that *Dramatics* was written for the benefit alone of nostalgic alumni reciting Shakespearean soliloquys over their brandy is further strengthened by such features of the book as the *Index Personarum*, which lists all those undergraduates of yore who were connected in one way or another with the plays. Not just the directors and actors, but the members of the stage-crews and the musical ensembles and the various committees (finance, tickets, publicity, etc.), make up the long roster. It would seem that only those veritable dropouts and confirmed misanthropes who had refused to come within hailing distance of the plays have been left out of the list.

Indeed, alumni from "Abad, Orlando, 271" to "Zuzara, Francisco, 264" hundreds of entries later, should find *Dramatics* a thoroughly appealing work, with its detailed accounts—in some instances, much too detailed, one feels—of what transpired behind, in front of, above, and even under the stage (as in the 1923 *Macbeth,* with the stage crew in the pit below producing smoke for the witches' cauldron). But Father Bernad's history of Ateneo dramatics is more than an essay into Ateneo de Manila nostalgia. The passages from *The Guidon*, the Ateneo student newspaper, and the footnotes referring to campus lore dear perhaps only to the hearts of true-blue Ateneistas, can turn off, as the mod expression goes, readers who would have nothing to do with the Jesuits or the college they founded in 1858. And there are quite a few such readers, to be sure, not only the old-fashioned 19th-century freethinking types, but also Catholics otherwise devoted to the

Holy Father and his soldiery. They do themselves a disservice if they fail to appreciate the story of the Ateneo stage in the context of Philippine culture and history. That this chronicle of the Ateneo theater is in fact intended to be viewed in such a context is evident in the author's prefatory remarks:

"This present monograph is an attempt to tell the story of the Ateneo stage during three exciting decades: from 1921 to 1952. The reason for choosing those decades is as follows: In 1921 a new era began for the Ateneo: the school passed from the control of the Spanish to that of the American Jesuits. Almost immediately, they produced their first play: *Julius Caesar*. The following year they staged another— but not in the Ateneo *salón de actos*: they staged it in what was then the largest and best theatre in Manila, the Grand Opera House. This was a bid for public recognition and an attempt to reach a wider public. In the eight remaining years of the Ateneo in Intramuros, one production succeeded another, each one trying to break the record of the previous. . .

"The fire of 1932 destroyed the Ateneo in Intramuros; yet within two months of that disaster, the Ateneo Players' Guild was performing on the stage of what by then was the largest and finest playhouse in Manila, the Metropolitan Theater.

"There followed four years of experimentation, carried on in spite of great odds . . . Those years were dominated by a dominant stage presence: that of Father Irwin. . .

"The completion of the Ateneo Auditorium in 1936 ('the finest theater in the Orient') ushered in an era which we have described as 'The Opulent Years' of drama. The facilities of that fine playhouse with its well-equipped stage made possible a variety of productions: from mystery thrillers (*The Bat; The Blue Ghost*) to classic tragedy (*Hamlet; Alcestis*). These were the years for innovations in staging: the introduction in the Philippines of the cyclorama; the scrim; the illusion created by lights; the use of the loudspeaker-from-behind-the-scenes; the use of the bare stage with no scenery but creating the impression of rich simplicity.

"This golden era was abruptly ended by the war and the consequent destruction of the Auditorium. . .

"After the war, despite the total destruction of the Ateneo (the second time in less than two decades), dramatics again claimed a good deal of the attention and activity of students and professors.

Among the ruins at Padre Faura a multitude of one-act plays were produced, climaxed by the full-length production of *Hamlet*.

"After 1952 the Ateneo moved to the new campus at Loyola Heights and a new era in Ateneo history had begun. . .

"The Ateneo story after 1952 is a different tale, perhaps requiring a different narrator than the present writer. But the story of those three decades is exciting and worth telling. . . ."

Thus has Father Bernad set forth the structure, the broad outlines, of his history of the Ateneo stage during those decades which, it scarcely needs to be said, brought about profound changes in the interior and exterior landscapes, the psyche and consciousness of the Filipino nation. At the Ateneo, the shift from Spanish to English, the extended dominance of English and of English-language plays, the cycle of destruction and rebirth, the move from Padre Faura to Loyola Heights, the gradual Filipinization of the Society of Jesus, the resurgence of Pilipino, the reaffirmation of Filipino priorities and values as more Pilipino plays took the spotlight—all this reflected, sometimes anticipated, even illuminated, what was happening in the country at large.

Dramatics tells part, a substantial part, of the history of the Ateneo de Manila during those "three exciting decades"—a history which, in turn, not only forms part of, but vividly, dramatically parallels, the history of the Filipino people through war and peace, through old and new eras, from the placid 1930s to the restive 1950s.

IN RECOUNTING THE HISTORY of the Ateneo stage, Father Bernad exhibits a playwright's or novelist's flair for narrative, for drama; a storyteller's concern for atmosphere, the meaningful gesture, the significant detail. All this, plus the historian-essayist's lucid commentaries, as when he moves some distance from the action the better to view it in the correct perspective, makes for an engrossing tale, indeed. Only one other Jesuit writer, the late Horacio de la Costa, could have matched the author's talent for capturing, as he does, the surface movements and the deeper levels of an incident, a cultural trend, a historical period.

Dramatics, which might have become another tedious tract in the hands of, say, a historian who would rather die than write well and clearly (to paraphrase a non-Jesuit author, Bertrand Russell), is eminently readable stuff, one of the finest examples of history-as-narrative as anyone can hope to find these days, and calls to mind such gifted practitioners of the craft as Kerima Polotan and Nick Joaquin. Father Bernad's chronicle is replete with those "great moments," those crucial, memorable highlights which propel the story even as they underscore a theme, a meaning in a larger context. These "great moments" alone are sufficient reward for those who want their history to be as vital, colorful and engrossing as life itself. Doubtless, the first duty of the historian, whether he is writing of student dramatics or the drama of a nation, is to be interesting; for all in vain would be his splendid perceptions and pronouncements if he should fail to arrest the attention of his audience.

The "great moments" recorded in *Dramatics* occurred on and off the stage. The 1922 *Julius Caesar* occasioned a mini-demo on the campus, when high school and college students engaged in a ticket-sales contest and the controversial decision of the judges brought about an uproar. A grade-school boy named Lamberto Avellana, one of the spectators at the 1923 *Macbeth*, was so fascinated that half a century later, he could still recall the sight and feel of his first inspiring contact with Ateneo drama. Jesus Martinez as Poo Bah in the 1926 *Mikado* "acted his character so admirably and sang it so forcefully" that the audience broke into frequent "prolonged applause." At the gala performance of the 1928 Passion Play at the Grand Opera House, when Moises Diaz as Judas spoke his despair, "every word came distinctly, every emotion vibrated" in the acoustically perfect hall, and the entire assembly rose as one to give the student-actor a standing ovation.

In the title role in the 1931 *Cyrano de Bergerac,* Narciso Pimentel, Jr., when he realized that the enormous nose glued to his face was falling off, yanked the thing off his face and flung it imperiously to the wings, and delighted with this bit of theatrical ingenuity, "the audience went wild with applause." The 1932 *Treasure Island* at the Metropolitan Theater, which featured a high-school lad named Teodoro M. Locsin in the role of the drunken pirate Billy Jones, had for its gala night patrons "the cream of Manila society headed by Archbishop Michael J. O'Doherty, Governor General and Mrs. Dwight Davis, and Senate President and Mrs. Manuel L. Quezon." A "mammoth crowd" and the Manila press went ecstatic over the 1932 *King Lear*, directed by Father Irwin and with Leon Ma. Guerrero in the title role. "He was a hit!" exclaimed Father Irwin of Mariano Yenko, who played the role of the Japanese butler in the 1935 *Officer 666: A Melodramatic Farce*. The audience shivered and screamed at the 1936 *Blue Ghost*, Father Irwin's first major production at the Padre Faura auditorium. The "sensation" in all four performances of the 1937 *Hamlet* was a college sophomore, Teodoro Arvisu, Jr. (who was to die as a Jesuit in 1957), whose performance as the loquacious Polonius was hailed as a "tour de force." The 1938 *Alcestis,* whose cast included Francisco B. Romualdez as Apollo and Raul Manglapus as Thanatos, was the "first public, full-scale presentation in the Philippines (at least in recent decades) of a Greek tragedy."

Candles enhanced the 16th-century atmosphere of the 1941 *Who Ride on White Horses* when a practice blackout plunged the Ateneo Auditorium in darkness, and the candle-lit scenes entranced another of the Ateneo's future dramatists, a first-year high school boy named Onofre Pagsanghan. The 1948 *The Man Who Was,* billed as "serious drama," produced "uninhibited laughter" in the audience when Juanito Ordoveza's "false moustache (improperly glued) turned from horizontal to vertical" so that he had to hold it "with his four fingers every time he spoke his lines," a farcical crisis compounded by the noisy collapse of the backdrop when the other actors unwittingly leaned on it.

The 1950 *Hamlet*, directed by Father Irwin and the Ateneo's second production of that play (the first had been staged in 1937), saw four performances acted by two different casts, but with three actors—Jose Manalo, Teofisto Guingona, Jr., and Carmelo Quintero—alternating in the leading role, prompting *The Guidon* to remark that "three Hamlets died four times" in the "biggest Ateneo production since the war." The 1952 *Francis of Navarre*, written and directed by Father James B. Reuter, S.J., to commemorate the 400th anniversary of St. Francis Xavier's death, was for the Ateneo a "radical innovation," for the college had not only admitted girls to the cast, but had "actually deluged the stage with them." It was a harbinger of things to come—not only more plays with mixed casts, but an Ateneo turning coeducational, and other things besides, in the not too distant future.

In 1952, the Ateneo had moved to Loyola Heights and, as Father Bernad observes, a new era in Ateneo history had begun.

259

GREGORIO C. BRILLANTES

THE EXCITEMENT, THE COLOR, the prodigious efforts, the moments great and small of Ateneo dramatics during those three decades—what did it all signify? What did it all try to accomplish, what did all this achieve?

Those who took part in the plays would know just how the illusion and reality, the grease paint and the lights and shadows, the kaleidoscope of the Ateneo stage touched and, in varying degrees, influenced their lives.

Father Bernad himself provides an answer, or rather, answers, and these are set forth in the homily which he delivered at the funeral Mass for Henry Lee Irwin, S.J., at the Loyola House of Studies on August 24, 1976, and which is printed toward the end of *Dramatics at the Ateneo de Manila:*

" . . . Father Irwin had clearly seen the value of dramatics. For him theatricals were not an end in themselves; they were an instrument—a potent instrument—in the total development of the human personality. Here are his words: The first aim of school dramatics is to impart facility in self-expression. And again: A youth trained in dramatics is never at a loss. And again: I deplore certain types of modern plays with their trivialities and slang, which we are unhappily cultivating in our schools today. Such inferior plays are simply defeating our purposes in dramatics. They afford very meagre opportunity for lofty character portrayal and are little apt to elevate our students' tastes and ideals.

"You see from these remarks by Father Irwin that he was not primarily a director of dramatics. He was primarily—first, last, always—a teacher. I hope I shall be forgiven for saying that he was not a good teacher of philosophy. His students have told me that. Nor was he a good teacher of literature. Again his students will testify to that. But he was a magnificent, a splendid, an incomparable teacher on the stage. *There* was his genuine classroom.

"I say that this his last period of involvement in dramatics—the four-year period from 1948 to 1951—was his most glorious. The proof was that, in the course of those four years, he had become superfluous. Indeed, he had become an obstacle. He had taught his students so well that they no longer needed him. They actually improved on his techniques.

"That is the genuine test of a good teacher: to be able to produce students better skilled than himself.

" . . . He sometimes said things and he sometimes did things that gave offense; but they were forgiven him, because people realized that, underneath everything, this man had a deep respect for the people among whom he lived; for the Filipino. And he had a genuine love for the Philippines.

"It was deep, and it was genuine. . .

"And so, we are here this morning . . . to show our respect for this man, who, in 54 years of involvement in the Philippines, in 61 years in the Society of Jesus was—recognizably—the genuine article."

At the Ateneo, the play was not the only thing, to revise Shakespeare a bit. Always, there were more things in heaven and on earth than were dreamt of in the philosophy of those who did not share Father Irwin's faith and vision.

Dramatics at the Ateneo de Manila is history at its readable best, a wise and presuasive guide to a truer understanding of our culture and our national identity. It is, also, tribute par excellence to the memory of that excellent Jesuit teacher, Henry Lee Irwin, he of the intense gaze and the theatrical voice and the flowing gestures, who left his authentic, indelible imprint on the history of the Ateneo de Manila and in the life of many an Atenean, *ad majorem Dei gloriam*, and the glory, too, of Philippine theater.

(*The Manila Review,* 1977)

To the Rescue of the Creative Spirit in a State of Siege

RESTRICTIONS ON THE CREATIVE SPIRIT in our time, those persons, places and things that could stop or inhibit one from writing, are many and various, and include dictators, generals, detention camps, electrodes, libel suits, censorship, literary critics, brown-

---

Adapted from a paper read at the National Writers Conference sponsored by the Philippine Chapter of International PEN, in Manila, June 1984.

outs, in-laws, arthritis, coronary infarction, metastasis, malnutrition, glaucoma, sloth, hospitals, mortuaries, beerhouses, bankruptcy, success, television, the human condition, publishers and chicken feet.

The last two phenomena, though not so reprehensible and oppressive as most of their companions on the list, could serve to demonstrate the above proposition with singular vividness and urgency, as I shall forthwith attempt to show in this determinedly analytical paper.

There's a story I have been thinking of writing for over a year now, which I haven't written, partly because of nonliterary obligations and preoccupations, and partly because of certain restrictions on my creative spirit stemming from the fact that the distinguished journal which to my mind should be the most congenial outlet for this particular story offers in payment to its contributors not a four-figure sum inscribed on an instantly cashable check, but three copies of the publication, collectible within a month of the date of issue from the publisher's office in Ermita.

It used to be two copies before the present restrictive regime banned this journal from circulation some 12 years ago, reportedly for reasons of national security that had nothing to do with the unrest of poets, essayists and other contributors, actual or prospective. The magazine, which has an international audience, has since happily resumed publication; and perhaps in response to insistent private demand it now rewards its writers more handsomely—with three copies of the issue containing one's story or essay or poem, plus a bowl of beef mami and an order of asado siopao, either at the Carlton Noodle House on Jorge Bacobo Street, or at Mrs. Ho's Café on Padre Faura. If at the latter, and if the famished writer happens to be the editor-publisher's friend of long standing, that is to say, he has faithfully read and expressed fervent admiration for this literary luminary's short stories and novels over the last 30 years or so, he, the fortunate contributor, is likely to receive a gastronomical bonus—the Ilocano editor-publisher's favorite merienda, a plate of chicken feet.

Such uniquely unforgettable remuneration, together with the stimulating company—for two or three other writers or journalists or aspiring gourmands might drop by and join the party—is a boon to be relished and devoured, especially in hard times like these when chicken parts once customarily discarded as less than edible now go into the making of spicy delicacies, as indeed they have been so appreciated by the publisher's loyal friends. All the same, while I think I am no less devoted in my friendship with this person of exceptional merit and virtue, I cannot quite dismiss the notion, due most probably to some grievous flaw in my by now permanently unregenerate character, that the three precious copies and the Chinese specialties do lift one's creative and overall spirits—but only for an afternoon.

What of the night ahead, with its stack of bills to be reviewed and toted up by candlelight in case the power has been cut off, not to mention that existential three o'clock of the soul, when one is visited by chill visions of further restrictions, not only on the creative spirit, but on the spirit of life itself? And beyond the night, what about tomorrow morning, and the days and the weeks after? Unless the owner of the sari-sari store on the corner, a college dropout from the Eastern Visayas to whom Teodoro Valencia is the apotheosis of Philippine writing in English, is willing to accept your three copies in exchange for a tin of corned beef or, in keeping with your celebratory mood, a six-pack of beer, very bleak indeed would be the prospect of your post-publication days.

But not, one hastens to add, as distressing and calamitous as the circumstances writers of the future may have to contend with, as I intend to suggest in that story I mentioned at the outset, the story I haven't written—a piece of fiction which, as already sketched out in my mind, is set in the distant future, but which has much to do, I daresay, with our concerns as writers today striving to achieve whatever each one of us envisions as the fulfillment of his creative spirit, his art's desire.

IT IS THE YEAR 2084. The Philippines a century hence looks very much like the underdeveloped, heavily indebted country we have long known and yet is radically different in many ways. The English language has been banned, finally and totally, its proscription sanctioned by horrendous penalties under a dictatorship beside which Mr. Marcos' martial rule would appear as benignly cheerful as a convention of United Field Technologists. All about the crumbling, poverty-stricken, overpopulated landscape are giant billboards and signs extolling the dictatorship in the sole official language, which is called Tagilocan. The regime has burned, destroyed, practically everything and anything printed in English, in a manic zeal of ideological and linguistic purity. Only Tagilocan must be spoken and heard, read and written; only in this language may the citizenry sing and dream and make love; only in this tongue—the supreme distillation of all the Filipino languages ever spoken in these islands from even before the Sri Vishayan Empire, or so the obedient citizenry is made to believe by the Ministry of Cultural Enlightenment—only in this language, which actually contains more Ilocano borrowings than from any other vernacular, may the people communicate with one another. (In what language the state conducts its foreign trade and diplomacy and advances its science and technology is a minor detail I will merely hint at in the story.)

But what is this tense and secretive group doing on this night, in this house, in this town on the outer limits of Megalo-Manila? What has brought together in this hidden candlelit room this group of eight or ten elderly men and women gathered round a reader, even older than the rest, their host for the evening? He is reading—from a tattered, ancient-looking book—in English. It is Nick Joaquin's *Prose and Poems*, published well over a century ago; and the old reader's voice falters from age and emotion and then, recovering, goes on in the dim, quiet room: "October in Manila! But the emotion, so special to one's childhood, seems no longer one's own; seems to have traveled ahead, deep into time. . . And time creates unexpected destinations. . . ."

And the night hours pass, and they take turns reading, with a kind of reverent affection, selections from an old, rejected, prescribed, virtually extinct literature—the fiction of Manuel Arguilla, Bienvenido N. Santos, N.V.M. Gonzalez, Carlos Bulosan, F. Sionil Jose, Francisco Arcellana, Edith L. Tiempo, Edilberto K. Tiempo, Estrella Alfon, Kerima Polotan, Gilda Fernando, Wilfrido Nolledo, Ninotcha Rosca, Jose Dalisay, Antonio Enriquez and some others. They read from books with fragile yellowish pages and cracked bindings, or from laboriously handwritten sheets creased and faded from having been folded and flattened many times over, the better to hide them from the eyes of the army and the knowledge police. Their reading is interrupted sometimes by voices or footfalls outside; once or twice, they blow out the candles at the approaching whir of airborne night patrols.

They are members of a dwindling group, a subversive society under siege, meeting once in a long while in some member's house to remember and celebrate the stories and poems and plays written in a banished language more than a hundred years ago.

In the morning they are gone, in the room linger the smells of candlewax, time and memory, and the old man, the reader, the host, whose house this is, drowses in his rocking chair. He wakes when his grandson, who is about 15, comes into the room to call him to breakfast. But first, can he show his grandfather something he has written? A poem, Lolo, the boy says, somewhat shyly but with a mischievous gleam, and gives the old man the sheet of yellow ruled paper on which is written in pencil, in an adolescent's untidy longhand:

First, a poem must be magical,
Then musical as a sea-gull.
It must be brightness moving
And hold secret a bird's flowering.
It must be slender as a bell
And it must hold fire as well. . . .

"Did you really write this?" asks the old man in fearful yet gentle amazement.

"Yes, Lolo," says the boy.

"Strange, but I seem to have read something similar, the same words and music, somewhere," murmurs the old man. "When I was very young, like you, before the burnings, long ago. . . ."

That is how the story will go, more or less, when certain restrictions to my creative spirit are lifted and I get around to writing it; with a touch here and there of Orwell and Bradbury and perhaps Borges, and with those lines from Jose Garcia Villa meant to induce an ironic chuckle at the end—of the story, of Philippine literature in English. And it occurred to me, while reflecting again on this still unwritten story, that in regard to writers and writing, the futuristic fiction is far more stark, appalling and oppressive than present reality, increasing militarization and all. For we writers can still meet as a tribe, a society, a fraternity. We need not meet in secret fear and trembling, as writers do in other countries. Books are published even if not widely read, the works of writers still see print, including some that are decidedly uncomplimentary to the present dispensation. A visitor from a more embattled country or a more regimented society may well wonder whether our writers, specifically our literary artists, ever produce anything worthy of the ire and vengeance of their governors, or whether the latter, like the majority of their subjects, do not bother to read our authors at all. The same perplexed visitor may likewise ask why Nick Joaquin has written only two novels instead of five or seven or a round dozen, or why, for that matter, the admirable prolific creativity of F. Sionil Jose remains the exception rather than the rule among our foremost writers of prose fiction. The answers to such queries concerning our two most eminent writers, both of whom have lost neither their passports nor their freedom to write, might well suggest that perhaps recent communiques on our state of siege could be slightly exaggerated.

All this is by way of underscoring the nature of our situation today, which is that even in the shadow of authoritarian rule, we still have access to an area, a buffer zone, of relative freedom, in which we can meet and discuss our concerns and practice our craft and follow where the creative spirit will lead us. But this zone, even as we assemble and hail one another within its boundaries, could now be narrowing, diminishing, and the time may come, sooner than we expect, when it can no longer give us shelter. What we now enjoy, limited as it now must be, could be no more than a reprieve from the fate that has befallen such writers as Kundera in Czechoslovakia, Kenedi in Hungary, Sinyavsky in the Soviet Union, Pa Chin in China, Theodorakis in Greece, Leroux in South Africa, Timerman in Argentina, Pramoedya Toer in Indonesia. What have our writers individually and as a community, done and are doing with this diminishing time, this narrowing margin of freedom? Prudence if nothing else should move us to employ our time, our resources and energies more judiciously, in order to bolster the creative spirit, now and against the day when writers' groups are banned and literary activity and publication suppressed altogether except that in the service of the dictatorship or the ruling junta.

TO THIS END THERE CAN BE as many plans and proposals as there are writers convened in any one place. A number of such projects and programs we have heard of before, expressed in tones of solemn urgency, at various forums and conclaves beginning with the

National Writers Conference sponsored by the Philippine PEN in Baguio City, in 1958.

"The Filipino Writer and National Growth" was the theme of that conference, which saw earnest participants dissecting such momentous questions as the role of the hula hoop in our culture, the feasibility of translating Shakespeare into comic-book form and whether Winston Churchill won the Nobel Prize for Literature as a historian and polemicist, or as a fiction writer, in the manner of Hemingway and Faulkner. It was attended by some 150 delegates, out of whom one will be hard put to find more than five today who can be said to have overcome restrictions to their creative spirit. There has been some national growth—of the list of writers who no longer write, who are prevented from writing, who gave up writing.

That conference, perhaps the first and last one when our writers were most hopefully united, was more than a quarter of a century ago; and looking back on all those conferences and symposiums and panel discussions since, one is sorely tempted to ask, prompted by the theme of this conference: What have we really done, as a group, as a fraternity, as a community, to bestir and energize, protect and strengthen the creative spirit? What do literary conferences achieve in terms of enhancing our creativity aside from the writing of critical papers that at best might ensure one's academic tenure or provide quotations and footnotes for someone else's paper at the next conference? Has any writer, of any race, nationality, sex, color, creed or club, been moved to write a play, a novel or a poem by attending a literary conference and listening to his fellow writers holding forth as pundits and panelists? Don't such activities tend to be mere substitutes for that which N.V.M. Gonzalez back in Baguio in 1958 called the writer's only business, which is to write; what John Updike at a PEN-sponsored conference in Sydney in 1974 defined as the writer's only reason for being, which is to write and delight in seeing his work *printed*, never mind all those theories, treatises and discourses on the subject from Aristotle to the structuralist critics of the present day. . .

And what in heaven's name am I doing, posing these dismal questions, talking about restrictions and a story I haven't written, instead of writing it? Why am I impersonating a critic, a literary scholar, a wise man? Why are we gathered here pontificating on the art and craft, and the hazards and rewards, of literature and journalism, and in the course of these three days writing nothing but names, addresses, autographs and witticisms on the backs of envelopes and mimeographed conference papers?

The burden of these uneasy questions is the modest proposition that there may be other efficient and effective ways of countering certain restrictions that besiege the creative spirit besides holding writers' conferences and participating in literary discussions and passing the usual resolutions on truth, justice and freedom. There is a need, and a singular pleasure indeed, for which we are all grateful, to gather as a clan, if only to reassure ourselves and remind certain authorities of our craft and maybe our cunning; in a state of siege such tribal rites should comfort us, even exorcise our anxieties and our fears. But after we disperse, what? Between conferences and meetings, what ought writers to do, individually and in isolation—and, more urgently, as this conference would suggest, as a collective, a community, in solidarity?

More than ever since we first gathered as a tribe, we should as a group go to the rescue of the creative spirit under siege; and to lift the siege, or at least help repel it in one vital area, one crucial segment of the front, reinforcements have to be rushed to the beleaguered defenders in that sector. Now if there are high-minded cultural foundations, oil corporations and other agencies generous enough to fund, say, an annual writers' conference, might they not perhaps think it more worth their while to support other enduring forms of literary enterprise? The idea is by no means novel or startlingly new, but viewed from the diminishing zone, from the shrinking space, time and freedom on which our writers now stand as in a circle of land under siege, any possible assistance ought not to be despised and spurned.

Why not annual, or better yet, semi-annual or even quarterly awards (and not just varnished plaques and embossed certificates) for fiction, poetry, the feature article or the essay? Why not achievement awards (and not just tin medals and wooden trophies) for the novel, the short story, drama and poetry? Why not special grants and fellowships to beginning writers? Why not add to already established awards, so that a given work could win more than one prize in a single year? Nothing can beat that boost to the creative spirit derived from having created, having produced a work that's a prize winner twice or thrice over. Why not a literary quarterly devoted to new writing in place of a newsletter dedicated to club chitchat of the writer-bureaucrat? And at the very least, how about annual anthologies reprinting the better writing that's being done—with contributors receiving, in advance, aside from a thank-you note, a pat on the ego and a treat of chicken feet, the equivalent, say, of an assistant director's Christmas bonus from the Ministry of Mass Media and Information or half the New Year's salary increase for a beautification inspector in the City of Ma'am? And while we are at it, why not a writers' union, a real one, not that union spawned by martial law and designed, we have been assured, for the glorification of the powers that must be obeyed, but a union of and for writers that will, through manifesto, lawsuit, boycott, picket and strike, gain for writers and journalists greater recognition and more substantial compensation for their labors? In sum, while raising fists and banners against restrictions of a certain order, to raise support and standards for the writer's sake, that he may go on writing, that he may not fall and be foiled and confined, overrun, overwhelmed: one more extinct statistic in the New Republic. (They who write well and voluminously while about to keel over from dehydration, depression, detention or premature senility need not apply for humanitarian relief and benefits.)

TO SPEAK OF WHAT SOME of us might regard as degradingly petty and mundane may not sound to the rest of the world as ennobling as pronouncements on the role of the writer in society, on his duty and privilege to write in the face of all adversity, on truth and justice and the imperatives of art and vision, and the frontiers of freedom, and the invincibility of the human spirit. But it is the stuff which we can turn into bread, rice and wine, or sinigang, sisig and beer, and if fate be more generous, a car, a trust fund, a house, a lot, that will help in countering and defeating the restrictions that the writer confronts in our time, and in rendering more valid and credible and truly encouraging all that talk about the role of the artist and writer in society, and the parameters of art and freedom, and the demands of this issue and that ism, which we all have heard before and very likely will hear again next year and the year after next and again the following year, unless constitutional, political, economic and other crises and upheavals finally impose an indefinite moratorium, on writing as well as on literary discussions and writers' conferences.

(*Solidarity*, 1985)

Language, Garbage and Assassins

1.

"BABABAPA?"

"Bababapa."

"Bababanaba?"

"Bababana."

This briskly cheerful Filipino dialogue, between a music-lounge patron and the elevator operator on the top floor of a five-star hotel, didn't go unremarked by a couple of foreign visitors among the guests waiting for their turn to go down. The tourist from Detroit or Delaware or wherever turned to his wife brightly: "Hon, did you hear that? These guys talk like they were sheep."

"Do they, now," said his lady. "I think they call it Tag-eh-lag."

I didn't make up this linguistic bit, as some scholarly skeptics might think. The tale's from *Graphic* librarian-researcher Sendong Bonifacio, who is pure Tagalog and Manila-bred, as his name would suggest; and it seems he was inspired to recount it, for the enlightenment of all present, by our editor in chief's discourse on "the language of the street" ("It's Tagalog slang that's the national language, not Pilipino!") during a happy hour (actually, close to three hours) at this resto called Obeertime, across from the Dominga Building on Pasong Tamo in Makati.

Some annotation, aside from maybe a few inebriated chuckles, is in order, though. The language in question is not "Tag-eh-lag," as the lady from Wisconsin or Winnepeg or wherever called it, nor is it Pilipino, as our editor in chief seems to prefer. It's Filipino, as mandated by the 1987 Constitution: our national language based on

Tagalog, which the same sacred law of the land and certain commissions and agencies enjoin us Filipinos to develop and propagate and cherish as our own, for the nation and for our sake and our posterity.

Filipino it is, constitutionally and officially, and no longer Pilipino, let alone Tagalog, although, as Nick Joaquin has pointed out in a more sober forum, it's street Tagalog that "builds, extends and enriches the national language." And this species of Tagalog, which is anything but sheepish or lamb-like, has been doing it all this time, building up and bolstering Filipino, "though academicians may be horrified by its vulgarity and shocked by any suggestion to dignify, by inclusion in their lexicons, such terms of the vulgate as *ebot* and *spooting*. Yet these are the words that Filipinos use; and these are the words that are fusing our various languages and dialects into one . . . The anonymous word-coiners on the street are doing more to speed the coming of a common tongue than all the schools and academies put together."

The first of these academies was the National Language Institute established under the auspices of Commonwealth President Manuel L. Quezon in accordance with the 1936 Constitution, which provided for the "development and adoption of a common national language based on one of the existing native dialects." In 1937, Quezon appointed the noted Visayan scholar, Jaime C. de Veyra, director of the Institute, which recommended that Tagalog be the core of the national language. Commonwealth Act No. 40 subsequently provided that the Tagalog-based national language would be one of the official languages of the Philippines—the others being English and Spanish—upon independence on July 4, 1946. In 1959, the national language was officially designated "Pilipino" by Secretary of Education Jose Romero, who decreed its teaching and propagation in all secondary and normal schools.

The latest of these official language institutions, one is informed by the distinguished poet and scholar Virgilio Almario's *Philippine Almanac*, is the Komisyon sa Wika, established by Republic Act No. 7140 on August 21, 1991. The Komisyon has at least ten members representing the various "ethnolinguistic communities of the Philippines, particularly Tagalog, Cebuano, Ilocano, Hiligaynon, the Muslim Mindanao Communities, the Northern Cultural Communities, and the Southern Cultural Communities."

The commission's mission is "to promote and develop Filipino as the national language." Unless it has been abolished for budgetary or other reasons (it must be so low-key, one doesn't hear or read about it), the Komisyon should be working mightily to promote and develop Filipino, in tandem with the National Language Institute (still, one supposes, under its durable director, Dr. Ponciano Pineda) and any number of agencies, public and private, committed to the same task, fired by the same vision.

But even if these language academies were to close shop, written off tomorrow by legislative fiat or executive decree, the growth and development and spread of Filipino would go on, a sociolinguistic fact and an irreversible, expanding cultural phenomenon that is, well, indubitably Filipino. More and more of us residing here in these islands, many of us not born and bred in Bulacan or Cavite or Laguna, are speaking Filipino which, by my own reckoning, and for all practical purposes (with the accent on the practical) is 96.9 percent Tagalog, never mind what the Cebuanos and the Ilocanos and the Ilonggos and those northern and southern cultural communities have to say. All this, in and by and for Filipino, thanks less to genes, geography and constitutional provisions, and more to Sampaguita Pictures, Viva Films, Star Cinema, DWIZ, Radio Veritas, *Bombo Radyo*, *Eat . . . Bulaga, ASAP, MTB, Bubble Gang,* Kuh Ledesma, Regine Velasquez, Ariel Rivera, Ara Mina and many other such icons and institutions.

It's one national development that seems as natural and almost effortless, and to this Tarlaqueño who grew up in a household mix of Ilocano, Pangasinan and occasional English, with Capangpangan across the street and Bisaya on the corner, a glad and encouraging state of linguistic affairs. Filipino has come, is here, and will grow and endure—just as English will, in our part of the Global Village—so much so that even Filipinos not raised in it end up speaking and even writing in the language. Like this kinsman of mine, in Ilocos Sur, the son of a cousin, and some of his friends in their town literary guild. They had all been writing poetry in Filipino, and getting better at it, too, according to a Vigan critic—until certain commissioners of culture and the arts managed to convince them, with the aid of funds, grants and the like, that no, Filipino is not the wave of the present and the future; rather, several waves are, or wavelets—Ilocano, for the Ilocanos; Bicolano, for the Bicolanos; Cebuano, for the Cebuanos; Waray, for the folks in Samar and Leyte, and so on.

272

In a word, regional languages and regional literatures—after all these many years and commissions and agencies devoted to the development and spread of Filipino. And, hey!—these officials and authorities now busily promoting regional tongues and cultural tastes rather than the national lengua appear to be the same academicians horrified not so long ago by the slightest sign of street slang, the vulgate and the popularly vulgar spoiling the purity of *their* Tagalog.

WHAT'S GOING ON HERE, on the language front? Something's rotten in the state of Filipino linguistics, is there, pare ko? The same language commissioners or is it their academic clones—all avowed nationalists or national democrats, by the way—are sponsoring a conference on regional literatures, curiously in that bastion of academic conservatism, the prosperous Catholic university of De La Salle, in this month that marks National Language Week and the birth anniversary of Manuel L. Quezon, who envisioned for all Filipinos a common national language. Three more such conferences, likewise funded with your tax money and mine, are slated for the next few months.

Is it perhaps all due to the anticolonial, ultranationalist desire to return the country to its glorious tribal past, a yearning for rebellious fragmentation, heroic separatism and the eventual dissolution of the Republic?

At the very least a puzzlement, to this non-Tagalog Filipino anyway, whose comprehension of the language has of late taken a quantum leap, or so he thinks, and who has been looking forward to reading the classics of Amado Hernandez and Lazaro Espinosa and Lualhati Bautista and Andres Cristobal Cruz, and projected bilingual works of Filipino history and literature. But nothing complex and mysterious really, about this preoccupation with regional arts and crafts, says an editor of a rather malicious ideological bent. It's all simply a matter of policy and strategy—the reflection and result of a revolutionary party's shift from the countrywide struggle for national liberation to simultaneous thrusts on different regional fronts. Having failed utterly in the former, the NDF and affiliate organizations would now concentrate their forces on the latter. Indeed, better late than never, as any dedicated cadre would recall from a once little well-read book.

A less political, more charitable view of all this to-do on the language scene is advanced by a poet-professor in the College of Arts

273

and Letters at UP Diliman. This zealous and diligent program to promote regional arts and letters is but a cover-up, asserts this Doctor of Literature, for the sick failure of the language commissars to impose their dogmatic Tagalog prescriptions on the body linguistic, or diagnostic words to that effect.

Interesting opinions, but surely not infallible, though both the editor and the professor are deeply involved and demonstrably savvy in these matters. This department is not wholly convinced by their pronouncements, so will those deep thinkers, language scholars and other authoritative experts out there please write in and enlighten this department—and the multitude of *Graphic* readers in all the regions of this multilingual archipelago—on the real score in this intriguing, some would say, confusing, regional language business?

Don Manuel must be turning in his crypt in the Quezon Memorial Circle. To think that, more than 60 years after the National Language Institute was created under the aegis of the patriot and statesman from Baler, the same commissioners or their successors and subalterns tasked to promote Tagalog and/or Filipino should now lay siege to it, oppose and oppress and suppress it. . .

If he were still with us this first August of the 21st century, Su Excelencia, el Señor Don Manuel Luis Quezon, might even be more dismayed and disgusted—*puñeta!*—over what's become of the city of his affections, what's being done in and to this city he had conceived as the nation's premier and model metropolis, now the setting for outrageous political fortunes, lawless blight, corruption and vice, wretched public services, all manner of anarchy, squalor and decay, man-made catastrophies, tragedies and abominations—like the fiery Ozone horror and, most recently, the horrid Payatas garbage avalanche, whose murderous stench lingers over this month of assassins, of the Plaza Miranda massacre and the murder of Ninoy Aquino.

2.

BASURA IS THE TALK of the town.

For over a month now, or since the Payatas trash avalanche buried several hundred constituents of Quezon City Mayor Ismael Mathay, Jr., people in high places and low, in upscale villages and depressed barangays, uptown and downtown, can't seem to stop talking garbage.

Elsewhere around the country, like in Camarines Sur and Cebu, Basilan or Jolo or Lanao, it's other things and aggravations people are talking about; but in Metro Manila it's mostly garbage. Its form and substance, nature and components. Its complex dynamics and omnipresent manifestations. Its density, solidity, solubility and volume by the day, and the collection and disposal as well as the economic and financial potential thereof. Its social, cultural and political significance; and not to forget, its capacity to go berserk and homicidal, to break loose from its managers or handlers and rear up and roar down and devastate and devour a whole community like a gigantic cannibal monster more terrifying than any beast from a Stephen King bog or Steven Spielberg nightmare.

That murderous cinematic metaphor may sound a bit too much for Mayor Mathay, Vice Mayor Connie Angeles, the Quezon City Council and certain trash agencies and contractors. It could be something of an understatement, though, to the survivors of the Payatas catastrophe, the Lupang Pangako folk who most certainly voted for the same officials now absolving themselves of any blame. The cab driver weeping on TV, recounting how he had lost his wife and four children . . . the laundrywoman, stunned and stammering before the flash-bulbs and cameras, whose three children and mother and sister were buried in the trash-slide . . . the *turo-turo* waitress still hoping, more than two weeks after the black soggy mountain came crashing down, that seven of her nine children didn't lie entombed under all that nauseating mud and filth. . . For them, no words could describe nor any image diminish the horror, the tragedy, the grief, anger and despair.

Amid the death and destruction at the dumpsite, words are of no avail, whether from politico, bureaucrat, garbage management expert or the trash-terrorized. Not aid funds and relief goods, either—the cash assistance and provisions of rice, canned food, medicines, clothes, blankets, disappeared as soon as these arrived at refugee centers, carted away by steal-and-sell operators from adjacent shantytowns. As if they weren't oppressed and tormented enough, the inhabitants of these squatter dumps—a separate class of the wretched of the Filipino earth—must yet prey on one another. Heaven knows, and now probably the public, too—they know how these most

275

dispossessed of our country's poor, they who must live on and amid garbage, have been misled and deceived, alternately ignored, neglected and exploited by their professed saviours and protectors for more profitable business and politics. Mass slaughter complexed with dirty politics and filthy lucre. . .

So the talk went, and more, all over, in Metro Manila, anyway, which produces more than 6,000 tons of *basura* every day, and in nearby precincts like Antipolo and San Mateo, where the landfill, the "controlled" dump, is filling up rapidly to erupting point and threatening to unleash another Payatas-like avalanche . . . So we all heard and learned, from all the talk, indignant sound and authoritative fury; the discussion, argumentation and knowledgeable discourses on radio and TV, all inspired by garbage, dealing with all sorts of garbage, including, as suggested by several callers on Emily Marcelo and Vic Milan's *Kalikasan Vigilante* radio program, the two-legged *trapo* kind. As late as the other day, eight out of ten callers to Emily and Vic in as many minutes sounded off on the garbage problem, the specifics, the whys and wherefores of the rotten mess and pollution, and how citizens courageous can cope and counter. . .

So it went, that chat and revelations generated by the garbage crisis, which was, according to certain presumably trashy types, just that, and no more, that is to say, harrumph, ahem, nothing but talk. . .

But a lot of talk there has been since mid-July and it seems not to have abated, which is more than you can say for any other putrid subject and offensive issue since maybe the Cory Power Revolt on EDSA. Oral complaints and testimonies, verbal protests, indictments, verdicts and remedies, delivered on the airwaves, over fences, across backyards, by phone and wireless, in jeepneys and FX taxis, in forums, sermons and congressional hearings—talk rivaling in volume and quantity those thousands of tons churned out daily by the garbage mills. And along with the queries and answers, the assertions and denials, a great deal of head-scratching, eye-blinking and finger-pointing, this last mostly in the direction of Mayor Mathay and the Quezon City Hall, of Chairman Jejomar Binay and the MMDA, the Metropolitan Manila Development Authority which, as one more loquacious caller to Emily Marcelo put it, is as undeveloped as Jojo is short on wisdom and efficiency.

Glaring at the finger-pointers, Hizzoner Ismael, Jr. maintains that he is not to blame, ever, for the Payatas garbage disaster and the plight of the dumpsite denizens before and after. Not only presumed innocent but unaccountable, absolutely fault-free, guiltless in truth and in fact—in spite of mounting evidence apparently to the contrary, the disregarded situation reports and warnings of impending disaster, and all this talk, so unkind and painful, about the garbage crisis, the garbage anomaly, the garbage squatter colony, the Payatas tragedy, and, for goodness sake, enough already, even his son Chuck's irregular garbage hauling business, they say it stinks, and how, when everyone in City Hall from the top to the janitors can vouch for Ismael Mathay III's passion to serve the poor of Quezon City, for his integrity as unsullied as his solid waste management. (This enterprising gent may get to be mayor yet, and soon, as his doting dad's been dreaming, if QC congressmen Feliciano Belmonte and Dante Liban, former veep Herbert Bautista and action star Rudy Fernandez, who are all for taking over Mathay Sr.'s seat, don't get their act and flock together. Or unless, providentially, astoundingly, the people of Quezon City discover a great, noble, unrivaled, irresistible leader. . .)

SO HE IS BLAMELESS, Mayor Mathay is; and as far as he and Chuck and his councilors are concerned, it's other VIPs who should get the axe, maybe literally, for the Payatas trash and muck attack that killed some 300 people. (As many as a thousand dead, most of them unidentified and unrecovered, according to one unofficial casualty count.)

In Mel Mathay's verdict, it's former President Ramos who deserves to be pilloried as Fidel "did nothing" about the city government's proposal back in 1994 to put up an incinerator that would have done away with the need for a crowded dumpsite. As worthy of Mayor Mathay's malediction are former MMDA chairman Prospero Oreta and the Metro Authority's current chief, Jejomar Binay—both public servants offered "bureaucratic resistance" to the city government's plan to operate "waste plants" rather than open dumps. And finally, the Payatas squatter folk themselves are to blame, too, for the trash tragedy—they had been deaf and dumb to their mayor's repeated appeals for them to be relocated, after a mini-slide swept away a row of shanties in August last year.

Unimpressed by the good mayor's apologia announced in a Senate hearing, Ombudsman Aniano Desierto has urged the filing of administrative charges (with the prospect of dismissal) against Mayor Mathay and Chairman Binay, together with the entire QC Council and barangay capitana Emerita Pecson and some other minor local government characters, for having "neglected to institute the necessary measures despite recommendations regarding cracks which had developed . . . after an August 3, 1999 landslide"; and for "allowing Payatas to be a major dumping facility" in defiance of "several directives and mandates."

Also in a "bitay" mood against Mathay and Binay are human rights lawyer Romeo Capulong, his colleagues in the Public Interest Law Center, and relatives of the Payatas victims. They have filed a P1-billion class suit (P3 million per death) against Mathay and the Quezon City government, Binay and the MMDA, a real estate firm that owns the Lupang Pangako disaster site, and a garbage trucking company. The respondents have been charged with "gross neglect" for the dumpsite deaths, and with the "slow demise" of Lupang Pangako, once a livable settlement that they had misused as a dumpsite over the last 12 years.

More than ten years of rank, rotten dumping? And in the process the poor and the dispossessed made even more impoverished, and abused, and oppressed? Which raises a few more garbage-inspired questions. . .

Why protest and condemn such outrageous acts and operations only now? In all this time, why did these now implacable human rights militants, these champions of the urban poor and defenders of the downtrodden neglect to take up the cause of the Payatas folk?

Why no demos, die-in rallies, marathon pickets at City Hall by the proletarian legions of Bayan, KMU, Gabriela and the NGOs, all otherwise wrathful and raging on short notice against imperialism, fascism, bureaucrat capitalism, the AFP, the PNP and the oil companies? Must a mountain of garbage first collapse and bury hundreds of the poorest of the poor, before demanding justice and a billion progressive smackeroos in damages? In order that the squatter poor would squat and scavenge no more, but live in luxury and style and maintain more than one wife and car and maybe even run for mayor or senator?

That about covers the whole gamut: the remedies to the garbage problem, the science and technology of garbage, the economics and the politics of waste disposal, the ideology of waste management and so on. As far as can be gathered, in the righteous talk and leftist outcries, in the probes and hearings, the charges and indictments following the Payatas catastrophe, what's been left out may well be the most consequential aspect of this multilayered upheaval. The morality of garbage, the ethics of trash—ignored, disregarded even by those bishops and evangelists who could be as vocally indignant when properly aroused as any politician-demagogue lambasting the neocolonial despoilers of the land.

BUT TO HIS CREDIT and the benefit of all appalled or at least disturbed by the Payatas tragedy, one Rene Saguisag, by repute a man of law and principle for all seasons, a Thomas More crying in our wilderness, has spoken out or, rather, written down for the record this judgment on the Payatas infamy. For *Graphic* readers particularly and fellow Filipinos of democratic faith and good will who might have missed Atty. Saguisag's column in *Today*, this department takes the liberty of bringing his majestic discourse to these pages:

"The birthday celebrant Mayor Mel Mathay with Vilma Valera . . . seated, Sec. Lenny de Jesus, DBP Chairman Ramon Abad . . . This caption we owe to the *Manila Bulletin* . . . President Estrada was also seen in photographs with Ms. Guia Gomez in Negros or with a love child in Cebu. . .

"These public servants do not seem to understand the meaning of prudence or of role modeling. They make it harder to teach certain of the Ten Commandments. What people do in their bedrooms may be their business, but not what public officials do in public. . .

"I try not to sound like a zealous fundamentalist. But the day following the disappointing *Bulletin* publication, my dear friend Mel, a member of Class '57 of the College of Law of San Beda, where I as a prelaw student would see him from afar as one of the outstanding Mathays, went international, as it were.

"This time the story in the *International Herald Tribune* . . . was prominent above the page-one stuff. 'The mayor of Quezon City, Mel Mathay, said residents were ordered last week to move out of the area because of the danger of landslides as a result of the typhoon's onslaught. But they refused, he said.'

"The government was helpless, it seemed . . . But then maybe he and Lenny de Jesus might precisely have been discussing how to

279

drive out those 80,000 souls from the Promised Land. If nothing else works, maybe the President can try to be faithful to the Ten Commandments for the rest of his term. That goes for Mel and Vilma and Lenny and Mon and those who ape these egocentric non-role models of Christian family life. . .

"At this writing [July 14] around 150 people were verified killed on Monday. Scores are missing after that mountain of rain-loosened garbage collapsed and burst into flames. Three hundred houses, mostly barong-barong, were lost in the squatter colony at the foot of the dump in the place called Lupang Pangako.

"Let us all hope that the victims are now all in the true Promised Land, without the garbage we see in the newspapers.

"The *Herald Tribune* said survivor Gloria Alano sobbed and yelled at rescuers using a heavy bulldozer on a heap of garbage to search for survivors and bodies. 'Backhoes, use only backhoes, not bulldozers. I want to get the bodies of my loved ones,' she cried. Her husband and three children were buried under the tons of garbage. Maybe the remains may yet be recovered. . .

"The Film Center victims in November 1981 had it worse. Some of them are still there, thanks to the vanity of Imelda, who had wanted to speed up the project. A scaffolding of the center being built collapsed on November 17, sending the entire sixth floor and its six giant beams crashing down to the second floor. Tragedy struck at 2:35 a.m. while more than a hundred workers were putting fresh cement on the sixth floor of the building. . .

"When we look today at the idle and unused Film Center or Lupang Pangako, would we hear the breeze carrying the plaintive wails of the dead and those they left behind? At night, would the pale moon tell us that some accounts have to be settled in the name of plain and simple social justice?

"Charges should have been filed against those concerned, including Imelda, whose minister on the job said, 'The incident was a normal risk in construction.' Today, we have Mel saying he wanted to save the people 'but they refused.' This is leadership?

"What should we really put as the cause in the death certificates of those who died in the Land of Broken Promises?

"Garbage suffocation? The poor and the unwashed deserve something better than seeing their top officials in glittering parties crooning with great passion, 'If our lips should meet, inamorata.'"

To which supreme summation of the case by the citizenry's counsel, we all should say Amen, and Peace, and God be praised, though the heavens fall . . . though we must recall every ignominious August of our time, that our nation's best and brightest are slain in the blaze of noon, and the poorest of the poor must die in their prisoners' sleep at the break of dawn; though in a certain state of the nation conspirators and assassins will protest their innocence as they preen and prosper, sing, dance and make merry and tempt the fates with great passion, gold, guilt and savage fashion hidden like rot and ruination under so much murderous garbage, and all not yet disposed to be hauled away to the inglorious dumpsite of history.

(*Graphic*, 2000)

Writing for the Broad Masses, Singing for the Broadway Muses

IN THE WAKE OF SEPTEMBER'S cultural extravaganzas, artistic revelries, multi-book launch parties, literary beer festivals, the Book Fair, the Manila Critics Circle Awards, *A Portrait of the Artist as Filipino* in English, Tagalog and Spanish, and *Miss Saigon*, too, imported from Broadway or is it London by the impresario J.V. Ejercito in collaboration with the Cultural Center of the Philippines, with Lea Salonga as the golden-throated whore trilling for all she's worth above the Pinoy protest howls and catcalls providing an unmusical background for it all, and finally the *Sunday Inquirer Magazine* devoting its first October issue to writers and publishers and their works—following all this, like the last lone atonal note in the grand symphony there came to the *Graphic* this communiqué dispatched from what the poet-professor Gemino H. Abad might call the English-language clearing in the groves of UP Diliman: actually a photocopy of a letter to SIM editor-publisher Karla Delgado-Yulo, which arrived even as the echoes of the arts still vibrated in our editorial cubicle and that began, arrestingly, fascinatingly:

"Why is the man laughing?"—referring, it turns out, to a mirthful mug shot of Dr. Bienvenido Lumbera which appeared in that issue of the *Inquirer* mag.

The concerned co-authors wished, we were told, to share their reflections or, rather, questions with *Graphic* and other readers interested in literature, writing, the arts and such. So then, with no intention whatsoever of preempting a response from the original addressee, or presuming to come up with one, we reproduce hereunder, slightly edited for reasons of space, clarity and civility, Danilo F. Agbayani and Sherwyn Liu Laurel's inquiring, inquisitive missive to the *Inquirer* editor-publisher, dated October 3, 2000, as follows:

"Why is the man laughing?

"Why is Dr. Bienvenido Lumbera laughing in the photo illustrating the article, 'The Babel Unified' (SIM, Oct. 1, 2000)?

"Is it from progressive hilarity, nationalist exhilaration, democratic delight and cultural cheerfulness? Or, as the old song goes, is he laughing on the outside but crying and groaning on the inside? Because the Pinoy Babel refuses to be unified and still prefers to go to the (liberal, non-Tagalog, Western-oriented) dogmas? And because his own romantic bubble continues to be defiled, his academically profitable if historically counterfeit bauble disowned even by his avowed disciples who persist in writing in English, for English language publications like the *Sunday Inquirer Magazine* instead of *Liwayway* or *Hiligaynon*?

"Or is the man maybe laughing because he has once more announced the folly and futility of writing in English, in the Sunday magazine of the *Philippine Daily Inquirer*, the nation's foremost English-language newspaper? *Naka-isa na naman si Ka Bien sa mga elite at capitalistang burgis,* that Lenin called the 'friendly fools' helping to dig their decadent, reactionary graves?

"Is he also laughing at his own joke about F. Sionil Jose, the darling of the U.S. Embassy, the Magsaysay Foundation and other agencies of U.S. cultural imperialism? That over the last 50 years, Mr. Jose has been writing his great stories and novels not in English but in some provincial vernacular that Random House and his legion of readers around the world have somehow deciphered, comprehended and acclaimed?

"Is he laughing, triumphantly, because he is 'writing for the masses' in English-language periodicals rather than in Tagalog publications, which have all but disappeared since the great national language reawakening of the 1960s? Is he rejoicing at the prospect of a great national literature slouching closer to be born, heralded by a chorus of various tribal angels, the Seraphim of the Internet, Taglish tabloids, Pinoy Mills & Boon romances and Pilipino intellectuals being translated into English for the next Book Fair?

"And what is meant, really, by writing for the masses, which he has been propagating since the school year 1958–59? Did Rizal, with his *ilustrado* Spanish, write the *Noli* and the *Fili* to be read by the masses? Did Carlos Bulosan and Manuel Arguilla, with their newly learned English, write for the enjoyment of the rural multitudes? Do Dr. Lumbera's literary idols, the grassroots poet Jose Ma. Sison and the American critic E. San Juan, Jr., write in English for the pleasure and appreciation of the proletariat? Do Nick Joaquin, Gregorio Brillantes, Alfred Yuson, Jose Dalisay, Gemino Abad, Cristina Pantoja-Hidalgo, Charlson Ong and Lakambini Sitoy? Also Amando Doronila, Neal Cruz, Conrado de Quiros, Ceres Doyo, Pennie de la Cruz and Alya Honasan? Do they consider it patronizing and vulgar to write of our people's dreams, aspirations and struggles as the finest of them do in their fiction, poetry and journalism? Isn't there a difference between literature and propaganda, between the art of fiction and agit-prop, between writing about the masses and writing for and to the masses? And if writers were compelled or duty-bound to write only in one manner or another, wouldn't they and their readers be better off trying to strive and survive in people's republics like North Korea or Cambodia? (Let's not bring in the big powers like Russia and China but stick with our more modest and accessible Third World models, shall we?)

"Should the man be laughing at all?

"Could we faithful readers of the *Sunday Inquirer Magazine* expect to be enlightened on these issues and questions by the SIM's sagacious critic and humorist, Lito B. Zulueta, himself a distinguished man of letters from the Pontifical University of Santo Tomas, who would define and embrace all Truth (not Lito Z. but St. Thomas A.)?

"Thank you, and may we hope to read Mr. Zulueta's dissertation in the SIM very soon?

"(Sgd.) DANILO F. AGBAYANI, Vice Chairman

(Sgd.) SHERWYN LIU LAUREL, Secretary

UP Diliman Chapter
Filipino Party of Utopians United for Correct Contemporary
Knowledge (FPUUCCK)
c/o Office of the Dean
College of Mass Communication
UP Diliman, Quezon City"

THE ARTICLE IN QUESTION, "The Babel Unified" by Lito B. Zulueta, indeed raises quite a few questions—even more, perhaps, than are posed by Messrs. Agbayani and Liu Laurel. Which, we suppose, is as it should be, considering the burden of Mr. Zulueta's exposition that begs irreverent questions but demands serious and definitive answers. The latter may be simply beyond one's ken, but as writers and readers of the national literature—for Nick Joaquin said it right a half-century ago: literature that a Filipino writes in any language is Philippine literature, is the Filipino nation's literature, because the writer is Filipino—in that capacity, we can't just shrug off these questions and still pretend to be of the more literate and enlightened citizenry, can we? Should we? Shall we? (Hey, the interrogative style of those FPUUCCK fellows—law frat brods? investigative journalism studes?—is sure infectious, 'di ba?)

Mr. Zulueta's treatise, which is also a writer's profile and apologia, cites Dr. Lumbera's prognosis, that literature will become "less of the literature that we know now, printed and published. It will, in fact, go back to the oral tradition, when literature was recited, intoned and performed." This will come about, says Doc Lumbera, because people are "reading less and listening and looking more," prompted by the "impetus that wants literature to be tactile and visual."

Well, that could be true to a certain cyberdotcom extent. But literature as we now know and read it, in books and journals, printed and published as Gutenburg (and Cervantes, Tolstoy, Dickens, Melville, Kawabata, Tagore, Rizal et al.) must have envisioned it— will that literature perish, pass away forever from readers of the lost art? And more people are reading less. . . ?

Tens of thousands flocked to the recent book fair. National Book Store has not done better business with its cut-price holidays. Anvil Publishing, the UP University Press and other publishing houses are thriving. BookSale shops in the malls draw as many patrons daily as Jollibee and McDonald's, confirming at least that Filipinos relish reading as much as consuming cheeseburgers and spaghetti. The vast yearly crop of college-bred unemployed read the classified ads. With each weekly issue, *Philippine Graphic* gains a dozen or two more readers from Batanes to Tawitawi, not to mention OCW subscribers abroad.

Surely, more Filipinos now are reading more. Since Dean Worcester and the Thomasites came over to teach Filipino pupils the ABCs and XYZs, we've become the most reading people in Southeast Asia. What's arguable is the class and quality, the form and substance of our reading.

In Ray Bradbury's classic SF novel, *Fahrenheit 451* (the temperature at which paper burns), books, publications, any literature in printed form, novels, poetry, plays, histories, the humanities, the arts and sciences of mankind, of a nation, a people, a race, memorialized between book covers, are forcibly erased, brutally banned, burned—as totalitarian saviors and reformers of unhappy memory decreed for their subject masses in the last cruel century. . . .

Out-of-this-world fiction, that Bradbury opus, okay; but not the Hitler Youth and the Red Guards tossing books, journals, paintings, works of art and the human imagination into the bonfires. Neither fanciful, we would contend, are the reality and endurance and ever widening power and influence of the book, this thing, this artifact composed of paper, typography, printer's ink, a book designer's handiwork, and glue, thread or staples . . . And was it Graham Greene, in our book the foremost of the great novelists of the 20th century, who once remarked that many good things could be said for the book, not the least of which is that you could carry the small, lightweight, easily hidden copy of a subversive novel or proscribed poetry undetected across a dangerous dictatorship's frontier . . . Maybe not any more; but you get the point: the book and its worth, and the devotion and fidelity it can inspire in a person, an individual apart from the collective, the commune or the refugee crowds driven into exile.

But the quantum electronic leaps and bounds in technology—Western technology! U.S. ally Japanese as well!—ensure the end of the book as we know it, we are assured by the intelligentsia otherwise denouncing foreign S&T prowess as so much neocolonial anathema. To replace the book in the affections of writers, readers and publishers is a portable, palm-size device into which you'll feed a diskette, a capsule or whatever that will screen a story, a poem, a film on a monitor or something—already, Microsoft and Sony and Panasonic have introduced "theater in your hand" models in the computer market, that sell for about $1,000: a terrific bargain, of course, compared with the price of, say, a battered BookSale paperback, to our literary futurists and the masses they must write for, or so they say.

A mass of fortunate and fulfilled writers and cyberlit readers then; but how about the rest of the populace, the unregenerate book lovers, the obstinate print browsers and page scanners, authors and audiences with neither income nor inclination to enjoy oral-visual literature in techno-theaters? Not to say the reading folks who habitually do it in bed, in the bathtub or in the john, this last accounting for over 85 percent of the males (no figures available for females) in any literate community familiar with flush toilets. These readers will have to bother not just with the plot and the whodunit, the marvel and the message, the power of the prose and the beauty of the verses and so forth, but also about the batteries and the buttons and the warranty and where to plug the blasted thing without short-circuiting it or its owner. Since it's only digital, audio-visual literature that's available, you can't pluck out a love poem from a book in your pocket and recite it to your lady love enraptured on the seawall or under a tree in the park as in courting days of yore. . .

Numerous and forbidding are the hazards, complexities and deprivations of a world without books and, conceivably, newspapers and magazines . . . But that won't be on next Friday or the week after tomorrow or maybe till the end of this century or the start of the next, as even Orwell before 1984 might have imagined all too well. So flashback to the present, imperfect and tense as it's subject to progressive surveillance, investigation, the analysis of the concrete literary situation and so on.

THE PREEMINENT QUESTION to be resolved, in the matter of the writing and reading of Philippine literature, as Dr. Lumbera has defined it, concerns the "masses" whom the "committed writer" is obliged to address, in order to advance their decolonization and national liberation—640-peso words, these, but here the jargon of the hermeneutically disposed pedagogue can't be helped, and neither will most of us who are academically inadequate, within the parameters of this dialectical excursion or, more plainly, discussion.

Where are the masses that, we are informed, are ready, willing and eager to read literary works especially written for their pleasure, instruction, fulfillment and perfection? But before they can do so, that is, read novels, poems, essays, etc. and then declassify, deconstruct and demodulate these works of literature for their edification, they, which is to say, the masses and, it goes without saying, also the right or, rather, left kind of books, must first exist since being precedes reading and never vice versa.

Who or what are the masses which or whom the committed critic enjoins the committed writer to revere and serve? A nationwide census has yet to determine their numbers and identities, so for the purposes of this particular literary colloquium-cum-happy-hour at Obeertime on Pasong Tamo corner De La Rosa St., the objective, non-committal critic would have to proceed from the progressive premise that the masses alluded to consist of the heterogeneous horde, at the most a few thousand strong, that's gathered on occasion in places like the Liwasang Bonifacio and the Quezon Memorial Circle to protest against American imperialism, the U.S.-Malacañang dictatorship, unemployment and poverty.

But two or three thousand rallyists braving the barricades to political and economic liberation—are these the broad masses, the great militant majority, in a nation of 80 million? If not, then take the far larger crowds congregating at Rizal Park under the banners of Jesus Is Lord and El Shaddai; but what do they care to read? The Bible, most certainly, and newsletters from Brother Mike and little else.

Government employees, public school teachers, garment factory workers, fisherfolk, land reform beneficiaries, tribal folk, squatters, sidewalk vendors, dissidents, national democratic tax collectors— lumped together in a miserable union, as the committed writer might say a vulgar unity, they do add up to several millions; but will they bother to read and profit from the literature of the committed? Wouldn't they rather read, assuming that they could and without too much prodding, those Taglish sex and scandal tabloids, local imitations of the DC Comics and maybe how-to manuals on the disposal of bureaucrat capitalists, multinational managers, landlords, the AFP, the PNP and biodegradable garbage? Which hypothetical categories of reading should only magnify the need for liberating literature, and for bolstering the committed writer's political will to create his national literature of struggle, decolonization, liberation and freedom.

In any event, there's the vision, reports a noncommitted writer, a UP poet-professor, that one night visited a committed colleague as he sat composing on his Compaq laptop a Tagalog/Filipino epic poem exposing and opposing Western cultural imperialism, including the Old and the New Criticism: a dazzling vision of Dr. Lumbera's masses striding onward in regimented cadence, in the course of their Long March to the heights of literature and liberation; a vibrant, dynamic multitude marching, chanting literary slogans and waving their little black palm compureaders, as other marchers in some revolutionary poet's wakeful vision advanced in triumph and glory, marching jubilantly and chanting and holding aloft their little well-read Chinese books that, by the way, have since been spurned or forgotten, decanonized and consigned to the ideological dustbin if not capitalist incinerator.

For the present, though, one thing is sure about the concrete situation of the broad masses, if they are not the unified and homogenous abstraction of the committed literati: none of them, not even a symbolic few or a discriminative representation, have been privileged to watch J.V. Ejercito's lavish, splendiferous musical still showing to elegant SRO audiences at the Cultural Center of the Philippines.

The melodious fantasy entertainment starring our very own Lea Salonga as the golden-throated whore killing herself for love of her faithless American lover . . . The celebrated novelist and feminist activist Ninotchka Rosca, manning another sector of the Pinoy cultural front located somehow in New York City, assails and condemns the production as a neocolonial showbiz fraud and degradation of Filipino womanhood, in a critique that's decidedly more astute and penetrating than the pronunciamentos of committed artists and art devotees who haven't left home. Which may well demonstrate the creative intelligence and wisdom of maintaining a certain distance from the critical free-fire zone, the better to analyze, decolonize, deodorize and then galvanize the concrete cultural situation before it hardens, solidifies hopelessly beyond repair, modification or alteration, and must submit to radical demolition in the Great Pilipino Cultural Revolution.

2.

SO NOW, PEOPLE, FILIPINOS, countrymen, rather, countrypersons, to be politically and genderly—is there such a word?—correct, after that happy if rather rowdy coffee break, welcome back to our colloquium-workshop on the committed arts and letters and what the committed critic condemns as their reactionary, colonial, anti-Pinoy opposite, and again it's with the fervent hope that we'll all be enlightened, encouraged and empowered in, by and through this colloquium, four syllables, with the accent on the second, from the Latin colloqui, "to speak," which should remind all and sundry about what Dr. Bien Lumbera said, that literature, Philippine literature, is well on its way back to the oral tradition, not away from the ancient reciting and chanting and intoning, as Dr. Nick Joaquin wrote contrarily in his "Small Beer" column in the *Graphic* last July 17, which we'd thought was the last word on the subject but now probably is not, because Doc Lumbera, one of the indomitable few left to uphold the former view, could be right, as more and more Filipinos are, as he put it, "reading less and listening and looking more."

About *Miss Saigon*, which we touched on last week, that assessment appears or sounds to be the case—Filipinos looking and listening more, many of them, the majority of theatergoers and stage lovers in Metro Manila if not the nation, though surely not the broad masses; sighing and swooning and raving about the colossal musical that Erap's enterprising son J.V. and the Cultural Center of the Philippines saw fit, fantabulous and profitable enough to bring to the Philippines despite protests from both patriotic theater artists and plain Filipino Philistines.

We're all agreed, no debate—we've read and heard and seen more than enough, about *Miss Saigon* as the world-renowned gigantic high-tech musical spectacular, how many millions in dollars or devalued pesos it costs to produce and stage, its record-breaking runs in England, the U.S., Canada, Japan, Germany, Denmark, the Netherlands and Australia, and the trophies and awards showered on the show and its magnificent stars, the brightest, the most acclaimed and beloved (by foreign audiences and Filipino fans alike) being the luminous Lea Salonga. Yet not all, it should be duly noted, are ga-ga about Ms. Salonga and what's been called the vicious and vulgar vehicle on which she has sung and swung to world-crass stardom, or demo diction to that effect.

Demonstrably the most capable and coherent of these dissenters and oppositors is the celebrated writer and feminist militant Ninotchka Rosca, author of *State of War* and other novels and works of fiction and nonfiction, now declaring war from her cultural outpost or bunker in Manhattan on everybody and everything associated with the Cameron Mackintosh-Ang Bayang Makulay-Saigon Company Philippines-CCP (not CPP, ha) production.

Ms. Ligaya, you'll all agree, is a delight to see and hear, a beauteous exemplar, one should say, of the oral tradition. May we call then on Ms. Ligaya to read out for our benefit Ms. Rosca's penetrating critique of *Miss Saigon* that appeared—was printed!—in the *Inquirer*, which happens to be the country's biggest and most popular newspaper. A newspaper published in English, which may or may not have made its multi-million-strong readership captives of the language that the gringo imperialists, we are told, imposed on this archipelago, although the reality of a culture's being imposed on a people is open, we think, to doubtful discussion and debate, especially if the people, which is not necessarily the same as saying the broad masses, don't prove to be, ah, so narrow-minded as to revile, reject or renounce any stuff that's not deemed purely Pinoy, indigenous or native but which, say our committed confreres, shapes and forms, painfully, perversely, our society and culture, our arts and letters, our very lives and our posterity and the destiny of the nation and so on. . .

Ms. Rosca's piece is entitled, "Take 'Miss Saigon' to Ho Chi Minh City"—a progressive, provocative proposal that the cultural commissars of the People's Democratic Republic of Vietnam may now be prone to welcome, in a pragmatic bid for more foreign investment and World Bank-IMF loans, and maybe more cordial ties with their rich and generous former imperialist enemy, to support and strengthen their struggling economy. But all that is another script, another show, production and topic we could take up in our next scheduled Obeertime colloquium-workshop.

The article by our friend Nina Rosca starts off with a comparison of *Miss Saigon* with another Broadway show of the same season, *M. Butterfly*, written by Filipino-Chinese-American David Henry Wang.

Ms. Ligaya, please proceed to read the following excerpts from Ms. Rosca's critique of the successful super Saigon musical that, alas and aray, seems only to have made her sick. Ms. Ligaya. . . yes, read. . .

"*Miss Saigon* was supposedly a modernized version of Puccini's *Madame Butterfly* while *M. Butterfly* was an Asian analysis of Puccini's fantasy. . .

"It was the oddest romance ever told. We all hoped that (Monsieur) Butterfly would lay to rest Puccini's stereotype of the Asian female. After all, in this production, it was the Frenchman who committed suicide. He failed, of course, thus mocking even more Puccini's opera.

"Boom and behold, the Vietnam war-era *Miss Saigon* opened. Worse, Filipinas and Filipino-American singers and performers saw it as an opportunity to get to Broadway. So *Miss Saigon*, which was supposedly about Vietnamese women, became identified with women from the Philippines.

"This underlined what was beginning to be a reality: that Filipinas lent themselves very well to the stereotypical sex/love fantasies of the West. It came at a time when sex trafficking of Filipinas to the West was intensifying. . .

"Look at the premise: Kim is a golden-hearted prostitute. Off the bat, you have the bookends of the female stereotype. Wanton in bed but virtuous in everything else; self-sacrificing to the point of suicide; bonded to lover and child, not to national cause, self-pride, sisterhood or even survival, not to mention even an iota of intelligence.

"While *M. Butterfly* was based on a true story, I haven't heard of any Vietnamese woman who abandoned cause—whether left or right— and killed herself for love. . .

"Now, irony of ironies, the world's top exporter of women, the Philippines, true to its role as pimp, turns over the Cultural Center of the Philippines, paid for by tax monies clawed off the populace by the Marcos family, to a *Miss Saigon* production. . . .

"*Miss Saigon* is obsolete; productions have closed down in Europe and the U.S. No one buys this dream of a sexually wanton but submissive Asian girl. . .

"There's simply no audience there for this production any more.

"So they take *Miss Saigon* to the Third World where the poor, the helpless, those bought-and-sold, can watch their destiny—a destiny created for them by globalization—in fake glory for one night as all these gentlemen of the West and their local cohorts run laughing all the way to the bank.

"They play with your mind and take your cash."

They didn't take any cash from our spouse and eldest daughter, the artists in the family, who went to the invitational premiere. We can't tell, though, whether their minds were played with, not till breakfast tomorrow anyway, when as usual we and the Mrs. discuss matters of state, the human situation and the condition of the domestic economy.

Now we have yet to see this splendid if controversial spectacular, and we hope, shamelessly, for another gift of free reviewer's tickets before the show winds up its run in March. So, for the nonce, and for the purposes of this colloquium-cum-happy-hour, we'll just have to go by what the critics and reviewers have said about this showbiz production.

"It's only commercial gloss, darling," says Dr. Lumbera, also in the *Inquirer*, the nation's foremost English-language paper.

Ms. Ligaya, please read on, from here, these marked portions of Dr. Lumbera's composition:

"Manila lovers of *Miss Saigon* will do well to learn to distinguish between artistic quality and plain commercial gloss. The mammoth production now occupying the CCP main stage—by virtue of its $10 million budget, a 10-year polishing process that began in London in 1989, and full-time employment for its amply paid cast and staff for the duration of rehearsals and actual mounting—definitely has gloss, and commerce is obligated to keep that gloss there till the very last performance date. And it is essential that the gloss stay, for on it rests the effectiveness of *Miss Saigon* as a bearer of Western anti-Communist propaganda.

"Superior craftsmanship and attractive packaging make Miss Saigon irresistibly desirable. It is a product that blandishes the consciousness of middle-class consumers in a country like the Philippines which has its own problems with Communist and separatist Muslim insurgency and nationalist resistance to the presence of U.S. military troops on Philippine territory. . .

"When Kim commits suicide in hopes that her son would be able to enjoy a good life in America, Filipino audiences are reminded of their own colonial dream of finding paradise across the Pacific Ocean in such cities as San Francisco, Chicago and New York . . . Kim's son in time will be waking up to cold realities of inner city poverty, racism and maniacal violence in the U.S.

"A merit that Filipino theatergoers might derive from spending on a ticket to *Miss Saigon* is the preview it gives of how globalization could shape our entertainment fare in the coming decades, if they would allow it. . .

"And where do the Filipinos come in? The actor-singers were the hired hands that provided artistic labor for the Manila production, and yes, Filipinos also served as the vendors that peddled the play, using social, economic and political pressure, within the Manila business community.

"Filipino artists, we have been told over and over again, are 'world class.' They do not need convincing, they know they are. What they need is ample time and space for rehearsals, near-inexhaustible funds for production, and a controlled market which will assure performances for months and months."

Salamat sa pagbasa mo, Binibining Ligaya. . .

"But it's only entertainment, honey," those theater-loving folks, and they are a vast throng, able to fill the Cultural Center main theater many times over for months and months, would likely say of these up-your-ass protests and put-downs.

"And it's only a story, a fantasy, showbiz, not a historical pageant or documentary," the same enthralled middle-class consumers—whose numbers and buying power, by the way, grow by the day—might say of the artistic indictment and verdict that *Miss Saigon* succeeds only in dumping upon these shores the foul garbage of neocolonial "unreality."

Be that as it may, we promise to bear in mind Ms. Rosca's analysis and proscriptions, and Dr. Lumbera's diagnosis and prescriptions, if and when we get the chance, *gratis et maxima amore*, we hope, in these hard times, finally to see *Miss Saigon*. We hope, too, that all this committed, rather, cantankerous criticism and debunking won't spoil our enjoyment of this reputedly jolly good show, as it's a matter of principle, of faith and courtesy with us, blame it on our Ilocano genes, to enjoy to the fullest a play, a performance, a program, a party, to which we are treated most generously for free.

PENDING THAT NIGHT of perhaps glorious musical revelations, may we offer to all concerned, in and outside of this and future colloquia, some committed observations, prescriptions and proposals for the defense, preservation and advancement of our national sovereignty, not only geographically and geopolitically, but maybe even more crucially, in the realm of culture and the arts, as eloquently propounded by Dr. Lumbera in a paper presented in a conference on "The Arts and the Struggle for National Sovereignty," at the College of Arts and Letters of the University of the Philippines, on February 2, 1996, thus:

"Militant analysis of U.S. imperialism does not rest solely on the bodily presence of troops on Philippine soil, but also assumes that cultural domination by the U.S. takes many forms and the most insidious is its use of the Philippine educational system, which continues to employ English as medium of instruction, to prolong its hold on Philippine society. Doubtlessly, writers in the coming century will continue their quest for national sovereignty through their works, for the task of liberation is no less arduous now that the U.S. military bases have been dismantled. The rejection of the Military Bases Treaty was just the beginning. The decolonization of the minds of Filipinos young and old, age-old victims of a colonial educational system, remains to be thoroughly pursued. Committed Filipino writers have a long struggle to sustain."

This struggle of the committed writers—poets, playwrights, fictionists, essayists and critics, journalists and literature professors, too—can be made less arduous and protracted, the task of decolonization made easier and the objective of liberation more attainable—if, for starters, our committed writers (and aren't we all, in one passion or another?) desist immediately and henceforth from writing, reading, teaching, discussing, publishing or otherwise using English, and instead employ only Filipino or Tagalog or the favored vernacular. (Exceptions may be allowed where necessary: surfing the Internet, signing vouchers and contracts, issuing or encashing checks printed in English.)

Because, we humbly submit, the continued, widespread, persistent, unrestrained use of English by committed writers and artists is at the very least counterproductive in the arts and letters and at the most a treasonous catastrophe inflicted on our nationhood and national sovereignty. And come to think of it, we can't really, truly write for and to the broad masses and be read, not in the next 50 years anyway, can anyone, committed or otherwise?

The commitment to stop writing, reading and speaking in English . . . To illustrate: will not the use of English in the discourse, publications and preachings of our committed writers and artists, not to say educators, lecturers and the like, make it more difficult, if not impossible, to guide the generations of freshmen in our universities and colleges along the path of decolonization and liberation? Will not the task and mission for the greater good and glory of the nation be rendered more excruciating and unprofitable if the youths always see and hear—the oral! the audio-visual!—their committed mentors setting a bad English example? Just as the teaching of the Ten Commandments and the application of the Penal Code, said the brilliant human rights lawyer Rene Saguisag soon after the Payatas garbage-slide, would become that much more difficult if not impossible if the youth of the land, and their elders as well, particularly lawyers and trial judges, saw prominent personalities like President Estrada and Mayor Mel Mathay and Secretary Lenny de Jesus partying and setting an illegitimate extramarital example in public?

That's to deal with the language issue, in Philippine education and Philippine literature. About the performing arts, our stage plays, theater productions, musicals, operas and so forth, our committed writers, artists and producers can consider doing a *Miss Saigon* of their own, that is, the reverse or opposite, which seems to be their progressive art's desire. In the concrete and objective situation, as they might say, they can import another kind of stupendous showbiz production complete with special effects, rousing lyrics, dazzling sets, the works, along with a controlled market, guaranteed ticket sales, a long run and all the rest, and all to ignite and propel the broad masses' advance to decolonization, liberation, prosperity and freedom.

The committed literati and their business-minded associates could bring in *East Is Red*, the famous Beijing opera of the Mao era that, like *Miss Saigon*, has had its long run in theaters abroad but should still be good for many a tremendous reprise elsewhere. In Manila, for instance, with funding and logistics and an ample venue and pressure on the business community and ticket peddlers provided by the most affluent Beijing loyalists in these parts, beginning with the charming, ever smiling fellow, Ka Lucio somebody, who had that multibillion tax case with the BIR . . . They can maybe retitle the thing *The West Ain't Read*, something of the sort, or Tagalize it, and insist that the stars not be the original veterans but at least Chinoy, like the dashing Atong Ang, the formidable Tessie Ang See, the kittenish Kitty Go and so on.

These, as we said, are but for starters.

We'll present and take up more of these proposals and propositions in another colloquium-cum-happy-hour, same place, same mag, same mugs with which we'll drink more toasts to our literary decolonization and cultural liberation.

(*Graphic*, 2000)

Stories

FROM JANUARY 6 TO DECEMBER 29, 2001, the *Philippines Free Press* published 51 stories by almost as many writers of fiction.

That so many writers and stories saw print in the *Free Press* during this year is a consummation devoutly to be celebrated, and not only by the literary or the literati, the creators of imaginative literature, the inventors of tales and parables, and their publishers and readers. That the *Free Press* has been publishing that many stories every year since at least the second decade of the last century, when Jose Garcia Villa won the very first *Free Press* Prize for his short story, "Mir-i-nisa," in 1929—a span of more than 70 years, excluding the intervals of the Pacific War and the martial law regime—that such a stupendous number of stories were printed and, one presumes, properly read and appreciated is certainly cause for proud commemoration.

All these writers and their works, and the *Free Press* that published them, have put our people in their debt. The nation owes them much in the currency of the mind, the heart and the spirit, the treasure of the humanizing arts and letters, the fine—not gross—national product of their writings, and a lot more beyond any measure.

From the *Free Press* and these fiction writers, the Republic received gifts and favors perhaps even more beneficial to the soul of the race and the body politic. Foremost is the singular fact, the reality, not the fiction, that there are enough Filipinos, at least 50 of them in the year 2001, and about the same number annually for the better part of the 20th century, and most probably for a couple of hundred years more, unless the Philippines and the world come to an end sooner than later—there are enough Filipinos who are preoccupied with the art of fiction rather than with the friction of political faction; who are dedicated to the making of short stories and not to the fashioning of short fuses for seditious bombs and separatist explosives; who write for themselves and their fellow countrymen about love and honor and sorrow and joy and compassion and sacrifice and justice (even if they don't win a prize in the process) instead of writhing in vainglory or wringing their artistic hands in vain.

In a word, Filipinos who will not give up on their art and craft, their conscience and their vocation, and their fellow Filipinos and native land—which, I think, is a fairly encompassing definition of the Filipino writer; for our purposes on this auspicious evening, the Filipino short story writer. Without the short story written by Filipinos in English (from Arguilla and Bulosan to Yuson and Zafra) there would be no Filipino literature worthy of our readership, pride and acclaim, whether the literature be in English, Spanish, Tagalog, Ilocano, Cebuano or any other language still to be dictated perhaps by a totalitarian future. That future let us leave to the linguistic zealots and cultural commissars of the National Diliman Front who are devoutly awaiting it. Let us attend to the present liberal, capitalist, democratic moment and the *Free Press* Literary Awards. I say liberal, because only in liberty, in freedom, can the writer live fully in truth and spirit and serve the faith; capitalist, because he needs more than symbolic bread and should not disdain to profit from private property and public prizes; democratic, because there exists a rich diversity, a populous variety of voices, visions, messages, systems and creeds in the union of writers, in the republic of letters.

OF THE 51 SHORT STORIES published in the *Free Press* during the year under review, four were disqualified for having won awards or having been published elsewhere, which left 47 stories for the three jurors to read and evaluate. For our second meeting, we each came up with a shortlist; mine had ten stories, including the three eventual winners. Among the essays, "Unspeakable Evil" by Sean V. Bigay, on the September 11 terrorist attacks and Osama bin Laden and what they mean to us Filipinos, was a unanimous choice, the lone and unrivaled winner.

"Gizzard Boy" by Menchu Aquino Sarmiento was likewise ranked first by the three jurors. In my own estimation, it has all the qualities that make for an award-winning story: a wry, sardonic yet compassionate vision that is rare and unique in our contemporary fiction; an agile, unsentimental style that can deal all at once with the hilarious and the absurd, the comic, the poignant and the tragic; characters we recognize and empathize with in their situation; and not least, an episodic, unconventional structure that directs and controls the narrative. In varying degrees, the second and third prize stories share the same attributes: "Exiled" by Maria L.M. Fres-Felix, an arresting portrayal of rebellious, amoral youth in the shadow of martial law; "Dragonseed" by Leoncio P. Deriada, fascinating with its atmosphere and suspense in a conflict that threatens to destroy a family—a Chinese-Filipino family, which for me enhanced the story's interest and originality.

"There was a time when Gizzard Boy was not Gizzard Boy"— thus begins Menchu Aquino Sarmiento's story. "His real name was Hero, a ridiculous name, suitable for a dog, but not as ridiculous as Gizzard Boy."

There you have it right at the start—a sign, a portent, that you might discover "Gizzard Boy" to be a good, remarkable, memorable, even a great short story. For the story, the biography, the history, the human if not divine enterprise that attracts, inspires our commitment, remembrance and fealty, begins with the question or the suggestion of it: who is this person, and why is he or she called by this name? It is conceivably the greatest question and puzzle and mystery, the profoundest subject and theme and revelation that confronts every man born into the world, not just artists, philosophers, and census-takers—the question of identity, the matter of being and becoming, the name and personhood of a human being, in time and eternity.

Who is this man coming to be baptized in the river Jordan, is he the promised Messiah? Who is the subversive *ilustrado* from Calamba whose name is invoked by the Katipunan at the dawn of revolution? Is Simoun's real name not Crisostomo Ibarra? Who in truth is this Marcial Bonifacio on the China Airlines flight awaited by assassins at the Manila International Airport? Who is this lady with the pet dog strolling on the esplanade in Chekhov's Yalta? Who is this Filipina in Hong Kong who claims to have two navels? Whose warm hand touched the face of the girl Elay in the night, in a season of grace? And how did this poor, suicidal victim of a boy acquire the name Gizzard Boy? Which, by the way, doesn't sound too bad or nasty, and might even strike one as clever and snappy. In Tagalog, I suppose it would translate into "Batang Balunbalunan," which is the title of a tale that you and I might not care to read; but that is another story which again I shall leave to the language commissars.

At the end of Sarmiento's story, the birthday party for the boy Hero has turned into a family fiasco, a painful shambles, with Hero's classmates, children of the rich, refusing to eat the barbecued gizzards, the fried gizzards, the gizzard *tinola*, the gizzard *adobo*, laughing at it all instead, mocking it—the feast of chicken gizzards and skins provided by Atty. Bayani Tan Agbayani, the father to whom Hero was an unwanted illegitimate son.

When his classmates have gone, the boy sees that Francesca, the girl he loves, has left her purse, a pretty silken pouch containing over two thousand pesos. He pockets the money, then hides the purse in his Nanay's closet underneath her clothes.

"One day, Nanay would discover [the purse] and be enchanted by its frivolous beauty," writes Sarmiento, assuming the consciousness of the boy or the man that he will be. "She would believe that it had been meant for her all this time . . . She would believe that at last, she had found something she had lost, and it had been here all along. Suddenly, this would make her smile, if only for a little while."

It is the story's final illuminating moment, from which it derives its power, and resonance, its significance and memorableness as a work of fiction. "This would make her smile, if only for a little while"—such are the modest joys and simple consolations of the abused and wretched of the earth, until it all explodes in outrage and wrath before the palaces of their overlords.

In this and earlier award-winning stories, Sarmiento demonstrates her mastery of the form in her design of the crucial closing scene, the end that is in a sense a beginning. A story has ended yet in the ensuing silence we begin to see and hear and wonder about life and the lives beyond the page and the reading. That is what a good story should do, that is what a great story can do to us, for us.

Listen to Isak Dinesen, the great Danish writer whom Hemingway said should receive the Nobel Prize in his stead. In a short story, "The Blank Page" by Dinesen, an old woman who earns her living by storytelling is speaking to her granddaughter who wishes to be a storyteller. The grandmother tells the girl to be ever loyal to the story. "Because," she explains, where "the storyteller is loyal, unswervingly loyal to the story, there, in the end, silence will speak. Where the story has been betrayed, silence is but emptiness. But we, the faithful, when we have spoken the last word, we will hear the voice of silence."

The voices and the words and the visions formed on the page, and rising from the blank space following the end of a loyal and magnificent story, poem or essay—for these and more, we praise and thank our most faithful writers, the award-winning fictionists and poets and essayists whom we are gathered to honor tonight. We salute and thank the corporate sponsors of the *Free Press* Literary Awards, and Teodoro M. Locsin, who made the *Free Press* the magazine and the repository of the best writing in the country, including his own distinguished fiction and poetry; his exemplary successors, the Gentleman from Makati, Teodoro L. Locsin, Jr., and the Master Mason, Señor Enrique L. Locsin, and the excellent editors and staff of the *Philippines Free Press*.

(*Free Press*, 2002)

Last
Laughs

A Brief History of Martial Law

IT WAS NOT SEPTEMBER 21, but September 22, 1972, that signalled the actual start of Ferdinand Marcos' martial law regime. To be exact, 9:11 p.m. on that day 17 years ago—a Friday, as is the 22nd of this the first "Marcos Month" to be proclaimed by the admirers of the deposed despot.

The correct date of what Canor Yñiquez, Turing Tolentino and Annie Ferrer should commemorate as "Thanksgiving Day," and the exact hour of the commencement of that infamy, are provided us by I.M. Escolastico, our friend and associate of long standing (though he prefers to take things sitting down).

He cites as his authority no less than the prolific author of Proclamation 1081, who was to write, says he, in *Notes on the New Society,* now mercifully out of print, that "the instrument 'Proclaiming a State of Martial Law in the Philippines' had been signed on the 21st of September and transmitted to the Defense Authorities for implementation . . . clearance for which was given at 9:00 p.m., 22nd of September, after the ambush of Secretary Juan Ponce Enrile at 8:10 p.m. at Wack Wack Subdivision, Mandaluyong, Rizal."

As for "implementation" being 11 minutes behind martial schedule—that, claims this scrupulous student of history, was Enrile's driver's fault. The man, on learning that he was supposed to have been waylaid at Wack Wack, had called it a day and gone home to his second common-law wife, leaving the defense chief driverless for crucial minutes on that fateful night. As for that ambush, Enrile has since humbly confessed, under the tender gaze of Our Lady of Fatima at EDSA, that it was faked, to justify the desperate need—of his boss, as it turned out—for martial law.

So all that business about the Inglorious 21st had more to do with Apo Marcos' superstitious obsession with numbers—dates divisible by seven were deemed most auspicious, until of course the 21st of August 1983—than with the facts of history, before which Escolastico can only bow down in reverent humility.

Anyway, that Friday night in September, Escolastico remembers sharing a convivial table at the Acapulco Bar of the Tower Hotel in

Ermita with the *Free Press'* Napoleon Rama, the *Pilipino Star's* Ruther Batuigas and the *Economic Monitor's* Willie Baun, watching, together with two-thirds of Manila's licentious press, an alleged fashion show of the latest-style lingerie.

Nap Rama and some other connoisseurs of avant-garde fashion were nabbed on the way or when they got home in the pre-dawn darkness of September 23. To his surprise, dejection and eventual relief, Escolastico was spared the attentions lavished by the Metrocom on his subversive media colleagues. It seems his mother's own cousin from Camiling, a rather short but high official close to Mr. Marcos, and a couple of Palace friends with no little influence at Camp Crame had managed to have a few names, including his and that of a future National Artist then working on a biography of Ninoy Aquino, deleted from a colonel's mission orders.

Whatever the real lowdown, which has never been confirmed or denied, the net result for Escolastico was an injustice, one of the most dastardly in that long dark night—denying him accommodations among the brave, the true and the honorable in the Crame gym, and depriving him of such manly ordeals, such inspiring tales of faith, valor and egoism as Max V. Soliven hasn't tired of recycling to this day.

Denied that transfiguring encounter with destiny, Escolastico now reveals that he sought redemption and peace of soul by writing down his impressions of the martial law years, for the benefit, as the former Malacañang tenant was wont to say, of our country and people, of all Filipinos and their posterity. By the time Apo Marcos and Imelda got settled in Makiki Heights, our friend had produced more than a thousand pages of jottings, enough for a hefty volume that can brain a thick-skulled loyalist if dropped from, say, the top of the Post Office building.

But is Escolastico's chronicle of martial law, like Soc Rodrigo's in this distinguished journal, worth the telling? What can he possibly recount that hasn't already been recorded in far more vivid detail and memorable style since the Marcoses took that flight to Hawaii?

People have a point there, he concedes; but not one to be so quickly squelched on the subject, he offers us this condensation of his massive work—a history of martial law, all in one paragraph:

"Contrary to oft-repeated allegations, it wasn't honest-to-goodness one-man rule. Like any good dictator's wife, Imelda helped ruin the country. Johnny, Danding, Bobby, Hermie, Rudy, Jun and other business-minded pals pitched in, too. So did Richard Nixon, Ronald Reagan, George Bush and Michael Armacost. Not to be forgotten are the contributions to the erection of the New Republic from Kokoy, Bejo and other hard-working relatives. Marcos & Co. indeed had a lot to do. The 1973 Constitution, delayed by the abrupt disappearance of many Con-Con delegates, had to be finished, naturally in 1973. A group of diligent delegates, led by somebody who looked like Diosdado Macapagal, worked overtime in the Malacañang library, often forgoing dinner and floor show, to complete the Charter. The self-appointed constitutional authoritarian liked the results. Marcos thought the people should, too. Multitudes expressed their approval by cheerfully raising their hands as they were photographed. The photo industry, along with other trades, was thus given a big boost. The Muslims, who had been requested to surrender their guns, had to be placated, also with guns. Generals added the mortuary business to their portfolio of lucrative sidelines. The Department of Public Information promoted developmental journalism. This led to some interesting developments in the media. Doroy Valencia developed Rizal Park and environs and was hailed as the Dean of Philippine Journalism. The cultural scene was enlivened by visiting artists like Van Cliburn, George Hamilton, Gina Lollobrigida and Muhammad Ali. Ninoy Aquino, the regime's most famous detainee, and Soc Rodrigo, Tany Tañada, Tito Guingona and other irrepressible souls ran for the Interim Batasan. They lost to Imelda, Cesar Virata, Vicente Paterno and other beloved figures. The ensuing noise barrage failed to shatter Marcos' eardrums or his equanimity. Then, Francisco Tatad resigned as information minister to campaign for the Opposition's surprised presidential candidate, the heroic and semi-senile Alejo Santos. The old guy was trounced, too, but that didn't seem to depress him or his pious campaign manager, who kept his job as media psychology consultant to the Office of the President. Marcos went on making speeches, something he had always liked to do since his UP days. Florentino Makabenta, not Adrian Cristobal, as was long wrongly assumed, wrote for Marcos something like 1,369 speeches, on subjects ranging from Absolutism to Zoning, without pronunciation guides. Consequently, Marcos kept saying 'le-jeés-lah-tive,' and 'to-wárds' and 'Sar-tre,' things like that, until aggravated Ateneans just had to launch the Light-a-Fire movement to stop the atrocities. Imelda also delivered her quota of speeches, with titles like 'City of Man in the Kingdom of God' and 'The Moral Dimensions and Aesthetic Parameters of the Green Revolution." On the side, with the audio-visual assistance of Jolly Benitez, she gave lectures on the 'Synergy of the Good, the True and the Beautiful,' and the 'Bountiful Hole in the Sky.' The gap widened between rich and poor, with more and more of the latter falling into it. The NPA featured Marcos' portrait on its recruitment posters, with unprecedented results. Amnesty International discovered that there were now more human wrongs than rights. Metro Aides lent zest and color to often flooded streets and June 12 parades. Earlier, the Afro-Asian Writers Conference had for special guest the famed punctuation poet, Jose Garcia Villa, who, without really trying, almost caused the confab to lapse into a coma. Enrile and Danding put up a foundation to fund research on stem borers and other pests, thus increasing the earnings of coconut farmers playing the stock market. All this time, Marcos and his spouse were amassing a fabulous fortune by venturing into new investment areas. This single-minded interest in financial matters would have some negative effects on the Philippine economy and the international banking system. Justice Secretary Ricardo Puno improved the syntax of the laws on detention. Chief Justice Ikeng Fernando penned his landmark annotations to the jurisprudence on the umbrella. Imelda borrowed at least two 747s from PAL and several millions from the GSIS, all without collateral and just by phoning Roman Cruz, Jr. Around this time, Marcos decided to lift martial law, transferring the decree to a higher drawer in his Malacañang study, and throwing in some fresh mothballs to boot. This was before Ninoy came back from exile, despite General Ver's solicitous warning that some people would shoot him in the head if he wore a bullet-proof vest. This was exactly what happened, at the airport, as Ninoy was gingerly helped down the passenger tube stairs. He was shot dead in the head from behind and above, although his shorter assassin was seen standing on the tarmac several feet away in front of the tube stairs. This led to a lot of confusion and bad feelings throughout the land. Yellow confetti donated by Bea and Ting-Ting blocked traffic on Ayala Avenue, while Butz and Nikki alternately marched, skipped and jogged from Tarlac to Tarmac. Then Marcos snapped at the chance of winning his sixth or seventh mandate from the people. But faced with the popular and saintly Cory, he found his macho appeal failing him, followed by his kidneys, or vice versa. He tried to do a repeat of his '69 election victory. That was when, as they say, 'the shit hit the fan,' which is more graphic, rhythmic and onomatopoeic in Ilocano. Finally, God, Enrile, Ramos, RAM and Cardinal Sin brought about the EDSA Revolt, which gave the gringos the chance to repay Marcos for being their right arm or hand or whatever appendage in Asia. In a semi-comatose state the toppled constitutional authoritarian was flown out by the U.S. State Department or the CIA or the Green Berets to involuntary exile, and retirement in Honolulu, with Imelda on the plane singing 'Killing Me Softly' and 'New York, New York,' looking and sounding like Tessie Tomas, only heavier, mournful and melodramatic."

"Now," says Escolastico as he looks us reprimandingly in the eye, "what did martial law, Marcos, Imelda, Enrile, Danding, Ver, EDSA and all that teach us Filipinos? What have we learned?"

He answers his own momentous query:

"Next to nothing."

(Times-Journal, 1989)

Mutters of Humble Opinion

AREN'T WE SHORTCHANGING our esteemed readers and society at large and humanity as well, says our ever concerned friend, the occasionally gregarious and allegedly brilliant Escolastico, by confining our periodic commentary to just one subject or two when there's room in this space for a dozen and more?

Instead of dealing with only one theme or topic, says he in a tone of solemn rebuke, why don't we let the laser beam of our insightful perspicacity (his extravagant words, not ours) probe the whole spectrum of Philippine reality or at least a goodly chunk of it in one sitting, in the manner of famed columnists like the late Teodoro F. Valencia and his indefatigable disciples, notably Art Borjal and Jess Sison, who habitually pack as many as ten topics and 15 opinions into a column on weekdays, more on Sundays and holidays?

What this country needs, Escolastico points out, is not pompous analysis in essay form but several pompous certainties packed into a readable capsule that the intellectually famished can switch on and peruse with their morning coffee. (His mixed-up metaphors.)

All right, we'll do it that way this time around—with the help, which we hereby acknowledge, of an analytical brother-in-law, an introspective neighbor with a green card now having second thoughts about going back to San Francisco, and our highly politicized barber from Apalit, Pampanga. But we intend to go back next Tuesday to the style and format we started out with in this corner—faster to write, some say—unless we get an avalanche of mail from our countless readers (a count has yet to be made) imploring us to continue being lavish and variegative in dispensing our humble opinions on the Philippine as well as the human condition.

* * *

During President Aquino's state visit to Washington, the imperialists, all Americans, of course, were quite forthright about their plans to hold on to Clark and Subic and other so-called facilities on our sacred soil, while she fell far short, alas, of her goals in the matter of aid and investments. This was because, either out of shyness or due to Press Secretary Azcuna's failure to locate the right speech in her cosmetics case, she limited herself to just beating around the Bush.

* * *

Our solons seem bent on doing their work under a common roof rather than in two distant locations. But the PNB ceiling they want to hold their sessions under is anything but common, as just propping it up has already cost this cash-strapped nation something like P2 billion. They should just wait for the opening of the gargantuan hotel that the beauteous Bien Bien (Dr. Emilia Roxas to you) is building along Manila Bay. A portion of the hotel's coffee shop alone is designed to accommodate the Senate and the House in joint session, plus the lawmakers' staffs, private armies and relatives within the first degree of consanguinity.

* * *

The Most Profound Statement of the Month may well be Assistant Majority Floor Leader Raul Roco's comment on the move to house both chambers of Congress in the PNB building by the Bay: "Nearness and familiarity may breed all sorts of unwanted ill will unless

307

mutual respect is strengthened." True, true, but let's not forget that there will always be all sorts of wanted ill will among even our more respectable politicians.

* * *

Militant teachers have vowed to go on strike again to protest Education Secretary Quisumbing's "no work, no pay" order. The citizenry, too, should stage rallies—against these public school teachers who all these years have insisted on turning out "no read, no write" graduates.

* * *

As announced by Professional Regulation Commissioner Julio Francia, the country has just gained 785 new dentists, out of some 1,530 who took the licensing exams last May. We pray that, in these trying times when one can only hang on by the skin of one's teeth, they will not be demolarized by a hand-to-mouth existence.

* * *

After all these years of following the PBA and PABL cage tourneys, we've come to the conclusion that there's no duller and sillier sport than basketball as it's presently played—ten full-grown males running up and down the court dribbling, blocking, passing in predictable motions, each trying to shoot or stop the dunking of the ball into one or the other hoop. That's all, over and over, till the last buzzer—monotony is the name of this game. To revitalize the game, the rules should be overhauled without delay. For instance, instead of the all-male quintet, a team could consist of three gents and two ladies. Imagine the color, excitement, crowd appeal and popularity generated if we had these lineups pitted against each other at the Ultra or the Big Dome: Jaworski, Cesar, Loyzaga, Sharon Cuneta and Alma Moreno vs. Patrimonio, Lastimosa, Codiñera, Dina Bonnevie and Zsa Zsa Padilla. And with imports along the lines of Kim Basinger, Farrah Fawcett or Rene Russo, the possibilities are simply fantabulous. As a former President of the Philippines, himself a champion shooter and play-maker, was heard to say, basketball in this country can be great again.

* * *

While President Aquino was abroad trying to get more money to stabilize the economy, Cabinet and other officials dutifully took turns echoing what she had asserted before she departed, that the present government is most certainly stable. That's a proposition to which oppositionists with or without horse sense will always say neigh.

* * *

In our previous columns, "Filipino-speaking Filipinos" got printed as "Filipino-seeking Filipinos"; "lawn grass and shrubbery" came out as "lawn grass shrubbery"; "converging points" appeared as "converging pointed"; "regular basis" was turned into "regular bass," etc. (All since corrected, in this space or elsewhere.) Is the Port Area chapter of the Proofreaders United for Tangible Rewards, Inducements and Dividends (PUTRID) trying to tell us and this paper's management something?

(Times-Journal, 1989)

The Party, the Proletariat, Perestroika and All That

"AND SO IT CAME TO PASS THAT MARX was allowed by the Almighty to come back from the afterlife and give his message on global TV. He was given only a few minutes so he had to think real hard what to say."

"And what did good old Karl say?"

"'Workers of the world—I am really very sorry.'"

"Hahahaha. Wherever did you pick that one up? A sorry joke, and it's no joking matter, 'padre."

"I agree. Absolutely. A very serious matter indeed, as you well-Red intellectuals have long known. And surely the workers in Eastern Europe and the Soviet Union and elsewhere aren't taking it lightly, or haven't you heard?"

"You started this off by saying those smart-ass things about Marx and Lenin and Gorbachev. . ."

"Ah, yes, as I was saying, my dear progressive friend, if Mikhail Sergeyevich Gorbachev, the General Secretary of the Communist Party

309

of the Soviet Union, the Great Red Father of *glasnost* and *perestroika*, *Time* magazine's Man of the Decade—"

"Please get to the point as I don't have all day. After this round, I'll have to drive out to Diliman for a meeting at five p.m."

"As I was saying, if Gorbachev should fail in his bid to reform, actually to revolutionize Marxism-Leninism, what you fellows call scientific socialism, at least four groups outside the Soviet Union would be beside themselves with joy. Not that they are already beside themselves with other things."

"I'm just dying to hear what kind of reactionary crap has collected between your bourgeois decadent ears."

"I'll make you eat your words yet, you well-fed closet Communist . . . If Gorbachev fails, there are all these people who are going to be very glad. These would be Deng Xiaoping and his aging gang in Beijing; the imperialist warmongers of the U.S. military-industrial complex—to use your nice terminology—and the anti-nationalist, pro-bases politicos and businessmen in our Bayang Magiliw. And last but surely not least, the more radical and therefore more ambitious cadres of the Communist Party of the Philippines."

"Kindly elucidate, elaborate, clarify. I might need a few footnotes for my next lecture from a typical benighted burgis like you."

"If Gorbachev fails in this revolution of his to make Marxian socialism more democratic, more human and humane—sounds great, doesn't it—if he's shown not only to be a monumental flop, he is overthrown, ousted, maybe even killed in a coup by the true believers in the Kremlin, Deng & Co. will be very happy. Why? Because that would prove exactly what they tried to teach those pro-democracy demonstrators at Tiananmen last year, that Marx couldn't have made any mistakes about history, socialism, capitalism, human nature and all that, and Gorbachev and his ilk should know better than to wash their dirty Lenin in public."

"Hahaha again. The subject really brings out the neocolonial witless—I mean, the wit in you."

"That won't wither away, unlike the state in your sacred scriptures. To resume—besides those hardline characters in China, the capitalist warlovers in the Pentagon would celebrate Gorbachev's downfall, too, as that would mean the real fire-breathing ultraconservative comrades lording it over again in Moscow. Which would mean back to the cold war, back to the arms race, a bigger budget for nuclear missiles, Star Wars and all the rest, and more reason to hold on to Clark and Subic. And what's good for the health and wealth of those warlike gringos would be just fine with our pro-American operators, like that guy Gordon in Olongapo and maybe more than half of the Senate . . ."

"That accounts for three of the interested parties. Where do our friends in the NDF-CPP-NPA come in?"

"If Gorbachev should succeed—imagine, calling for an end to the Communist Party's monopoly on power, for a multiparty setup, and no more violence, no armed revolution to achieve socialist goals. And more—freedom of the press, of assembly and the rest. And most heretical to Party hardliners, the legalization of private property—by God, even private ownership of factories, of the means of production! And all this because Marxism-Leninism has succeeded only in distributing misery equally—except among Party bigwigs, of course—in making the proletariat suffer under the dictatorship of poverty. So Gorbachev's now batting for multiparty democracy, democratic freedoms, free markets, etc., to keep Soviet society and the Soviet economy from going under . . . Well, if you were a thoughtful Marxist revolutionary still maybe 50 years away from what Ka Joma or Ka Satur would call the strategic stalemate in your jungle headquarters on Mount Makiling or the Bondoc Peninsula, what Gorbachev's doing to the one true faith would kinda depress you, wouldn't it?"

"Well, I don't know, since I've never been anywhere near the Bondoc Peninsula."

"It took the Soviets 72 years to find out that Marxism-Leninism doesn't work. The Poles, Hungarians and their neighbors took about 40 years. Sooner or later—the domino theory at work, but not where people once thought it would—China, Vietnam, North Korea, Cuba will follow suit. The people getting sick and tired of the dictatorship of the proletariat, any dictatorship, for that matter, and clamoring for real democracy, more of it, and more food, jobs, peace and prosperity. You know something?"

"OK, let's wind this up. Just one more beer before I take off. I'm expected at the UP before the happy hour. There's this pubhouse near the campus called Trellis, where they serve classy, elitist sisig. . ."

"It's going to take your revolutionary friends less time than the Soviets and the Poles and the East-Germans and all those people in Eastern Europe to wake up to the fact that communism doesn't work."

311

"What makes you say that, 'padre?"

"Because Filipinos are smarter, that's why."

"You think so?"

"You can bet a case of beer on it. Less than 40 years."

"Make that 72, like the Russkies. Filipinos may be smarter, but they like to take their time."

"So let's take our own sweet time—and one more for the road."

(*Times-Journal*, 1990)

Dear Erap, Do Not Resign

YOUR EXCELLENCY:

Greetings, hail to the Chief Executive, warmest regards to the families, good luck, good health and all—which glad tidings I would have extended personally to your exalted if embattled and now impeachable self, had you found the time to attend the alumni reunion of St. John's Academy the other week, at the Club Filipino.

I am no alumnus of that venerable institution in San Juan town (where your jolly boy Jinggoy still holds sway), a school founded by the beloved educator, Concepcion Marquez-Gil. But my wife is, and so are you, whose family was neighbor to hers in your grade-school days, in Pinaglabanan. She remembers you as the charming, kindhearted rogue who coached her all-girl basketball team, which she captained.

Likewise a graduate of St. John's is lawyer Eric Nubla, who organized this year's Club Filipino reunion. I happened to be seated next to him at the dance and dinner party, and the talk was, no surprise, mostly about St. John's most distinguished and absent alumnus, and Attorney Nubla, Chinoy eyes turning more merrily chinky, wondered aloud if people still told those Erap jokes every other Filipino seemed to have a stock of even before your glorious Barasoain inaugural.

312

They still do, said a slightly tipsy guest; and this gent proceeded to regale the table with one of the newer "Eraptions," as your Ateneo High teacher Emil Jurado and your old class buddy Reli German called these tales in that supposedly funny book they put out some years back when you were still the Veep and couldn't have imagined, even in your most hallucinatory Blue Label daze, all the troubles, the profound muck and mess into which the presidency, your office as well as your administration, has sunk up to nearly its nostrils. A foot or two lower and you'll go under, recalling that bit about your late idol Macoy standing on Imelda's shoulders submerged in the fiery mud of their hell, remember?

In the process dragged down to the pits, too, are the economy, the peso, the stock market, not to say tourist attractions like the casinos and high-yield enterprises like Dante Tan's Best World Resources Corp. and lucrative ventures like Bingo 2-Ball that would have legalized jueteng to the relief and joy of the PNP, the cobradores and the gambling masses.

Anyway, the "Eraption" one picked up at the Club Filipino that evening went something like this. When informed by your Executive Secretary, Ronnie Zamora, that a lot of people were demanding that you resign, and resign pronto, you merely smirked and shot back, "Me resign? But why should I? I've already signed what it is I'm supposed to sign! So why am I being asked to re-sign?" This, followed presumably by presidential gasps and groans bemoaning the lack of justice in this world, kindness and plain common sense.

"Re-sign . . . ?"

It's rather lame, even stupid sounding, in print; but recited with certain facial contortions, winks and blinks, it could draw some titters and a few guffaws around a party table. As it did, at the St. John's shindig. But Eric—you must know the guy as he comes, like you, from an old San Juan family—you'll love him for this: he kind of put a damper on things when he said the crisis this time of the year calls for anything but levity, these are times that try men's souls. Their soles, too, one should add, what with all the protest marches and demos and *welgas* going on.

Yes, Your Excellency, our friend Attorney Nubla, VP of the Integrated Bar of the Philippines, was being judicious, proper, precise and politically, legally and constitutionally correct in counseling sobriety, reflection and gravity amid the current crisis. For my part, hopefully, humbly, and in the same fraternal spirit, I hereby add my voice to the voices crying in the chaotic wilderness to make straight the path of truth, justice and constitutional wisdom; I dare to raise before Your Excellency, Joseph Ejercito Estrada—most prominent graduate of the elementary department of St. John's Academy, honorary member of the Ateneo High School Class of 1955, former movie actor, mayor, senator and vice-president, and now still the incumbent President of the Republic, of 75 million Filipinos—I present this request, this appeal, this petition:

Please do not resign.

Don't quit. Don't step down or go off or drop out, as the case may be. Or go on leave. Re-sign not, and go on being President . . . our President . . . (Note the absence of exclamation points, of a demanding pitch and excitable tones such as anti-Erap solons and Makati Business Club stalwarts are wont to use these days.)

Do not resign. Not now. Not yet anyway.

You may well ask in your sober, somber moments: In the face of all these aggravations and agonies that beset the Office of the President as well as my person, why should I not resign? Why, oh, why not give up, quit, at least go on leave, take a vacation or otherwise make myself scarce, defunct, put away and mothballed, a resigned ex-President?

Why not? Why indeed not?

Your Excellency, the presidency may be what Cardinal Sin calls an occasion of sin, a seat of temptation for public servants like you. As if, by changing your address or visiting your various domiciles alternately only on odd or even-numbered days, you would confuse the tempter and dispel his wily spell. But yield not, I beseech you, to any sweet narcotic weakness promising escape to either bliss or oblivion, to tempt you in your hour of supreme travail and possibly darkest despair to just give up and resign.

Don't—for the sake of the country and the people, your people, our people, especially the more than 10 million adoring Filipinos who elected you President over six or seven or was it eight rivals by an unprecedented majority in the annals of Philippine democracy, freedom and suffrage only some two years ago. . .

Consider, Your Excellency: Suppose, soon after your old drinking buddy, mahjong mate and jueteng collector Chavit Singson told a presscon about those more than P500 million jueteng and tobacco tax payoffs that you allegedly—incredibly! shockingly!—pocketed (which explains, it's also alleged, why you walk with that weighed down twitch and wobble) . . . suppose, following that October 6 presscon of Gov. Luis Singson and as soon as Cory Aquino and Cardinal Sin, Rep. Roilo Golez and Sen. Ramon Magsaysay, Jr. and Vice-Pres. Gloria Macapagal-Arroyo and former president Fidel Ramos and the Ayala-Forbes-Alabang activists asked you, not so politely, to resign, you heartily agreed, you packed your bags and maybe those attaché cases Chavit said he often used to bring you your share of the loot, you announced your resignation on nationwide TV and without much ado or addenda departed for good from Malacañang?

Suppose you had done that, just like that—just because Cory and the Cardinal and politicians like Golez, Lina, Macapagal-Arroyo and concerned citizens like Ramos and Jaime Augusto Zobel and Jose Concepcion and later 130,000 rallyists at the EDSA Shrine had demanded that, being morally bankrupt and absolutely unfit and incapable as President, you should immediately, unconditionally and permanently resign?

If you'd done their bidding then and made a quick, ignominious exit, you would have spared them and the resign-now or impeach-Erap crowds a lot of suspense, and much fear and dread, and worry and anxiety over the worsening state of the nation and the deterioration of the economy. But at the same time you would have deprived them and the rest of the nation, both those for and against your summary removal or retirement, of so much good, such a tremendous range of bounties and benefits as to reduce to comparatively trivial annoyances what the people presently endure; such a cornucopia of blessings, virtual manna or the equivalent of dollars, not devalued pesos, falling from heaven, that the people will praise and thank you for, if not this Christmas, surely in the more secure and enlightened future.

What are these good things, these blessings that the people might lose, might never have, had you quit as soon as you were asked by Cory, Sin & Co.?

Well, páre, I mean, President Erap, Your Excellency—let us count the ways.

First that comes to mind, it's so clear and real and there's no avoiding it—we have this ongoing super political roadshow that's far more stirring and gripping than several dozen Thalia telenovelas rolled into one, to say the least; and heaven knows how badly, really badly, we Filipinos in our dire straits need such dramatic distraction, such excellent entertainment. A sure indication that we desperately need such an enthralling production—if DILG Secretary Alfredo Lim and PNP Chief General Panfilo Lacson are to be believed, there are fewer criminals and psychos on the loose these days as even these characters now stay indoors, watching TV and reading the papers, following the fortunes of their beleaguered hero from one thrilling episode to another.

With performances on the national stage, as it were, every day of the week, and with more mesmerizing plot twists, many more lavish scene changes and special effects than you can shake a critical finger at in *Miss Saigon*, the all too real *Estrada in Extremis* that you inspired but didn't write, direct and produce, and in which you are the constant star attraction even when you are off-stage, is certainly the splendiferous show of the season, the critics' unanimous choice, the talk of the town, and in impact and consequence the acme, the standard, for years to come.

Aside from you, the casting alone is impossible to beat—from Chavit and Atong, Jinggoy and J.V., Yoly and Bong to Cory and Jaime and Fidel and then Loi and Guia and Laarni and also Nene and Frank and Blas, Johnny and Miriam and Kit, and any number of congressmen, and with the impeachment trial proceeding in the Senate, the Chief Justice no less. . .

All that you may call the showbiz part. Then there's the educational part, all the lessons you must continue to impart as Chief Executive, Commander-in-Chief and paterfamilias, which should prove to be more meaningful, beneficial and rewarding over the long haul, for our people and our posterity.

Already, you have done your fair share of educating our people—a daunting task for any teaching President as we Filipinos, especially those of us who elected you by a massive unprecedented majority, are a stubborn, unruly, ungovernable lot. Though sometimes we can also be as meek and docile as lambs, like Ka Eddie's and Brother Mike's loved flocks congregating in Rizal Park to pray and fast for your salvation.

The romanticized masses who idolize you, who would suffer most from your continued stay in Malacañang—by rights they should be the first to benefit from your example and your instruction.

(*Graphic*, 2000)

YOUR EXCELLENCY:

Greetings again, warmest regards to the families, to old friends and new, Chavit, Atong, Dante, Mark, Laarni, Joy, Rowena—especially Rowena, that willowy beauty from PAL.

Did Weng, as the former flight attendant is fondly called, come with the government's bail-out package for old pal Lucio Tan's ailing airline? If not, Mrs. Lopez has lent wings to your heavily laden heart anyway, hasn't she? You do need such a boost for your cardio-vascular and other systems these terribly trying days, don't you, sir? But will she be subpoenaed, too, and be grilled by those heartless House prosecutors and unsympathetic Senate jurors on whatever she knows about the "P1 billion worth of land and property" that, reports the Philippine Center for Investigative Journalism, you allegedly own and share with loving friends old and brand-new?

I hope they'll spare Weng Lopez any anxiety and distress as a summoned witness in full view of the gallery and nationwide TV—they should, solely for her sake, and never mind you and yours as, in this instance, you and lawyers Andres Narvasa, Estelito Mendoza and Raul Daza can very well look after your protective macho self. One look at the *Inquirer*'s front-page photo of her—so lovely, sweet and oh so vulnerable, smiling radiantly, trustingly, beside you on that PAL flight to the U.S. in March last year—and anyone will have to agree that it would be a gross violation of her gorgeous constitution to subject her to even the slightest cross-examination. In Rowena's case, let insistent pubic, uh, public demand go hang, if you know what I mean.

But some of the more ungallant senators, the likes of Tito Guingona and Rene Cayetano, who seemed to enjoy reducing to tears yet another sweet tender friend of yours, the ledger-keeping Yolly Ricaforte, tend to heed the demonstrating public's clamor, and might just decide to subpoena Rowena. And, of course, there's no telling at this point—for even loquacious Miriam Santiago seems to have clammed up—exactly who and when and how many they will summon to testify at your impeachment trial. That's adding to the suspense, the high drama, the low blows, the tall tales, the puzzles, questions and arguments, including the real score on your impeachment agenda and game plan.

Are you in truth and in fact for a just, thorough, expeditious, most of all speedy trial, as you've announced more than once, to resolve the case and decide your fate once and for all and salvage our society, the economy and the nation? But why did your ever obedient LAMP cohort in Congress, in the aptly named Lower House, try mightily, anomalously, idiotically, as Joker Arroyo might say, to stop the justice committee from forging the impeachment bill and then block the delivery of the indictment articles to the Senate? Had Speaker Manuel Villar not banged down that gavel when he did, precisely at that historic instant on November 13, the impeachment bill ensuring the early trial that you seemed to wish for so ardently might have landed instead in some moronic congressman's trash can. And even after Senate President Aquilino Pimentel had formally received the stuff, the hastily elected Speaker, Arnulfo Fuentebella, a fervent Erap loyalist if ever there is one, went about mobilizing majority congressmen in a bid to nullify both the impeachment bill and Villar's legislative feat that had caused Rep. Jose Mari Gonzalez to throw a fit and also a fist in the House sergeant-at-arm's face, which barbaric action is typical of politicos from your home town, San Juan, or so say the Opposition ladies in Congress who want you impeached and thrown out of Malacañang.

YOUR EXCELLENCY, are you really for a swift, fair, just, expeditious trial? Or is it the reverse, as your allies, your partymates and partners in the House, and in the Senate, too, appear to have been agitating for since the NGOs called for your impeachment even before Chavit Singson's jueteng bombshell?

Are they out to slow down, derail, dismantle the impeachment proceedings, against your express will? Are they following a script you haven't even heard of, with dastardly subplots you don't know about? What's going on out there?

A few things, though, we can all be sure about by now. One is the trial kicks off on December 7, unless a giant asteroid slams down on Metro Manila or an earthquake swallows up the Senate or you make up your mind to resign today, this afternoon before the close of office hours. But you've vowed repeatedly never, never to resign, so I guess that option is out, between now and Christmas, anyway.

Another thing I don't have any doubts about is this educational business I mentioned in the first part of this epistle, missive, whatever, after the showbiz production offering the unhappy populace so much entertaining distraction.

Surely, by not resigning now, not calling it quits yet, you carry on in your role as the teaching President—no lean, mean achievement, since our people or, as you may prefer, the *masa*, the masses, are a difficult, hard-headed, wayward, generally ungovernable, uncontrollable lot, as thousands and tens of thousands and still more of them are even now demonstrating for your information and benefit.

And what, you and your families and friends old and new may ask, are these things you are teaching the people, the masses, just by hanging on and not resigning and now going through the impeachment trial and all?

The first concerns the people or, rather, the masses, there's a difference there, according to the historians and political scientists and sociologists and, not to forget, politicos like you whom they elect to inflict on the more informed and discriminating minority, including Cory Aquino, Cardinal Sin, Jaime Zobel, Joe Concepcion and maybe Fidel Ramos, too, and Joe de Venecia.

As they watch and see all that's being done and undone under your administration to make this nation far from great again, in fact more wretched and impoverished than ever before, and bankrupt in more ways than one, the folks on the farms and the toilers in the countryside, the factory workers and laborers and daily wage earners, squatters, sidewalk vendors and domestics, jeepney and tricycle drivers and their passengers, a great many of them perhaps still nostalgic film fans of the romantic rogue Asiong Salonga—as they see and take it all in, and sweat and grumble and groan in the process, they should begin at least, at last, to realize the costly enormous folly of thinking little and voting big for president or senator, for congressman or governor or mayor, a candidate of dubious merit but who happens to be an immensely popular charmer, a spellbinding entertainer, like, say, a Grade-B movie idol. So that, hopefully, should the painful lesson sink in this time around, the same folks who gave you an unprecedented poll victory—over ten million votes that buried your half-dozen rivals for the presidency—will resolve that, beginning in the May 2001 elections, they will never, never again vote carelessly, stupidly, for somebody just because he or she happens to be dashing, debonair, pretty or popular.

Wouldn't this mean only the ugly, the ungainly and the unpopular might be elected to office? Small price to pay, I'd say, for good government and a sound economy—not a sagging one, as in a banana republic. (I think that's from our buddy, your Ateneo High classmate Reli German: banana . . . "saging" economy . . . you get it?) Which the crisis that has descended on our heads might still lead us to, if it's not resolved though this impeachment trial, to the people's relief and satisfaction, as you have prayerfully hoped, not later but soon.

Some more lessons remain to be taught and, it's to be hoped, learned by the populace, so long as you stay in office and don't resign but hold on to your tenure, presidential, extramarital as well as professorial. Really, what further loss and impoverishment would be visited on this nation if, by resigning at once when Cory Aquino and Cardinal Sin first urged you to, you had eliminated from the people's curriculum the object lessons, the instructive theses and demonstrations that should mold and motivate democracy's greatest asset—an intelligent, principled citizenry zealous of its rights and obligations.

By staying on, not giving up although pummeled black, blue and pink by all kinds of accusations, charges and indictments, twisting in the wind, as they say, yet neither resigned nor resigning, you go on teaching our people many an invaluable and, it's to be wished by all Filipinos who love our people and country, truly effective and enduring lesson on—don't laugh, please, Your Excellency—the moral values of an upright citizenry.

Here, maybe people will see, too, that God does write straight with crooks or crooked lines, and makes things right—with the probably unwitting collaboration of assorted scoundrels, jueteng lords and collectors, stock market manipulators, PAGCOR consultants, poker and mahjong-playing cronies, drinking and womanizing buddies, unscrupulous friends old and new, and enterprising ladies in the real estate business. And, Your Excellency, there's the special irony, of profound educational import in itself, in a high school dropout's capacity to serve his people as preeminent mentor and guide, without your intending to but effectively just the same, just by being your natural, glandular, irrepressible self, and not resigning, staying where you are, bravely, stolidly carrying on.

And what are these other courses of study that you're giving for the benefit of the people, rather, the masses—subjects that are all the more memorable and striking for bearing the imprint of the Palace, the seal of the presidency?

Quite a number, and they come complete with texts and lectures from all quarters, with audio-visual aids, field trips and lab experiments, daily quizzes and, if certain educational authorities have their way, one final decisive exam. And these courses cover the evils of drink, especially all-night boozing, what it does to the brain, the heart, the liver, the kidneys and the executive department . . . the economic woes and chaos spawned by polygamy, chasing and keeping one skirt too many . . . the misfortunes brought on by mahjong, especially if played for multimillion-peso stakes on a presidential yacht or in a log cabin . . . the hazards of transporting bundles of jueteng and tobacco tax money in sacks, boxes and attaché cases . . . the exorbitant burdens in maintaining several mansions . . . carousing till dawn with a jolly midnight Cabinet instead of reading books such as Will and Ariel Durant's *The Lessons of History*, Machiavelli's *The Prince*, Thomas Merton's *Thoughts in Solitude*, Peter Drucker's *Management for the Third Millennium*, Francis Fukuyama's *The End of Ideology and Future Politics*, Nick Joaquin's *Culture as History* and other such works that should prove more salutary and rewarding to presidents, whether impeachable or not, than the consolations of Johnny Walker and friends. . . .

The academic program isn't strictly for the masa, to be sure, as demonstrated by the learning experiences and educational transformations we've witnessed in recent days—among the members of your Cabinet, and in the ranks of the House and the Senate, and in the elite enclaves of Makati, in the media, the colleges and universities . . . with Mar Roxas and Lito Banayo and other members of your official family calling it quits, and demoralized or disgusted defections following one after another in your dimming LAMP party, and Frank Drilon, Jun Magsaysay, Dolfo Biazon and other enlightened, emboldened solons bolting the majority party to range themselves against you, Fidel Ramos preaching about morality in government, Cory Aquino appealing to the big fat businessmen to fight poverty and malnutrition, one "Jimpol" in your employ giving up on bribing more media people to slant their reportage and columns in your favor, even the pious Kit Tatad, the Senate majority leader and your staunch defender now after long denouncing your dissolute ways, suddenly seeing the light again and abandoning the ruling party to become an "independent" as he sits in solemn judgment during your impeachment.

SO IT GOES, YOUR EXCELLENCY . . . And after the trial, what? Senate President Aquilino Pimentel, Jr. says this "nightmare"—he must have trouble sleeping these days, look at those eye bags, what with all these ponderous issues and weighty responsibilities pressing down on his dedicated shoulders—this terrible crisis should be resolved in a month's time. Not so, said Senator Santiago before a lesson or two also got through to her and she stopped shooting off her pugnacious mouth—the proceedings could last till May and the rules don't favor a quick, short trial, the senators could ask an infinite number of questions, two minutes' worth of questions could result in one or two hours of debate, scores of witnesses might have to be cross-examined for days on end, and so on. The over-eager Gloria Arroyo may have to wait that long to take over, which is a crying shame since she is surely the lesser evil, being no more than four-feet-seven, says my mother-in-law, your old San Juan neighbor, Señora Felipa Yupangco Castrillo, and I'm not one to dispute my dear mother-in-law.

Some scenarios have come up, all dealing with the resolution of this Trial of the Millennium, in which I suppose you take pride, being the veteran trouper that you are, as principal protagonist and star. Here's one plot outline, the most dramatic and fascinating, I think, that I got from a slightly tipsy St. John's alumnus, at that Club Filipino reunion I told you about—not Attorney Nubla, whose first name, by the way, isn't Eric, but Maurice, and who is with the Philippine Lawyers Association, not the IBP.

The scenario goes this way: the trial winds up around the middle of January 2001 at the latest, and the Senate jurors hand in their collective verdict, and Chief Justice Hilario Davide pronounces you not guilty.

You are not culpable. You are declared innocent. Blameless. Off the hook. Exonerated from the alleged offenses: graft and corruption, bribery, perjury, polygamy, betrayal of the public trust and culpable violation of the Constitution.

You are acquitted.

A stunned silence, then gasps of disbelief and despair, shouts of triumph and jubilation, pandemonium in the Senate Hall, dancing and delirium and devastation all at once in the streets, prayer rallies and angry protests all over again throughout the land as prices skyrocket and the peso slides down to 60 to the dollar and the expiring economy goes from coma to terminal.

Then you resign.

You quit, give it all up, retire from the scene.

You resign because you've done your bit for the nation, you've imparted those lessons for the good and welfare of our people, your classes are dismissed and you know the party is over. Because maybe Christ the Lord and his mother Mary and Joseph your namesake and the prayers of Cardinal Sin, Mike Velarde and Ka Erdie, and the counsel of loving friends old and new have convinced you finally that it's time to let go, give up, make the supreme sacrifice, resign.

Your Excellency, you are not resigning right now, not yet, not this minute, this weekend, this December, this Christmas. But according to this scenario—and you are famous for acting out lesser, mediocre, less than monumental scripts—you will resign in January. By then, it would be about time, too. The right time.

It's called starting the New Year right.

(Graphic, 2000)